RECITAL OF A LIFETIME

A SCIENTIST'S CAREER IN THE WORLD OF MUSIC
A MUSICIAN'S QUEST IN THE SERVICE OF SCIENCE

RALPH KOHN
accompanied by
GRAHAM JOHNSON

RAPHAEL EDITIONS
www.raphaeleditions.co.uk

University of London Doctor of Music (honoris causa)
at the Royal Academy of Music, July 2014

RECITAL OF A LIFETIME

24 Preludes & Fugues in major and minor keys

A SCIENTIST'S CAREER IN THE WORLD OF MUSIC
A MUSICIAN'S QUEST IN THE SERVICE OF SCIENCE

RALPH KOHN
accompanied by
GRAHAM JOHNSON
and in well-tempered conversation

RAPHAEL EDITIONS
www.raphaeleditions.co.uk

ISBN 978-0-9932013-0-1

Raphael Editions, 14 Harley Street, London W1G 9PQ

Printed in England by Caligraving Ltd

For my beloved Zahava, Hephzi, Michelle and Maxine
and in affectionate memory of
Professor Allan St. J Dixon OBE MD FRCP,
19 August 1921 — 19 June 2014
Physician, scientist and humanitarian,
whose selfless aim and greatest reward was always
the well-being of his patients and friends

A few more kind words …

'Ralph Kohn is a force of nature … the depth of his cultural background—
from the early days in Leipzig to his enlightened contribution to British life—
informs this engaging and heart-warming story'
PROFESSOR JONATHAN FREEMAN-ATTWOOD Principal, Royal Academy of Music

'An extraordinary life-story lived at the pinnacle of medical science and music'
JOHN GILHOOLY Director, Wigmore Hall

'This book tells a compelling story of science, music, history and business about a
remarkable individual, Ralph Kohn. I cannot recommend it highly enough'
DAME NANCY ROTHWELL President and Vice-Chancellor, University of Manchester

'An amalgam of music, science, business and courage that is unique,
a story told with rich anecdotal charm'
SIR JOHN MEURIG THOMAS former Master, Peterhouse, Cambridge

Foreword & Acknowledgements

I have been putting together the material for this autobiography for a very long time. For years I have carefully noted anecdotes, stories and quotations on separate sheets of paper, carefully filed; some of these have found their way into the various addresses and speeches I have been invited to give over the years, particularly those in connection with the work of the Kohn Foundation for charitable causes. Unfortunately, I am not a spontaneous public speaker—everything has to be carefully considered and written down—but this has been to my advantage when it came to gathering the materials that have been necessary in the writing of this book. My wife and children have long encouraged me to tell the story of my life in systematic fashion, but as anyone knows who has attempted to turn his hand to autobiography, this is far easier said than done. At work I have a marvellous secretary to whom I dictate letters and e-mails, a perfect solution for that kind of correspondence, but a book like this is another matter entirely. I can think of many distinguished friends of the past, now no longer with us, who spoke from time to time about intending to write their life-stories, and never got round to doing so.

Or perhaps, like me, they tried and it seemed too daunting a task. I confess to being very afraid that a book about my life would end up in that same category of might-have-beens.

Some years ago I thought the solution may be to hand everything over to a professional biographer, someone whom I did not know, and who did not know me before he took on the task. This was not a success. The book, worthy in its aims, reached draft form, but I am not an important historical figure or politician, and friends told me that none of my personality came over in the solemn recounting of the facts of my life and times—if my story was going to be told, it seemed I would have to do it myself. In the following years I mentioned my ambition to write a book to various friends, including the pianist Graham Johnson with whom I have made quite a number of recordings. During rehearsals or recording sessions (see *Interlude 7*) Graham would sometimes ask me how my book was getting on (he was working at the time on his own monumental three-volume encyclopaedia devoted to the Schubert songs). I was rather ashamed to admit that whereas I had a lot of written material to hand, I did not see how it would ever coalesce into a readable book. This was not laziness on my part I can assure you—I do not shy away from hard work, but even I found most of it heavy going whilst retaining confidence in the fact that there was a worthwhile tale to tell. Graham asked if he could see some of the material and I agreed whilst being rather afraid to hear his verdict.

His response was immediate and clinically precise: there was much fine material here, some of it exciting and moving, but the style was too dense, and I had failed to explain myself sufficiently when it came to dealing with scientific matters. I had forgotten, he said, how most people were confused by highfalutin scientific terms. He was kind enough to say that it was a delight for anyone to engage me personally in conversation, but he was frank about the fact that not enough of that delight came through in my factual prose. He advised me to adopt a lighter touch, to attempt to write less formally, as if I were speaking directly to a friend. I was willing to work on this, and I did, but I doubted if it would make sufficient difference. Graham then proposed an extraordinary solution: what if I were to send him each chapter to look at after it were written? After reading the material and researching some of the background, he offered to visit me in my office, ask me questions, and we could record and transcribe the conversations. As he put it, I would be responsible for the 'preludes', and he would add the extra contrapuntal voice when it came to the following 'fugues'. I think he got this idea from the remarkable conversations between the composer Igor Stravinsky and the younger musician, Robert Craft. And needless to say the reference to 'preludes' and 'fugues' is a result of the Bachian thread that has joyfully and fruitfully run through my life, just as it runs like a faithfully recurring theme through this book.

At first I found this idea of being interviewed about my life rather daunting, but I had momentarily forgotten that Graham Johnson is one of the world's great piano accompanists. He had often played for me in lieder recordings, and he was now skilfully doing exactly the same thing to help me, and see me through, in verbal, rather than musical, terms. I found that his questions were as carefully and tactfully placed as chords on the piano: his support enabled me to expand in relaxed fashion on what I had written, as if I were singing my heart out at a recording session. These conversations, each of about one to two hours, were mostly led by me, but occasionally Graham took the reins and steered them into new areas, as if he were modulating while playing one of Schumann's wonderful piano interludes. On those occasions, in true recital fashion, it was up to me to follow him, and thus the whole book is a collaboration between two people performing, as they say, from the same hymn-sheet—or perhaps song-sheet would be a better metaphor. As well as the twenty-four so-called 'Preludes and Fugues' in this book, there are also eight 'Interludes' where we both agreed that the subjects of these chapters were better treated as solos from me, rather than as duets with participation from us both; we have given these subtitles—in each case one of the dance movements from Bach's English Suites. Sometimes the written material of the preludes was altered after the fugal conversations—being able to talk at length about certain aspects and episodes of my life had a freeing effect on my ability to write about them.

with Graham Johnson

Photograph by Clive Barda

This book therefore, in its collaboration between a singer and a pianist, has something of the two-way give-and-take that characterizes the working together of two artists giving a recital. It was subsequently a short step in the same direction to consider including a CD as an integral part of the entire project—and this was not as complicated as it would have been with other people because the tracks already existed, and this was going to be our CD. The same two people who are in conversation in this book had already made a number of CDs together over a twelve-year period, encompassing a number of great composers, and we had many tracks to choose from. Great songs (and particularly those in the lieder repertoire) are always about something, and always relevant to human situations—the great poets that are set to music ensure that this is the case. It was amazing, as I went through my story, to realize how many of the situations I faced in my own life were mirrored in one way or another, and sometimes very subtly, by these lieder texts.

We have chosen twenty-five tracks from our rather large discography; it is entirely up to the listener, of course, if he or she wishes to engage with the musically illustrative part of this book (and one can easily read the book without listening to the music), but I do believe the CD adds something unique to this publication. It is also a reflection of the fact that music, and the great German poetry that goes with it, has always been an absolutely essential part of my life.

In writing this book I must thank my dear wife for her exemplary patience. There have been times when I have got up in the middle of the night with a new thought that I have wished to put down on paper before it slips my mind (as it does at my time of life). She has to put up with me switching on the light and searching with excessive and exasperated zeal for the pen which, for some reason, always seems to elude me at that hour of the night! My daughter Hephzibah has been, as usual, an indispensable helpmate, taking the lion's share of responsibility in the preparation of the book's illustrations, many of which had to be painstakingly sourced and selected from various family albums. Apart from examining old photographs, Hephzi excels in taking new ones; I am proud that some of the most beautiful images in this book bear witness to her own skills with the camera. My daughters Michelle and Maxine have also supported me in this large task—indeed, my entire family has had to be very patient with me when I found myself absorbed in the creation of a project as time-consuming as this.

There are a number of people who have played a significant part in ensuring this autobiography was more than an unfulfilled pipe dream. It is my pleasure and privilege to thank them here:

Celia Ballantyne who gave valuable advice concerning the CD included in the book; the supremely talented Clive Barda with whom I have enjoyed many photographic sessions and who took the portrait on the book's cover; my teacher, the distinguished Talmudical scholar Dayan Ivan Binstock, who read the manuscript and raised various points on religious matters; Mark Brown, my record producer of many years who effected the CD compilation with his customary skill; Nick Flower whose meticulous proof-reading and designing skills magically turned typescript into a real and, hopefully, vibrant publication; Tony Forwood, my right hand in all contractual and business matters; Jonathan Freeman-Attwood, outstanding principal of the Royal Academy of Music, whose friendship has given me great joy in the later years of my life; my imperturbable PA for many years, Vivien Kemeny; Sir Michael Rawlins who very kindly read the draft and raised various important scientific questions; Martin Shaw, the photographer, for his skill in turning many pictures hanging on home and office walls into viable images for reproduction as well as photographing me with my grandchildren; and Richard Stokes whose translating of song texts sets an unrivalled standard.

As *Recital of a Lifetime* went to press I received the sad news of the death of Professor Allan Dixon whose work and significance in my career is described in later pages. I feel sure that the book's principal dedicatees, my wife and daughters, will understand my having added Allan's name to theirs as a token of my deep gratitude for his friendship and counsel over many decades.

RALPH KOHN

London, July 2014

PRELUDE I

With Johann Sebastian Bach in Leipzig

I CONFESS to reflecting a great deal on the country of my birth where music and philosophy flourished, a land that gave Europe some of its greatest artists and scientists. This is a land of fairy tales as well as unspeakable nightmares. In my youth I lived through the terrible twelve years in which millions of lives were destroyed and the reputation of one of the greatest countries on earth was blackened to an unimaginable degree. Seventy years after the destruction of the Nazi regime we are better able to see these years as a terrible, but temporary, aberration. One can never be complacent about these things, but in the later part of my life it has been my happy experience often to be made welcome in Germany where the hard lessons concerning the dangers of state tyranny seem to have been learned better than anywhere else in Europe. My wife Zahava (together with my daughter Hephzibah) has given many talks in schools as part of a Holocaust awareness project regarding Zahava's childhood experiences in Bergen Belsen. The warmth and interest shown by young people has been extraordinary, and nowhere stronger than in Germany itself.

Sometimes I imagine the 1930s and '40s as if history had gone in another direction, with me and my parents and siblings living in a peaceful and prosperous country without Hitler at its head, a country benefiting from the skills and talents of all its citizens, a gentle giant rather than an uncontrollable monster. I would have regarded myself as loyal citizen of Germany and our upbringing and schooling would have made us feel part of that romantic tradition; this cradle of composers, poets and philosophers seemed to be a safe and good-hearted place. *Der Lindenbaum*, one of Franz Schubert's most famous songs from his *Winterreise* cycle, describes the cosiness of a German village with a linden tree at its centre where lovers plight their troth under its shady branches. All of us who love the German language have felt part of that poetic tradition with its idealized villages and linden trees. In Schubert's great song cycle the reality that has to be faced by the winter traveller is harsh and brutal; that linden tree (the genus *Tilia*, commonly called a lime tree in the British Isles) is reduced to a fading memory of the past, but what a beautiful symbol it was for us all.

Der Lindenbaum No 5 *of* Winterreise, D911 FRANZ SCHUBERT (1797–1827)   *see page 325*
CD Track ☐1   *for text and translation*

How could I describe the city in which I was born? For most English-speaking people it is just a name. It is not a world-hub like Berlin or London, and yet it is a very special place. The poet Karl von Holtei (a friend of Brahms, one of my musical heroes) once wrote: 'Leipzig is the only city in Germany that represents the whole of Germany … a place where one can forget being Hessian, Bavarian, Swabian, Prussian or Saxon; the only city where even the man who possesses nothing but his personality is honoured, and where all the advantages of a world-metropolis are to be enjoyed.'

Leipzig Marktplatz *circa* 1900 with the old Town Hall

Leipzig was a cosmopolitan and commercial centre with a well-established orthodox Jewish Community. It was practically the first place eastern European Jews would reach from Poland and the Ukraine. It was a large city, but not uncomfortably so. All these things contributed to my parents' decision to move there in 1919, immediately after their marriage—my father had formerly lived in Hanover, and my mother in Berlin. They were both supremely happy in Leipzig, and were treated honorably there until the nightmare of 1933. My family lived comfortably in this lively city for fourteen years, and then events caught up with us, as they did for millions of others. I was exiled from the country of my birth, but in recent years I feel at home and welcome in this city; not even Germany's terrible years of aberration can take that away from me.

Leipzig may be less imposing and exciting than Berlin to the north; it is far less architecturally magnificent than Munich; situated deep inland it is less open and bracing a city than Hamburg by the sea; and it lacks Cologne's connection with the Rhine and its wine-growing surroundings. For about fifty years after the Second World War it was somewhat hidden from western visitors, swallowed up by the East German state, but now, after twenty-five years of a united Germany, it has reclaimed much of its distinguished former identity.

Quite apart from the city's importance as a business centre (trade-fairs have long been a regular

The Thomaskirche with Bach's statue

feature of Leipzig life), its musical background and literary connections are second to none. Some would say that Leipzig, in terms of its architecture, is less interesting than Dresden, the other important city in Saxony, about seventy miles to the south. Dresden is famous for its striking buildings (the celebrated Semperoper, for instance) and the beauty of its outlying landscapes. But it is not for opera, or for anything worldly, glamorous and showy, or even for its surrounding countryside, that Leipzig has earned the respect of serious musicians, writers and thinkers all over the world.

Certainly, for any music-lover the word 'Leipzig' conjures up any number of lively and moving associations. Philosophers may well choose to salute the birth here of Gottfried Leibniz (1646–1716), but for musicians Leipzig has a more important hero: it was first and foremost the working and final resting-place of Johann Sebastian Bach, in my opinion the greatest of composers. Bach moved to Leipzig in 1723 and worked here indefatigably, both at the Thomaskirche and the Nicolaikirche (where the demonstrations of 1989 helped to precipitate the fall of the Berlin Wall).

An early drawing of the Nikolaikirche in Leipzig

It is perhaps Bach's overwhelming industry, writing music for performance in these two great churches among others (masterpieces that were often unappreciated by some of the petty bureaucrats of the time), that set the seal on Leipzig's reputation for hard work and artistic inspiration. Bach's remains were eventually returned to the Thomaskirche in 1950, where his unassuming gravestone is set into the floor of the crypt beneath the choir. One would not expect a showy mausoleum in a city like Leipzig: the simplicity of this site is overwhelming in its modesty and has become a place of international pilgrimage.

Leipzig has always been a city where achievement is expected, and then taken for granted, a tragedy in Bach's case where he composed like a god and was treated as a servant, but a salutary experience for those who wrongly believe they can get away with less than their very best. There is something about Leipzig, or perhaps it is simply the Saxon temperament, that is rigorous, even severe: this is hardly a town full of gratuitously charming people (it is a long journey to Vienna, as we will find out when it comes to telling the story of my father's visit there before my birth) but the Saxon nature despises duplicity and gives, and expects, value for money: intellectuals were always welcome—the University was founded in 1409—and those who went into business were expected to abide by the rules. The city's reputation for probity was underlined by the choice of Leipzig as the location of the German Supreme Court in 1888.

Much of Leipzig was destroyed during the war and as part of the old communist East Germany the city was a shadow of its former self. As everywhere in cities from the former Eastern bloc, one can still see a number of ugly buildings that reflect the grim lifestyle of Communist rule. No one can minimize the human and intellectual cost of that pitiless era, but when I now visit the city I rejoice that large parts of it were spared the relentless advance of modern architecture during the sixties and seventies (the fate of Birmingham comes to mind). Inaction on the part of the Communist authorities allowed much of the infrastructure to decay without it being razed to the ground. Since the collapse of the old politics, much of the city has been sensitively and painstakingly brought back to life and an increasing number of restorations have made it possible to appreciate Leipzig's beauties.

For students and lovers of Bach this means the possibility of a journey back in time. Much later in my life it has been an unforgettable experience for me to be able to go to the Thomas Church and hear a Bach cantata performed in the building, and in the same acoustic, where the composer worked and performed. The instrumentalists, singers and boy choristers (the 'Thomaner') perform with heart and soul in the large gallery above the congregation; they are as true to the composer as if he were there to direct them himself. My lifelong devotion to the Jewish faith of my fathers has never precluded me from rejoicing in this composer's work; he was inspired by a different religion but his expression of his love of God has universal significance. How many times in the last twenty years have I emerged from the Thomaskirche, stunned by the music and the authenticity of its performance, and walked into a magical part of the old city that now resembles if not exactly Bach's

Leipzig, at least something like the town Johann Wolfgang von Goethe knew when he was a student there in the 1770s. He referred to it in his play *Faust* as 'klein Paris', a miniature Paris.

One can still eat and drink at Auerbach's Keller built in 1530, the hostelry where the character of Mephistopheles in Goethe's *Faust* sings the famous 'Song of the Flea'. A number of composers have set this text, none more humourously than Beethoven.

Auerbach's Keller in Leipzig

 Aus Goethe's Faust 'Flohlied' Op 75 No 3 LUDWIG VAN BEETHOVEN (1770–1827)
CD Track 2   *see page 326 for text and translation*

Even before Bach arrived from Cöthen (his previous appointment), the firm of Breitkopf & Härtel had been founded in Leipzig in 1719. It has remained one of the most important of all music publishers for some three hundred years, printing the complete edition ('Gesamtausgabe') of the works of Schubert at the end of the nineteenth century. Leipzig was also a world centre of book publishing of course—F A Brockhaus, founder of the most famous of German encyclopaedias, began his Leipzig business in 1819. At the end of the nineteenth century the book trade employed 15,000 persons in Leipzig; five hundred newspapers and periodicals were published there, and more than nine hundred publishers and booksellers had their headquarters in the city, with representation for eleven thousand firms in Europe.

After Bach, the musical links are almost too numerous to list: this is where Felix Mendelssohn held the position of music director of the Gewandhaus (from 1835 until his death in 1847). There have been actually three buildings of this name—the building in modern style we see today replaced the gracious building from 1880–1884 which was destroyed in the Second World War and which, in turn, had replaced the orginal Gewandhaus (literally, Drapers' Hall) which Mendelssohn knew. The musical conservatory, or Hochschule, that Mendelsohn founded in the Grassistrasse in 1843 remains one of Germany's finest, and it is possible to visit the Mendelssohn House in the Goldschmidtstrasse (formerly the Königstrasse), now a museum.

The music-making here set standards for everywhere else in Europe in terms of symphonic and chamber music. Robert Schumann, born in nearby Zwickau, studied and worked in Leipzig, where he also lived (between 1840 and 1844) after his marriage to Clara Wieck. This was after the court case where the composer had to fight Friedrich Wieck, Clara's father, for permission to marry his daughter. The Schumann house in the Inselstrasse is now a museum and concert hall.

A music-lover in Leipzig could easily walk around the important sites in the inner city: from the Mendelssohn House (Biedermeier furniture and an atmospheric ambience) to the Neues Gewandhaus on foot is easy, and then due north to the Nicolaikirche with the opera house in the near vicinity. Turning due west on the Grimmäische Strasse one walks past the Altes Rathaus (Old Town Hall) with the Alte Börse (Old Stock-exchange) behind it, and arrives with a rush of emotion (at least that is what I always feel) at the peaceful oasis of the courtyard of the

Thomaskirche with its statue of Bach. This landmark by the Leipzig sculptor Carl Seffner seems always to have been there—in fact it is less than twenty years older than me—erected in 1908.

The Thomaner in 1930 assembled beneath Seffner's statue of J S Bach

Fugue I (in 2 voices)   RALPH KOHN *with* GRAHAM JOHNSON

GJ   With this reverential return to the name of Bach, and his statue in Leipzig, you have put your cards on the table. Is he, for you, the greatest of all composers?

RK   Absolutely. As you know I have spent many years studying the song repertoire of the nineteenth century, and you and I have recorded together many great lieder. I cannot imagine life without the music of Mozart, Beethoven, Schubert, Schumann, Brahms and so on, but for me Bach is the irreplaceable apex of western musical achievement. He has also become increasingly important to me as a musical companion as the years have gone on. One of the greatest joys of my life is to attend the Bach cantata concerts on Sunday mornings at the Royal Academy of Music, an ongoing project supported by the Kohn Foundation to include the performance of all two hundred or more of these immortal works. The Royal Academy of Music/Kohn Foundation Bach prize also recognizes musicians who have contributed to the performance and study of this composer.

GJ   A list of the prizewinners is almost a Who's Who of Bach in this age of the world, and it's very international too—representing Britain, Germany, Hungary, the USA and Japan. And that is just so far!

RK   The pianists Murray Perahia and András Schiff, the conductors Sir John Eliot Gardiner and John Butt, the conductor and harpsichordist Masaaki Suzuki, the tenor Peter Schreier (also a conductor), the musicologist Christoph Wolff (who certainly knows more about Bach than anyone else in the world) … all these remarkable people, some of them my close friends I am honoured to say, have contributed enormously to the performance and study of Bach's music. Not content with being a renowned Bach conductor, John Eliot has recently written a fascinating book on the composer. And what a joy it was, only recently, to listen to the 'Goldberg' Variations played by András Schiff at a special performance given at the Royal Society which I was privileged to organize. I can think of few more wonderful ways to spend an evening than this. The marriage of music and science on that occasion, and in that hallowed institution, was a summary of my own life's twin passions.

GJ   You and I often enjoy speaking German together, particularly when we work on the lieder repertoire. Over the years I have seen you slip into German with the greatest ease when speaking to musicians. I have had to learn the language the hard way but it is second nature for you—it is, after all, your mother tongue.

at the Royal Society with Paul Nurse (president of the Royal Society) and the pianist András Schiff

RK From the very beginning I realized that one had to master more than one language in order to communicate with different people. I always spoke German with my mother because she spoke nothing else—her beautiful German was that of an educated woman from Berlin—and I was lucky to learn *Hochdeutsch* at her knee. With my father, on the other hand, I spoke Yiddish. Like me, he spoke only German with my mother—with a bit of a Galician accent—but with me he spoke Yiddish, that wonderful mixture of German, Polish, Russian and Hebrew. My father used this language superbly and I love it very much to this day; I am always delighted to hear it skilfully spoken, something rather rare now, with the richness of its vocabulary, its very many allusions to Talmudic learning, and its unique humour. I was delighted to break into speaking Yiddish recently with Lord Weidenfeld who was born in the Austro-Hungarian Empire, and whose background makes him hugely knowledgeable about this aspect of Jewish culture. The language is very nostalgic for me, it represents a vanished age and it reminds me overwhelmingly of my father and his roots.

When I speak of my own roots it seems difficult to imagine where they actually are. I sometimes imagine what would have happened to me if our family had been permitted to continue living and working in Leipzig. I was far too young to know anything about Bach when we left, but perhaps I would have been permitted by my father to study music at the famous Hochschule in Leipzig if things had worked out that way. Certainly, everything in my life would have been entirely different. My family left Leipzig towards the end of 1933, an early departure by the standards of many. Our destination was Amsterdam, but we stayed in Berlin for six months before going by train to Amsterdam in the spring of 1934.

GJ And when did you next visit your home town of Leipzig?

RK Twenty-eight years later, in 1961, in the days of the DDR! I was sent there for business reasons by my employers at the time, the pharmaceutical company Smith Kline and French (later Glaxo Smith Kline), and was told that I was to be 'einquartiert'—given lodging—with a family called Kötz. I found myself staying in a house, built in 1904 on the site where Bach had lived and where the Thomaner choirboys lived also. It is hard to describe how thrilled I was by this; the address was Thomaskirchhof 18 and for me this was more magical than any luxury hotel. This enthusiasm was not shared by my colleague, Dr Leo Stevens, who was travelling with me. I was so delighted to be living in the ambience of the great composer that I had clearly failed to notice that the living conditions were more than somewhat primitive with antiquated plumbing. 'Go hang yourself with your Bach,' Stevens said to me, 'give me a decent bathroom.' I suppose this goes to show that one man's hero is another man's inconvenience. These are the circumstances in which I came back to Leipzig, and back to the composer whom I revere above all others and whose music means more to me than any other music. Despite everything that had happened in the world since we left Leipzig, I felt I was in some way returning to a place with which I had a strong connection.

GJ I am certain your London home had a 'decent bathroom'! Over the years you have grown ever closer to Bach, and to Leipzig and you visit there once or twice a year. In June 2011 you received the Medal of Honour from the Lord Mayor of the City of Leipzig for your substantial contributions in promoting J S Bach and your support of the Bach Festival in Leipzig. And you have also been honoured by the Thomaner.

RK I forgot to say that the chorus of the Thomaskirche, the Thomanerchor, was the collective recipient of the Royal Academy of Music/Kohn Foundation Bach prize in 2011. They recently celebrated their 800th birthday and theirs is a tradition that goes uninterruptedly back to the composer himself. Some people may think it strange that a Jewish boy from Leipzig, a naturalized British subject, immensely grateful to live in the United Kingdom, should feel drawn back to the town of his

birth, and after so many years. I truly believe that it is the power of Bach's music
that has made this reconciliation not only possible for me, but also the most natural
thing in the world. No one, and certainly not the deranged thugs of the Third
Reich, could take away from me the fact that I was born in a great city of music,
science and culture, and that I have the right, after many years away, to enjoy and
celebrate that connection.

The Kohn family in Leipzig in 2011. *from left to right* My daughters Michelle, Hephzibah,
myself, The Lord Mayor (*Oberbürgermeister*), my wife Zahava, my daughter Maxine

GJ According to the President of the Federal Republic of Germany you do indeed have
the right to celebrate that connection! In 2012 he honoured you with his country's
Cross of the Order of Merit for your contribution to Germany's musical life.

RK Did you know that the tombstone in Leipzig of my brother Simon, who died in
1927, ten months before I was born, was mercifully untouched by the upheavals
of the Nazi era? He died six years before the onset of that terrible time.

On a monument in Leipzig's Old Jewish Cemetry, Berliner Strasse 121, are
inscribed the following words: 'During the time of National Socialism Jewish
children were forbidden to play in public parks and green spaces. Here was the only
place in Leipzig where they were permitted to play *im Grünen*—out in the open.'

Simon's grave is a reminder to me that my family will always be associated with Leipzig. The Order of Merit, from a very different kind of German government than the one that we fled, reminds me that I was born there with German as my mother tongue and with the great composers, poets and scientists of this country as part of my own cultural heritage.

There is no doubt that I feel myself to be overwhelmingly British, and London is my home. But I am grateful that the Lord Mayor of Leipzig and the musicians of the Thomaskirche have been generous enough to welcome me back there from time to time. And it is a matter of huge pride to me that the names of Zahava and myself are now engraved on one of the walls of the Thomaskirche as donors to that institution. It is said that Euripides once wrote that 'the first requisite to happiness is that a man be born in a famous city'. As far as my own happiness is concerned, Leipzig is more than famous enough to prove the wisdom of the great Greek poet! As a city it has been through some truly terrible times, but it remains a very special place.

The tombstone of my brother Simon Kohn

PRELUDE II

The Kohns of Leipzig

MANY MUSIC-LOVERS have explored Leipzig and visited landmarks associated with the great composers, but now I want to propose a slightly different journey that will explore less familiar aspects of the city. Before the war or, to be more specific, before the destructive orgy of *Kristallnacht*, the Lutheran Thomas Church, bastion of Christianity, stood happily near to a synagogue in the Elsterstrasse, such was the city's diversity.

In the 1920s we would have been able to take a tram from this synagogue and wind our way due north without being disturbed by the large ring road that now encircles modern Leipzig, and which marks out the perimeters of the old city walls. On our left there is the Schauspielhaus (once called the Centraltheater) and progressing up the Grosse Fleischergasse we come to the Romanushaus, one of Leipzig's finest old baroque buildings. We turn right into a long thoroughfare known as the Brühl which runs west to east. This was formerly a part of the city's Jewish quarter and was an important part of the fur trade—indeed, in the 1920s, this street accounted for one third of the world's trade in furs.

The Brühl was also Richard Wagner's birthplace in 1813, an ironically inappropriate address for an anti-Semitic composer to have made his entrance into the world, but this accounts for the naming of the Richard-Wagner-Strasse which

runs in parallel to the north. In my opinion, and however great his music, he hardly deserves this honour from the city of Leipzig, a town which he scorned because of its enthusiastic connection with Jewish musicians. Wagner's own prejudices notwithstanding, Leipzig was a liberal city open to foreigners, including many thousands of Jews, who were prepared to come here and work hard; it had an enlightened belief in diversity.

There had been a Jewish community in Leipzig since the twelfth century, a school and a synagogue in the city since the thirteenth. By the end of the nineteenth century all anti-Jewish restrictions had been abolished and the city became a magnet for the persecuted Jews of the east, often victims of

The interior of a Leipzig synagogue, *circa* 1900

Russian or Polish pogroms. In
the first quarter of the twentieth
century the Jewish community
nearly doubled in size. Many of
them were drawn to the city by its
standing in the selling of leather,
hides, wool, cloth, linen and glass.

The Leipzig Hauptbahnhof

Behind the Brühl on the
other-side of the Willy-Brandt-
Platz lies the Hauptbahnhof. This
large railway station, originally
built in 1915, is a symbol of a
modern age that Bach never knew. By the end of the nineteenth century Leipzig
had the biggest railway terminus in the world and was the nerve-centre of German
trade and industry. This was the first long-distance railway and an important hub of
Central European railway traffic. This fact plays a significant role in the story of my
family because it determined Leipzig as the residence of choice for immigrant
businessmen, particularly those who dealt in furs, textiles or other commodities that
could conveniently be sent and received by rail.

Most of the tradesmen and dealers that lived and worked here before the Nazi
era were from eastern Europe and were so-called *Ostjuden*—Jews from the east. A
present-day synagogue in the nearby Keilstrasse is the modern manifestation of the
Bernstin Broder Schul—a name that shows that the original worshippers in pre-
Nazi times were indeed *Ostjuden* from the city of Brody in the Ukraine. Around the
corner is the Nordstrasse which is famous as a shopping district and in the old times
many of the shopkeepers were Jews. A little to the north west lies a large and
beautiful park, the Rosental, which is attached to the zoological gardens and
planetarium. This is part of an important area known as the Waldstrassenviertel
where, before 1933, over twenty percent of the population was Jewish—some
2,500 people. These were undoubtedly the well-to-do among Leipzig's thriving
Jewish population and my family was fortunate to be of their number.

It takes quite some imagination to enter into an entirely different pre-war world
where the local hospital of the area, the Eitingon-Krankenhaus, was endowed by
Chaim Eitingon the Russian 'king of the fur trade'; there was also an old persons'
home called the Ariowitsch-Stiftung. These resonantly Jewish names are now the
empty echoes of a vanished age—an era that did not slip quietly into history but
was ruthlessly destroyed. In the present-day the Waldstrassenviertel remains a highly
desirable part of Leipzig thanks to the imaginative restoration of the beautiful large

houses, painted in their original colours, that now make sumptuous apartments. The residential streets here have been named and re-named after such diverse famous personages as the Russian composer Tchaikovsky, the philosopher Leibniz and the owner of the famous music publishers, Peters Edition, Henri Hinrichsen. A gracious street overlooking a pleasant canal, Liviastrasse, is named after the soprano Livia Frege (1818–1891), daughter-in-law of Christian Frege, a member of a famous Leipzig family of merchants and bankers. She was the favourite lieder singer and close friend of Robert and Clara Schumann. Leipzig was a city of lieder singers and so it has remained. Gustav Mahler, one of Leipzig's more celebrated Jewish visitors, composed some of his Symphony No 1 in a house in Gustav-Adolf-Strasse in 1887/8. He was replacing Artur Nikisch at the time as conductor of the Leipzig Opera.

The streets in this area have changed character since the war because ring roads have been built to facilitate the movement of traffic in a modern city, but the whole area remains amazingly accessible to the town—rather like having a house in London's elegant Regent's Park with its illusion of country greenery and quick access to the West End on foot. I have always enjoyed living near to green open spaces, which is perhaps why my London home is only minutes away from Hampstead Heath. For my father, a businessman working in one of the streets near the Brühl, it must have been blissfully convenient to leave his house bordering on the Rosental and be at his desk after a ten-minute walk. There were few European cities in the 1920s where it was possible for a Jewish businessman to lead a more comfortable life with everything that he might need in terms of his religion close at hand, and also instant access to the best theatrical and musical experiences in Europe.

We have a special destination in mind on this journey, at least very special as far as I am concerned. Without further ado we reach it on foot, although according to the maps, access would have been even easier in the 1920s. We have arrived in another street named after a composer, albeit one less famous than Tchaikovsky: Albert Lortzing (1801–1851), a former director of the opera who had lived in the vicinity and had written the well-known opera *Zar und Zimmermann* that had been premiered in Leipzig in 1838. And it is at 13 Lortzingstrasse, a house on six floors in the elegant Waldstrassenviertel, a few metres away from the Rosental park, that this tour of Leipzig ends. It is also the beginning of the story of my life as it is recounted in this book.

Albert Lortzing

Let us imagine our starting point as being early 1927, a year or so before my own birth. Living in this house in the Lortzingstrasse were my father, in his late thirties, together with my mother, a few years younger, and their young family. My father was Max Kohn, a successful and prosperous dealer in textiles; my mother was Max's wife Lena. Max's mother Rachel, a widow, was also living with the family. Although Max and Lena had first met in 1913 they had married only in 1919 at the end of the Great War. Their first child, my elder brother Moshe or Maurice, named after my grandfather, had been born in 1920, shortly after their move to Leipzig. A second son, Simon, had been born in 1921 and in early 1927 the health of this six-year-old boy was a cause for grave concern. Two daughters, my sisters Celia and Toni, had arrived in 1923 and 1925 respectively, and both were healthy children. Apart from Simon's illness these were optimistic times for the Kohn family. They were untroubled with financial concerns and had every hope for a happy future— a future as rosy as the Rosental gardens laid out in the park near their house.

In February 1927 Max and Lena's worst fears were realized and their son Simon died of bronchial pneumonia. After the tragedy of his death everything seemed exceedingly bleak, especially for my mother who had a breakdown. The death of a child where the parents have to bury their offspring is one of the worst things that can happen in any family. We know how deeply affected the poet Friedrich Rückert was on the death of his children and I have always thought that his *Kindertotenlieder* poems, later set to music by Gustav Mahler, convey something of the anguish my mother and father must have felt on Simon's loss.

Wenn dein Mütterlein No 3 *of* Kindertotenlieder GUSTAV MAHLER (1860–1911)   *see page 327*
CD Track ③   *for text and translation*

Little did they know that by December of the very same year their lives would be changed with the arrival of another baby in the house in Leipzig. And that event marks my entrance into my own story.

Fugue II (in 2 voices) RALPH KOHN *with* GRAHAM JOHNSON

GJ Do you believe you were born under a lucky star?

RK To answer this question I would like to quote the famous medical researcher, father of chemotherapy, Paul Ehrlich. He said that success in medical research depended upon the '4 Gs'—*Geld, Geduld, Geschick* und *Glück* (money, patience, ability and luck). My definition of luck is placing all your money on a number at the gaming table and winning. But the odds are stacked heavily against you.

GJ Well what about the innate gifts with which a person is born? Is that not also something of a lottery? I looked up your birthday: in Chinese astrology you are a Fire Rabbit—active and adventurous, you love anything that sparks your creativity or curiosity. You have a burning desire to get out there and live life to the fullest. In western astrology you are a Sagittarian … an archer, independent, confident, generous, very career-orientated. It's a sign famous for singers—Maria Callas was a Sagittarius, and so was the German soprano Elisabeth Schwarzkopf—she shares your birthday, actually, of 9 December …

RK That proves, if I may say so, how questionable astrology is … the only thing I have in common with Elisabeth Schwarzkopf is an interest in singing. And I think you would agree that our experiences of growing up in Germany were rather different! I would have to confess, however, that I do have a touch of what the Germans call *Aberglaube*—superstition. My father would always kiss the mezuzah on the doorpost, and I do share something of his religious mysticism. Although I am a scientist by training I sometimes feel—if I fail to make the right observances—that I might be unlucky. I have inherited this from my father …

GJ … perhaps that's your artistic side, rather than the scientific …

RK And talking about being born under favourable circumstances, there is a rather extraordinary story about my coming into the world. It certainly indirectly affected many subsequent events in my life.

After the death of my brother Simon in February 1927 life at home must have been completely unmanageable. My mother, normally a woman of great discipline and self-control went to pieces, and hardly surprisingly. My father, a successful businessman but also a man of mystical faith, travelled all the way from Leipzig to Vienna to consult a famous Hassidic Rebbe and ask his advice. My father regarded this famous man, Rebbe Ysroel Friedman as a very saintly individual; he was known as the Chortkover Rebbe (he lived from 1854–1934) because his rabbinical dynasty had originated in Chortkov, a small town in the Ukraine where the Russians had earlier massacred an entire Jewish community.

My father set enormous store by this holy man's learning and his wisdom, and on several occasions consulted him about important decisions that related to our family. On one very special occasion the Chortkover Rebbe and his considerable retinue even stayed as our guests in Leipzig, a huge honour for us. This Rebbe had thousands of followers, my father Max Kohn among them. On that occasion in Vienna he had the following words of advice for the bereaved father: 'In order to reverse this tragedy, you must have another child as quickly as possible. If it's a boy, call him Rafael.'

Ysroel Friedman, Rebbe of Chortkov

Rafael is the name of an archangel of course and the literal meaning of the name is 'God will heal'. In Orthodox families it often happens that a child is given a name to commemorate someone else in the family, but Rafael was a name that had never figured in our family. It is perhaps for that reason that I always regarded myself as Ralph although my given name was Rafael. I should also say that we were fond of nicknames, usually used only within the family—my brother was Meue, my sister Celia was Zilli, Toni remained Toni and I was Futtel.

GJ Do you think your birth had the predicted effect?

RK I do think so. My birth, so soon after Simon's death, gave my mother a new focus in life. I was the youngest child and I daresay I was very spoiled. On looking back I remember nothing but receiving the greatest love from my parents and I am sure I was allowed to do things that had been forbidden to my older siblings. My brother Maurice was nearly eight years older than me, and my two sisters, Zilli (Celia) and Toni, were six and three years older. Because the age gap was quite large between us I had a rather separate upbringing from theirs; I never felt that I was in the shadow of my brother and sisters, nor that I was deprived of anything as a result of being younger, rather the reverse in fact. I was born rather a sickly child with respiratory problems. My mother, having lost my brother, was very protective about my well-being. There was a certain amount of playful understandable jealousy from my siblings who saw me as a favourite child.

GJ Do you remember anything about the house of your birth in the Lortzingstrasse?

RK Not really—I was very young when we lived there and my brother and sisters had
much more vivid memories of that period. It pleases me now to know that we lived
in a street that was named after a composer. I also like to think that even when I
was a toddler I was in walking distance of the stamping grounds of my beloved
Johann Sebastian Bach. It is as if the option of listening to his music was always
waiting for me to follow up. The house in Lortzingstrasse was on six floors with
a flat in the basement and a nursery in the attic. My father was a very successful
merchant in textiles so we were able to afford a governess, a nurse, a maid and a
cook. This may seem embarrassingly showy by today's standards, but in Weimar
Germany such employment was prized, and many middle-class households in
Britain in the 1920s were similarly staffed. Of course the houses in the
Ehrensteinstrasse where my uncle Jacob lived (he was my father's elder brother)
were more magnificent, but our house was full of fine furniture, numerous
paintings, a grand piano and a gramophone—my father loved playing records of
Caruso and Italian opera. The house survived the war and is still standing in good
condition in Leipzig. I have seen it several times since, but only from the outside.
It has been converted to a number of apartments. Because I was so young when we
left I had always wanted to visit the house again and see if the interior prompted
any memories. After the fall of the Berlin Wall, some time after 1989, I was bold
enough to ring the bell and speak to one of the inhabitants. I explained to her that
this had been my home before the war. Her very rude response was 'Na und?'
('So what?'). I think she might have been terrified that my intention was to try to
reclaim the house as my family's property—there was a great deal of that happening
at the time. Mostly, however, I have been met by incredible kindness among the
people of Leipzig.

GJ You must have been too young to remember clearly the disruptive move from
Leipzig in 1933.

RK Yes, but the events leading up to that decision are hardly personal to me, they are
part of my family history as well as the history of Europe. Looking back it seems
that the campaign against the Jews was achieved by means of what we musicians
would call a slow crescendo. Nazi Brownshirts killed the first Jews in early 1930,
eight of them, in Berlin, a few weeks after my second birthday. In that year the
Nazis got six million votes and Jews were increasingly intimidated. As early as 1931
fifty synagogues were sacked and Jewish tombstones were defiled. This is seven
years before the notorious *Kristallnacht*. When we look back at these events it seems
that the fate of the Jews was sealed long before that fateful day of 30 January 1933

when Hitler finally became
Chancellor. The unemployed
were manipulated by the Nazi
press and with so many of
Germany's Jews in law, finance
and business, either as sole
operators or successful owners,
it was easy to persuade a great
many uneducated people that
the harsh economic conditions
were the fault of the Jews.

I felt nothing of this tension
of course, I was surrounded by
a protective cocoon of love and
affection. There were regular
family holidays in Kolberg
on the Baltic coast, the present-
day Kołobrzeg in Poland. There
is a surviving photograph of the
family on the beach in the very
early thirties, my two sisters
seated on either side of my
mother and father, and with me
in the centre of the snapshot
with my elder brother standing
behind me.

The Kohns in Kolberg, a north-German holiday resort

Whatever the anxieties of my parents I never felt them. I went to a Jewish
Kindergarten so I would not have experienced the discrimination against Jewish
schoolchildren that was instigated at the beginning of 1933, just after my fifth
birthday. It was a different matter for my father of course, and to a lesser extent for
my older siblings—although they too were protected within the *Gemeinde*—the
Jewish community.

My father knew all the important Jewish movers and shakers in Leipzig.
Prominent owners of department stores or banking families were particularly
threatened: names like Kroch, Hodes, Ury, Bamberger and Held, and most of these
decided to leave. Nationwide, 10,000 Jews left for Palestine in the last nine months
of 1933 alone. One must remember that many of the Leipzig Jews were *Ostjuden*
conditioned by fairly recent experiences of Russian persecution, and acutely

sensitized to the danger-signs of a similar thing happening in Germany. Many of the long-established assimilated Jews of Berlin, for example, the so-called *Jeckes* or *Yekkes*, had lost this inherited sense of perpetual danger that kept the *Ostjuden* or *Galizianer*, like my father, always on their toes. As we now know, complacency, and a feeling of 'that could never happen here' proved fatal for a great number of them. The older people, often decorated heroes from the Great War, found the imminent danger most difficult to grasp.

GJ   I am reminded of the varied fortunes of different generations of the Hinrichsen family, proprietors of Peters Edition in Leipzig—you know them from the volumes of lieder that every performer has on their shelves. When Hitler came to power the two sons Max and Walter left for London and New York respectively and they founded different branches of the family firm in those places. They could not persuade their father Henri Hinrichsen to go with them—he was a famous philanthropist, he had endowed the city of Leipzig with a museum of instruments, and he had been awarded every honour imaginable by city and country. In the end he was murdered in Auschwitz.

RK   This is an all-too familiar story. As soon as the Nazis came to power, Jews and Communists were being rounded up and sent to concentration camps (Buchenwald, Dachau, etc) which were enlarged to accommodate them. Many of the Jews were convinced that Hitler was a passing phenomenon, but my father was in the minority that believed, from very early on, that the whole situation was extremely dangerous. He knew that the Nazis kept meticulous records of their opponents and that arrests always followed. As far as I know he had never been politically active, but for some reason he feared they would be coming for him. The midnight knock at the door—that's how the Gestapo used to work. They carted off people suspected of 'anti-national behaviour' and on all other manners of flimsy pretext. Father would not sleep at home and things could not go on like that. It was a big decision to leave that beautiful home behind us with many of our belongings, but my father was completely decisive.

My beloved parents—Max and Lena Kohn

PRELUDE III

My parents

L EIPZIG WAS NOT THE FIRST staging-post in the story of the Kohns. My father, Marcus Kohn, known as Max or Mottel, was born in 1889 in Polish Kalusz (now Kalush in western Ukraine), nestling in the foothills of the Carpathian mountains, sixty miles from the Russian border. His father Moshe, my grandfather, ran a small business there. The nearest city of any importance is Lvov or Lviv (formerly known as Lemberg) which is the capital city of Galicia. For centuries Galicia had been one of those unfortunate areas in central Europe that had been the subject of constant dispute between warring countries or factions. It was possible to become very confused about one's nationality or allegiance if one lived there for any length of time. I should point out that our original family name was Hoffmann but this was changed sometime around the turn of the century to avoid conscription into the Tsar's army—Russian officers had come to Kalush looking for able-bodied men listed under the name of Hoffmann, but they found only a family by the name of Kohn! It is little wonder we tried to avoid being drawn into the endless troubles of the region, conflicts that continue, in one way or another, to the present day with simmering violence between the

Mickiewicz Street in Kalush, Ukraine, *circa* 1910

recently independent Ukrainian state and Russia. During World War II, Ukraine suffered terribly under the successive rival tyrannies of Nazis and Communists. Some 28% of the population of Lvov was Jewish, and a Jewish community had flourished there since the sixteenth century. In 1941, in a fashion brutal even by their own depraved standards, the Nazis eliminated the Jews of this region almost entirely.

The demographic make-up of the area has now entirely changed on account of the Holocaust and the transferal of the Polish-speaking minority to the so-called Polish 'recovered areas'. This was before Russia incorporated Ukraine into the USSR. After the collapse of Soviet communism with an independent (though troubled) Ukraine, Lvov (Lviv) is now considered a cultural jewel and the most comfortable city in that country in which to live—perhaps this accounts for its nickname as 'the little Paris of the Ukraine'. It was fortunate, in architectural terms at least, to survive the Nazi and Soviet occupation of World War II almost unscathed; the buildings and the pleasing lay-out of the city recall its former glory as an important provincial city on the far-flung borders of the Austro-Hungarian Empire. The town has an air of civilized urbanity going back to the time when my father, young Marcus Kohn, was a boy. With the incorporation of Crimea into Russia in 2014, Lviv has become a city of refuge for those choosing to leave Crimea.

Kalush was provincial to say the least and I'm certain that the Kohn family journeyed to the metropolis of Lvov many times. My father's later success as a businessman in Leipzig suggests that he was already familiar with the workings of a big city rather than having been merely an inhabitant of a *shtetl*. When he left Galicia Max brought with him, as part of his heritage, the shared apprehensions of the Jews who lived in small, threatened communities in eastern Europe. They had been unjustly blamed for the assassination of Tsar Alexander II in 1881. Between 1881 and 1884, in countless revenge attacks in 166 towns in the southwest of the Russian Empire, including the Ukraine, thousands of Jewish homes were destroyed, many families were reduced to poverty, and large numbers of men, women, and children were killed and injured. Things were to get considerably worse in the early years of the twentieth century and of course worse still in the 1940s.

This moving poem by Antoni Sionimski was written about Poland in the wake of the Holocaust, but it expresses a nostalgia that Max Kohn, in the wake of family memories of the Galician programs, would have entirely understood, even as a boy:

Gone now are those little towns where the shoemaker was a poet,
The watchmaker a philosopher, the barber a troubadour.
Gone now are those little towns where the wind joined

Biblical songs with Polish tunes and Slavic rue,
Where old Jews in orchards in the shade of cherry trees
Lamented for the holy walls of Jerusalem.
Gone now are those little towns, though the poetic mists,
The moons, winds, ponds, and stars above them
Have recorded in the blood of centuries the tragic tales,
The histories of the two saddest nations on earth.

ANTONI SIONIMSKI (1895–1976) *Elegy for the Jewish Villages*

The two sad nations are Poland and Russia of course. Max Kohn left Galicia at an unusually young age with a Polish passport and before the large wave of emigration following the 1905 pogroms. His father, Moshe, had died in 1901, aged only thirty, leaving my grandmother Rachel and his family of five children penniless. This sad turn of events forced young Max to leave Galicia to begin a new life, and to find a new way of surviving, in a strange new country. Family ties are always extremely strong in Jewish communities, and in this case the extended family in Germany came to the aid of the widowed Rachel. Relatives in Hanover offered to give a home to both her eldest son Jacob and young Max. Jacob went to Germany first and Max joined him later.

My father arrived safely in Hanover and joined his elder brother Jacob in a rag-and-bone business, pulling a handcart along the city streets. They traded rags, then cloth, and built up a viable business, sending money home to their mother. They gradually built up relationships with other traders in northern Germany and Holland. At the same time Max set about educating himself by attending night classes. Essentially he was going to school to learn aspects of a completely different culture from the one in which he had grown up, but he was careful not to neglect his Jewish education—Talmudic studies where he learned, among other things, the discipline of argument. His religious commitment was lifelong, and he remained devout and Orthodox, rooted in his belief.

To understand what that belief was we need to make something of a digression, because to say that someone is Jewish is like saying that someone who is a Roman Catholic or a Presbyterian or a Mennonite is simply a Christian. They are all Christians, it is true, but this description is hardly detailed enough to describe the subtleties of a particular religious background. My father was Jewish of course, but he was specifically Hasidic.

The Hebrew for Hasidism, *hasidut*, denotes piety or saintliness, a devotion to the spiritual aspects of Jewish life. This movement goes back to Rabbi Yisroel Ben Eliezer (who was born in 1698 or 1700 and died in 1760—almost an exact contemporary of J S Bach, and also a visionary) who was often called he 'Baal Shem Tov' (literally, the 'Master of the Good Name'), or 'Besht' for short. He was born in

Rabbi Yisroel Ben Eliezer, the 'Besht'

western Ukraine. From an early age he found himself unsatisfied by the traditional modes of Jewish worship and study. He became friends with other like-minded individuals who were also seeking to infuse traditional modes of worship with a new spiritual content. He stressed the role each individual could play in the service of God; he emphasized the importance of joy in religious worship and the commandments; he vigorously opposed fasts and asceticism; he taught that physical pleasure can give rise to spiritual pleasure. His teachings were regarded with deep suspicion, even as heretical, by the rabbinical establishment, but the Baal Shem Tov's movement rapidly caught the imagination of the community, especially the common people. He inspired a group of outstanding disciples who became leaders of the movement in their own right, spreading their teachings to many parts of eastern Europe, and founding dynasties, many of which continue to this day. These leaders were known as *Zaddikim* (literally, 'righteous ones') and the followers became known as Hasidim.

We have already had an indication of the power of such an individual in the Chortkover Rebbe, the *Zaddick* for whom my father, Max Kohn, felt lifelong devotion. Each *Zaddick* (with the title of Rebbe to differentiate him from the ordinary town rabbi) had his own court with devoted followers who travelled to visit him on great festive occasions. It was common for one Hasid to ask another: 'To whom do you journey?' ('To which *Zaddick* do you owe allegiance?').

Although there were some Hasidim in western Europe—and even in Israel as early as 1777—the vast majority stayed in eastern Europe where, before World War II, hundreds of different dynasties flourished. These dynasties were known by the name of the town in which the Rebbe resided—European town names continued to be used as part of their title even when a Rebbe moved to the United States or Israel—the exception being the Hasidic master who held court in Boston with the title 'The Bostoner Rebbe'. The meetings for prayer, study and companionship took place in a small meeting house known as the *shtiebel*. These places of worship, like small-scale intimate synagogues with fewer formalities, were also to be found throughout Europe and were used for worship by eastern European Hasidim— such as the male members of my family. Even today contemporary Hasidic sects are linked to powerful Rebbes of former times: the Chabad-Lubavitch, now prominent in Israeli politics, the anti-Zionist Satmar in the United States, and the esoteric Breslov sect.

The first meeting between my parents took place in Berlin in 1913. My mother, born Lena (Lene, or Lea) Aschheim, was a native of Berlin and she was twenty-two years old at the time she met Max. Her parents, my maternal grandparents, were Leo and Rosie Aschheim. One of the oldest pictures to survive in the family archives is of my maternal grandparents with my mother, Lena, the tall teenager in the middle of the photograph.

The Aschheim family in Berlin

Leo Aschheim was a milliner who supplied hats to the German African colonies—countries like Tanganyika—before the First World War, and his wife Rosie came from a prominent family named Kurz. Leo and Rosie had five children, all born in Berlin. Although my mother had been raised in Berlin (her German was excellent and she was completely at ease living there), she came from a family of *Ostjuden* who had come to Germany a generation earlier. For this reason the marriage was deemed suitable, and so it turned out to be. Like my father she never possessed a German passport. My father was born in Poland of course, but my mother, despite the fact she was born in Germany, retained the Polish nationality of her parents.

Many members of my mother's family emigrated to the United States. When I first visited America in 1952 I was made much of by my Kurz relations on my grandmother's side—all high–flyers in the academic, legal and accounting professions. At this point I must also mention my mother's relative, Dr Selmar Aschheim, although I never actually met him. He was a star gynaecologist at the Charité, one of the great hospitals of Berlin and Director of the Laboratory of the Universitäts Frauenklinik. He later became chair of research in gynaecology at Berlin University but was dismissed from this post in 1933 and later emigrated to Paris. When Professor Max Planck had bravely argued with Hitler that German learning and science were endangered by the dismissal of people on racial grounds, the Führer's reply was: 'Our national policies will not be revoked or modified, even for scientists. If the dismissal of Jewish scientists means the annihilation of contemporary German science, we shall do without science for a few years.' In 1928, together with Bernhard Zondek, who was an endocrinologist, Selmar Aschheim had developed what became known as the Aschheim-Zondek test for pregnancy in women—this was colloquially known as 'the rabbit test' and it was used worldwide before more sophisticated means were discovered to detect pregnancy in women without the use of laboratory animals.

In 1913 the marriage between Max and Lena was agreed, but then 'events' (as Harold Macmillan once described them) intervened. My father travelled a great deal for business reasons and at the outbreak of the First World War he found himself in Holland. Although he had lived in Germany for a long time he was a Polish citizen and he really wanted to avoid being conscripted into Franz Josef's Austro-Hungarian army. So he decided to stay in Holland, and chose as his base Scheveningen, a sophisticated seaside resort on the outskirts of the Hague. He built his business from there, and made quite a success of it considering the adverse conditions of the war. But he was far away from his betrothed Lena and he was not certain whether an arrangement made in 1913 would still be binding on both sides after what amounted to six years of waiting. This is one of those occasions when he decided to consult the Chortkover Rebbe. My father wrote to Vienna from Scheveningen asking what to do about his fiancée in Berlin. The Rebbe counselled patience and, following that advice, my father returned to Berlin after the war and married my mother in 1919. Fortunately she had also thought it worthwhile to wait for Max.

Fugue III (*in 2 voices*) RALPH KOHN *with* GRAHAM JOHNSON

GJ You never knew your paternal grandfather, Moshe Kohn, who died in Kalush in 1901, but his presence was clearly felt in your family …

RK My elder brother, as well as my eldest cousin, was named after him—in the Ashkenazi Jewish tradition you must never name a son after a living parent or grandparent and of course my grandfather had been dead for quite some time when both my cousin and brother were born. My father's mother, my grandmother, was supported by remittances to Galicia, sent by my uncle and father when they were working in Hanover. But as soon as business was better and they moved to Leipzig, she came to live in Germany, at first with her elder son, my uncle Jacob.

  She then came to live with our branch of the family in the Lortzingstrasse from 1920 onwards. She wore a wig and was very Orthodox; she was like a second mother to us, kindly and loving, sacrificing everything for her children and grandchildren. My father revered her—don't forget that in those days, if it was at all possible, you had one of your elderly parents staying with you—there was no such thing as sending them to an old peoples' home. When we left Germany for Holland she came with us, going to live once more with her elder son, my uncle Jacob. In 1935 she moved with that branch of the family to Palestine and they settled in Haifa. We never saw her again.

GJ This must also have been very hard on your father. We know what a brave and resourceful boy he was in leaving his mother and going out in the world to support her as well as his younger siblings. Can you tell me something about his appearance?

RK He was a smallish man, 5'4" or 5'5" but very sprightly—he liked to swim, to ski, and to walk. He was quite lean with no extra fat. He had a somewhat protruding nose, and by the time I was a child he had lost most of his hair.

  That's what he looked like. In terms of personality he had different sides to his nature, just as he had different names—Marcus, Max or Mottel (my mother called him Mottel) as well as Mordechai—the name used when he read from the Torah. For me he was simply Papa. He was very affectionate and all the children adored him. He was warm, also in a physical sense. I remember getting hugged a great deal more by my father than by my mother. On the other hand, he had an extraordinarily quick temper; he was capable of working himself up into a frenzy about nothing at all, and speaking recklessly in the midst of his fury. My father was very hurt when he didn't receive sufficient recognition for services rendered. On certain occasions he had very little self control, but his saving grace was that he bore no grudge or resentment for long. I have scarcely ever known anyone whose temper could be so volcanic and whose anger was so quickly forgotten once he had got it out of his system. With him the bright sunshine always came immediately after the storm.

GJ Goethe writes 'Vom Vater hab ich die Statur' ('I get my build from my father'). What did you inherit from Max? Do you also have a volcanic temper?

RK Physically I am not at all like him, and I think I do have a different temperament. I am generally even-tempered and even 'well-tempered'! Of course I learned a great deal from him, but that is another matter. I am offended by bad manners of every kind, but I am much more controlled than my father and when I have 'let go' I have always regretted it. There is a Talmudic saying and it goes something like this: 'Who is a strong man? A man who controls his temper. Who is a wealthy man? He who is satisfied with what he has.' But to be truthful, and in answering your question, just like my father I can be hurt by ingratitude.

GJ Did your father's temper lead him to punish you?

RK Hardly ever. From time to time, although I was spoiled greatly (as I have already said) he would give a little slap—but this was never severe. One minute later he would kiss me. I remember that he would sometimes shout at my mother, but this was only occasional and, as a very strong personality, she was more than capable of answering back. On the whole he was a great diplomat and very much loved for his affectionate nature and his humour. His health was never very good however, and he was dogged by illness. He had suffered so much anxiety in his life that it wore him down; he was fifty-one when we came to England as refugees—I know I am jumping ahead in the story—but as a result of losing everything twice in rather quick succession he seemed more like a man of seventy, and he never really recovered any momentum or true joy in his life. There were all sorts of crises to overcome—at first permission to work as a Polish citizen was very difficult to obtain. I remember him receiving the letter that refused his first application to work in England. It began with words like 'we have given very careful consideration ...' and ended 'but we have reluctantly come to the conclusion ...', and so on. An undersecretary had signed the letter with the usual 'your obedient servant' and this made my father believe that there was light at the end of the tunnel—after all this man professed to be his obedient servant!

It is to his credit that later on he managed to make a living in England after setting up his own company, but it was an uphill struggle. He was always generous to others in need—I can never forget him bringing home from the synagogue poor members of the congregation who needed a decent meal, obeying the Hasidic emphasis on behaving lovingly towards one's fellow Jews. He really lived his faith. One of my greatest personal treasures is a letter from the Leipzig days written in Hebrew script which is so exotic in appearance that some people would think it came from another planet. This letter is signed by the famous Chortkover Rebbe in acknowledgement of what seems to have been a very substantial donation from my father—the kind of sum that only a very prosperous businessman would have been able to send to his spiritual leader. It is certain that after about the age of forty, which I would guess was his financial peak, my father never made such money again.

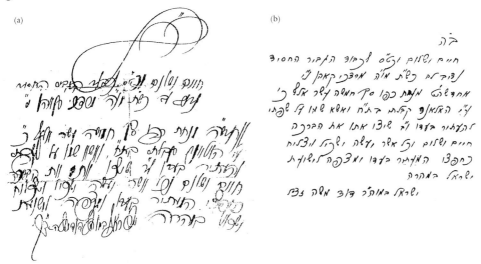

(a) Letter to my father from the Chortkover Rebbe, a prized family possession
(b) *the same text transcribed into modern Hebrew script*

I can't stop myself from thinking how contented he would have been to have remained in Leipzig—regularly attending the *shtiebel*, listening in his spare time to his beloved Italian opera records, and working hard in a way that brought him some kind of fulfilment and reward. He was very good at his work, completely honest, and he has been a role model for me throughout my life in my own business dealings. Life could have been a lot worse for him, but it could also have been a lot better. He never regained the happiness of his earlier years, and I still mourn him deeply.

🔊 *Chanson hébraïque* No 4 *of* Chants populaires MAURICE RAVEL (1875–1937)   *see page 328*
)) CD Track [4]   *for text and translation*

GJ From everything you have told me about your mother over the years of our friendship, she must have been very much a personality in her own right.

RK She certainly was!

GJ Can you describe her?

RK She was a good-looking woman, middle-sized in build, half a head taller than my father. She was light in colouring and of normal weight, except in very old age. She was very active and even with staff in both Leipzig and Amsterdam she was very hands-on in terms of running the house, although she was not a good cook—I remember much of the cooking was done by my grandmother Rachel. Mother was not an intellectual. She was very down-to-earth—you would expect as much from a born Berlinerin—and there was never any boasting or pretension about her. She was a kind, good-hearted woman.

   If my father was something of a dreamer, a mystic as I think we have already discussed, she was an absolute realist. My mother leapt to my brother's defence when my father worried that Maurice was playing too much sport—she admired his prowess on the playing field, and I must confess I also envied him this ability; in fact I was so protected by my mother (who was concerned for my health) that I was never allowed to learn to swim. Maurice was a confirmed Zionist, meaning he was an ardent supporter of a future Jewish state, and ultimately wished to live there. My mother admired this down-to-earth and practical side of his nature far more than if he had been an ardent student of the Classics. She used to remind my father that not everyone was interested in that kind of thing ('Nicht jeder kann ein Lateiner werden'). She was calmly confident that Maurice would make his way in life very well without concerning himself with Latin, and this turned out to be an entirely accurate prediction.

GJ I notice when you speak of your mother you often slip into German …

RK I associate what she said with the German language and she spoke it so well that even today it is a pleasure to remember her tone of voice and vocabulary.

   However, she never really learned any other language, even English, although she lived in England for nearly forty years. This failure to adapt cut her off from a great deal of happiness and communication—in not being really able to speak with her grandchildren for example.

GJ Was she a religious woman?

RK   She was Orthodox and believed in prayer, but she was not really interested in Hasidism. Unlike my father she was not convinced about *kvitel*—the writing of notes with petitionary prayers for health or success that are handed over to the Rebbe in order to receive his blessing. Perhaps you have seen pictures of all these *kvitlech* placed between the stones of the Western Wall in Jerusalem? My mother hated hypocrisy and she could not accept the idea of sinning and then nullifying your guilt by saying certain prayers and writing petitions without addressing the core of one's behaviour. Instead her faith was pure and simple and direct, with a certain dignity and nobility about it.

GJ   If I was to think of a musical equivalent of that description it would be one of the Beethoven settings we have done together—you remember, completely forthright religious texts by the poet Gellert who was a Leipzig man for much of his life. In the songs the sentiments apply as much to the Jewish religion as to the Christian.

Die Ehre Gottes aus der Natur No 3 *of* Sechs Lieder von Gellert   LUDWIG VAN BEETHOVEN
CD Track 5   *see page 329 for text and translation*

RK   Beethoven's music sometimes seems to have been carved out of stone it is so heroic. My mother had almost a heroic determination always to separate truth from lies and she displayed a stoic sense of resolve when the time came for us to leave Germany, and later Holland. She never said anything that was not one hundred percent true and sometimes, just like Beethoven himself, she would blurt out things that were better not said. I would say she was honest on occasion to the point of self-destruction. When she went on and on being critical (she had difficulties with my uncle Jacob for example), my father would say 'Hör endlich auf' ('Just stop it!'). Nevertheless, I would say my mother had intelligent judgement and that my father listened to her opinions increasingly as the years wore on.

GJ   Would you say you were close to your mother?

RK   I loved her and she loved me, but it was always easier to communicate with my father who was more flexible, less rigid. On the other hand she was proud of my achievements and she lived to see me established in my career. At the end of their lives my mother and father moved down from Manchester to live in Hendon and we would visit them there with the children. After my father died we often took mother on holiday with us to Switzerland and Holland. We remained a close family. But I think it very sad that she once said to me that the happiest years of her life were those of her youth in Germany. In 1947 she wrote down an abbreviated story of her life for a family newsletter circulated by her American relatives and she referred to the 'tale of a family'—our family—'that was once very happy'. The story of my parents' lives could easily have been far more tragic, and the story of how we all escaped the Holocaust is a remarkable one—we will talk about that in detail later—but the *joie de vivre* they both deserved was taken away from them by a tidal wave of history over which they, and millions of others, had no control. My father died in 1971 and my mother seven years later, in 1978.

My parents in Amsterdam in the 1960s

PRELUDE IV

Leaving Germany

We Jews are a seismic people. We are often the first to note forthcoming events and upheavals! VICTOR KLEMPERER (1881–1960)

IT IS PERHAPS the greatest piece of luck in my life that our family left Leipzig in late 1933, although it did not seem lucky to us at the time. We owed this decision to my father's in-born wisdom, something in the blood. He was unhappy about living in Germany even before Hitler was elected Chancellor in January of that year. Perhaps a Jew from Galicia is less complacent than those who have become completely assimilated, and he certainly sensed mortal danger. Quite a lot of people were prepared to shrug-off the Nazis as a passing phenomenon, a temporary unpleasantness, but my father seems to have instinctively understood their deadly intentions from the start. He still had his Polish passport (this was to be particularly fortunate for us seven or eight years later). He was prepared to abandon all that he had built up in Leipzig on the strength of a gut feeling that Nazism, and its danger to Jewish people, was something that was bigger than anyone could control, and that it was not all simply going to fade away.

Our final destination was Amsterdam, and again it was fortunate that my father had spent a great deal of time in Holland twenty years earlier. It seemed natural to him to choose the Netherlands as our place of refuge. We did not journey directly to Holland, however, but first headed for Berlin where my mother's relatives lived. In comparison with the escape stories of many Jews in the later 1930s, our family made a comparatively leisurely exit. In those early days of the Third Reich there was a great deal more time for Jews to leave according to their own timetable. Nevertheless, even if we were not actually being thrown out, we were made to feel unwelcome. There was a background of tension and regret on that winter journey—hardly surprising considering what we had left behind.

In Berlin we stayed briefly with my grandfather, and then moved to a house, Holsteiner Ufer 11, which we rented for six months. From the Bellevue tram station further along the quay you can take pleasure cruises on the Spree, but we were not in the mood for such excursions—in any case it was the wrong time of year. I am certain that nothing about the amenities in Berlin for visiting Jews made my father regret his decision to leave the country. It was from Berlin that my father prepared, as best he could, for our new life in Amsterdam.

For over four hundred years Amsterdam was known as 'The Jersualem of the West' because of its large Jewish community. Even though Jews represented no more than 2% of the population in Holland as a whole, they made up 10% of Amsterdam's population—thus about 66,000 people. The community lived in the eastern part of the old city: the Jodenbreestraat and Deventer Houtmarkt—the first of these where Rembrandt had lived and worked, and the second a wood market. By the time our family arrived this area was declining in favour of areas like the Weesperstraat or the Oosterpark. The Jewish community formed an important part of the city's life. Most were self-employed and worked in commerce—the diamond trade for example, or textiles (like my father) or the production of food and drink. Just before my family arrived in Holland, a Committee for Special Jewish Interests was formed whereby refugees had to prove that they were economically productive and not a burden on the state.

Largely on account of my father's business acumen we were fortunately not regarded as refugees and were thus not registered with the Dutch Jewish Refugee Committee. We sought no financial relief and were able to stand on our own feet. We were aware, however, that thousands of other people from Germany had chosen to make their lives in Holland and that the Dutch authorities were hypersensitive about upsetting the balance between Jews and non-Jews in the Netherlands. There was no need for a visa between citizens of Holland and Germany because of reciprocal treaties; in practice visitors and tourists were free to come and go and faced little risk of discovery if they stayed. My father, on the other hand, had a Polish passport, infinitely less desirable at that time. Fortunately he had lived in Holland before and, because of this, and because he had a self-sufficient business, we were allowed to stay. Nevertheless each year he was obliged to reapply for a stamp in his passport permitting him to live and work in the Netherlands. This he did for every year between 1934 and 1939. I think this must have been a constant reminder to him that we did not really belong there.

After we arrived we moved into a modest house in the Tweede Boerhaavestraat, No 66, in the east of the city. I was not able to stay long there with my family because as soon as we had arrived in Holland I was diagnosed with a suspicious lung condition and spent six months in a sanatorium. Fortunately I was not suffering, as the doctors had feared, from tuberculosis. My first school was the Palache (primary) school on Lepelkruisstraat, and I could easily ride there on my bicycle. It was one of three Jewish elementary schools in Amsterdam before the war (and it is just a coincidence that my wife Zahava was a pupil there eight years later). We had regular holidays at Scheveningen and we moved subsequently into a house in the Sarphatistraat, No 76, a long and elegant street, east of the Amstel river, part of an area known as the Jewish Canals. Some of the family furniture had arrived from Germany—this included paintings and a grand piano. There was often liturgical music at home—music sung and recorded by famous Jewish cantors—and on the Sabbath the family would sing traditional Jewish songs.

The house we attended as a *shtiebel* in Amsterdam is still in the Nieuwe Achtergracht, but it has not been in use as a place of worship since the war. In the eastern European Hasidic tradition a *shtiebel* is not a grand or ornate building but is more like an ordinary house. We also attended, although less regularly, the famous Portuguese synagogue (also known as the Spanish Synagogue) in the Meester Visserplein. This was built during the age of Rembrandt for the large Sephardic community in the city. These were the descendants of the Jews who had been expelled from Spain by decree of Ferdinand and Isabella in 1492—and those of the Jews similarly expelled from Portugal in 1497. Like my family in 1934 they had found refuge in Holland. This synagogue was built at the end of the seventeenth century for the Spanish Jewish community of course, but Spain was at war with the Dutch Republic at the time so the worshippers tactfully preferred to refer to

Interior of the Esnoga in Amsterdam

themselves, and their synagogue, as 'Portuguese'. This building, also known as the 'Esnoga' or 'Snoge', is very simple—a high rectangular space with the original wooden benches—but in proportion and effect, with its large and lofty windows, it is a magnificent architectural jewel, one of the most beautiful synagogues in the world. I read the other day that Barbra Streisand had visited it recently, and even that very demanding lady was silenced into reverence by the beauty of the building. In fact the Bevis Marks Synagogue in London, which dates from 1675, was influenced by the Amsterdam 'Snoge' and in many ways is a smaller replica of the Dutch building.

How well I remember all the old gentlemen standing in their top hats on the Sabbath. I also remember fine sand on the floors—an old Dutch Sephardic tradition—to absorb dirt and moisture and to muffle noise. In fact, sand on the floor dates from the time of the Marranos, the Jews who had undergone a mock conversion to Christianity and who continued to worship 'underground' with extreme caution. To muffle the sound of their prayers, they placed sand on the floors not to be overheard. Sand on the floor in the 'Snoge' thus commemorates the time of the Spanish persecution.

During my time in Amsterdam I remember that the name of the Chief Rabbi was Saarlouis, and that the cantor was the greatly gifted baritone Israel Eljasz Maroko. What a magnificent voice he had! He was born in Poland in 1896 and became the Chief Cantor of the Ashkenazi synagogue in Amsterdam in 1926. In July 1943 he was deported from Westerbork transit camp to Sobibor where he was murdered, as were his wife and three of his children. One son survived.

Despite many lively memories of life in Amsterdam, I cannot say that my family felt truly welcomed into the community. There was something about the Dutch mentality that seemed quite closed (not all of them of course—I have marvellous Dutch friends). On the other hand my father made a reasonable living and the conditions were a thousand times better than in Germany. In fact he was more successful in dealing with the Dutch than I was. When I started my own activities many years later, my links were mainly with Switzerland, Germany, Italy, France and Scandinavia. Despite my knowledge of the Netherlands, and being able to speak fluent Dutch, I found it difficult to do business there.

Amsterdam is a city with a reputation for 'anything goes', but the rural Dutch can be extremely censorious. My friend Professor Victor Dubowitz, the great paediatrician, was once in Holland on his way to Den Helder, the northernmost point in the North Holland peninsula. Vic is a South African and on this occasion his accent got him into trouble. One Sunday morning he set off by car to the Horn of Holland. On asking a Dutch worthy directions to the 'Hoorn' (which he pronounced 'Hoeren' in Afrikaans), he received the following admonition: 'You ought to be ashamed of yourself—going to visit the whores ['Hoere'] at 8am on a Sunday morning!'

Fugue IV (*in 2 voices*) RALPH KOHN *with* GRAHAM JOHNSON

GJ At just over six years old, you were already a seasoned traveller. You had left your Leipzig home, spent time in Berlin, and then almost as soon as you arrived in Amsterdam you were separated from your parents and sent to a clinic.

RK I had been rather a sickly child and X-rays were taken of my chest which were an immediate cause for concern. The physicians saw what looked like a lesion on one of the lungs. Tuberculosis was rampant at the time, and diagnosis and treatment entailed long-term observation and hospital visits. This was the era before the discovery of anti-tubercular drugs. I was sent to the Amsterdamsch Kindersanatorium Hoog-Blaricum which is near Hilversum …

GJ … famous for the radio station?

RK Exactly, southeast of Amsterdam. This sanatorium was famous for the treatment of tuberculosis and, in comparison to some of the other old pre-war hospitals it was rather a lovely place in which to be—full of light and air with a tall roof and high ground-floor windows, and lots of outdoor activities. This was an important stay for me in every way. My parents came to see me, mostly on Sundays, bringing all sorts of treats, but I was so immersed in coming to terms with a new country and a new language, that the time melted away. Perhaps my mother had been over-protective of me as a child; this was my first taste of a kind of independence. I returned home after six months with a clean bill of health, thank heavens, and able to speak Dutch fluently. I was fitter, and more robust. What could have been a terrible episode in my life really did me a lot of good.

GJ And Blaricum provided you, surely, with your first exposure to the world of hospitals and clinical treatment which was to play such a large part in your professional life. And you came back from there with fluent Dutch. Do you still speak it?

RK Certainly! My accent is still good although
I have forgotten some of the vocabulary.
During the Wigmore Hall singing
competitions those famous Dutch singers
Elly Ameling and Robert Holl have been
surprised that I can speak to them in their
own language. My wife Zahava gets really
annoyed with me when I tease her by
speaking Dutch in a rough working-class
way—a *Zeedyk* accent it is called. 'Stop', she
says, only half jokingly, 'I really can't stand
it.' Zahava has excellent Dutch of course, she
lived in the country far longer than I did.

GJ What are your memories of the house in
the Sarphatistraat?

RK Well it was quite a change from the first
house in the Boerhaavestraat which was
near a brewery—I can still remember the
pervasive smell in the air of beer—Heineken

Outside Sarphatistraat 76, Amsterdam,
where I lived in my youth

perhaps. In moving to the Sarphatistraat we had many facilities lacking in the
previous house—a bathroom for instance! The new house was large enough to
have a live-in girl as a cleaner and housekeeper. A number of items of furniture
had arrived from Leipzig. One of the family treasures was a large watercolour of
a *shadchan*—a Jewish matchmaker. He had a beard, was wearing a hat and was
smiling, making a circle between his thumb and first finger that signified he had
been successful in finding his clients a good match. I also remember a magnificent
copy of the complete Talmud, twenty leather-bound folio volumes containing the
sixty-three tracts that had come from Vilnius, at that time the world centre of
rabbinical scholarship. People used to come to the house to consult these volumes,
but my father did not permit people to borrow them.

GJ Who else do you remember coming to the house?

RK My father was always a generous host and there were no doubt many visits from
people he knew from the synagogue. But there is one man in particular, in his
middle to late thirties at the time, who remains strongly in my memory. His name
was Dr Burg, or that was the name he chose to use when he came to visit us in
Amsterdam. I shall come later to why he may have needed to use a pseudonym at

the time. His real name was Kolomán Lauer and my father befriended him in the 1930s. He was a Hungarian Jew (born in Szinérválja, now Seini in Romania) who lived in Budapest travelling widely on business. He was a *Kohen*, which is to say a member of the priestly sect. He sometimes even came to synagogue with us on the Sabbath in Amsterdam and if he was staying with us during the Holy Days, he recited the priestly blessing at the *shtiebel*. My father said that he had never come across a man as smart and able as Lauer. As young as I was, I remember that he had a charm and a sophistication about him that made each of his visits to our home a special event. He was a trained lawyer and was addressed as 'Herr Doktor'—as were most men who had been to university in those days.

From time to time at Sarphatistraat 76 we would receive parcels from Hungary that clearly came from Lauer. These parcels were labelled 'Muster ohne Wert' (samples without value) and they contained small bottles of Tokay. I don't need to tell that this was the famous sweet dessert wine from Hungary which was said to be highly prized by Schubert.

GJ Schubert actually wrote a song in praise of Tokay: *Lob des Tokayers*.

RK So I believe, although I've never sung it—and I myself haven't drunk alcohol for years. Receiving these kinds of samples would have made more sense if my father

had been a wine merchant or even lover of wine. I suppose we might have thought at the time that he was thinking of expanding his business. It was only years later, when we were in England, that my father told me that in these boxes—with their special compartments for the bottles—large amounts of currency were hidden. It seemed that Hungarian Jews, many of them foreseeing trouble ahead, exactly like my father had done, were being helped by Lauer to smuggle money out of the country ahead of their exile. My father never spoke about how he dealt with the money at the time, or where he sent it, but it was clearly an ongoing arrangement that worked. I would think my father had been chosen as middle-man because he was utterly honest and reliable.

Kolomán Lauer

You would no doubt be surprised if I told you that Lauer was connected with Raoul Wallenberg, the Swedish diplomat in Budapest who turned out to be one of the heroes of the Holocaust?

GJ That is a surprise! The name of Wallenberg is very famous of course, also because after all his heroic efforts he suddenly disappeared, taken prisoner by the Russians, and was never seen again. But what was his connection with Lauer?

RK Lauer, together with a Swedish businessman named Sven Salen, had set up an import-export business in Stockholm with the name of the Mid-European Trading Company (Mellaneuropeiska Handels AB) shortened to Meropa, although he continued to travel on a Hungarian passport. In 1936 he had met a young Swede by the name of Raoul Wallenberg, twenty-four years old at the time, who had trained and qualified as an architect. Apart from spending time in South Africa, Wallenberg had already worked at a Dutch bank in Haifa in Palestine where he met a number of Jews who had been exiled from Europe and whose stories had had a profound effect on him. Wallenberg was partly Jewish—only a sixteenth Jewish, I believe—but he was proud of this part of his ancestry. In 1942 Wallenberg joined Lauer's company and within eight months the young man had become a major shareholder and international manager of the Mid-European Trading Company. From 1942 to 1944 on his business travels throughout Germany and Nazi-occupied France he became adept at understanding, and circumventing, German bureaucracy. He also made several visits to Hungary where he met Lauer's family and experienced the oppressive circumstances under which Hungarian Jews in Budapest were living with German violence a constant background threat.

Raoul Wallenberg

GJ　I think many people are not aware of how complicated the political situation in Hungary was at the time—especially in regard to the fate of the Hungarian Jews.

RK　Although Hungary had joined forces with the Nazis in 1941 in the war against the Soviet Union, the Jews had enjoyed relative safety there—if not any sense of comfort or security. The Hungarian leader Miklós Horthy was right-wing and anti-Semitic, but he was not interested in systematic persecution of the Jews. In 1943 when the Germans lost the Battle of Stalingrad—and it seemed clear that the war would not be won by Germany—Horthy, attempted to negotiate a separate peace with the Allies. Hitler demanded continued solidarity from Horthy and, when this was refused, Germany invaded Hungary on 19 March 1944—although Horthy remained nominally in power. A few month's later the full horror of the Nazi 'Final Solution' became known to the world and the Nazi destruction machine went into overdrive. There were eye-witness accounts of the gas chambers. Adolf Eichmann had also arrived with the German army, and began his deadly work. Thousands of Jews from the Hungarian countryside were rounded up by the train-load and deported to Auschwitz. Tens of thousands of Hungarian Jews fled to Budapest in the hope of acquiring refugee papers from the foreign embassies in the capital. For a while Budapest was the only safe-haven for about 700,000 Jews. The Swedish Embassy, one of the few neutral powers, issued about 700 protective passes but this was an inadequate response to an unprecedented refugee crisis.

GJ　So now it was up to the heroic Wallenberg to alleviate the problem.

RK　No, it was not nearly as simple as that. It was at this point that President Roosevelt and the government of the United States became involved and established the War Refugee Board—the WRB. A committee of prominent Swedes was convened to discuss the growing problem of the besieged Hungarian Jews, among them Kolomán Lauer who was known to have great expertise in Hungarian matters. The original Swedish representative to Hungary was Folke Bernadotte, but the Hungarian government disapproved of him; another man was needed. The committee called for the recruitment of a suitable non-Jew to go to Budapest on a rescue mission. This person had to be a citizen of neutral Sweden and empowered to represent his country. Lauer had come to know Raoul Wallenberg well and admired his great qualities—courage, initiative and an idealistic passion for doing the right thing. It is true that Wallenberg was only thirty-two and some people thought he was too young for the job, but Lauer persisted in his wholehearted recommendation—and he won the day. In putting Wallenberg's name forward I believe Lauer proved himself one of the greatest talent-spotters in history. He found exactly the right man for a truly impossible job. I knew Lauer both before and after the war and he struck me as perhaps the most astute person I ever had the privilege to meet.

GJ   I wonder whether Wallenberg realized at this point what he was taking on.

RK   I would have thought it very likely that Lauer remained Wallenberg's adviser at this critical juncture. The young Swede demanded, and eventually received, very special powers and unprecedented freedoms. These were so wide-ranging that they required the ratification of the King of Sweden himself. This outcome was no doubt influenced by the fact that Wallenberg came from one of the top aristocratic families in the country. Lauer no doubt played a significant part in these negotiations. Wallenberg was allowed to use any method he saw fit to achieve his ends, including bribery; he required very substantial financial resources; he was free to rise above all diplomatic niceties and protocols and deal directly with the Nazis, as well as appealing directly to Horthy if necessary; he was also empowered to provide asylum in legation buildings for those holding Swedish protective passes.

When Wallenberg arrived in Budapest on 9 July 1944, 437,402 Jews (by the Nazis' own count) had already been deported in 148 trains destined for the east between 14 May and 8 July. This is an astonishing number in a very short time. It was clear that Wallenberg's greatest enemy was Adolf Eichmann, Chief of the Jewish Office of the Gestapo and answerable to Heinrich Himmler. Fortunately, there were set-backs to Eichmann's ambitions: Auschwitz, having received five trains a week from Hungary, each containing four thousand men, women and children, was now finding it impossible to 'process' so many people. The over-zealous Eichmann, always hopeful of promotion for his efficiency, was told to slow down. His hopes of removing the whole of the remaining Jewish population of Budapest in a twenty-four-hour blitz in the last weeks of July were prevented by Miklós Horthy having a severe case of 'cold feet'. The Hungarian leader (soon to be deposed by the Nazis and imprisoned in Bavaria) feared the reactions of the world press, not to mention the advancing Russian army. Without Hungarian troops to police his orders, Eichmann's hands were tied. As it happened, Himmler himself, hoping to play a part in a separately negotiated peace treaty, and believing that lessening the pressure on the Jews would improve his chances of survival, agreed to the cessation of trains.

GJ   This is truly a bizarre twist of fate.

RK   Not even these events could stem the fanaticism of Eichmann who had appealed to Berlin over Horthy's head for permission to continue his deadly task; he was no doubt surprised, and deeply disappointed, by Himmler's response, where another slightly more humane functionary might have been relieved. Adolf Eichmann remained at his desk as determined to destroy Jewish lives as Wallenberg was to save them. When the two met for dinner at Wallenberg's headquarters, Eichmann initially found the Swede 'charming'.

GJ This bureaucratic image brings to mind Hannah Arendt's description of Eichmann as the embodiment of 'the banality of evil'.

RK Quite so. In a few months Wallenberg had given out 13,500 protective passes; he had set up soup kitchens, hospitals and nurseries, purchasing food, clothes and medicine with the large funds at his disposal. He built thirty Swedish safe houses. In November 1944 Eichmann instituted 'death marches'; when there were no trains to take his victims east, Hungarians Jews were forced to walk the route from Budapest to Vienna under appalling conditions, and Wallenberg was there to hand out food and medicine, bribing and threatening as he handed out yet more Swedish passes.

Hungarian Jews assembled for deportation in 1944

Like a man possessed Wallenberg used every means he could, diplomatic as well as physical, to save Jewish lives. Eichmann was still determined to send trains out to Auschwitz, whether or not authorized by Berlin. He managed to do so on a couple of occasions. There are stories of Wallenberg jumping on the roofs of cattle trucks in train stations, handing Swedish passes through the air vents. The German soldiers were ordered to open fire but, impressed by Wallenberg's courage, they aimed too high. The gallant Swede leapt to the ground and demanded that the Jews with passes should be allowed to leave the train.

In January 1945 Wallenberg discovered that Eichmann, frustrated by his inability to transport his victims to Auschwitz, was planning a total massacre in the largest Jewish ghetto. Through an intermediary, a powerful ally in the Hungarian police, a note was delivered to Eichmann's superior, General August Schmidthuber, who was warned that he would be held personally responsible, and hanged as a war criminal, if such a massacre took place. Wallenberg's quick action at this time saved the lives of many thousands of Budapest Jews. Indeed, they say Wallenberg saved 100,000 lives in all. And none of this would have happened if Lauer had not recruited him and put all the pressure he could on the Swedish government to appoint Wallenberg to this post. I am very proud to think that my father, very early on, played some role in the good works of this remarkable man.

GJ What happened to Lauer? I hope he didn't vanish behind the Russian lines like the unfortunate Wallenberg.

RK Lauer was a man who thrived on working in the background. As a result he has always been treated merely as an adjunct to the Wallenberg story. He survived the war and went on working, but I feel his role in the whole saga of the saving of the Budapest Jews has been underestimated and remains insufficiently acknowledged and rewarded.

The tragic story of what happened to Wallenberg is a long one, and it has not been entirely resolved. It is believed he died in Russian captivity in 1947, but there have been any number of theories. There is a moving letter that Lauer wrote to Wallenberg in late 1944 ending with the words: 'Gratitude for your work you can probably not expect. So be very careful before you throw yourself into any adventures.' As for Lauer himself, my father was in touch with him again after the war. In 1959 or 1960 I met Lauer again for the first time since 1939. This is jumping forward in my story of course, but I was working for Smith Kline and French at the time and my brief was to go to Basel in Switzerland for my pharmaceutical work. I met him at the Hotel Euler, and he seemed very pleased to see me again after over more than twenty years. He questioned me about my work and I told him about my pharmacological activities. His reply to my explanation was among the shrewdest things anyone has ever said to me in my life, in fact it was life-changing: 'You have a lovely job, but frankly, you should aim to work as an independent and not work for a company.' This was the first time I had ever thought about taking an independent course in my career. He really had my best interests at heart I am sure. He had a sister living in Israel and a niece he was keen for me to meet. I was, after all, of marriageable age!

GJ A bit of a matchmaker then? That brings us round full-circle to that picture of the *shadchan* in Amsterdam. In this case however Kolomán Lauer had not made a match. His successful matchmaking in helping to save 100,000 Jewish lives might be slightly more important!

RK Zahava and I were happily married three year later (see *Prelude XIV*) and I was spared the fate of poor Heinrich Heine running after girls who were probably in love with other people. This is music I love to sing, but it is a fate I was fortunately spared.

 Ein Jüngling liebt ein Mädchen No 11 *of* Dichterliebe, Op 48 ROBERT SCHUMANN
CD Track [6]   *see page 330 for text and translation*

Lauer was invited to our wedding in Amsterdam in 1963 but was unable to come; he did, however, send a telegram.

After that we lost touch. He faded from my life, and I fear he has rather faded into the background of history. I have found it impossible to find out what happened to him, and when he died, although I am sure that many people reading this will be able to enlighten me. He almost certainly died in Israel but I am not sure when. He was a great and good man and I honour his memory.

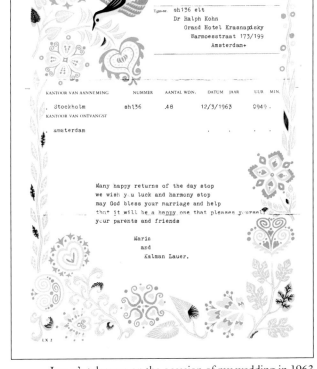

Lauer's telegram on the occasion of my wedding in 1963

Amsterdam in the 1920s

PRELUDE V

Storm clouds over Amsterdam

MY FATHER'S BUSINESS PARTNER in Leipzig had been his elder brother Jacob. It was Uncle Jacob who had sent for my father when he was in Kalush, and the two brothers had a rag-and-bone business together in Hanover.

Later they moved to Leipzig, although their paths diverged in terms of business. Our family had left Leipzig in 1933, but my Uncle Jacob, Aunt Netti and my cousins left for Amsterdam immediately Hitler became Chancellor. This was really only a staging post on their journey to Palestine—the British-mandated territory. Jacob had decided that Europe was now a dead-end in terms of business opportunities and there was an unknown future for Jews. He preferred to take his chances in Palestine, despite the flaring up of tension between Jews and Arabs the year before. I did not realize it at the time, but my future in-laws, shortly before the birth of my wife, were also leaving for Palestine at this time, and also via Amsterdam.

There were in fact nearly 7,000 German refugees admitted to Palestine in 1934 alone, and Jacob believed that it was a safer destination than anything Europe had to offer. In this he clearly differed from my father who was unrepentant about having left Germany, but saw no reason to emigrate to Palestine. Holland was a fiercely independent nation, and although it was far from ideal in its attitude to immigrants, he felt safe there.

Looking back on those times it seems incredible that Jews should have felt safe anywhere in Europe. Although the term 'anti-Semitic' had come into use in the late 1870s (a sentiment typified by the Prussian politician and historian Heinrich von Treitschke with his famous phrase 'Die Juden sind unser Unglück'—'the Jews are our misfortune'), Germany was not the only country that displayed anti-Semitic tendencies. I am thinking now of France and the disgraceful case of the Dreyfus trial, long before there was such a movement as Nazism. Jews had always known that there was a part of society where they were loathed, and not only in Germany of course. What made Germany a special case could be the subject of endless discussion; some people would argue that it is the nature of the German people themselves, as if they were all somehow intrinsically evil. I would refute that; rather was it that country's tragedy that for centuries it had fostered an attitude of dutiful obedience to its rulers who were, in this case, a group of psychotic criminals.

At the time nobody could look into the future; would the Nazis represent a real intensification of that hatred to a dangerous degree, or would the whole thing blow over? My father took the former view, but there were others who, in the wake of *Kristallnacht*, hoped somehow to survive under a new dispensation of moderate practical restrictions and legal strictures. Many people believed that in the long term this would be the worst thing that could happen. There was even some more hopeful news: in the opening months of 1935 prisoner numbers had fallen in Dachau and most of the Jews taken there in 1933 had been released. In 1936 for the period of the Olympic Games in Berlin, all antagonism to Jews ceased—on the instruction of the Minister of propaganda—Goebbels, and all negative references were forbidden.

The bad news, however, consistently overpowered the good. Conditions in Germany had considerably worsened since we left. In May 1934 *Der Stürmer* ran a fourteen-page anti-Jewish issue which depicted Jews as ritual murderers—this was designed to stir-up hatred in the Christian community. In September 1935 the Nuremberg Laws defined 'Reich Citizenship' and set out rules for 'the protection of German Blood and German Honour'. All Jews were defined as being not of German blood, and marriage between Jews and German nationals was forbidden. In London *The Times* wrote: 'Nothing like the complete disinheritance and segregation of Jewish citizens, now announced, has been heard since medieval times.'

Thousands of Jewish professionals in Germany—professors, teachers and academics in the arts and sciences—were summarily sacked. As early as 1933 the Academic Assistance Council (AAC) was established in the UK. This supremely practical organization negotiated with universities, and government departments to find new jobs for these refugees, some of them men and women of the greatest distinction. The founders of AAC (it changed its name in 1936 to the Society for the Protection of Science and Learning, and subsequently in 1998 to the Council for Assisting Refugee Academics, or CARA) were Sir William Beveridge, A V Hill, J M Keynes and Lord Rutherford, assisted and advised by Esther Simpson and Leó Szilárd. Thanks to this and similar organizations in America, there was at least a chance for well-known, respected and gifted Jews to leave Germany and continue their work in another country, and in an atmosphere free of harassment and fear. (My association with CARA many decades later, and my support for its work, has been a source of great pride to me—see also *Prelude XXIV*.)

For the ordinary German Jew, the man in the street with no family connections abroad, there was no such organization to help them. Throughout 1935 and 1936 more Jewish-owned businesses were summarily transferred to Aryan owners. There were violent anti-Semitic incidents in Poland in 1936, and Hungary and Romania followed suit, racist thugs in all these three countries taking their cue from Germany's shameful example. Nothing in this gradual escalation of violence, however, could predict a decisive turning point, the so-called *Kristallnacht*, in the history of what would turn out to be the Holocaust. The assassination in Paris of a junior German official Ernst vom Rath at the hands of Herschel Grynszpan, a young Polish Jew who was incensed by the expulsion of his family from Germany, gave the Nazis the excuse they needed. The result was the 'night of broken glass' of 9/10 November 1938 when a thousand synagogues and thousands of shops, businesses and homes were ransacked. Over 30,000 Jewish men and women were rounded up and shipped to concentration camps, and hundreds killed.

In my home town of Leipzig an American official described what he saw: 'Having demolished dwellings and hurled most of the moveable effects into the streets, the insatiably sadistic perpetrators threw many of the trembling inmates into a small stream that flows through the zoological park, commanding horrified spectators to spit at them, defile them with mud and jeer at their plight.' I knew the zoo in Leipzig, it was only walking distance from where we lived in the Rosental district. These terrible things could have happened to members of my own family.

The great poet Heine foresaw the potential evils of totalitarianism: 'In a country where they first burn books', he wrote, 'they will end up by burning people'. Of the many lieder I have sung over the years, one of the most frightening is a song by Robert Schumann to a Heine poem—this is *Belsatzar*, the story of the Babylonian king Belshazzar who derides Jehovah, orders the Jewish temple to be plundered, and sets himself up as a God. He pays for this blasphemy with his own life after reading the handwriting on the wall. The Rembrandt painting of this scene from 1635, *Belshazzar's Feast*, has always been a favourite of mine.

It was *Kristallnacht* that revealed Hitler to be the Belshazzar of the twentieth century, and he too died ignominiously, less than seven years later.

Belsatzar Op 57 ROBERT SCHUMANN (1810–1856)   *see page 330*
CD Track ⑦   *for text and translation*

My uncle Jacob left Leipzig before we did, five years before this catastrophe. Although he lived for a while in Amsterdam, he departed for Palestine in 1935, taking almost his entire family with him, as well as my grandmother Rachel Kohn. He left behind his son Gershon who was in the middle of medical training at the University of Amsterdam for Medicine, and who naturally wanted to complete his degree. It was arranged that Gershon (whose nickname was Gegi) would stay with us in our family home. This decision, made on very practical grounds, had enormous repercussions for me and for the entire Kohn family. As it turned out, Gegi was the greatest parting gift that Uncle Jacob could have left us.

Belshazzar's Feast by Rembrandt van Rijn

Fugue V (in 2 voices)   RALPH KOHN *with* GRAHAM JOHNSON

GJ   Uncle Jacob seems to have been quite a character!

RK   He was indeed, and a great deal more affluent than my father. Some people would have said more 'successful' but my father was a careful man, and this precluded him from some of the more adventurous business dealings that appealed to Uncle Jacob. That branch of the family, including my cousin Gegi, lived in a much bigger and grander house in Leipzig than anything we could afford. The address was 22 Ehrensteinstrasse, a villa imposing enough later to be requisitioned by the Nazis as a headquarters for officers. Uncle Jacob was rich. I remember him as a most affable and lively man; he could charm the birds from the trees as they say. We children adored him, he was definitely our favourite visitor to the house, but my mother disapproved of him. To get my mother's approval someone had to be completely above board—she was that kind of straightforward Berlinerin.

One of her favourite expressions was 'Ich kenne meine Pappenheimer'—I doubt if she knew she was quoting Schiller in using this old saying, more or less the German equivalent of 'I know who is who' or 'I know on whom I can rely'.

For her, Uncle Jacob did not come into this category—he took risks, he had chutzpah. When he arrived in Amsterdam in 1935 he had managed to bring quite a lot of money out of Germany and he lived in high style.

GJ Were you already close friends with Gegi from your Leipzig days?

RK No, the age difference between us was too large for that. My relationship with him began in 1935 when he came to live with us in Amsterdam, in the Sarphatistraat— I was eight and he was already twenty-one. He was almost six foot tall and very handsome. He had had a very different upbringing in the sense that his father had the money to pay for nannies, tutors and special lessons. He was the star of the family and doing brilliantly in his medical studies at the University of Amsterdam under the renowned Professor of Medicine, Isidor Snapper. By the time he came to live with us he had already travelled extensively with his father and had a knowledge of the world that was very unusual for a young man of the time. These days young people take travel for granted, but this was not the case before the war, except for the privileged few.

GJ What were Gegi's special abilities?

RK They were almost too numerous to mention. He was a talented linguist, speaking a number of languages. He was a promising pianist and greatly loved classical music. This was particularly fascinating to me because I was taking violin lessons at the time. In this respect, and many others, he was a role model, although I don't think that expression was used in those days. He was also a fine soccer player and an athlete—specializing in the 100 and 200 metres. He came third in these sprinting events for middle Germany. (He had already suffered the humiliation of being forced off a national track team in Germany on account of being Jewish.) He was also a good chess player and well-versed in Talmudical studies.

GJ What fascinates me about Gegi is how almost all his enthusiasms are reflected in your own life-story—apart from athletics perhaps! He studied medicine, and you made your life in medicine; he was a gifted linguist, just as you are; he had a passion for classical music which has been one of the strongest influences in your life and, like you, he played chess. You continue to study the Talmud in depth on a weekly basis with an eminent Talmudical scholar.

RK Well, there is no doubt that Gegi had an enormous influence on me. He was a friend and mentor as well a first cousin. It is difficult to imagine what my life might have been if he had not come into our home at precisely the time I was eager to learn from someone with enormous enthusiasms completely different from those of the rest of my family. It was the breadth of his interests that was astonishing, and I must say, probably thanks to him, my passions, both scientific and artistic, have always been as diverse as his. No one else in our immediate family (apart from my mother's relative, Dr Selmar Aschheim of Berlin) had gone to university and this made him an absolute icon. For those crucial five years between 1935 and 1940 he took me under his wing.

GJ This is such a hymn of praise that I must ask whether Gegi had any unattractive qualities?

My athletic cousin Gershon (Gegi) standing on the right of the picture; on the left is his brother, another first cousin, Nachum Kohn. Between them is my aunt Netti Friedlaender Kohn. The picture was taken in Palestine in 1936

RK Of course he did, don't we all? He was on bad
terms with my older brother Maurice for no
apparent reason—I think he felt somehow
superior. That must have hurt Maurice who
was an ardent Zionist and would probably
have preferred to go with Uncle Jacob to
Palestine. Gegi was capable of arrogance on
occasion, as if he were too accustomed to
getting his own way in everything, and he was
also at times a poor loser in chess when I
managed to beat him, young as I was! By the

Max Euwe (on the left) playing Alexander
Alekhine at the Chess World Championship,
Holland, 1937

way, this game was an abiding passion between us and it has remained a lifelong
enthusiasm, I still play regularly with my grandson Alex and try to solve the daily
chess problem in *The Times*.

It is difficult to appreciate these days how chess was something very political
in the 1930s, and how it remained so throughout the Cold War period—think, for
example, of how Bobby Fisher contested the world championship with Boris
Spassky in Reykjavík in 1972. The championship series in 1935 was held in
Holland between Dr Max Euwe who was a Dutch mathematics teacher, and
Alexander Alekhine, a Russian-born Grand Master, living in France. The
championship lasted eighty days and took place in thirteen different cities in the
Netherlands. I can still feel the excitement of it all because I followed all the moves
religiously and replayed the games. After thirty games Euwe was declared the
winner. When Alekhine regained the title in 1937 by beating Euwe he is reputed
to have said: 'I have also beaten World Jewry whom he represented.' Alekhine was
later to collaborate with the Germans—but the story is a complicated one: he did
this, so he claimed, to protect his Jewish-American wife, Grace. He was a serious
alcoholic and was found dead in his hotel room in Portugal in 1946. There is still
uncertainty about what really happened to him, and there is some speculation, pure
conjecture, that he was murdered by Soviet agents.

GJ Tell me something about how Gegi influenced your musical development?

RK My lifelong passion for music is something that grew thanks to Gegi, there is no
doubt about that—I have already mentioned that he was a good pianist. We would
go together on Sunday mornings to the youth Concerts of the Concertgebouw
Orchestra. These were conducted by the legendary Willem Mengelberg as well as
his deputy Eduard van Beinum who was later to inherit Mengelberg's mantle. I also
remember Pierre Monteux and Bruno Walter as guest conductors at some of these

concerts. It is thanks to Gegi that the first orchestral concerts I attended were of this marvellous quality. We also discussed music non-stop—he had definite opinions regarding performances and interpreters.

GJ Did these include singers?

RK Not as far as I remember. In fact it was my father who had a passion for operatic voices and had his favourite records. Gegi was more of an instrumentalist and we both regarded the young Yehudi Menuhin as a special icon. There had been many fine Jewish violinists at the time—Szigeti, Huberman, Elman, Heifetz—and there were to be many more after Menuhin, but his fame was a special inspiration in the face of the anti-Semitism spreading across Europe. We lived safely in Amsterdam, but we still felt somehow extremely unloved and marginalized. And suddenly, there was Yehudi Menuhin playing his magical violin. In spite of everything that had been said about us, here was a young Jewish boy playing like an angel.

Yehudi Menuhin in 1938
Photograph inscribed to the accompanist
Gerald Moore, teacher of Graham Johnson

The great Dutch conductor
Willem Mengelberg

PRELUDE VI

Leaving Holland

IT WAS CLEAR that the international community had to help Jews leave Germany under any circumstances, and by any means. It is true that until the borders closed at the start of the war, Jews were allowed to emigrate, albeit without all their possessions or money, but many were trapped within the Reich because they were unable to find a country willing to let them in. Before *Kristallnacht* there had been many Jewish children allowed into England on an ad hoc basis, but now a more concerted effort was required. After this watershed catastrophe, the British Jewish Refugee Committee appealed to members of parliament. On 21 November 1938 a debate was held in the House of Commons and it was agreed that an unspecified number of refugee children, under the age of seventeen, were to be admitted into England. There were some doughty British parliamentarians who fought hard for this outcome, among whom was that extraordinary MP Eleanor Rathbone who later did so much for Jewish causes. The system of *Kinderstransport*—a name with deep historical resonances—was thus brought into being by parliamentary agreement. This scheme ran effectively for nine months between December 1939 and the beginning of the war, although there was a final *Kinderstransport* from Amsterdam in May 1940 which I will describe in considerable detail a little later in this narrative. In the end some 10,000 children were saved in this manner. All formalities were to be waived for these arrivals, but a £50 bond had to be deposited for each child 'to assure their ultimate settlement'. The children were to travel in sealed trains, but the running of the scheme had nothing to do with the British government. Many of the heroes were individuals, Jews and Christians of many denominations working together: Lola Hahn-Warburg set up the structure when she was still in Germany; in England Lord Baldwin, Rebecca Sieff, Sir Wyndham Deedes and Viscount Samuel all played an important part, as did Rabbi Solomon Schonfeld, and Professor Bentwich who was the organizer of the Dutch escape route. The Quaker leaders Bertha Bracey and Jean Hoare were also very active, the latter personally escorting a plane-load of children from Prague. The stockbroker Nicholas Winton arranged the transport of over 600 children from Czechoslovakia. Also crucial was the role of such non-governmental organizations as the Refugee Children's Movement, the Friends' Committee on Refugees and Aliens, the Chief Rabbi's Emergency Relief Council and the Central Jewish Fund for World Jewish Relief.

We were living in Amsterdam, so there was no question of being rescued from a country that no one expected to be under the jackboot of Nazi rule. If we had still been living in Leipzig at the time I would have qualified, being still four years under the age limit. The pressures on parents in Germany, becoming more dangerous by the day, to part from their children and let them take part in this scheme in order to survive, must have been enormous—a kind of Sophie's Choice. I wonder whether my mother would have let me go, and I am almost certain I would have refused to travel without the whole family. My sister Toni would have qualified, and maybe even Celia by the skin of her teeth, but my brother Maurice and my cousin Gegi were too old. We were indeed fortunate as a family not to have to face this predicament, and even more fortunate that our lives were all saved by an indirect connection with this famous scheme.

The first *Kindertransport* arrived at Harwich on 2 December 1938, less than a month after *Kristallnacht*. It brought 196 children from a Jewish orphanage in Berlin that had been burned down by the Nazis. Trains full of children arrived from Vienna, Berlin, Prague and other cities. One of the refugees from Vienna was Gitta Deutsch, the thirteen-year-old daughter of Otto Erich Deutsch, the greatest Schubert scholar of all time, and to whom we owe the catalogue numberings of the composer's songs. The famous musicologist would soon also arrive in England as a refugee; in this way children were often split from their parents who had claimed asylum separately. All the children were unaccompanied and a few were babies carried by children. The experiences narrated by Gitta Deutsch in her book of memoirs—*Böcklinstrassenelegie*—show that some were luckier than others in terms of their new homes. Children who could not speak a word of English were taken in by families—some found love and affection, but others suffered terrible loneliness and heartbreak. The English foster parents were seldom less than dutiful but were also sometimes cold and patronizing, treating the young refugees as charity cases, and certainly differently from their own children.

Typically the trains crossed the Dutch and Belgian borders, the children travelling on the German Reichsbahn to the border crossing at Aachen. In the Netherlands their first stop was Utrecht. The journey continued via Hoek van Holland and by ship to England. Some children remained in Belgium and Holland and were doomed later to perish in the camps. Nevertheless, in the two years of its existence the *Kinderstransport* saved the lives of 10,000 Jewish children born in Germany, Austria, Poland and Czechoslovakia; three-quarters of their parents were victims of the Holocaust.

The heroine of *Kinderstransport* in the Netherlands was a woman named Truus Wijsmuller-Meijer. She was born in 1896 as Geertruida Meijer. She married a Dutch banker by the name of Wijsmuller—hence her double-barrelled name. The couple had no children of their own but Truus came from a family that had fostered children in the wake of World War I and was a gifted social worker. She was tough, resolute, modest and unpretentious in defending the interests of deprived children. After the horrors of *Kristallnacht* she realized that only radical action could save Jewish lives. She journeyed into Austria to collect train-loads of children and personally harangued Adolf Eichmann (the arch-villain of a previous chapter in this book), then in an earlier part of his career and in charge of the newly formed Central Office for Jewish Emigration in Vienna. Truus Wijsmuller asked Eichmann for permission to release 600 children into her care. (He joked with her that he was only too glad to get rid of them.) She was no respecter of geographical boundaries and as efficient in organizing a transport from Riga in Latvia to Sweden as she was in smuggling children onto the illegal ship *Dora* bound for Palestine from Marseilles. She set up the Burgerweeshuis orphanage on Lijnbaansgracht in Amsterdam and converted it into a refugee hostel and staging post for the *Kindertransport*. The many children who passed through these doors often needed medical attention. My cousin Gegi, now Dr Gershon Kohn, had recently qualified as a doctor at Amsterdam University, and it so happened he was one of the physicians on the hostel's roster—some miraculous fate had brought him into contact with Truus Wijsmuller-Meijer.

It goes without saying that the declaration of war in September 1939 weighed heavily on all of us, but we did not feel immediately threatened. It took six months for us to realize that Hitler intended to exercise his insatiable ambitions for European domination with all possible speed. On 9 April 1940 German forces invaded Norway, defeating French, Polish and British forces at Narvik. On 10 May German troops—preceded by air bombardment—attacked Luxembourg, Belgium, the Netherlands and France. The British, trapped in northern France, retreated to Dunkirk and withdrew by sea after heavy losses. The story of how a fleet of small, individually owned British boats braved the seas to rescue the stranded soldiers, vulnerable to attack from the air, embodies the kind of spontaneous gallantry typical of the country to which I would soon belong.

By 13 May German troops were pushing through Holland to Amsterdam. It seemed inevitable that Amsterdam would fall, but the speed with which this was accomplished came as a terrible surprise. Some 140,000 Jews, including refugees from pre-war Germany, Austria and Czechoslovakia, were trapped behind the German lines. A few thousand escaped southwards through France. Only a few hundred managed to reach the safety of neutral Switzerland, Spain or Portugal.

It must have been all but impossible at that time to muster any sense of optimism. When I sing the second of Brahms's *Vier ernste Gesänge* (*Four Serious Songs*) I think of the darkness of this period of history, and the sense of utter hopelessness that so many people experienced.

Ich wandte mich No 2 *of* Vier ernste Gesänge, Op 121 JOHANNES BRAHMS (1833–1897)
CD Track 8   *see page 332 for text and translation*

The intrepid Truus Wijsmuller was aware of the danger facing seventy-one children from Berlin who were now trapped in Amsterdam at the Lijnbaansgracht orphanage. She had to find a way to get them out of Amsterdam. In this same period she travelled to the German border in an attempt to save an eighty-six-year-old blind Jewish woman and encountered the implacable hostility of the Gestapo. This sinister encounter redoubled her determination to save her children by whatever means possible. Fortunately she was well known, and respected, by the Dutch military establishment. On 13 May she was summoned by the garrison commander in the De Lairessestraat and informed there was a ship waiting in the port of IJmuiden that would take her children to Great Britain. The ship was a coal-freighter, the SS *Bodegraven* of the KNSM—the Koninklijke Nederlandsche Stoomboot Maatschappij (The Royal Dutch Steamship Company). It had a gross registered tonnage of five-and-a-half thousand tons and her design allowed for fifty-four crew members. During the 1930s she had sailed between Hamburg and Chile. Safe passage for this vessel was being negotiated with the Royal Navy in London.

Everything now was a race against time. Truus Wijsmuller had to arrange to hire buses to take the children to IJmuiden; the road between Amsterdam and this naval town in north-west Holland was lined with military checkpoints. With only seventy-three children as passengers, there was room on the ship for other members of the Jewish community without endangering the welfare of the children. Wijsmuller had the children as her highest priority, but she saw no reason why the boat should not take as many Jewish refugees, of whatever age, as it could hold. With only hours to spare she alerted several Jewish organizations about this departure but everything had to be on a first-come, first-served basis. The news that the SS *Bodegraven* was due to depart for an unknown destination—anywhere being better than under the Nazi jackboot—spread like wildfire among the Jewish community, but the fact is that there were many thousands of people who did not know about it until it was too late. We had the unbelievable luck to hear the news from a very special messenger.

Fugue VI *(in 2 voices)* RALPH KOHN *with* GRAHAM JOHNSON

GJ   The invasion of Holland must have been a terrifying turn of events for your family.

RK   Yes indeed, this was a horrific time—I was not yet thirteen years old but I can still recall the gravity of the situation like a feeling of panic in the pit of the stomach. Of course, some of the Jewish community believed that a German occupation might be bearable; some advocated leaving the women and children while the men escaped. But the speed with which the invasion of Holland was accomplished left the majority of people with no options, above all those who believed it was imperative to leave immediately. My father was resourceful but under the circumstances there was little he could have done to get us out of Holland.

GJ   But you *did* leave Holland!

RK   And in telling you this story we are moving into the realms of a once-in-a-lifetime miracle. On that fateful day my cousin Gegi happened to be tending the *Kindertransport* children at the orphanage. His relationship with Truus Wijsmuller was close; as a result he knew when and where the buses would be waiting to take the children—and whomever else—to IJmuiden.

GJ   This seems to me to be an almost unbelievable coincidence that he had first-hand access to this information and that your family were the beneficiaries.

RK   Late in the morning of 14 May he arrived at our house with the news that five or six *Kindertransport* buses would be leaving the city from Lijnbaansgracht, with sufficient space for other refugees. The choice was stark. If we wanted to get out we had to be at the Jewish Community Centre—the address was 26 Van der Boechorststraat, southwest of the old city—within a few hours. He believed, rightly as it turned out, that this would be the last boat to leave IJmuiden before the Germans tightened their grip on Amsterdam. He gave us this information at 11 in the morning, so we had to make up our minds on the spot. He himself was forceful in encouraging us to leave.

GJ   I simply cannot imagine what it must have been like to make that decision, particularly without the hindsight of knowing that the Jews who were left behind would later be deported and murdered.

RK   I remember it so well: what do we do? Do we stay, do we go, do we simply lock up the house and leave? There was some talk about sending the children to England on their own. My parents told me later that I spoke out most emphatically: 'We go together or not at all. We're not going to split up the family.' I take credit for that. My mother agreed: 'Forget the house, forget about everything. If we're going out, we're leaving now, as a family.' Only a few days before I had been on a school trip to Oosterbeek, a small town on the Rhine, just west of Arnhem. By some lucky chance the expedition had returned to Amsterdam a day before the invasion of Holland. It was an act of Providence that we were all together now at this crucial moment in our lives. Gegi was very clear about the conditions: we had to go as we were, without luggage. Even if Truus Wijsmuller was determined that her children would have a doctor accompanying them on their dangerous voyage, the Kohns had no special privileges or reserved seats thanks to the connection with Gegi—at that stage it was unclear how many people would be waiting at the Community Centre for the buses, and we simply had to take our chances.

GJ You've described your house in the Sarphatistraat with its fine furniture, grand piano, pictures on the wall, your father's precious edition of the Talmud …

RK We never saw any of those things again. My father had a few items of hand luggage: money, jewellery, documents, passports, prayer shawl and books. Assembling these took a little time; after the ten-minute walk to the buses we arrived *en famille* at about 1.30 pm. By now there were crowds of people trying to get out of the city and everything was noise and confusion. My father kept a cool head and opened a rear door of the bus and got all of us inside. If we had joined the queue in orderly British fashion we would have been left standing.

Truus Wijsmuller was very much in charge of this convoy. We began our journey only at about 3 pm and there was a distinct feeling of a race against time. Throughout the journey the buses were repeatedly stopped by Dutch police and soldiers, but she had papers provided by the military commander in Amsterdam that allowed us to proceed. It took us four hours to reach IJmuiden which was in a state of complete chaos. The Dutch military were there in force, but there were also British soldiers who were landing in a last-ditch attempt to bolster the Dutch defences. It was impossible to move the buses beyond the sluice gates.

SS *Bodegraven*

GJ   I would guess this would not have defeated Truus Wijsmuller.

RK   She was extraordinary! She emptied the buses and walked the refugees along the quay. She was completely determined that her children and her refugees would get through. We passed cars and cyclists. I can still see in my mind's eye a picture of a slim and energetic woman walking towards the harbour with the greatest determination, and leading us to our destination.

      Once we had reached the SS *Bodegraven* there was another delay. In fact we discovered only years later that the captain had been informed on 13 May by the British that the fate of the *Bodegraven* was to be scuttled in order to block enemy access to the port of Amsterdam. Explosives had been consequently brought aboard the day before. The authorities then changed their minds: another ship that was 40m longer, the *Jan Pietersz. Coen*, was chosen for this dismal role, leaving the *Bodegraven* free to take refugees, but there were still explosives aboard. Wijsmuller was nevertheless convinced that the refugees should board and take their chances …

GJ   … *anything* was better than falling into the hands of the Germans?

RK   Yes, she was utterly convinced of this. Looking back on it now, it is as if she could see the unfolding of the whole tragedy of the Holocaust before it had actually happened. Within a few minutes she managed to speak to the naval commander in charge of the port—his name was Cornelius Hellingman and he was one of the heroes of this episode. He ruled that the children and refugees should be allowed to board the *Bodegraven* and the explosives to scuttle the ship were to be removed from the hold. There was one more delay that threatened our departure: apparently there was a British plan to destroy the sluice locks at IJmuiden but this idea was fortunately abandoned when a Dutch official pointed out to British officers that the whole of Amsterdam would be flooded if the sea were allowed to come into the locks. Truus Wijsmuller came on board with the children and the captain of the vessel, Huibrecht Regoort, invited her to come on the voyage with us. She declined of course; she felt she had too much work left to do on behalf of her refugees. She later wrote that she left her coat and handbag on board to reassure the children that she was planning to come with them. They had come to rely so much on her warmth and optimism that she feared they would be afraid of making this voyage without her. The *Bodegraven* left the harbour at 7.50 pm, less than nine hours after Gegi had walked into our house in the Sarphatistraat with the piece of news that changed our lives for ever.

GJ   And what happened to Truus Wijsmuller?

RK 'Auntie Truus', as she was known, continued her work tirelessly during the war, smuggling children out of Holland whenever possible, and providing food parcels. She was arrested by the Gestapo in 1942, but she somehow faced them down and they let her go. She was probably second only to Wallenberg in terms of saving Jewish lives during the war. In 1966 she was named a Righteous Gentile by Yad Vashem, the Holocaust Martyrs and Heroes Remembrance Authority in Jersualem. She died, a legendary figure in her own lifetime, in 1978.

Truus Wijsmuller together with the sculpture erected in her honour in Amsterdam

INTERLUDE 1: ALLEMANDE

At sea

THE VOYAGE on the SS *Bodegraven* was undoubtedly the most dramatic, and most terrifying, five days of my life. In telling the tale of this journey I draw here and there on the memoirs of fellow-passengers like Norbert Ripp and Heinz Hirschberg (later Rabbi Harry Jacobi), the latter a couple of years older than me, a refugee from Berlin who remained a close friend of Truus Wijsmuller. It seems that because of the narrow window for the ship's departure, Captain Regoort had to leave behind some hundreds of refugees who had not yet succeeded in embarking. Fred Keulen who was a member of the crew later claimed 'we could have taken hundreds more people on board'. The captain also lost his second officer, Roetering by name, who had been ashore trying to organize the embarkation of the remaining refugees. The Kohn family were lucky to have come aboard at the same time as the children from the *Kindertransport*. As we sailed away huge columns of black smoke were visible from deck—these were from the oil storage tanks that had been set on fire to prevent the Germans taking them over.

Each one of us had different visual memories of the journey. The story as I tell it has now been pieced together from various sources after many years, but at the time we had almost no idea of what was going on. We were kept almost completely in the dark—and that is a literal description in view of the blackouts at night to prevent enemy attack. It was a May evening in the beautiful summer of 1940; sailing conditions were calm, from the point of view of the weather at least. At 9 pm news came though on the ship's radio that the Dutch government had capitulated. The Queen of the Netherlands and the royal family had gone into exile. We had literally left the country with just over an hour to spare. It turns out that the *Bodegraven* was the last ocean-going ship to leave the Netherlands, although a number of coasters managed to depart that same evening, including the *Friso* on which the Dutch war journalist and radio reporter Lou de Jong managed to find a place.

As dusk set in at 9 pm or so, we were attacked for twenty minutes by gunfire from two German aircraft circling overhead; it was fortunate for us that these planes had clearly already offloaded their bombs elsewhere. The captain ordered the refugees below decks as the enemy aircraft strafed the *Bodegraven* from prow to stern. There were many tracer bullets among the ones aimed at us, but no one was hit. I remember later seeing these shells lying all over the deck. During this incident one of my sisters and I had somehow managed to get separated from the rest of the family—frightened by the chaos on deck we took refuge in the engine room; I can still hear the cacophony of the machinery ringing in my ears. In view of the two terrible accidents that occurred later in the journey, we were lucky that no harm came our way. Of course my parents were beside themselves when we disappeared, if only temporarily. We had all experienced the most tumultuous day of our lives, and tensions were unbelievably high. We were later all successfully reunited of course.

We were spared any more enemy violence for the remainder of the voyage. According to a radio newscast the next day in Holland, the *Bodegraven* had been sunk without any survivors. But once this danger was past there was little sense of relief: we felt we were sailing into the terrifying Unknown. As far as we knew there was no guarantee that we would be permitted to land in England. The captain was evasive when questioned and he offered no guarantees. It seemed to us at the time that he simply had to improvise while his human cargo waited, some more patiently and calmly than others. There had been no time to load adequate supplies on board before the ship's departure and for five days the Orthodox Jewish passengers, forbidden to share the rations offered them by some of the crew, survived on tea and coffee and biscuits. Norbert Ripp remembers eating rice cooked with either dried prunes or apricots, two or three people sharing the same tin plate. He also remembers the cook baking bread and receiving a big ovation from the passengers. We had no change of clothes of course, and we slept in the hold on coal sacks. The ship took what appeared to us a seemingly aimless route along the south coast of England. For reasons we did not understand at the time we stopped at Falmouth but we were not allowed to disembark. After this we continued around the south coast, circumnavigated Cornwall and then proceeded northwards through the Irish Sea. At one time we expected to land in Belfast, but were subsequently told this was not to be. Our most likely destination was Liverpool.

There were a number of distinguished people on board including several VIPs who, completely unbeknown to us, were on secret government business. The Chief Rabbi of Vienna (his position before he escaped to Amsterdam) was also one of our passengers. His name was Rabbi Josef Babad, with a reputation as one of the greatest Talmudists of his era. And then there were people that none of us in the Kohn family had heard of at the time. One of these was Jacques Goudstikker, a world-famous dealer in the paintings of the Old Masters.

He had a famous gallery on the Herengracht in Amsterdam that was packed with the works of Vermeer, Rembrandt and other famous painters; he lived in a beautiful mansion on the Amstel, and gave legendary parties in Nijenrode Castle (where some of his finest pictures were hung) on the Vecht River near Breukelen. I discovered much later that Goudstikker, together with his wife and son, had travelled to IJmuiden by car with an important museum official from Brussels (anxious to return home, even via England if necessary) and that this man, Puyvelde by name, had met up with Goudstikker earlier in the day. They agreed to make their journey together; Puyvelde had a diplomatic passport and this enabled the party to move easily through the roadblocks on the way. Although they managed to board the *Bodegraven* successfully, Goudstikker, on that fateful day, must have been a man with the bitterest regrets. He was so famous in the

Jacques Goudstikker

international art markets that it would have been relatively easy for him to have transferred his hugely prosperous business to London or New York in 1939, but he had gambled on the fact that the war would pass Holland by, as it had done in the First World War. It was only on 14 May, with Rotterdam in flames, that Goudstikker realized that he would have to leave everything behind. The decision to do so was, like that of the Kohn family, taken on the spur of the moment. Under these conditions he had had no time to transfer his business into hands that may have protected his interests in his absence, a move that might have secured the long term financial security of his family once the war had ended.

On board Goudstikkers's wife, Desi, and her son, were assigned a cabin (such facilities were offered to women and children only, and not to those of us who had arrived with the *Kinderstransport*) but she refused to be separated from her husband. They all slept as well as they could in the same part of the ship to which we had been assigned (although we did not know it at the time, this was known as Hold IV). On the night of 15/16 May Goudstikker went up on deck to get some fresh air. He was a man of the world, used to international travel, and had been a privileged passenger on many an ocean liner. Conditions in the hold were unpleasant and up on deck it was a beautiful summer night. It must have been tempting to go in search of better air—an opportunity to clear his head that must have been terribly distracted by the momentous events engulfing us all. He had to find his way in the pitch dark, of course—blackout conditions were enforced to avoid the attention of the enemy.

Desi Goudstikker waited anxiously for her husband to return. After some hours had gone by she went to the bridge—as it turned out negotiating the blackout conditions more successfully than her husband—and asked the captain for help. A navy recruit by the name of Dekker, unfamiliar with the ship, was dispatched to look for the missing man, but he also failed to return. It was only at first light that the ship could be searched and two bodies, only a few

Jacques Goudstikker

feet apart, were found lying in the bottom of Hold III. Goudstikker had apparently descended the wrong staircase in the dark while attempting to return to his family and had fallen some twenty feet down an open hatch. I had often wondered whether Gegi, one of the doctors on board, had been involved in the aftermath of this incident, but it was apparently a gynaecologist from Amsterdam named Wijszenbeek who pronounced Goudstikker dead—he had broken his neck and died almost instantly. The young naval recruit Dekker had made exactly the same mistake while searching for Goudstikker; he had been critically injured by the fall, but was still alive.

There were plans made to bury Goudstikker at sea but these were abandoned when it was decided that an emergency stop was needed to convey the young sailor to hospital, and that Goudstikker's body could be taken off at the same time. The boat was permitted to land briefly at Falmouth on the Devon coast. Mrs Goudstikker was permitted to attend her husband's funeral in Falmouth, but this was only after protracted negotiations with the authorities. There was no question of any of the other passengers (many of whom held German passports and were technically enemy aliens) being allowed to land.

I often thought of the terrible plight of Goudstikker's wife having to go ashore in a foreign country to bury a husband who had died in such a way. It was only relatively recently that I found out she was twenty-eight when she boarded the

Bodegraven, fifteen years younger
than her husband, and had
already enjoyed a career in her
own right as an opera singer—in
fact she was the daughter of the
famous Jewish soprano Selma
Kurz; her father, Joseph von
Halban, had been a distinguished
Viennese gynaecologist. Desi
Halban (appearing sometimes
under the name Halban-Kurz)
sang Verdi roles—Gilda and
Violetta—in Budapest and

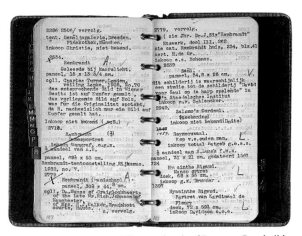

The notebook of Jacques Goudstikker

Vienna; after marrying Goudstikker she performed under Mengelberg's baton in
Amsterdam. Following her husband's untimely death she made her way to Canada
and bravely continued her singing career; she appeared with the New York
Philharmonic conducted by Bruno Walter, who also accompanied her in lieder
recitals. After the war she returned frequently to Holland where she continued to
sing and later to teach.

A detailed list of all the art works belonging to Goudstikker was found in a
small notebook on his person. In Amsterdam we had also abandoned all the
belongings in our home, but Goudstikker had left behind art treasures of almost
incalculable value. The Nazis seized these without delay. There is a photograph
from June 1940 of that famously light-fingered art-collector, Reichsmarschall
Hermann Goering, leaving Goudstikker's gallery in the Herengracht in Amsterdam
looking like a cat who has just eaten a large bowl of cream.

Hermann Goering leaving the Amsterdam atelier of Jacques Goudstikker in 1940

Thanks in part to that list, the Goudstikker heirs were beneficiaries of a settlement of $20,000,000 from the German and Dutch governments on account of these stolen masterpieces. It is an indication of the bureaucratic and legal difficulties facing Jewish Holocaust victims who had been robbed in this semi-official way (difficulties exacerbated by a series of recalcitrant Dutch governments) that this outcome was only arrived at in 2006, over sixty years after the event and far too late to benefit Goudstikker's immediate family. A few years ago Zahava and I went to the Jewish Museum in New York to see an exhibition of the paintings that had belonged to Goudstikker.

The grave of Jacques Goudstikker in Falmouth

My family's voyage with the SS *Bodegraven* came to an end on the fifth day of our journey, 19 May 1940, and not a moment too soon for any of us. We disembarked at the Seamen's Union building in Liverpool hungry, confused and bedraggled, but safe from the Nazi menace. In the pocket of my father's coat was the letter from the Chortkover Rebbe that he believed to be his talisman; he was no doubt convinced that the document had played its part in this happy outcome. It was the end of a long journey, and the beginning of a new one, the ending of an old life and the birth of a new existence in an unknown country. The *Bodegraven* continued in valiant service until sunk by a German U-boat off the coast of Liberia in July 1944. According to the testimony of Fred Keulen, a sailor who had been a member of the crew on the ship's voyage with us to Liverpool, and had stayed with the ship until its final demise, survivors from the *Bodegraven* spent a week in lifeboats before reaching Freetown.

SS Bodegraven

I did not know much about the music of Bach at that stage of my life, but the sense of exhaustion, and also of release and gratitude, of the aria 'Schlummert ein, ihr matten Augen' from Cantata 82 (*Ich habe genug*) comes to mind when I think of the conclusion of that terrible journey for me and my family. Misery was where we had been in Holland, in terrible danger; our new English homeland represented peace and a refuge against evil. The great composer was not of my faith, nor I of his, but I make no apology for singing the words that the Christian Bach set in this wonderful music. This is a universal language of gratitude to the Lord on high for deliverance from all the trials that life is capable of throwing at us.

Schlummert ein, ihr matten Augen *from* Cantata 82 JOHANN SEBASTIAN BACH (1685–1750)
CD Track 9   *see page 333 for text and translation*

PRELUDE VII

On English soil

WE STAYED at the Seamen's Union in Liverpool for two days and two nights. This was merely a transit stage. The eventual destination of our group of refugees had already been decided by the British Ministry of Health which worked through the War Refugee Committee. The northwest and northeast coasts were 'protected areas' where the government would not allow the residence of aliens. Incoming refugees had to be moved from Liverpool. For those on the SS *Bodegraven* this meant Manchester or Wigan.

My father was travelling on a Polish passport that was no longer valid—it was just as well there were no document checks when we embarked at IJmuiden. His passport had expired in 1938 and he had wisely decided not to travel to Poland to renew it. It was also impossible to get it renewed by the Polish consulate in Amsterdam. We were therefore all classified as stateless on our arrival. I did not have a travel document of my own but was listed on my father's no-longer-valid passport. This state of affairs, catastrophic under normal circumstances, turned out very happily for us. The British authorities accepted us as friendly aliens. Poland was an ally, indeed the reason for going to war when it was invaded by the Nazis.

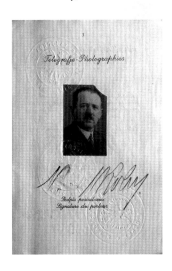

The Polish passport *opposite* with which we arrived in England, with pictures of my father and mother

We were not sent, like so many Jews of German and Austrian nationality, to a holding camp on the Isle of Man. Instead we were dispatched, along with the *Kinderstransport* children, to Wigan, the first stop en route to Manchester.

It was here that I had my first experience of the generosity of the British, and the warmth of northerners in particular. We had escaped from our fear of soldiers with dogs, the instruments of Nazi hate, to find ourselves enthusiastically welcomed at Wigan Wallgate station by a sympathetic crowd. We moved on to the Drill Hall on Powell Street (a famous building that has since been demolished). Here we were greeted by the mayor (with a speech considerately translated for us into Dutch and French) and were then billeted in Baptist and Methodist Chapels where we stayed for the first month.

The fact was that Manchester was preparing for our arrival. It had had a thriving Jewish community for 200 years and had long been used to accommodating victims of misfortune and political reversal. The Manchester Jewish Refugee Committee had been founded in 1933 to help Jews find a way out of Europe and offer them support on arriving in Manchester. The city had already received an influx of 6,000 refugees and now they had to find homes for thousands more. 650 private homes were offered to the Manchester Town Clerk by the end of May, all available to refugees. The Committee that handled my family's settlement in Manchester was expressly working for those who had escaped from Holland and Belgium. In June 1940 the children from the Lijnbaansgracht orphanage were moved from Wigan to Manchester and accommodated in two houses in Heaton Road, Withington, south of the city centre. My mother and father were part of a group of forty-two adults with their families who were placed in houses all around Greater Manchester.

A picture taken soon after my arrival in Britain
Note that I am wearing a tag for identification

We shared a house with other refugees at 2 Mayfield Road, Salford, on the borders of Prestwich. The day of our arrival was 22 June 1940. There were two bedrooms and we all ate together. After a year, and as the other residents gradually left, we found ourselves the sole occupiers of the house. We stayed in Mayfield Road until 1942 when we moved to 3 St Paul's Road, a smaller house in a parallel street. This was north of the Jewish quarter of Cheetham Hill. There was no difficulty in continuing our religious observance as Orthodox Jews of the Dietary laws, the Sabbath and other Jewish holidays. Rabbi David Feldman had come from Leipzig in 1936 and created one of the strongholds of Orthodoxy in the Broughton Park area of Salford where there were many synagogues. We attended one that was very near our house.

Like all other inhabitants of Britain we had to endure the heavy air raids, the night-time sirens and the blackouts. My bar mitzvah on 9 December 1940 (celebrated with a bit of herring and a bottle of whisky) coincided with Manchester's first air raid; in the distance we could see the city centre glowing with fire, but Salford was not hit. My father, who was suffering from a severe infection, signed up as an air raid warden. My mother had a series of gynaecological problems—the strain of years in exile was beginning to tell in both their cases. It was easier for the younger members of the family to adapt. Both of my sisters were able to find work and my elder brother joined the army—he was among the first troops to land in France shortly after D-Day in 1944.

There was now the question of my education to consider. I started off at the Grecian Street Primary School (situated between Albert Park in the south and Lower Broughton Road in the north) and then moved on to secondary school in 1942. I was enrolled at Salford Grammar (a marvellous school with some 20% of Jewish pupils—sadly, it no longer exists). I already knew many of the boys there and settled in very quickly. I was fourth in my class of about thirty in my first year at the school and remained very proud of that achievement considering where I had come from—having arrived in the country without a word of English.

I still remember my teachers—mostly men who were too old for military service, but highly experienced at their job. There was the remarkable headmaster Cyril Gill, then in his late thirties, who was later to become an expert in counselling and guidance. Today, in an era of educational mayhem with 'Acadamies' created everywhere to varying effect, he would probably have been one of those extremely highly paid 'Super Heads', but in those days he accomplished miracles simply as part of his vocation as a remarkable teacher. He encouraged each of us to be different, inspiring us to be the best possible version of ourselves. I wanted to study biology, for example, and because that subject was not available at Salford Grammar he arranged for tuition at Broughton High School for Girls. The rules were strict: if the air raid 'all clear' sounded before 2 am, homework would be due the next day; if the sirens sounded after 2 am, the boys were excused homework. Gill created what would in later years be called a multi-faith school and left in 1945, passing the baton on to E V Simm.

My schooldays ended in 1946. I was a school prefect and I look back on my time at school with the greatest pleasure.

The prefects at Salford Grammar School, 1946. I am in the back row, second from left

In 2005 I made a speech to the Old Salfordians' Annual Dinner recalling those years:

> My years at Salford Grammar were really happy in spite of the hardships of the war. At one stage, we spent every night in the air raid shelter, and frankly the atmosphere was so pleasant that we came to look forward to our nights out! On one occasion an incendiary bomb landed in our back garden but was quickly extinguished by the ever-alert air raid wardens who included my father.

Fugue VII (*in 2 voices*) RALPH KOHN *with* GRAHAM JOHNSON

GJ Your description of your arrival at Wigan Wallgate in 1940 is very moving. I don't suppose a large consignment of asylum-seekers would receive a welcoming committee today!

RK To encounter this kind of humanity was not only very touching, but also an enormous relief. We were treated in the most wonderful way by the local people. They brought food and clothes when they heard about us. In Manchester a clothing depot was set up in Deansgate to gather clothes with the slogan 'Don't put off until tomorrow what the refugees need to put on today'. This was all part of an exceptional kindness, something I will never forget. Of course everyone has their own memories, and not every refugee has such positive reminiscences. I know that some of the *Kinderstransport* children felt extremely deprived in Britain, while others—like the two Jewish girls adopted by the famous Attenborough family and who became the adored sisters of Richard, David and John—were blissfully and deservedly happy. I can only suppose we also were very lucky.

GJ It is often said that people make their own luck. Perhaps it was your positive attitude to life that enabled you to survive more happily than others?

RK Well I did look for the positive side of my new life. I was young enough to adapt. I was in a privileged situation as a child. Our family was intact, and we had left no one behind. We were simply in a different environment. As a new immigrant I never allowed homesickness or regrets for the past to get me down. I even enjoyed the Manchester winter fogs—so thick on one journey that the bus conductor had to shine a torch so that the driver could see the kerb. In a way, for me as a child of twelve, there was a slightly romantic element: 'Isn't it fantastic, another country and the adventures that it holds!'

British life was strange—the traffic system was most peculiar, and it was not possible to bike around Manchester in the same way I had in Amsterdam. At school it mystified me as to why I had to make so many choices so early in my education: history or geography, German or French, and so on. But there were so many other wonderful diversions. I don't think I understood what had happened. I had little idea of the scale of the upheaval. I was with my parents and I had their love and attention. I honestly considered myself as a normal child who had happened to go from one country to another with the loving care of my own family.

GJ I don't suppose you had the time or the inclination to feel sorry for yourself …

RK You wouldn't make a special case of yourself and say 'I'm a refugee'. I thought of
the countless people in the army, and the millions whose loved ones were fighting;
their fathers, their brothers, their sons. So I don't think I felt particularly
unfortunate because I looked around me and I saw that we were all going through
difficult times.

GJ I must now ask you about something that you hardly mention as having been a
problem. You arrived in Britain, five months after your twelfth birthday, and you
didn't speak a word of English. How on earth did you manage?

RK I had originally wanted to go to Manchester Grammar School and I went for an
interview with the High Master there, Douglas Miller. But Gegi—my admired
older cousin Gershon—had to come with me. He did most of the talking and I
most of the listening: what they were saying during their discussion was
incomprehensible to me. I was told (via Gegi) to 'Go and learn the language' and
to come back in two years when my English would be fluent enough. I was very
disappointed, but I was fortunate in going to the Grecian Street Primary School
because of the care and kindness of the teachers there, and one or two of the top
boys. They were determined to help me with my English and as a result I took to
it like a duck to water, if I may say so. I also briefly attended the Hope School in
Salford where I have very grateful memories of the kindness of the school's head
boy, whose name was McAlpine. He came to our home on many occasions to help
me with my English. As you know in the end I went to Salford Grammar, rather
than Manchester Grammar, and I have no regrets about doing so.

GJ And what about the teachers at Salford Grammar? Do you remember any of them
vividly?

RK Oh yes! The German teacher Mr Bird was disorganized and kind, very tall and
full of bonhomie. I had a certain advantage in this subject of course. His favourite
phrase in controlling unruly behaviour was 'If there is any more of it, there'll be less
of it'. He had little wooden pipes that he would break over our heads with the
words 'Pipe down, Schweinehund!' The English teacher Mr Stell was a brilliant
teacher and I remember studying *Macbeth* with him. It was said that you could
get through School Certificate on his notes alone—and this was years before the
availability of printed cribs. He was no good at discipline and he spoke in a high-
pitched voice—we were told that he had been gassed in the previous war. The
chemistry teacher, Mr Duckworth, was way past retirement age—he was a self-
styled expert on chemical reactions, but his forecasts were always wrong. He would
prophesy if you mix this liquid with that powder, the resulting colour would be

blue. Lo and behold, the colour was red! Undiscouraged, Mr Duckworth would—with a shrug of the shoulder—exclaim: 'Well, what do you expect—wartime chemicals!' Everything that went wrong—even chemical reactions—was due to the war …

GJ And what of your schoolfellows? Speaking for myself, I can remember the names of many of the people with whom I went to school even if I have lost touch with them for decades.

RK Well, I remember the names of all my fellow-prefects in the sixth form: Hymie Goldberg, John Steel, Keith Iverson, Peter Whitmaugh, Bernard Super and Allan Briggs. I also remember Ted Buchwald, a refugee from Czechoslavakia, who was a marvellous chess player. We formed a school chess team together and it was the best of its kind in the northwest of the country. Another prefect was Dave Hessayon; he had abbreviated his name to Hess, and he remained a friend for many years. He was of Cypriot and Jewish descent, but he grew up in Salford. He was, like me, a beneficiary of the enlightened educational attitudes of our headmaster Cyril Gill. Gill allowed Dave to do wrestling as a sport, rather than football or cricket, and Dave studied biology alongside me at the Broughton High School for Girls, thanks to Gill making a special arrangement enabling us to do so. Dave was extremely clever. He won a scholarship to study botany and chemistry at Leeds University and then went on to Manchester University to study soil science.

Dave eventually became the most successful gardening writer of all time, beginning with *Become Your Own Gardening Expert* in 1959, published under the name D G Hessayon. Apart from developing the enormously successful houseplant product Baby Bio (now marketed by Bayer), he is listed in the *Guinness Book of Records* as the biggest-selling non-fiction author in history. There was a gap in the market for this kind of self-help manual; his writing was down to earth—literally—with charts and photographs, just what the gardener needed. He provided something that was not available elsewhere. In a way, that was what I did within my own professional sphere when I started my own company. But that is jumping forward in my story. Dave became something of a recluse in later years but he was brilliant and enormously successful.

GJ Your story about Gegi, your cousin Gershon Kohn, coming with you to Manchester Grammar because you could not yet speak English, prompts a question about what happened to him. The role he played on getting you aboard the SS *Bodegraven* was crucial, and yet after you all came to England he seems to have faded out of your life.

RK We grew apart for a number of reasons. As I have told you, Gegi was one of the most gifted people I have ever known. My debt to him as a mentor is enormous. In many respects his talents were such that he led a charmed life. For example as soon as he reached England with us in 1940, his medical credentials found him some position in the Manchester Royal Infirmary from where he went from strength to strength. He joined the Royal Army Medical Corps in 1943 and in 1944 changed his name to Geoffrey Kent. Jewish officers at the time were encouraged to Anglicize their names in case they were taken prisoners of war. He left the army with the rank of Captain.

In 1950 'Geoffrey Kent' and his family emigrated to provincial Canada— although he was doing very well in Britain—and he later moved to the United States where he occupied a leading post as a renowned liver pathologist in Northwestern Memorial Hospital, Chicago.

Gershon Kohn (Gegi) in the British army— known by this time as Geoffrey Kent

GJ In recent years you have been in touch with Gegi's son, your second cousin Paul Kent, who lives in Chicago. Your correspondence with Paul has been most amicable, and he sent you a document he prepared about his father's life with a great many illustrations. I have it here … Paul's mother, Gegi's wife, was a very pretty English woman, Katharine Ruscoe. He met her at the Manchester Royal Infirmary in 1940 when they both worked there and they married in 1944, a partnership that lasted for more than sixty years.

RK Katharine was indeed a charming woman, and she and Gegi raised a fine family in America. It comes down to the simple fact that Gegi's marrying a Christian— 'marrying out' is the expression used among Jews—was a shock at the time as far as my entire family was concerned. In his earlier years he had been a model of Orthodoxy. Among Gegi's many other gifts he had been a talented Talmudical scholar and, in those days, someone from his background marrying a non-Jewish girl was almost unheard of. It represented a considerable problem for the rest of the family. And yet Gegi was so loved, and so respected, I don't think it would be true to say he was condemned for his choice. I just feel there was an enormous bewilderment and sadness that he had taken this path, and that we had somehow lost him. That was the Orthodox attitude in those days and mostly also the Orthodox thinking today, although intermarriage is of course very much more common nowadays.

GJ May I say something from an outsider's perspective? Gegi's own discomfort about stepping outside the family tradition seems to have played an equal part in the estrangement that developed between you. Whether your family punished him, or whether he was punishing himself, seems unclear. Perhaps he felt hard done-by by your family's reaction after all he had done to save your lives? Perhaps he decided to reinvent himself to get on better in a profession where there was, let's face it, a certain amount of anti-Semitism in the higher echelons? Dr Geoffrey Kent seems to have gone to extraordinary lengths to expunge all traces of his former life as Gershon Kohn.

RK He kept much of his life-story to himself as far as his family was concerned—he had three sons and a daughter. His children knew almost nothing of his Jewish back-ground until much later in life. After his death in 2008, aged 94, some of his family, including his daughter-in-law Fran, touchingly explored the family's Jewish heritage with genuine interest and enthusiasm.

GJ It is very interesting to me that Gegi had asked for his ashes to be dispersed over Holland. His son Paul did not comply with this request and the ashes of his mother and father were scattered over Lake Michigan instead (their family had once lived there). Of course this decision is understandable from their point of view. And yet, Gegi, born in Leipzig like you, had wished his ashes to go back to Holland, the country where he lived between 1935 and 1940. At this time he was your best friend and mentor, the person who took you to orchestral concerts at the Concertgebouw. This was the country where Gegi was involved in the work of the *Kindertransport*, and where he helped save lives as a young and idealistic doctor. Was this perhaps the time in his life, despite all his later achievements, when he really felt happiest? It seems to me that this final request to return his ashes to Holland was his way of showing a love for his roots and the faith into which he was born.

RK   I must gently remind you that no Orthodox Jew would allow himself to be cremated; it is always burial as the belief is that there will be a resurrection involving the whole body. This is an immutable law, but Gegi's children had not been brought up to realize this. As I look back on my youth I realize that Gegi played a greater part in helping me discover my lifelong enthusiasms than anyone else, and I remain hugely grateful to him. I regret how things turned out, and as you say there are two sides to every story. It is true that he seems to have retreated from us as much as we retreated from him. Perhaps everything would be entirely different today without that dangerous background of exile and war. If he had remained in Amsterdam Gegi's life would have been entirely different, but that is also true of mine.

     And as far as I am concerned, this story has a happier, or at least a more civilized, ending than you may imagine. Gegi and I resumed our relationship during the year I spent as a Research Fellow at the Albert Einstein College of Medicine in New York in 1957. Geoffrey Kent (as Gegi was now known) worked with the world-renowned liver pathologist Professor Hans Popper at Mount Sinai in New York, so we met frequently and stayed in contact after I had returned to England. The greatest British liver physician, Dame Sheila Sherlock, was also a good friend of mine. She knew Geoffrey Kent very well (they worked in the same field of course) and was absolutely astonished to discover that he was my first cousin—she had no idea even that he was Jewish. She then told me that, yes indeed, she could detect a family resemblance between the two of us. Subsequently, when Geoffrey went to Chicago and I worked for Smith Kline and French, we often met in New York. He liked nothing better than to meet for dinner and talk in Yiddish about the old days. We also met at family gatherings from the 1960s onwards, mainly in the United States.

You know, times have changed so much since the early 1940s. Having someone 'marrying out' within a family remains a challenge for Jewish parents of an Orthodox background, but it is not the insuperable challenge it once was. At least that is true for me and my wife Zahava. Our youngest daughter Maxine has a Christian husband. We have enormous respect for our son-in-law who is a good and loving family man. We also adore the beautiful grandson that has blessed that marriage. In the end it is love for those close to you, and concern for their happiness, that overrules all other considerations. This much a long life has taught me, and it is also part of my faith. Love and respect—what two important words those are—however imperfectly we show them in the course of our lives. Johannes Brahms memorably sets these biblical words to music: 'Though I speak with the tongues of men and of angels, and have not Love, I am become as sounding brass, or a tinkling cymbal.'

 Wenn ich mit Menschen No 4 *of* Vier ernste Gesänge, Op 121 JOHANNES BRAHMS (1833–1897)
CD Track ⑩   *see page 333 for text and translation*

This is a lesson that it sometimes takes a lifetime to learn, and it is equally important in the Jewish and Christian faiths.

John Rylands Library, Manchester University

PRELUDE VIII

At university in Manchester

WHEN I LEFT SALFORD GRAMMAR I wanted to study medicine—following in my distinguished cousin's footsteps I suppose, although I have already mentioned a famous gynaecologist in Berlin, Dr Selmar Aschheim, on my mother's side of the family. I applied to a number of medical schools to read medicine in 1946, but it was the worst possible time to do so. At the end of the war, ninety percent of all university places were allocated to returning ex-service personnel—this was a nation's way of thanking its returning troops, many of whom had put off pursuing their university education in their determination to do their duty and serve King and Country. This policy was to be in operation for three years, and I did not have the patience to wait for a place to become available.

Instead I decided to study pharmacology and was accepted onto the course at Manchester University for 1947/48. My school exam results had earned me a City of Salford Bursary to study at Manchester. How simple it was in those days, and how grateful I was for that scholarship. The funding of education under Attlee's recently elected Labour government was a different world from the student loans that are necessary today. Such a financial commitment for someone from a refugee family would have been all but impossible.

The decision to study pharmacology was not taken lightly. Already reading medical journals and papers, I was aware that the world stood on the threshold of a new era of pharmaceutical discovery. Research was all the rage, and I wanted to be part of it. This sense of imminent improvement in the conditions of life was part of the enormous optimism that seemed to grip at least some people after the end of the war. I can still recall this feeing, despite some of the worst winter weather ever to hit the United Kingdom in 1947 and the continuation of rationing.

For these very reasons many people were tempted to leave Britain to make new lives in sunnier climes like South Africa and Australia, but a few years later we would be speaking of a New Elizabethan age; by that time science and medicine were truly on the march—as, incidentally, were the arts in Britain. On a private level my father was able to resume his business when he was allowed to work after the war; I had been naturalized in 1947, and he and my mother were naturalized in

April 1948. He viewed the past with fortitude and stoicism. He had lost most of his relatives in Germany, Poland and the Ukraine but he never complained about his own hardships, always realizing that others were far worse off.

I completed my first degree in 1950—a BSc. I then spent the next academic year working towards my MSc and in 1951, with my sights set on a PhD, was ready to pursue my postgraduate studies. I lived at home for all this period and concentrated on my professional training. This also involved developing a certain kind of stamina which was to stand me in good stead in my later years.

I had also developed my intellectual resources to enable me to investigate a subject in an appropriate way. My doctorate, which followed seamlessly on from my MSc, involved demanding work in both pharmacology and bacteriology. I already believed that this kind of interdisciplinary research was the way forward in this sphere. After three years of meticulously conducted experiments, my doctoral thesis was entitled *Sensitization to Histamine by Haemophilus pertussis*—the last two of these words are simply the Latin tag for the bacterium that causes whooping cough. In essence my research involved a study of a histamine sensitization phenomenon induced by whooping cough vaccine—and this had possibly wider implications for the immunization of children against this illness. *Haemophilus pertussis* had been identified in 1906 and was also known as *Bordatella pertussis* or *Bordet-Gengou bacillus* after its discoverers, Jules Bordet and Octave Gengou, who worked at the Pasteur Institute in Brussels.

At the heart of my work was the question of anaphylactic reactions to the vaccine. Many people know that a bee or insect sting, relatively harmless to some people, can induce a potentially fatal anaphylactic shock in others. If it were understood why humans sometimes responded to a vaccine in this way, children could be immunized with far greater safety. There had been a great deal of research in this area going back to the 1920s. Particularly useful to me were the investigations done by Parfentjev, Goodline and Virion who had fairly recently published papers on hypersensitivity. They discovered that mice injected with large doses of *Haemophilus pertussis* vaccine were susceptible to extreme anaphylactic shock with very small doses of histamine. In other words, a bacterial organism was able to sensitize mice to histamine. This evidence was to have a bearing on the mechanism of sensitivity and anaphylactic reactions. Bearing in mind there was a good deal of anxiety in those days about the side effects of *pertussis* vaccination in children, this was regarded as important work at the time.

The connection between histamine and anaphylaxis was the subject of research by Meyer and Brousseau in 1946, Halpern and Roux in 1950, Pitman in 1951 and Dale in 1952. The reader without any medical knowledge will gather that this was a field that interested a great many scientists. For my thesis I set out four areas of investigation and exploration while looking at *Haemophilus pertussis* from different angles: first I made a biological assay of the histamine sensitizing fraction of the bacterium; then I determined whether the sensitizing activity was allied to any known fractions of the bacterium. Following this I investigated the histamine sensitizing fraction of *Haemophilus pertussis* and its possible relationship to side-effects in children vaccinated against whooping cough. Lastly I examined the mechanism by which mice are made highly sensitive to histamine. In this final section I also included numerous pharmacological observations.

Adam Davison Macdonald

I was thus working in two departments at the same time. Professor Adam Davison Macdonald was my remarkable mentor in pharmacology. He was not only an expert on histamine-related phenomena but also a brilliant administrator. Macdonald, who was Scottish, unsurprisingly, was a notable humanitarian with a number of refugee doctors working in his lab, including Dr Leo Wislicki who worked, and published, with Macdonald on carbohydrate metabolism, specialized in diabetes, and was a physician at the Manchester Royal Infirmary.

My supervisor in bacteriology was the Canadian-born Professor Hubert 'Hugh' Maitland, tall bluff and outspoken, who was also a source of great intellectual support. It was Maitland who had suggested I worked on *Haemophilus pertussis* in the first place. This won me the Wild Prize in Pharmacology in 1953 for the best MSc thesis of the year. Maitland was sufficiently impressed to recommend that I should continue researching this same topic for my PhD. Unfortunately all was not plain sailing in this regard. The presence of a pharmacologist in the Department of Bacteriology was unwelcome to the bacteriologists who were experts on whooping cough. This hostility was exacerbated by the uneasy relationship between Maitland, who supported my work, and some of his senior staff who argued behind his back that the research I was doing was a task for bacteriologists and beyond the competence of a pharmacologist doing his PhD. I was a young researcher caught in the cross-fire of departmental tensions and rivalries. I needed to grow the whooping cough bacterium but I had to rely on people who were not anxious to help me. There was a show-down with one of those alluded to above: he said he would have serious reservations about me getting my degree (expressing these thoughts, however, in a rather more abrasive manner). When I informed my superiors about this incident I was told not to worry about it. They clearly had words with the relevant individuals who kept well out of my way from then on.

In the end these difficulties were surmounted. I took my Viva on 31 August 1954 and successfully defended my doctoral work in the presence of the external examiner, Professor Robert Cruickshank of Edinburgh University, with my mentors Macdonald and Maitland on the same panel. Some time later Maitland asked me to prepare tables, graphs and summaries for the Wright-Fleming lecture he was invited to deliver at St Mary's hospital at the invitation of Sir Alexander Fleming. This important annual event was founded by Sir Almroth Wright, a famous immunologist, and by Fleming himself who was already the world-famous recipient of the Nobel prize for his discovery of penicillin. I could scarcely believe it when Maitland told me that he intended to place the research I had done for my thesis at the centre of his lecture.

This was a remarkable time for me and I was assiduous and energetic in my studies, as well as healthily ambitious. I think these are all necessary qualities in a young man, or a young woman, who desires to achieve their full potential. As influential as Maitland had been on my studies, it was Macdonald who saw that my real future lay in pharmacology. For this insight I must say I owe him a very great deal. He encouraged me to apply for the Charter Travelling Scholarship which was worth £300—a tidy sum in those days, and the only one of its kind in the country—sponsored by the Royal Pharmaceutical Society of Great Britain. This would enable me to go abroad and study with eminent pharmacologist Daniel Bovet. He was one of the world's outstanding drug researchers in the 1940s and '50s, and he lived and worked in Rome. He was to be awarded the Nobel prize in 1957.

I could scarcely believe that the time had come for me to return to the so-called Continent, albeit to Italy, a country I had never visited before. So it was goodbye to Salford, and goodbye to my parents with whom I had lived for the fourteen years since coming to England in 1940. It was also goodbye to my studies in Manchester. I don't know how aware I was at the time that Manchester University had stronger links with the nascent state of Israel than any other scientific institution in Britain. This was because the first President of Israel, the great Zionist Chaim Weizmann,

A graduate of Manchester University

had been Reader in Chemistry at Manchester University during the first decade of the twentieth century and had become the hero of the hour during the First World War when he was able to manufacture acetone from maize, thus enabling the manufacture of cordite and, in turn, the mass production of ammunition. Such was Weizmann's sway with the British government of the time that he was personally credited with the issuing of the Balfour Declaration of November 1917 that declared official British approval for the idea of establishing a national home for the Jewish people in Palestine—although this was not actually achieved until 1948. Half a century after leaving Manchester University, my close involvement with the work of the famous Weizmann Institute in Israel (see *Prelude XX*) is thus connected, in a way, with my earliest degree studies. I am also enormously proud that Manchester University saw fit, many decades later, to confer on me a Doctorate of Music, *honoris causa*.

These reverberations lie very many years into the future, of course. When one is young, one is scarcely aware of all the strands that will one day come together to form the definitive pattern of one's life. In the meantime this was still 1954, and I departed these shores in high spirits and with the greatest optimism. The happiness in this kind of departure and its understandable twinges of regret are wonderfully conveyed in *Scheiden und Meiden* by Gustav Mahler, one of his *Des Knaben Wunderhorn* songs.

 Scheiden und Meiden GUSTAV MAHLER (1860–1911)
CD Track 11

see page 334
for text and translation

Fugue VIII (*in 2 voices*) RALPH KOHN *with* GRAHAM JOHNSON

GJ You left school in 1946 and began university life in 1947, so you had something of a gap year. What did you do at that time—did you travel the world in the way that the young all seem to do today?

RK There was no money for that in those days! But I travelled the world in a manner of speaking—by reading more than I had ever done before, or probably since. I attended the Manchester Talmudical College and this was a journey into another culture that was part of my own heritage. With Dr Meir Wallenstein, a specialist in Hebrew language at Manchester University, I worked on Hebrew literature, continuing my studies there until 1954. This included a study of the Paytanim, the school of exuberant and lyrical Jewish poets of a thousand years ago. Thanks to the John Rylands University Library in Oxford Road (see illustration on page 84), I devoured a great amount of literature in both English and German. In English, my adopted language, the works of Oscar Wilde and Bernard Shaw were a revelation, and in my mother tongue I became a devoted fan of the novels and historical studies of Stefan Zweig who had committed suicide only four years earlier in Brazil. Zweig was not physically executed by the Nazis but they had destroyed his career and broken his spirit—I think the author's autobiography, *Die Welt von Gestern* (*The World of Yesterday*), is a fantastic book. No one has better described the ache of the Viennese refugee who feels cut off from everything culturally dear to him. The poetry of Goethe, Heine and Schiller fascinated and moved me; the Rylands Library also opened up that world to me. These writers were also a part of what I might call my German-speaking inheritance. I think this year of reading deepened my knowledge and understanding, and prepared me, without my realizing it at the time, for my later fascination with singing lieder.

GJ This raises the subject of whether you had been able to continue your musical enthusiasms that had been awakened with Gegi in Amsterdam.

RK My school music teacher in Salford had not been a very sympathetic type: he used to put on endless recordings of Wagner for us to listen to. There was no school orchestra and there was no question of being able to afford violin lessons. But Manchester was, like Amsterdam, a profoundly musical city. I benefited from an ambience where music was respected and performed at the highest level, and I attended concerts as far as money would allow. For me the most memorable concert in Manchester was at the Belle Vue Stadium in Kirkmanshulme Lane. Here on a summer evening in 1949, one of 5,000 in the audience, I heard two hours of bel canto singing by Beniamino Gigli. I fell in love with the music and the style, and

The great Italian tenor Beniamino Gigli

this revelatory induction into the world of great singing was to have repercussions for the rest of my life.

My university years coincided with the re-opening of the Free Trade Hall in 1951 which had been all but destroyed in the Manchester Blitz. These were the days of the Hallé Orchestra under Basil Cameron and Malcolm Sargent, and later Sir John Barbirolli who rebuilt the orchestra to its former greatness.

There were also foreign orchestras on tour. I could not afford a ticket for the visit of the Concertgebouw Orchestra under Eduard van Beinum, but I was fortunate enough to attend a rehearsal. To my intense astonishment and delight my old violin teacher from Amsterdam, Sam Tromp, was playing at one of the first-violin desks. Tromp had been leader of the second violins when I had known him in Amsterdam, and he had miraculously returned safely to the orchestra in 1945 after internment at Theresienstadt (Terezín). What a reunion that was! He had aged noticeably since those years of course, and he had last seen me as a boy. He could not believe his ears when I walked up to him and told him who I was. Tromp was a very well-respected player—Bernard Haitink knew him very well, and his son went to school with my wife Zahava. We later met him in Israel.

GJ   Do you remember anything about the music on that occasion?

RK   Of course! It was Bruckner's Symphony No 8 and the Wagner *Wesendonck Lieder* sung by Kirsten Flagstad. She arrived late for the rehearsal, dressed in a beautiful coat. I remember van Beinum was exceptionally patient with the great diva …

You see how fascinating I found, and continue to find, this world of music-making? The dilemma I was facing as a student was that I didn't really know whether to study music or medicine. It seemed that if I were to have a secure profession, medicine might be better than taking risks with music. I wanted to study medicine, but music was my great love. In later life I could not think of doing one without the other.

GJ   This duality is something like your insistence on having your cake and eating it by combining bacteriology and pharmacology! I understand this very well in my own profession as a lieder accompanist where my life is spent studying music and poetry that have been joined together by a great composer. This is a truly inter-disciplinary art form. Many musicians are purists in a way and find the addition of words superfluous to music, and many literary experts believe that music adds nothing to the beauty of poetry. There are some kinds of work, like accompaniment, and perhaps pharmacology, where one has to have a foot in both camps simply in order to do one thing well.

RK   It is certainly the unique combination of music and poetry that has always fascinated me about lieder.

As much as I loved music, I opted in the first instance to study medicine and that failed to work out. I moved sideways to pharmacology, perhaps as a result of my experience in chess! I suppose today people might call it lateral thinking. And in the meantime there was another important reason why I changed my mind. Dramatic developments had occurred in drug research and patient treatment. After the synthesis of the sulphonamides for the cure of infectious diseases in the 1930s, penicillin was discovered and the era of antibiotics for the treatment of a whole variety of infectious diseases had begun. It was a revolutionary and exciting time—many illnesses such as tuberculosis, cardiovascular disease and rheumatic disease, could now be treated with the ever-increasing number of drugs that were shown to be effective. Great strides were also made in the control of pain, prevention of viral diseases such as poliomyelitis, and so on. This captured my imagination and passion, and I decided to study pharmacology.

GJ   You've explained that you didn't get a chance to become a medical doctor because university places were reserved for ex-servicemen. Is it possible that the university selection boards were simply prejudiced against you as a Jewish refugee?

RK   No, I don't think so for a minute. There were far too many Jews in the medical world for that to have been likely. In any case, I never heard an anti-Semitic remark directed against me at school or university. In fact my relationship with people of all faiths has always been fantastic. I've always stood for what I believed: that might be a minority view, but I never hesitated to say it. I never hid who I was and what my background was. Equally I never tried to overplay it to my advantage.

GJ   From undergraduate to PhD is a gigantic step to cover in one chapter of your autobiography. I would like to ask you a bit more about the occasion that seems to have been the crowning glory of this period—Professor Maitland's lecture in 1954 where your thesis was the basis of his talk. I think you could allow yourself a little more retrospective pride about that!

RK I would not wish to be immodest about this occasion, but I could scarcely believe that my thesis would be presented in front of such a distinguished audience at the prestigious venue of St Mary's Hospital in London. Fleming, by far the most famous medical scientist in England at the time, was presiding. Maitland's opening words, after thanking Fleming for the honour of presenting the lecture, were 'The subject of my lecture is *The histamine sensitizing property of Haemophilus pertussis* based on the PhD thesis of my student Ralph Kohn who, I am pleased to say, is in the audience', or words to that effect. I was walking on air. Those words are still ringing in my ears; he was so generous. And at the reception after the lecture Fleming congratulated me on my work; it was indeed a day to remember for the rest of my life.

Alexander Fleming

The Istituto Superiore di Sanità in Rome

PRELUDE IX

Rome LA DOLCE VITA

IN 1954, thanks to the advice of Professor Macdonald in Manchester, I arrived in Rome. I was the Royal Pharmaceutical Society's Charter Travelling Scholar and my destination was the Istituto Superiore di Sanità, an imposing building opposite the University of Rome on the Viale Regina Elena. A centre of this kind was something relatively new in the 1950s. Medical science and drug research in Rome at that time stood high in international esteem. The institute had started off as the chief food and drug control laboratory in Italy, but in due course it also became renowned as a centre of medical research. It is to the credit of the Italian scientific community that they saw the need for such an institute as early as the 1920s. It was conceived in 1929 and its building was supported by a donation from the Rockefeller Foundation in New York, an organization that had an astonishingly generous record when it came to medical philanthropy outside the USA.

The institute was opened in April 1934 as a 'centre for investigations, researches and verifications' to quote its founding laws. Its third director general was appointed in 1935—Professor Domenico Marotta. He ran the institute for the next twenty-six years and shaped its standing and status both at home and abroad.

During the war the institute escaped damage and it became a leader in malaria research through its work in parasitology. Italy had a substantial malaria problem: the marshland around Rome was an incubation area for mosquitoes—the ideal place to conduct research.

In the post-war years the institute attracted international scholars who flocked to it from all over the world (I was among the thirty visitors on post-doctoral fellowships to do so that year). This enthusiasm was on account of the presence of two medical scientists of world renown. The first of these was Professor Ernst Chain (subsequently knighted) who had won the Nobel prize in 1945 for the discovery of penicillin (sharing his award with Sir Alexander Fleming and Sir Howard Florey). In 1948 Professor

Domenico Marotta

Domenico Marotta had invited Chain to set up the International Centre for Chemical Microbiology, which was handsomely housed in a separate five-floor building adjacent to the institute. The second world-famous medical scientist at the institute (one year younger, though equal in rank) was Daniel Bovet. He was to win the Nobel prize in 1957 (on this occasion not sharing it with anyone else, an unusual occurrence) for his discovery of drugs that block the actions of specific neurotransmitters. The presence of both these eminent scientists, under one roof, was a magnet for members of the younger generation, including myself, who were fascinated by the possibilities of biotechnological research.

The institute was generously funded and the presence of two such famous men as Chain and Bovet changed its status in the world. Its eight principal departments were biology, chemistry, biochemistry, engineering, microbiology, parisitology, physics and therapeutic chemistry. There were sub-departments in electronics, electron-microscopy, histology and infra-red spectroscopy. For each of these disciplines there was a specialist library. The institute had its own workshops, glass-blowing, design and photographic departments. It had fifty modern and spacious offices and laboratories on each floor, all finished in marble. In these were tested vitamins, hormones, vaccines, radioactive substances and drugs of all kinds. On a more domestic note it was a food and drink authority, standardizing wines, fats, oils, milk and bread.

Professor Macdonald's link with the institute had been through Professor Daniel Bovet, the great man in pharmacology, and Bovet was the reason why I had come to Rome. He was Swiss by birth; although we mostly conversed in either French or English, he had been brought up to speak Esperanto. He had researched at the Pasteur Institute in Paris where his work led to the use of sulfa drugs in the treatment of streptococcal infections such as pneumonia, meningitis and scarlet fever. In 1937 the so-called '933F' antihistamine was synthesized by Bovet and his research assistant, Anne-Marie Staub. This word antihistamine has become so commonplace that it is almost unnecessary to explain that these drugs block histamine-producing neurotransmitters. The products that are in common use today, and for sale at all chemists, derive from Bovet's first discovery.

Bovet went on to research new drugs for asthma and hay fever. By the 1940s pharmacologists and chemists could see the possibility of producing substances whose actions would interfere in experimental physiological phenomena, or even pathological processes. Later his interest in the Indian nerve poison curare led to work on its related analogues. This in turn led to the use of suxamethonium (succinycholine) as a muscle relaxant in surgical operations. When muscles are paralysed it is easier to separate one from the other in surgery, and blood loss is

Daniel Bovet

minimized. Bovet's research led to muscle relaxants being in wide use by the 1950s and beyond. In his Nobel lecture of 1957 Bovet spoke movingly of 'the pharmacology of the future … an ordered and defined science in which foods, drugs and poisons will have become integrated with metabolism of the simplest constituents of living matter'. This was entirely in line with the noble traditions of the purest scientific research and notably different from the rather less esoteric viewpoints of Ernst Chain discussed in this book's next chapter.

I immediately recognized in Daniel Bovet a totally dedicated man and an original thinker. He was always first in the laboratory and last to leave. His mastery of neuropharmacology was such that I could think of no one better qualified in the world with whom to study at the beginning of my own career in this field. Bovet had decided to live and work in Italy, I think, because his wife Filomena (whom he had met in Paris) was the daughter of Francesco Saverio Nitti who had been prime minister of the country shortly after the First World War. Nitti, by the way, was a famous liberal and anti-fascist who had left Italy in 1922 when Mussolini came to power, only returning with his family to his home country after the war. Bovet himself spoke Italian only up to a point. He was extremely shy socially and found it difficult to entertain groups of visitors to the institute—he was certainly at his best on a one-to-one basis when he was extremely tactful and approachable. He and his wife enjoyed an exceedingly comfortable life in Rome, but then it seemed to me that almost everyone in that glorious city was living an idyll at the time.

I soon realized that this palatial public building dedicated to science was the scene of a shifting power-struggle between two famous scientists and their respective wives, with the overall supremo, Marotta as a kind of referee. One could almost write a play about their rivalries—at times these seemed almost operatic and in danger of overshadowing the research. Filomena Bovet, a charming Neapolitan, was in charge of the administration of her husband's laboratory. She was a scientist and biologist and her name would sometimes appear in scientific publications as 'F Bovet-Nitti'. She was everything that her husband was not—outgoing, vivacious, outspoken, political, and a mistress of intrigue in the time-honoured Italian manner.

She was nothing like her husband in terms of temperament and she seemed to have a great deal more in common with the Sicilian-born director, Domenico Marotta, whose decisions regarding anything to do with the institute were government-sanctioned and final. Filomena Bovet and Marotta spent a great deal of time together and there was quite a bit of gossip at the time about their association. (I have no idea if this gossip was justified.) The Bovets were very left wing and friends with the leader of the Italian communists, Palmiro Togliatti, but their luxurious way of life suggested to me a 'smoked-salmon communism', or at least a 'champagne socialism', rather than the real thing. Marotta on the other hand was extremely right wing, although this did not in the least seem to affect his friendship with Filomena Bovet who almost always accompanied him at official and social events. Marotta was a fine scientist; it was he who understood the close relationship between Bovet's therapeutic chemistry and the biochemistry of Chain. It was crucial to Marotta's purposes and his ambitions for the institute that both Bovet and Chain were interested in drug discovery. It was a tragedy that in the early sixties he was charged with misappropriation of funds and sentenced to a jail term—there was, however, a last-minute commuting of the sentence, Berlusconi-style. Over twenty years later the distinguished and talented director of the institute was vindicated; it seems that the vendetta against Marotta at the time had been a trumped-up charge with strongly political overtones. Present-day Italian politicians, when charged with crimes that would be open-and-shut cases in other countries, are able to allege judicial corruption (even where there is none) because of a long history of genuine scandals, like this tawdry case.

My initial task at the institute was to work with Bovet to investigate the effect of histamine when administered with neuromuscular blocking agents. I was soon to meet the second great man under the roof of the institute, Ernst Chain, and that meeting was to change my life.

Fugue IX *(in 2 voices)* RALPH KOHN *with* GRAHAM JOHNSON

GJ I can think of few more glamorous places to be than Italy in the 1950s. This is the post-war paradise that is the background to Patricia Highsmith's *The Talented Mr Ripley*, an unspoiled playground for European visitors of means before the country was swamped with tourists. Here was some of the best scenery, the most clement weather, the most interesting history and art, the most beautiful music, and the most delicious food in the world. 'Et in Arcadia ego!' 'Even in Arcadia, there am I' … Or as Goethe translated Poussin's motto for his Italian Journey 'Auch ich in Arkadien!'

RK Yes I am also reminded of Goethe's 'Kennst du das Land wo die Citronen blüh'n?', that marvellous song by Hugo Wolf ('Do you know the land where the lemon trees blossom?'). German visitors like Goethe have always looked to Italy for warmth and enlightenment, the removing of Teutonic strictures, a kind of intellectual freedom …

GJ Or perhaps simply a freedom from being intellectual? Some scholars think that Goethe, who was in his thirties when he visited Italy for the first time, actually lost his virginity there. Before it, they say, sex was all in the great poet's head.

RK Well let me assure you that I am no Goethe—in this, or any, respect! My father was shy in discussing sexual matters but like a lot of men before the 1960s I became aware of the facts of life in school. I suppose I was no better and no worse than any other young man of that generation. I had already had an emotional awakening aboard ship on my way to New York in 1952—I'll tell you a little more about that later. But apart from times away on holiday, I lived at home until the age of twenty-six or so, and that certainly discouraged a great deal of romantic activity. I was relatively inexperienced and somewhat shy; although I was keen on certain girls over that period, there was no one in Britain with whom I had fallen in love. Things were very different in those days: had I ever attempted anything too bold I would have been rebuffed in the manner of the boy at the end of Brahms's *Vergebliches Ständchen*!

 Vergebliches Ständchen Op 84 No 4 JOHANNES BRAHMS (1833–1897)   *see page 335*
CD Track 12   *for text and translation*

I do think, however, that my journeys abroad opened me up and made me less inhibited and Italy was a crucial experience for me in this respect. Not only was Italy a land of milk and honey, but it was the first time I had been away from the parental home for more than a few weeks. On arrival I stayed at the Pensione Atena

In Rome, relaxing and studying the architecture!

which catered for Greek students studying in Rome. I then moved to an apartment on the famous Via Margutta, in the vicinity of the Piazza di Spagna. The owner was Marchesa Lupi who required a year's rental in advance. For this amount of money she moved out of her own flat and lived with her disabled son in an adjoining apartment. I had this lovely 'artistic' flat for about eighteen months. Via Margutta is still at the heart of the Roman bohemian life, with artists and pseudo-artists occupying most of the apartments. The film-maker Fellini lived there for his entire life.

I was naturally struck by the difference in the weather, and the fact that music in Italy seemed to be an everyday fact of life, not just something for inside a concert hall. The open-air life was very relaxed; from spring onward we ate outside; and there was music and song; people would sing going along the street, or voices would drift from out a window. And Italian food was a revelation.

GJ In Salford you lived in a home that kept the Jewish dietary laws, and when you left England there was still food rationing … I suppose that whereas every young person in Britain today has had pizza or ravioli, you had never experienced anything like it?

RK I never forget the glorious lunches at the Castelli Romani. I had grown up in the lean war years so this profusion of food was a culinary *terra incognita*. In the summer there were departmental lunches lasting from 2 pm to 4 pm, after which there was no question of going back to work (our working day began at 9 am). It's all too easy to become accustomed to a life at that pace—it was idyllic. The Bovets were stupendous hosts—they would invite groups of us, forty at a time, to Frascati, Castel Gondolfo or one of the hillside towns. After one of these lunches I also remember a conversation with Filomena Bovet—I wanted to have a few more days off over the Christmas period and needed to get her permission to do so. I told her I wanted to go with friends to Capri. 'Capri?' she replied with a smile. 'I thought you were heterosexual—only homosexuals go to Capri!' I had never encountered that kind of response from a distinguished professional—outrageously personal by

English standards. I was not homosexual, and there were many heterosexuals living in Capri, including the famous English singing star, Gracie Fields. But even as a joke disguising her displeasure at my proposed absence, Filomena's reply had a kind of directness and frankness that was something new in my life. Looking back on it now it seems to have been also rather flirtatious—although that interpretation of a remark coming from the wife of my world-famous professor would never have occurred to me at the time. There is no doubt, however, that I returned from Italy more worldly-wise and experienced in life than I could ever have imagined.

GJ Did you see a good deal of the country?

RK I did indeed. Actually, a one-day excursion from Rome remains in my mind for the wrong reason. Three of us (including Maria, the daughter of Marotta) visited Monte Cassino where the protracted battle between the Germans and the Allies took place between 1943 and 1944. This is the site of the famous Benedictine monastery of course—at that time still being painstakingly restored after its wartime destruction. At the foot of the rebuilt abbey there is a large and famous Polish War Cemetery with the graves of over a thousand Poles who died, under the command of General Władysław Anders, as they stormed the ruins of the Abbey in May 1944. There are three types of tombstones in this impressively laid-out cemetery—Roman Catholic and Russian Orthodox, inlaid with Christian crosses, and Jewish with the Star of David. I was standing looking at these simple and dignified Jewish graves when a group of Polish visitors came over to speak to me; they seemed perfectly affable. 'Do you know where you are?' one of them said. 'Yes', I replied. 'This is the Polish Jewish cemetery.' 'Right', he replied, as if taking me into his special confidence. 'What you should know about the people buried in this part of the cemetery is that they either belonged to the medical corps or were administrators, none of them were ever fighters.'

As you know I am a man who avoids controversy or confrontation—it is not in my nature easily to lose my temper, but I have seldom been so shocked and so angry. It was clear that whatever role these people had played in the battle, they had given their lives in that terrible campaign. My reply was immediate: 'Here we have an example of insane anti-Semitism beyond the grave. You absolutely disgust me … your disgraceful discrimination and prejudice dishonour the dead.' I was almost shaking with fury, but I walked away.

GJ You have often said that you have never been confronted with anti-Semitism on your own account but this is a most unpleasant story. At least it is not an anecdote that reflects badly on your Italian hosts. Your stay in that country lasted until 1957

The Jewish section of the Polish cemetery at Monte Cassino

and in the next chapter you discuss the work with Ernst Chain that kept you there for three years. Apart from the discordant incident you have just described, how do you think your lengthy stay in Italy—your *Italienische Reise* to compare you again with Goethe—benefited you?

RK Well, just in this case, I could compare myself to the great man and say I was enchanted—'bezaubert' as they say in German—by Italy in a similar way. Apart from the fact the mercenary Roman traders and taxi drivers took your money left, right and centre with a smiling face, Italy opened up for me a world of sentiment, warmth, laughter, sunshine—as well as cultural depth. It was, you may say, an absolute tonic, a holiday. I had a circle of friends in Rome which included a number of

Anna Reynolds

artists and musicians; we used to meet at each other's homes for musical evenings.
One of the most interesting personalities of this group of 'bohemians' was the
young British mezzo-soprano, Anna Reynolds, who was also a fabulous pianist.
She later became a distinguished Wagner singer, working at Bayreuth, and also sang
lieder most beautifully. When I read recently in *The Times* of her death, aged eighty-
two, I felt a wave of nostalgia for those carefree evenings of music-making in that
beautiful city when the whole of life stretched before us. In Rome I learned there
were different ways of reacting, feeling, loving, enjoying things. Living in Rome
was 'La dolce vita'—'The sweet life' as the famous film director Fellini would depict
it in 1960. It also represented a real and important step forward in my musical life,
something I will describe later in more detail. A piece of music by Raffaello
Rontani, *Se bel rio*, one of many beautiful *arie antiche*, describes the sense of
well-being I experienced in Italy.

 *Se bel rio* RAFFAELLO RONTANI (*c*1570–1622)
CD Track ⒔

see page 335
for text and translation

Ernst Chain

PRELUDE X

Sir Ernst Chain FRS

MY MEETING WITH PROFESSOR ERNST CHAIN at the Istituto Superiore di Sanità in Rome was a significant moment in my life. When I arrived in Rome he had already been there for six years, having begun his work at the institute in 1948. He had been Nobel laureate in 1945 for his work on penicillin and the speech he gave at the awards banquet in Stockholm set forth his philosophy. It made the bold point that scientists could no longer afford to inhabit the ivory tower of academe at the expense of being part of the real world. He wanted scientists to be rounded human beings, participating in the results of their research, rather than laboratory-bound boffins:

> During recent times the adventurous human mind has created several discoveries that are changing completely the character of our civilization and have immeasurably increased our control over some of the forces of nature. But unfortunately as yet we have not been able to master those forces within ourselves—greed, the lust for power, fear and intolerance, which so far dominated the structure of our society and human relationships. Shall we ever be able to achieve this most difficult of aims? … After the terrible and almost unbelievable experiences of the last six years we are not justified in making a lightheartedly optimistic forecast. It is absolutely certain, however, that unless we do succeed in building up a social structure that enables us to keep pace with and control over the scientific advances we shall irretrievably and completely lose all that civilization which has been our heritage, often bitterly fought for, over the last five thousand years. The construction of such an international society cannot be achieved by mere formulae elaborated by diplomatists at the green table or a handful of intellectuals … Scientists now realize what the cost has been of not having resisted with all their power the barbarism between 1933 and 1939 on the plea that this was the job of the politician. Some of my colleagues in the USA and in England have given proof of a new attitude of real humanism which rises above mere specialization and which integrates morality and scientific progress.

When Ernst Chain talked of 'adventurous human minds' that had changed our civilization, he was, with some justification, referring to himself. This larger-than-life character was born in 1906 in Berlin. He graduated from the Friedrich Wilhelm University in the late 1920s and earned his PhD from the Charité Hospital, one of the most renowned in Europe (this was the same institution where my relative Selma Aschheim was a distinguished gynaecologist). Erwin Chargraff, the distinguished biochemist from Vienna, spent some time in Berlin and described university life there in the following terms: 'The openness towards new ideas, the lack of jealousies, the large field of vision, had an immense effect on a young research-minded person, particularly someone who had come from the jealous and intransigent world of Vienna. When I look back on those days, it seems to me that the last rays of the setting sun were falling on my head.'

Chain was not only a scientist: he was passionately interested in the arts, music in particular. The Berlin of the 1920s, rich in great painters, conductors and musicians, was the ideal city in which to work. His scientific contemporaries, among others, were Albert Einstein, Max Planck, Otto Hahn, Fritz Haber, Lise Meitner and Otto Warburg. Chain studied both piano and conducting (he went on an orchestral tour in the Argentine) as well as writing music reviews for a Berlin evening paper.

Originally he was a left-wing Jewish firebrand (he became later in life a fiery right winger)—exactly the kind of academic who was prominent in the Nazis' firing line. In 1933, at the age of twenty-seven, he left Germany for England, leaving behind a mother and a sister whom he failed to persuade to leave Germany and who later died in Theresienstadt. He came to University College London, where he worked with J B S Haldane, one of the pioneers of genetics and biometry. He then moved to Cambridge, taking a PhD and working in the department of biochemistry which was chaired by Sir Frederick Gowland Hopkins, a Nobel laureate and one of the pioneers of biochemistry in Britain. He stayed in Cambridge for two years before moving to Oxford in 1936 and joining the Sir William Dunn School of Pathology where the Australian Professor Howard Florey was a lecturer in chemical pathology and director.

It was an extraordinary coincidence that before his work on penicillin, Chain worked on the enzyme lyosyme which had already been described by Alexander Fleming. Chain read Fleming's research on the mould *Penicillium notatum* that had been published in 1929. He saw that penicillin was mentioned as a constituent of this mould, and that it had anti-bacterial qualities. He revisited Fleming's work, isolated penicillin and confirmed its therapeutic action. He also contributed to demonstrating the structure of penicillin, confirmed by X-ray crystallography done by Dorothy Hodgkin. There is a famous story about this. Dorothy Hodgkin met the distinguished fellow crystallographer J D Bernal on the steps of the Royal Society in 1940. Hodgkin had succeeded in elucidating the β-lactam structure of penicillin, which had baffled the chemists for some time. Bernal said to Hodgkin,

'You know you will receive the Nobel prize for this', whereupon Hodgkin replied, 'But I would rather be a Fellow of the Royal Society'. Bernal's response was: 'This will be more difficult!' (see *Prelude & Fugue XXI*).

There was no contact between Chain and Fleming until 1940 when Chain and Florey published in *The Lancet*. Chain later told me that he received a call from 'out of the blue' from St Mary's Hospital, London, from a man who introduced himself as 'Fleming' and that it had taken him some time to realize who it was. Chain thought that he had died years earlier.

Much of the publicity over the discovery of penicillin focused on Fleming rather than Chain or Florey. Florey was reserved and modest, but Chain had no such reservations. He understood the necessity for industry and academe to work together (much more of a tradition in Germany than in Britain) and that drug research would benefit from the type of collaboration that had existed in the 1920s between Gerhard Domagk (Nobel laureate of 1939) and the German industrial conglomerate IG Farben for the development of the sulfa drug Prontosil and Sulphonamide therapy.

Chain was convinced that penicillin had a large-scale future, but Britain lacked the industrial base and tradition to make the drug in abundant quantities. It was in Oxford, under the care of Howard Florey, that the policeman Albert Alexander, the first patient to receive penicillin injections, had died in 1941. Alexander had initially responded very well to the drug, but there was an insufficient amount of penicillin available to continue his treatment. This inability to produce penicillin in sufficiently large quantities led to Howard Florey's travelling to the United States, with his colleague Norman Heatley (another crucial figure in the early extraction of penicillin) in search of American support to produce the drug using industrial methods of fermentation.

Chain pressed for the idea of patent protection, but both Sir Henry Dale of the Royal Society and Sir Edward Mellanby, Secretary of the Medical Research Council, opposed the idea of patenting discoveries that had originated from British academic research. 'Art for Art's sake' was the slogan of those who believed that art could serve no moral or didactic purpose, that it was a beautiful thing of itself. The reaction of these two eminent scientists was similarly 'Science for Science's sake', and typical of an entire academic establishment that believed it was somehow vulgar to mix the purity of scientific research with commercial enterprise. As a result Britain handed over to the USA its know-how on the greatest drug yet developed, and had to pay royalties to a US company, Pfizer, on a breakthrough which was the product of British science.

Chain was naturally very unhappy with this state of affairs. He believed in practical, applied research and the academic life in Oxford was not suited to his purpose. Important drugs like penicillin needed to be created in large quantities, and Chain was convinced that this aspect of drug research was part and parcel of his own work. He was a Zionist so he might have been tempted to go to live and work in Israel (he was, after all, a friend of his fellow scientist, Chaim Weizmann, who had taught at the University of Manchester many years before I was a student there, and who had become the first president of the newly established state). But at that time Israel would not have been able to offer Chain the facilities he needed. Domenico Marotta's invitation to come to the Institute in Rome was the kind of challenge he was looking for. This was to be a grand new departure, and Chain sought the help of the Rockefeller Foundation to build a pilot fermentation plant. He also established ongoing links with pharmaceutical companies.

On his arrival in Rome in 1948 the laboratories of the new International Centre for Chemical Microbiology (adjacent to the original institute) were still under construction, but it is clear that this building was being erected according to Chain's requirements, and that he had wielded quite some influence on the whole project from the very beginning. A plaque was placed in the foyer of the building with quotations from Louis Pasteur, aphorisms that Chain had selected because he felt they expressed the principles of his own thinking:

> Science knows no country, because knowledge belongs to humanity, and is the torch which illuminates the world. Science is the highest personification of the nation because that nation will remain the first which carries the furthest the works of thought and intelligence.

> In the fields of observation chance favours the prepared mind.

> Let me tell you the secret that has led me to my goal.
> My strength lies solely in my tenacity.

> There are no such things as applied sciences, only applications of science.

In 1970 I told Chain of my plans to go it alone in forming my own company to conduct clinical trials (see *Prelude & Fugue XVIII*). I told him frankly that the industry was not doing it right and that I could make a difference. As quick as lightning he turned around to me and said: 'I think this is fantastic, just what is needed. I believe you are just the man to do it. I will help you in any way I can.'

Six years later in 1976, when Advisory Services was a reality as opposed to a pipe-dream, we organized a symposium at the Royal Society to celebrate his seventieth birthday. It was entitled *Biologically Active Substances: Exploration and*

Exploitation and attracted an international field of delegates and a roster of twenty-five sponsors including major pharmaceutical and food production companies. I treasure the inscription Chain wrote in a copy of the proceedings of the symposium published by John Wiley in London; by this time of course my wife Zahava (see *Prelude & Fugue XIV*) had become so much a part of my life, professional as well as personal, that she was very much part of the symposium's success:

> To Zahava and Ralph with deep gratitude for their long friendship and the immense trouble and care they took in the organization of this symposium which became a reality and owes its undoubted considerable success mainly to their tireless and dedicated efforts, Affectionately, Ernst.

Ernst Chain died in 1979 in his country home in Ireland. In 1980 I was honoured to speak at Chain's memorial service in London, the third speaker after Chief Rabbi Lord Jakobovitz and Professor John Yudkin, one of the earliest and most vociferous opponents of sugar. (At the time many scientists thought that Yudkin's warnings about the dangers of sugar-consumption were unnecessarily extreme, but recent research increasingly vindicates his position.) Even after the farewell I took of my mentor at this memorial service, my professional association with Ernst Chain had not come to an end. Nearly a quarter of a century later the Kohn Foundation established an annual prize in his honour at Imperial College of Science and Technology (see *Prelude XIX*).

Fugue X *(in 2 voices)* RALPH KOHN *with* GRAHAM JOHNSON

GJ My father was a commercial artist—he would perhaps have preferred to paint what he wished, when he wished, but he had to make a living, so he went into advertising, using his drawing skills to sell products. Is this in any way a parallel case with pure science versus applied science?

RK Chain might have replied that the better your father was as an artist, technically, imaginatively and so on, the better equipped he would have been to be a useful commercial artist. Conversely, the more skilled he was as a commercial artist, the more likely it would be that he could achieve something worthwhile in the realm of pure painting. This goes against the grain of those who rigidly believe in specialists sticking to their own *Fach*—the German word which literally means 'box' or 'locker'. Today we would say that Chain 'thought outside the box'. He maintained that his renowned skills in academic research did not preclude him from exploring the nexus between academe and industry. He once explained the difference between pure research and applied research in the following way: 'In pure academic research, if your experiments give a positive result, you publish. If you obtain negative results, you still publish! In applied research, if you have a positive effect you have something; however, if the results are negative, you have nothing!'

GJ That sounds eminently practical and businesslike to me! How did you meet Chain?

RK It was in Rome, within a few weeks of my arrival at the institute. I was in the lift, with his technician, John Daymond, with whom I shared a flat in Rome. Chain joined us at a different floor and he heard me speaking with John in English. He then asked me who I was, and invited me to come with him to his office. He told me that he was working on carbohydrate metabolism and diabetes and that he needed someone to do pharmacological and surgical work in the laboratory. Of course I told Chain that I was working with Bovet. 'Tell him, by all means', said Chain.

I immediately went to see Bovet and told him of this encounter. 'Dr Kohn,' (Bovet was always very formal), 'I must tell you something', he said. 'You have not been here long: Professor Chain is not the easiest man to deal with, in fact we have never been able to publish anything with him—several attempts to collaborate have come to nothing.' On hearing this I said: 'Should I tell him "no", then?' Bovet's reply was: 'Ask my wife.' I went to Filomena and her laconic response was: 'See if you have more success than we have.' It was very clear from this that Chain was not an easy man, but I was walking on air. I was in a fantastic situation—I was now both a member of Bovet's department, and also invited to work with Chain, a Nobel laureate. What a start for a young man of twenty-six!

GJ A foot in both camps—this is by now becoming a familiar story! We have gathered that the Bovets found Chain uncomfortable to deal with, but what was he really like?

RK Well the Bovets were not the only people in the world to find Chain difficult. He was small and exceedingly dynamic. He took umbrage easily and flew into terrible rages. By some extraordinary coincidence the professional partnership of shared research between Bovet and his wife Filomena Bovet-Nitti was mirrored, on the other side of the building, by Chain and his wife, Anne Beloff-Chain. She was a fine biochemist in her own right, later recognized for her work on the metabolism of carbohydrates and the hormonal aspects of diabetes. He had married her in Oxford (she was the sister of the historian Max Beloff and of Nora Beloff, the journalist) and he used to lose his temper easily if something did not go according to his liking. She was fifteen years his junior and a delightful and clever lady. Anne and I had an excellent relationship, but at first it was simply not possible to get close to Chain himself.

GJ   What were you working on with Chain at this time?

RK   The research was into the intermediate metabolism of carbohydrates. We were working on glycogen synthesis in the liver. Our goal was to understand how the normal and the diabetic livers metabolize sugars and turn them into glycogen. We collaborated

Anne Beloff-Chain with their son, Benny

together for the next three years. At this point I must mention a long-standing colleague with whom I worked in Chain's laboratory, Francesco Pocchiari; Francesco was later to become a professor and succeed Marotta as director of the Istituto Superiore di Sanità; in later years he became an invaluable ally and colleague. As time went on my relationship with Chain, both professional and personal, deepened, and I think this was because of our shared background and culture. We also shared something else that was vital to our understanding of each other—a deep love of music. Chain was a very good pianist and an excellent sight-reader, and I was taking my singing studies in Italy extremely seriously. He used to accompany me in the German lieder repertoire that he had known very well since childhood and also in the Italian baroque music which I loved dearly—such things as the *arie antiche* which you and I were to record together many years later.

I learned too that Chain, as a young man, had also found himself facing the dilemma of whether to do music or biochemistry as a career. The biochemist Hans Krebs (another Nobel laureate) believed that Chain was actually more of a musician than a biochemist by temperament, and told him so. But Chain decided to stay in biochemistry. As he put it himself: 'If you are a biochemist, you'll always make a living. I can get a job wherever, publish a paper, then another, and so on. But in music, to make a decent livelihood, you have to be very good—in science you don't have to be all that brilliant.' In this case he was probably playing for safety on account of the upheavals he had already suffered in his professional life in Germany.

GJ   But you must have felt very brilliant! You had what you wanted: you were on
     the research teams of two very famous men in projects that interested you.
     The question is: 'Did this inspire you to work harder and with greater enthusiasm
     than ever before'?

RK   I worked hard, but not like someone possessed, certainly not like Bovet or Chain,
     who both invariably stayed late at the laboratory, while I made a point, at least once
     or twice a week, of leaving at 2 pm. These were the hours, incidentally, of all
     government departments. Chain once turned to me as I was going: 'Are you leaving
     already?' My reply was: 'Well, I've things to do.' He knew of course that I was
     involved in music (I was off to a singing lesson), as was he. He smiled broadly
     and said, only half jokingly: 'You know, Kohn, if you were to really put your mind
     seriously to research, you could get somewhere someday.' At other times he would
     say: 'If only you would use your time better in the laboratory.'

     I suppose you would have to say that I was beginning to realize I did not want
     Chain or Bovet's lifestyle in academia or academic pharmacology. That was a very
     important discovery for me. And it was thanks to Chain that I realized just how
     important an inter-disciplinary approach was in the modern scientific world.

Giving a recital accompanied by Ernst Chain

That stood me in very good stead in my later career as a scientific entrepreneur. I was also fortunate in establishing friendships with many of the researchers at the institute who had come from Europe, the USA and South America. These connections with colleagues worldwide were an invaluable asset in the following decades. I now knew that I could not imagine the rest of my life in a laboratory.

GJ And yet you stayed in Rome for three years in all.

RK Both Bovet and Chain wanted me to stay, and it seemed the right thing to do. I also had other reasons for wanting to remain in Italy—not a bewitching young lady as you might expect, but a certain Maestro Marcantoni, a friend and colleague of Beniamino Gigli, who had become my singing teacher. I was awarded the Charter Scholarship for a second year and my third year was financed, thanks to Marotta, by the Italian government—I received the Paterno Foundation Scholarship. In the end I was even offered a job at the institute which I declined. When I left Rome in 1957 there was a leaving party in the library. Filomena Bovet gave a speech in her usual forthright fashion: 'I don't know', she said, 'whether you are the greatest scientist we have ever had working here, but you are the only one who has succeeded in bringing the two departments together.' And it is true that the departments of biochemistry under Chain, and pharmacology under Bovet, had pursued joint research for the first time and published a number of joint papers, which had not happened before. (My colleagues accused me of having a 'diplomatic' approach to my work!)

I am certain I left Rome at the right time. The idyll was definitely over. A lot of the scientists were becoming very political; this was what led to Marotta's downfall. Chain was also aware that his time there was coming to an end; he felt Italy was in a mess and negotiated with Sir Isaac Wolfson for a return to London as head of the department of biochemistry at Imperial College of Science and Technology where he and his family occupied a magnificent penthouse at the top of the biochemistry building with two Steinway grand pianos (we often made music together there). Lord Blackett, a distinguished Nobel laureate and eminent physicist at Imperial College, also played a crucial role in this move to London. Chain was knighted in 1969, late in his life and twenty-four years after receiving the Nobel prize. Some people thought that this late honouring by the British establishment was as a result of his prickly personality and outspoken views, but it was also possibly because he had lived abroad for many years.

GJ So Chain had nothing more to do with Italy?

RK He was loyal to old friends. He wrote an open letter in defence of Marotta at the Istituto and was told by the left-wing Italian government of the time that if he returned to Italy he risked being arrested for the defamation of the Italian state. Bovet, too, had moved on to another university appointment in Italy—Sassari in Sardinia.

GJ All these years later, what would you say are your strongest memories of Rome?

RK For me memories of the 'Eternal City' are not only of the institute, but also of the Rome opera, the music at the Terme di Caracalla, the symphonic concerts at the Academia di Santa Cecilia … the music of Verdi and Puccini became very dear to me, the repertoire that my father loved. I fell in love with singing in Rome and that will be described in a later chapter of this book. And I shall always remember that Ernst Chain accompanied me with joy in German and Italian song. It is remarkable that such a formidable scientist would lose himself entirely in playing the delicate accompaniment to Scarlatti's *Le violette*. He was a great man in his field but in the end it was music that united us far more strongly than science.

Le violette ALESSANDRO SCARLATTI (1660–1725)   *see page 336*
CD Track 14   *for text and translation*

The Academia di Santa Cecilia in Rome

PRELUDE XI

America GO WEST, YOUNG MAN!

THE NEXT STAGE in my progress was a trip to America. I went to New York expressly to round off my international training. The city itself was a draw. I was a recipient of the coveted Riker Fellowship (Riker was the pharmaceutical firm that had produced the first pressurized dose inhaler in 1956). My destination was the recently founded Albert Einstein College of Medicine which at that time concentrated on research, teaching and clinical responsibilities. This was the kind of institution that appealed to Riker Laboratories when supporting the studies of young medical scientists.

The Albert Einstein College was the first medical school to be built within New York city since 1897, a private institution, part of Yeshiva University in the Morris Park neighbourhood of the Bronx. The college had entered an agreement with the city of New York that the care of patients in the new Bronx Municipal Hospital would be the responsibility of the faculty of the college of medicine. On his seventy-fourth birthday (15 March 1953) Albert Einstein had formally agreed to permit his name to be used for the medical school. Einstein's consent came only after the school agreed that admission would not depend upon race, religion, creed, colour, national origin, sex, age, disability, veteran or disabled veteran status, marital status, sexual orientation, or citizenship status. Here was a striking example of America's commitment to a future of equality. In fact Einstein's list predicts by fifty years the non-discriminatory precepts of western society in the twenty-first century.

At the time of my arrival the school had been open two years. In due course the college developed a global reputation in biomedical sciences and medical education and came to run the largest postgraduate training programme in America. The chairman of the department of pharmacology was Dr Alfred Gilman, internationally renowned and widely influential.

Alfred Gilman

Apart from his work as a pharmacologist Gilman was at the centre of what might be called the 'clinical trials revolution'. Together with Louis S Goodman he had done pioneering work in an early clinical trial that established the use of chemotherapy in the treatment of cancer. He was also known to me as the co-author (also with Goodman) of a very famous textbook which, as a student, I consulted on almost a daily basis. Gilman was born in 1908 and graduated on his dissertation at Yale in 1928. In 1931 he had been awarded a doctorate. Two post-doctoral fellowships ensued, first in the department of biochemistry at Yale, and then in the department of pharmacology. This switch to the latter discipline was to have happy consequences for pharmacology—one of which was the textbook I have just mentioned.

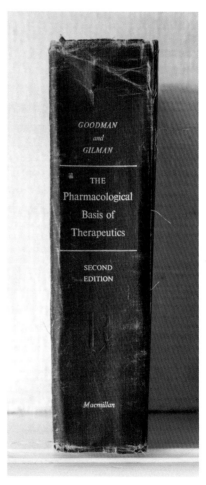

Gilman had met Goodman while he was at Yale; Goodman had completed an internship in medicine at Johns Hopkins University. Both were interested in pharmacology, and they taught together. It was clear that the current books on the subject were inadequate: ill-written, inaccurate and out of date. Gilman and Goodman decided to write a text for the use of Yale students—they wanted to integrate pharmacology with medical sciences, to interpret the action of drugs in the context of the medical advances being made at the time, and to emphasize the application of pharmacology to therapeutics.

The book was entitled *The Pharmacological Basis of Therapeutics*. The text, written in longhand, was a million words long and twice the length expected by the publisher Macmillan (a firm specializing in textbooks—such as Grove's *Dictionary of Music and Musicians*—owned and run by the family of the later British prime minister,

My battered copy of *The Pharmacological Basis of Therapeutics*, signed by Alfred Gilman

Harold Macmillan). This hefty tome first appeared in 1941 and was lengthier and more expensive than most medical textbooks of the time, but it became instantly indispensable. It was known as 'Goodman and Gilman' and medical students referred to it as 'the blue bible'. Within three years the book had sold 28,000 copies. This was a timely guide at a time when the sulfonamide drugs had already been introduced—over a hundred pages were devoted to them. The first edition had sold 86,000 copies by the time of the second edition in 1955. With later editions it was increasingly necessary to add antibiotics, anti-malarial drugs, and a range of chemotherapeutic agents that were specific against particular diseases.

What made the book remarkable was its emphasis on clinical practice. Gilman believed that medical students should be taught pharmacology from the standpoint of the actions of drugs in the treatment of disease. This entailed not only the pharmacology necessary for the rational use of drugs in daily practice, but also current advances in therapeutics. After the appearance of the second edition it soon became clear that the two authors were unable to keep up with all the pharmacological developments. A team of forty-two authors was recruited, all eminent in their fields. The two founding authors kept editorial control for more than thirty years, although Gilman's son, Alfred Goodman Gilman (a Nobel prizewinner in his own right in 1994) became senior editor for the sixth edition.

It was in the fourteen years between the first and second editions of this celebrated textbook that pharmacology changed radically. These were the years of my studies in Manchester, both undergraduate and doctoral, and the beginning of my Italian sojourn—truly exciting times for the drug industry. Treatment with antibiotics had become available in 1942 with the development of penicillin. My professional life started with penicillin—we have already discussed my close personal connection with Chain (as well as much more distant contact with Fleming). After that there was a proliferation of pharmaceutical advances. By the 1950s the most widely used antibiotics, apart from penicillin itself, were streptomycin and dihydrostreptomycin, chlortetracycline (Aureomycin), oxytetracycline (Terramycin), tetracycline, chloramphenicol, erythromycin, carbomycin, polymixin B, bacitracin, neomycin and tyrothricin. In essence, pharmacologists classed the antibiotics as penicillin G, the streptomycins and the tetracyclines. Their predecessors, the sulfonamides, were not strictly speaking antibiotics but chemotherapeutic antibacterial drugs. But there were many hundreds of antibiotics—produced by various species of micro-organisms (fungi, bacteria and actinomycetes) that became valuable in the treatment of infectious diseases. All varied in their action, in their antibacterial spectra, and in their physical, chemical and pharmacological properties.

Many of the drugs derived from plants were not commercially cultivated. Leaves, roots and rhizomes contained active pharmacological substances, but there was little understanding of how the process of chemical change worked on the metabolism. The story of pharmacology in the 1950s was the search for chemical substances which would interfere with the metabolic process—the search, in effect, for new medicines. Chain had achieved this with penicillin and continued with the development of the semi-synthetic penicillins in the 1960s. From the vantage point of the late 1950s, America was the place to be, the place where not only research was going forward but also an exploration of the many pathways to the commercial application of that research. Not since the start of the Industrial Revolution in England, a hundred and fifty years before, had the future of discovery and production looked so promising: ideas were being turned into products, and products appeared on the market that both benefited humanity and made money for their inventors. Many of the greatest scientific discoveries of recent times would soon become commercially applied, invariably using American money and production expertise. Within the context of Einstein's vision—work to be carried out without reference to creed, race, religion, colour or sex—we felt ourselves to be doing good at the same time as doing well. I had experienced the European view of the future as represented by Bovet and Chain, but for me in 1957, Alfred Gilman personified the American side of the vision.

When I met the great man for the first time in his small office, I was ready for him to say anything. For example, he could have told me that the department was interested in a particular type of work, and asked me to form part of the team. But he didn't. He said simply, 'I see you have a good deal of experience in the field of histamine; would you like to continue in that area of research?' This was typical of Gilman's relaxed and leisurely style—so very different from Chain's way of working. He achieved a great deal through warmth and kindness, modesty and good humour. His ability to understand others made him a great teacher and he enjoyed contact with medical students as much as with professional physicians. In the late 1940s at Columbia University's department of medicine he had seen the advantage of teaching by discussion. There, weekly staff conferences were attended by faculty with medical students in attendance. During the discussion of patients' cases physicians would often consult Gilman on treatment, although he was a PhD and not a medical doctor.

When giving his own lectures at Albert Einstein College, Gilman had the wonderful knack of communicating with the graduate students in pharmacology as much as with medical students. He was also able to comment constructively on the work of others without giving the least offence. I delivered lectures on histamine and its antagonists, one of my areas of research, and Gilman was present on every occasion (he attended all lectures by members of his staff when he was in New York). Afterwards, I was invited to his room for a discussion. With many big names in the research field this kind of post-mortem would have been a terrifying, even humiliating, experience. Gilman's comments to me, on the other hand, were helpful and sympathetic. What he thought could be improved was communicated in such a way as to concentrate the mind rather than lower morale. We struck up a friendship which lasted many years based on our shared Jewish cultural background, our scientific interests and our love of music.

Fugue XI (in 2 voices) RALPH KOHN *with* GRAHAM JOHNSON

GJ I've already said that Rome in the 1950s must have been a heavenly place to visit, but I would also have loved to know New York in the same period. Many people have told me that this was a wonderful time to be in the city from a cultural point of view—despite the aftermath of McCarthyism and the pre-civil rights attitudes that we would now find incomprehensible. And here you are in our story, travelling in 1957 to New York for the first time!

RK It was not my first visit to New York, actually. I had already travelled there in the summer of 1952 on a six-week holiday to visit my mother's relatives. My maternal grandmother's maiden name was Kurz, and my mother's cousin was Abraham Kurz, head of the Metropolitan Life Insurance Company in Manhattan. I also had any number of American younger relatives. I sailed, tourist class, on the *Île de France*, and financed my own passage.

On this journey I experienced the first emotional *coup de foudre* of my life. This was a shipboard romance—but I shouldn't even call it that because it was unconsummated. A young and inexperienced fellow like myself, I suppose you may even say callow youth, was just the type to fall in love rather shyly at a distance. I think the person concerned also liked me, but these times were characterized by a restraint that would hardly seem plausible to the young people of today. In those days there was a sense of propriety in such matters. For a while we corresponded with each other, but inevitably lost touch. This was my own version of that famous film *Brief Encounter*, and I left the ship a wiser and more mature young man than the unawakened person who had set sail in Southampton. There is a great Italian song in my repertoire that comes to mind when recalling these emotions.

Caldi sospiri RAFFAELLO RONTANI (*c*1570–1622)   *see page 336*
CD Track 15   *for text and translation*

GJ What were your first impressions of New York City?

RK In those days you still sailed directly into New York harbour. The first sight of the Statue of Liberty was as moving as I had expected it to be. When I arrived in New York I stayed at the New York YMCA—the 'Y' as it was known. The heat in August—over 100 degrees—was a real shock to the system, but the impression of the sheer vitality of life in New York was completely overwhelming for anyone from Europe. On the pharmacological side I was lucky enough to have lunch with John McKeen in Brooklyn, President of Pfizer; he had been responsible for developing the deep-tank fermentation technique of manufacturing penicillin in 10,000-gallon vats. On the cultural side, my relations made much of me and took me to museums, theatres, and concerts. I had a wonderful time.

GJ So by the time it came to travel again to New York, did you take a flight?

RK No, flying was very expensive and this was not yet the age of everybody taking transatlantic flights as a matter of course. Having written to Alfred Gilman, and having been accepted at Alfred Einstein College, I sailed once again to New York, sharing a cabin with three other people. When I arrived I stayed in New Jersey with Sheldon Gertner, a fellow pharmacologist and close friend whom I knew through Bovet. After a few weeks I moved to the Regent's Hotel on Broadway on 105th Street. From there it was very easy to take a subway downtown and go to concerts at Carnegie Hall and elsewhere.

GJ So just like Rome, New York was dear to you as a city of music?

RK Absolutely, and perhaps even more so because my own musical experiences—and here I should probably say my *singing* experiences—were becoming more and more varied. Now there was not just opera to admire, but also the world of German lieder—songs by composers like Schubert and Schumann. I was fortunate to work on the song repertoire with a wonderfully talented pianist and coach by the name of Charles Wadsworth, a couple of years younger than myself. We had enormous fun exploring the song repertoire together and became close friends. He later went on to be a central figure in New York music-making—playing a great deal of chamber music and accompanying singers—and has recently had an auditorium named after him in his home town of Newnan, Georgia. When Charles won a Rockefeller Scholarship and went to live in Paris in 1958, he invited me to live in his apartment on Riverside Drive at 96th Street. Apart from making music myself I was a voracious listener. I discovered the joys of the classical radio station WQXR, and I attended concerts at Carnegie Hall, as well as recitals at the 'Y' and the Town Hall. This was also a golden age at the Metropolitan Opera—and now I am speaking of the old Met, before it moved uptown to its present position. The baritone Robert Merrill was my idol, but I also revered the tenor Jan Peerce and his

The American pianist Charles Wadsworth

younger brother-in-law, Richard Tucker. And then there was that great Italian bass Cesare Siepi, and another amazing baritone, Leonard Warren.

GJ   This is an all-male list of names. You were clearly listening to these voices from the point of view of a student of singing—in my experience a young singer can listen to all kinds of singing with enjoyment, but pays very special attention to the masters of his own vocal *Fach*.

RK   Well it is true that Merrill and Warren were baritones, but I've included tenors and a bass on my list! Yes, I suppose that when one is really interested in singing one can't help comparing one's own progress with the people at the top of the tree—even if it is to be humbled by the enormous difference between their art and one's own.

GJ   What I find very striking about this selection of singers, all with extraordinary world-class voices, is that Cesare Siepi is the only one who is not Jewish. Robert Merrill was born Moishe Miller, Richard Tucker was Rivn—or Ruben—Ticker, Jan Peerce was Joshua Perelmuth and Leonard Warren was Leonard Warenoff. There was no similar flowering of operatic vocal talent in the British diaspora. Is this something to do with the sheer cultural differences between New York and London? Perhaps opera in New York was considered more as a branch of show business (as indeed it is today) rather than as the exclusive domain of high art.

Certainly Covent Garden at the time seems to have been rather more of a closed shop than the Met.

RK Some of the Met's greatest intendants have been Jewish—like Rudolf Bing during my time in New York City. At that time Sir David Webster was in charge at Covent Garden and was clearly a man of a very different temperament—he didn't go in for dramatic battles with his singers in the same way. I am thinking of the feud between Bing and Maria Callas of course! These are two very different cities, with two different musical cultures. America was the kind of country where people had the confidence to try anything—no avenue of advancement, in the entertainment industry at least, seems to

The great American baritone Robert Merrill

have been blocked to the children of immigrants. When I was a little boy the famous cantor Yossele Rosenblatt had visited our home in Leipzig when he was already world famous—do you remember the scene in the film *The Jazz Singer* (the movie from 1927 that was the first of any length to have a soundtrack) in which Al Jolson was moved to tears by Rosenblatt's singing? He had agreed to be filmed singing a secular song (not a sacred one) and had thought it beneath his dignity to appear in a starring role in Meyerbeer's opera *La Juive*. I had grown up in a family where certain cantors were revered as great artists. The New York Jewish diaspora, with its great cantorial tradition, was a source of rich and powerful voices, and being America there seems to have been no conflict between singing in the synagogue and singing on the opera stage. Opportunities were also there for a number of significant Jewish female opera singers—Regina Resnik, Risë Stevens, Roberta Peters and Beverley Sills for example.

GJ And not only opera singers—I am thinking of that extraordinary singer, Jennie Tourel, with her mastery of French and Russian song. Leonard Bernstein loved accompanying her and she was a New York phenomenon.

RK Tourel was marvellous—but just in case we are in any danger of forgetting to discuss the great singers who were not Jewish, I have to say that at the time I was also enthralled in New York by the Spanish soprano Victoria de los Ángeles—she made some of her greatest and most unforgettable appearances at the Met.

GJ And to think my first appearance in New York City was accompanying Victoria de los Ángeles in 1977 when she returned to America after an absence of many years! Returning to the roster of Jewish singers however, surely it was inevitable that someone, such as yourself, who had been expelled from the country of your birth, should have rejoiced in the far happier position in which Jewish artists found themselves in America?

RK I mentioned earlier to you what an inspiration Yehudi Menuhin was to us when I was a child in Amsterdam. My violin studies were immeasurably spurred on at the time by the thought of a young Jewish violinist reaching this kind of exalted level. The fact that these great tenors and baritones were Jewish was not the first thing I noticed about them when admiring their voices and artistry, but I must admit that it made me feel proud that a great opera house like the Met had admitted to its starry ranks quite a number of fine artists of Jewish origin. One must also remember that America was always more of a 'can do' culture. It is interesting, by the way, that these singers were all versatile enough to excel in more popular music—some of them even enjoyed stardom on Broadway.

GJ It sounds as though your New York stay was packed with cultural experiences. If I may be so bold, how were you able to achieve all of this on an annual stipend of $6,000?

RK It was Gilman himself who made it possible. When I first met him he said to me, in that very open way that was so characteristic of him: 'Tell me about yourself.' 'Apart from my scientific interests,' I replied, 'I want to travel and see the USA. I have other interests— music in particular, about which I am passionate.' I explained to Gilman that I had started singing in Rome and I'd like to continue that. He replied: 'You're going to be strapped for cash. We'll give you an additional $6,000, and you'll travel to scientific meetings at our expense.' Although generosity to visitors was, and

Victoria de los Ángeles

remains, typical of Americans in general, this was exceptionally kind. Of course I had no idea what kind of departmental budget he had at his disposal, but it was certainly a figure that would have made Gilman's opposite numbers in Britain, Professor Macdonald, for example, gasp in amazement. And of course it was very lucky for me that Gilman was also an enthusiastic musician—his father, a professional trombonist, had owned a music store in Bridgeport, Connecticut, and his wife Mabel was an excellent pianist. Gilman himself could play almost any instrument, and frequently did so at neighbourhood parties. In his student days he had learned to play the trumpet and played at weddings and bar mitzvahs to make extra money. The very idea of a famous British professor of pharmacology playing the trumpet with gusto at a wedding is a most unlikely picture, but this was America—and it is also part of an old Jewish tradition! In Schumann's famous song from *Dichterliebe* 'Das ist ein Flöten und Geigen' (the text by the Jewish poet Heinrich Heine), the lusty sound of trumpets ('Trompeten schmettern darein') is described at just such a wedding.

🔊 *Das ist ein Flöten und Geigen* No 9 *of* Dichterliebe, Op 48 ROBERT SCHUMANN (1810–1856)
CD Track 16   *see page 337 for text and translation*

The title-page of an early edition
of Schumann's *Dichterliebe*

INTERLUDE 2: COURANTE

Roving ambassador

TOWARDS THE END of my year-long stay in America Gilman said to me (he had a way of asking questions where there seemed no doubt that he had my best interests at heart): 'What do you want to do? Would you like to stay in America? Would you like to go into academic pharmacology or industry?' I was frank and honest in my reply. I said that I did not want to be an academic or researcher. I knew very well what it took to be either of those things, but I could not envisage long hours in a laboratory, or being permanently behind a desk. I was too fond of the outside world, travelling, meeting people and so on.

It was then that Gilman proceeded, almost magically, to pave the way for a job that seemed ideally suited to my abilities and my interests. I have to thank my lucky stars that he was a man of great vision in that he had a finely tuned appreciation of the fast-developing pharmaceutical industry, but he also understood my strengths (and weaknesses) and how these might be employed. He picked up the phone and spoke to one of the commercial firms with whom he had cultivated links over the years; indeed he was engaged as a consultant for this particular Philadelphia-based company, Smith Kline and French. And I also believe that even at this stage he already had in mind what my future with them might be.

What follows seemed almost too good to be true. After an interview in Philadelphia I was offered a role as head of a new unit of exploratory pharmacology at Smith Kline and French. This would involve my going back to England and working from London as my base. I was truly in the right place at the right time to land this extraordinary job—it was as if it had been created especially for me. My brief was not exclusively concerned with the research of actually developing new drugs (although I would of course need to be fully informed of all new developments) but to use my scientific expertise, linguistic skills and personal contacts to discover drugs in Europe which might be the basis of productive partnerships between European companies and my new American employers. The fact that I could speak English, German, French, Dutch and Italian was a considerable advantage. It was clear that only a trained pharmacologist could initiate the discussions that would lead to an informed opinion regarding the suitability of these ventures. This was no salesman's work but something far more complex, subtle and delicate. Apart from the technical side of the discussions, often with fellow scientists, this job was about getting on with people, winning their trust, and getting the best out of them to the advantage of both firms. It so happened that Smith Kline and French had been lucky, and astute, enough to benefit considerably from the fact that the drug chlorpromazine, developed by Rhône-Poulenc in France as a sedative and antihistamine, turned out to be the first important anti-psychotic. How this happened is a story in itself that I will recount in the next chapter. There were clearly other drugs being developed in Europe and elsewhere further afield that might benefit from a collaboration between European research and American marketing expertise.

In September 1958 I presented myself at the imposing Smith Kline and French headquarters in Spring Garden Street in Philadelphia. This was a firm that had started as John D Smith's drugstore in 1830. Mahlon Kline became a partner in 1875, and in 1891 they acquired French, Richards and Company, adding certain prized consumer brands. In 1929 the Smith Kline and French Company was renamed Smith Kline and French Laboratories. My arrival in Philadelphia was the beginning of a training period that lasted six weeks—and nobody could have wished for a better apprenticeship for what would follow in my career for the next seven years. The firm's President was Francis Boyer who had been chief of the firm since 1951 and was in his last year of tenure when I met him. I was also introduced to scientists, administrators and financial experts. This was a patrician group of people, including some very good linguists—Francis Grant, for example, who spoke excellent French and had been in the State Department, and J P Young, the grandson of Owen D Young, the man who had initiated the Young Plan in 1929 to alleviate the level of German reparations debt. It was only after the war that Smith Kline and French began to employ Jews, but as I have written elsewhere I never experienced the slightest anti-Semitism from anyone—on the contrary I had the impression of being welcomed with open arms. My life had changed utterly. This was brought home to me when Neil Osborne at Smith Kline and French arranged my trip home via a travel agent. This was an overnight trip on TWA, New York to London. 'You should have a sleeper on the plane', said Neil, and that was that. (There were four first-class sleepers on those piston-engined TWA airliners.) I was now part of a large firm that was sufficiently prosperous to look after the comfort of its employees. Even though I was just about to take a twelve-hour flight, I had already landed on my feet.

PRELUDE XII

Smith Kline and French

MY OBTAINING A JOB at Smith Kline and French, as if by magic, came about partly because of the ups and downs of pharmaceutical progress in the United States. The president of my new firm, Francis Boyer, was strongly in favour of opening the vast American market to European ideas and discoveries; this was a visionary move that was later imitated by many other firms in the industry. On the scientific front, advances in chemistry and in the synthesizing of amino acids and proteins were driving enormous changes in the worldwide industry resulting in a new 'rational approach' to drug discovery.

In 1951 George Hitchings and Gertrude Elion, working in Wellcome's laboratories in the United States, had employed a chemical approach to drug research. This led to the discovery of Purinethol (mercaptopurine), one of the first effective cancer treatments. Hitchings and Elion initiated many new cures and treatments. Their research was based on studies of nucleic acids and they searched for compounds to block the cellular reproduction of disease-causing organisms or cells. This dynamic new pharmacological approach (which eventually netted Hitchings and Elion the Nobel prize in 1988, together with Sir James Black for his work on beta blockers) suggested untrammelled progress and ever-increasing profits for the drug companies, but this was to reckon without the checks and balances demanded by the American Food and Drug Administration (FDA)—a regulatory body established in the early years of the twentieth century. In 1929 prescription drugs represented about a third of all consumer spending on drugs in the US; by 1949 it was well over half (the war had accelerated the therapeutic revolution) and by 1969 over four fifths. As new drugs appeared treatments became available, not just for infectious diseases but for chronic conditions: heart disease, ulcers, diabetes and pain. One must not forget that each one of those prescription drugs took a number of years, and millions of dollars, to go through the processes of research, development and manufacture, not to mention the clinical trials that led to its eventual licensing by the appropriate authorities. (Nowadays a new drug development might cost up to a billion dollars and take ten to twelve years to complete.) It was inevitable that with the profusion of available drugs, and after some very dramatic cases of toxic side-effects, the manufacture of drugs should become more stringently controlled.

Before the war American pharmaceutical companies like Merck, Pfizer and Lilly (firms employing many thousands of people) were the pre-eminent drug producers. Worldwide conflicts had driven the demand for penicillin sky-high, and then there was a similar demand for other antibiotics; these firms, and others, moved with alacrity into the manufacture of these substances. After the war Eli Lilly, for example, produced the new antibiotics vancomycin and erthromycin, as well as becoming involved in the production and distribution of Jonas Salk's poliomyelitis vaccine. In the early 1960s (and particularly after amended Food and Drug legislation in 1962) there was shift within the American pharmaceutical establishment: the number of therapeutic (or ethical) drugs developed from pharmacological and pharmaceutical research was greatly reduced. Firms like Merck and Schering continued to be involved in internal research and development, but both of these were originally subsidiaries of German firms, something which perhaps explains the reduction: the German pharmaceutical tradition held the imperatives of scientific research in equal esteem with purely business considerations.

John McKeen at Pfizer had developed the deep-tank fermentation method of making penicillin on an industrial scale. The drug that had been such a scarce substance in Oxford in 1941 was now being made in 10,000-gallon vats. Pfizer in America now concentrated much of its energy on developing a formidable marketing capacity. Eli Lilly, the company that had been the first to make insulin for diabetics in the 1920s, also had a very large sales force. Distribution was a paramount concern in a newly sophisticated age of rail and telegraph networks; the important challenge was the quick and efficient delivery of these products— existing, patented pharmaceuticals, proprietary drugs in other words—to pharmacists, drug stores and other retail outlets. These non-prescription products

John McKeen, president of Pfizer from 1949 to 1965

derived from natural vegetable and mineral sources could be sold over the counter; in the 1950s these products still accounted for a good proportion of all the money spent on pharmaceuticals. The drug firms needed mass-marketing expertise—advertising was an increasingly sophisticated industry—and also necessary was a strong public relations department.

The firm for which I now worked, Smith Kline and French, was in search of new ideas, new products, and new ways to find them; it was for this reason that I had landed my new contract. Their focus—typical of the US pharmaceutical industry of that time—was over-the-counter products. This is not to say that the firm was not involved in research of its own. In 1945, for example, it had begun evaluating the therapeutic advantages of coatings for tablets; at the same time its chemists had started searching for chemical or mechanical techniques that would release drugs to yield a therapeutic effect throughout 12 or 24 hours. In 1949 a chemist working for the firm, Donald McDonnell, found a solution to the longer-term release of drugs: capsules filled with pellets that would dissolve at different times. In 1952 the new capsule—the Spansule—was marketed. The capsule was first used with Dexedrine (dexamphetamine sulfate) for treating psychiatric, narcoleptic and depressive patients. This form of drug delivery was a therapeutic breakthrough. It formed the basis for one of Smith Kline and French's staple products, an over-the-counter cold treatment called Contac, launched in 1960.

Francis Boyer, while president of Smith Kline and French, had overseen an extraordinary expansion of the business: during his tenure, sales rose from $43 million to $124 million and earnings increased from $4 million to $20 million. Boyer had achieved this despite the fact that research expenses had increased fivefold in the same period. The reason for this was that he had learned that drugs—the intellectual property relating to their development and manufacture—could be acquired more cheaply and less riskily from other pharmaceutical companies than they could be grown and nurtured from within. Smith Kline and French continued its own internal research, but Boyer knew this was insufficient. The company needed access to pharmaceutical research in Europe, in the eastern bloc, in Japan, even in domestic American universities and research institutes. Preliminary testing, drug development and clinical trials were taking place all over the world and Smith Kline and French had no access to them without coming to the imaginative solution of sending well-trained scientists and commercially trained individuals to negotiate on behalf of the company. There were many firms in Europe that had developed and licensed drugs for their domestic markets, and which had not yet gained an entry into the USA. It would be very much to the advantage of these companies without American subsidiaries of their own to go into partnership with

Smith Kline and French who could provide them with access to the vast transatlantic market. There were also other sources: a university department may be well equipped to do the fundamental science of a new drug, but could not cover the work required in testing its pharmacology, toxicology or carcinogenicity, or large-scale clinical trials.

My task was to find new, developing or existing drugs that could be transferred to the American market under license to Smith Kline and French. Boyer also realized that such an operation was best run from the UK with its easy access to European countries; that is where my British background and scientific training was as important as my ability to speak several European languages. The firm had no foothold in the UK until 1953 when it bought an ailing company, Menley and James. With this purchase came a site in Welwyn Garden City on which modern facilities could be built; this became our headquarters. As soon as I returned from America in 1958 we operated from there in small, specialized teams. There were chemists and pharmacologists together with experts in the structure and function of drugs; there were also linguists and diplomats recruited from academia and the American State Department working in the US who were supported by operators from the UK.

Our work in the UK was closely co-ordinated with our colleagues in Philadelphia to whom I reported. I had the company's blessing and carte blanche to visit where I liked and to speak to whomever I chose. I refused to discuss anything

that was not protected, asking before each meeting: 'Have you applied for patents?' This was simply because I had no wish to hear about projects not covered by patents. Anyone I approached therefore knew that I was interested only in discussing those subjects that could be safely disclosed. We ran a totally ethical operation. People came to trust me and were able to judge for themselves how we conducted ourselves. In Paris, Copenhagen or Madrid I worked with a team of colleagues but in German-speaking countries I managed the bulk of the work on my own. On occasion there were awkward situations: I remember visiting the research director of a well-

with Daniel Bovet at the Smith Kline and French headquarters in Welwyn Garden City, *circa* 1960

known German company who had been the rector of Heidelberg University during the Third Reich. (This appointment lay within Hitler's control, and the man concerned had undoubtedly been an enthusiastic Nazi.) My companion on that occasion was the medical director at Smith Kline and French, the irrascible Dr Isidore Schrire. There was a very distinguished Talmudical scholar Sherira Gaon (906–1006) and my friend and colleage Isidor Schrire was a descendant of that family. I can only hope that the former rector of Heidelberg was as uncomfortable being in the presence of two Jews who knew about his past, as we were in having to keep company with him for professional reasons.

On the whole, the work suited me well. I enjoyed travel and I was at ease with the people I met. The happy-go-lucky attitude of Beethoven's travelling song *Marmotte* seems appropriate here.

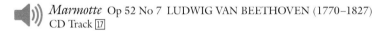

Marmotte Op 52 No 7 LUDWIG VAN BEETHOVEN (1770–1827)   *see page 337*
CD Track 17   *for text and translation*

Of course, I always tried to improve and raise standards—my own and those of people around me, where appropriate—and there was much to learn. As a group we had a highly developed sense of honour and commitment; we were scrupulous and meticulous, driven by a combined sense of duty and responsibility to those who had confidence in us. No one else did what we did, systematically, in the early 1960s, but others came to imitate us later. What was very important for my future was that I became well known in the international pharmaceutical community on scientific, medical and commercial levels.

Fugue XII (*in 2 voices*) RALPH KOHN *with* GRAHAM JOHNSON

GJ I am an absolute layman when it comes to pharmacology so I must ask you to excuse the naivety of some of my questions. It seems that you began to work at Smith Kline and French more or less at a turning point in the industry in America—a time when over-the-counter remedies were being slowly and surely overtaken by increasingly sophisticated medicines available only on prescription. You write of the tightening of regulations …

RK Yes, the industry was increasingly subject to public scrutiny, especially after the thalidomide tragedy in Germany, Australia and the UK, which had a huge impact on public opinion in America and led to changes to the law in 1962 when the US Congress passed the Kefauver Harris Amendment to the Food, Drug and Cosmetic Act. The government could now oversee and control not only the finished pharmaceutical products, but the processes that created them. There were stringent regulations on drug safety tests and on the procedures by which effectiveness was tested. This affected the way that clinical trials were run by pharmaceutical companies. Despite the fact that thalidomide had never been released in the USA, the Food and Drug Administration reacted very sharply.

GJ I'm sorry to interrupt, but after all the horrors of thalidomide—the births of deformed babies to women who had taken the drug for morning sickness—you must think this was a good thing?

RK Indeed I do. Almost my entire professional life in pharmacology, first working for Smith Kline and French, then Robapharm, and then as an independent, was spent working with, and within, these improved regulations. Nevertheless, this legislation made new drugs a great deal more expensive for firms to develop and the industry in the USA, and indeed internationally, was forced to change considerably. Smaller pharmaceutical companies had to close, merge or diversify. In the 1960s other countries were able to develop drugs more swiftly and cheaply. This knock-on effect of the tightened regulation happened to be an important factor in my career with Smith Kline and French where part of my task was acting as a link between America and Europe and Japan.

GJ I am fascinated that Smith Kline and French engaged you for this exciting and challenging work some years before the breaking of the thalidomide scandal, and before Congress had passed the new legislation. This was clearly something more complicated than a reaction to the new regime of government controls. I am interested in why they were so generous to you and offered a young Englishman the job of his dreams. They obviously liked you …

RK I hope they liked me, but I don't think this played more than a peripheral part in the arrangement. A few years earlier Francis Boyer had 'seen the light' as regards lively engagement with European collaborators. I would like to tell you one story because it is a fascinating piece of 'pharma' history. This concerns the drug chlorpromazine marketed in the USA as Thorazine. This drug had been developed by Laboratoires Rhône-Poulenc in 1950 in Paris and was used as an antihistamine and antiemetic. In the early 1950s a French doctor by the name of Henri Laborit attempted to reduce surgical shock in his patients. He knew that shock resulted from the action of chemicals in the brain. He wanted to reduce the amount of anaesthetic he used and chose chlorpromazine, a drug causing sedation without narcosis, to replace it. In fact he thought it possible (if used with pethedine and hydergine) to induce an 'artificial hibernation' in patients ...

Henri Laborit

GJ   This sounds rather sinister to me: was Dr Laborit something of a Dr Frankenstein?

RK   Far from it—he was a very bright and imaginative physician working for the army. His idea was that patients in shock—with severe trauma and burns— could stay sedated for a long time and, as such, would be easier to handle during surgery. But the property of the drug to keep patients quiet and passive required further testing.

GJ   I apologize to Dr Laborit, he seems also to have been admirably prudent ...

RK   The first clinical trial of the drug was conducted at the Ste Anne hospital in Paris in 1952 by the psychiatrists Jean Delay and Pierre Deniker. They treated thirty-eight psychotic patients with injections of chlorpromazine (used purely as a sedative) and they noted that patients were not only sedated, but also showed an improvement in cognition and emotion. This was the first synthetic drug to have been shown to be effective in psychosis.

GJ   So these were developments in France. What has all this to do with Smith Kline and French?

RK   As it happened Boyer, with little money for research at home, had gone fishing in French waters and acquired an option on the US rights to chlorpromazine from Rhône-Poulenc in 1952, but as an antiemetic. When news of the psychiatrists' trials in Paris began to spread he tried to persuade clinical departments in American hospitals to test it. Smith Kline and French invited Pierre Deniker to speak to psychiatrists in the USA. The economic advantages of the drug were outlined for state mental institutions and governments. Tests began in the institutions where the most severe cases were housed and convincing results were reported on television and in the press. By this time, by the way, the drug was marketed in Europe under the name Largactil.

GJ   I am utterly surprised! This word has a huge personal resonance for me—my elderly mother in South Africa suffers from dementia and is treated daily with

Largactil—and this is more than sixty years after the discovery of chlorpromazine. Smith Kline and French clearly had a huge success on its hands.

RK Not quite yet—by now there were scores of people involved in this new wonder drug. An important piece in this jigsaw was the work of the distinguished young psychiatrist Dr Nathan Kline, working in Albany in the state of New York, a pioneer in the work of antidepressants. It was these drugs that replaced electro-convulsive therapy, insulin shocks and even lobotomy. Nathan Kline tested chlorpromazine for Smith Kline and French and this led to the drug being approved for psychiatric treatment in 1954. The new drug became a standard against which all other tranquillizers were measured. The effect of chlopromazine in psychiatric disease was similar to that of penicillin in infectious disease. Partly as a result of this drug, psychiatry was reintegrated with the other medical disciplines. Pyschiatrists were fully fledged physicians who could now help their patients in ways other than listening to their problems. The overwhelming message for Smith Kline and French was that both scientific success and financial advantage could come from developing others' work; a pharmaceutical company did not necessarily have to own its intellectual property *ab initio*.

GJ This is an inspiring story—to think we have discussed a wonder drug like Thorazine or Largactil at the same time as a poisonous and useless substance like thalidomide.

RK Pharmacology is an extraordinarily complex subject—and here I must come to the defence of thalidomide. It is horribly toxic as far as the foetus of a pregnant woman in the first trimester is concerned, but it is used to this day as a treatment for certain malignant conditions (multiple myeloma) and for complications of leprosy. Another everyday example of this is the use of Botulinum toxin. This is a drug that is deadly in high doses but it is used clinically useful for the regulation of muscle spasms. As Botox it is increasingly employed in cosmetic procedures.

GJ You mean that many older people have come to rely on Botulinum toxin as a face-saving drug …

RK Well said, but joking aside, we must always remember that the value of a drug in treatment is also dose dependent, and that drugs are often poisons for some, and life-givers to others.

INTERLUDE 3: PASSEPIED

Exotic realms JAPAN, RUSSIA AND IRAN

IN MY NEW JOB I had to visit the chairmen, CEOs and research and medical directors of many French, German and Swiss companies, as well as in eastern Europe. In Germany and Switzerland I visited BASF, Bayer, Boehringer, Ciba-Geigy, Degussa, Hoechst, Roche and Sandoz, amongst the leaders. I was searching for demonstrably successful drugs ready for transfer to the substantial US market.

I also established an important relationship with Japanese research institutions. By the 1960s the country had recovered from the war and had a vigorous industrial and chemical base. As manufacturers and importers in Europe sought Japanese engineering and technology at this time, so the pharmaceutical industry turned its attention to Japan. The post-war Japanese economy grew by 10% a year between 1950 and 1970; Caterpillar, an American engineering company, had established one of the first joint ventures in Japan—with Mitsubishi Heavy—in 1963, and others followed. Panasonic, Technics and Sony were at the forefront of innovation in consumer products. Sony was the first company to offer a portable television (1962), video recorder (1965) and Trinitron colour television (1968).

After the war the Japanese companies sought to establish relationships with European and American producers by buying and selling licenses, by marketing agreements, and by joint ventures. In Japan I made contact not only with pharmaceutical manufacturers but also universities and research institutes. In pharmacological terms this was pioneering work. Together with my colleague Dr Don Hudson, who was a chemist, I arrived in Japan in 1961. We spent three weeks visiting biomedical university departments and research facilities and our journey took us to Tokyo, Kyoto, Yokahama, Osaka and other cities.

A part of my deep sympathy for Japanese culture came indirectly as a result of my enthusiasm for singing, and thanks to one of the people who helped and advised me on my musical studies when I returned to the UK from America. This was the accompanist Marcel Lorber; he was a refugee from Vienna who lived in Belsize Park, an area of north London that at one time was known as 'klein Wien'—'little Vienna'. After the war he had been with the Allied forces in Japan where he had entertained the troops and acquired a considerable knowledge of Japanese culture. When I knew Lorber, he was in his mid-sixties; he had no sense of humour, and he took himself very seriously. I had not expected that he would be quite so delighted to hear that I was off to Japan on a business trip for Smith Kline and

French. Far from being relieved that he no longer had to work with me for a little while, he asked me if I could do him a big favour. Would I kindly look up a certain Raymond Bushell, a world authority on toggles—small carvings suspended on the belts of Japanese costumes, sometimes as fasteners. I discovered these were called 'netsuke' (small Japanese carvings on an astonishing range of subjects in wood, ivory or other materials) and 'inro' (a traditional Japanese case for holding small objects). Lorber asked me to meet Bushell (who had been a member of the American occupying forces in Japan) and obtain from him a first-class netsuke and pay him whatever price he requested. Lorber would then reimburse me. Bushell offered me a beautiful animal carved in wood for which I paid him (on behalf of Lorber) the princely sum of £50—today the piece would be worth several thousand pounds. A few years later Bushell wrote a famous book entitled *An Introduction to Netsuke*.

I feel I would have to explain more about these fascinating artefacts to the reader were it not for the worldwide success of Edmund de Waal's *The Hare with Amber Eyes*, a fascinating story of a collection of netsuke that was passed down through the celebrated Ephrusi family (de Waal's relations on his mother's side); this assemblage of hundreds of precious and intricately carved objects moved from Paris to Vienna and then (having survived the depredations of the Nazis and the theft of the Ephrusi's other artistic treasures) to Tokyo. The netsuke then moved to de Waal's own safekeeping and he wrote the book about them which became an international best-seller.

On coming back to London I passed the little piece over to Lorber and discovered that he already had a substantial collection of these exquisite objects. (He later left these to the Israel Museum in Jerusalem where I have viewed them with great pleasure.) From 1982 onwards (this time no longer working for Smith Kline and French, but travelling as my own boss) I became a netsuke and inro

A netsuke

An inro

collector in my own right. I bought a number of beautfiul pieces in Tokyo and Kyoto and then found a leading dealer in Honolulu. I built up a lovely collection including the work of Tomotada (Edo period, 18th century), Shibata Zeshin (1807–1891) and one of the greatest nineteenth-century masters, Masatsugu Kaigyokusai (1813–1892). These exquisite little articles brought me and my family years of pleasure. Very sadly we had a burglary fairly recently and our collection was taken. We have acquired some netsuke since then, but it has not yet been possible to replace our entire collection. In the meantime the Kohn Foundation had the pleasure of sponsoring a talk by Edmund de Waal about his book at the Royal Society of Literature where he gave us a fascinating evening in conversation with the novelist Penelope Lively.

Of course, in later years my work regularly took me to Japan, often in the company of my wife Zahava. These pictures show us in 1995—visiting Hiroshima where, astonishingly, the famous cupola had survived the atom bomb. I am also attempting here to make music with local instrumentalists as my wife, slightly concerned, looks on. This was taken in a private room of a famous restaurant in Osaka.

 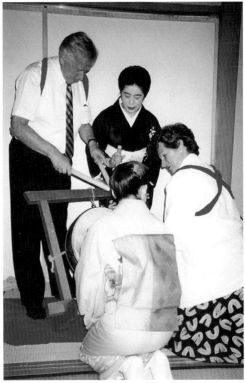

Travels in Japan

In 1962, during the height (or depth) of the Cold War, I flew to Moscow in the company of the UK chairman of Smith Kline and French, Dick Pfizenmaier, and another colleague from Philadelphia, Francis Grant, whom I had first met in the Philadelphia headquarters of the firm in 1958. On behalf of the company I made a scientific presentation to the Soviet Ministry of Health during which I stressed the importance of drug research—for both human health and commercial benefit. I dared to argue that proper patents would ensure that the intellectual property belonged to the individual or laboratory concerned; any subsequent international licensing agreements would mean substantial royalties might be earned.

The reply to this speech came from the formidable Mme Yakovleva, Deputy Minister of Health, who informed us that the Soviet system worked differently: 'Medicines should not be the subject of financial gains, but rather made freely available. No secrecy, no patents, but publication of results so that all could see the benefit.' I had the temerity to argue back that there seemed to be different views within the Socialist camp, citing our licensing agreements with Hungary and Czechoslovakia. These, I said, conformed with the principles I had just outlined. Without missing a beat, and without blushing, Mme Yakovleva countered with these words: 'There is no difference in our system. We all have the same philosophy, but I was talking of the ideal world, which we have not yet reached.'

Having made her impeccably Marxist position clear, she continued with the news that I had been hoping for: 'We would therefore be interested at this stage to collaborate with you.'

From Moscow I flew alone to Leningrad to visit two influential scientists at the Pavlovian Institute in the Russian Academy of Medical Sciences. One was Nikolai Nikolaevich Anichkov who had been president of the Academy of Medical Sciences of the USSR between 1946 and 1953. He was a strong party member and had on his desk a picture of himself in military uniform (he was a major general) as well as a signed photograph of Lenin.

Anichkov's work on cholesterol should have won him the Nobel prize. He had been the first to describe myocardial cells (Anichkov- or Anitschkov-cells, or cardiac histiocytes) and chart the significance of cholesterol in the pathogenesis of atherosclerosis, and thus heart disease.

The other famous Russian scientist was Anatolii Aleksandrovich Smorodintsev, a virologist who worked closely with Albert Sabin in immunizing millions of eastern European children with Sabin's polio vaccine. Smorodintsev told me that Sabin (a Polish Jew who became a naturalized American citizen) was forced to immunize the children in eastern Europe (rather than the USA) because the Food and Drug Administration did not at that time allow the live attenuated virus to be

Nikolai Nikolaevich Anichkov   Anatolii Aleksandrovich Smorodintsev

used for immunization; they feared it might reverse to parthogenicity and cause the disease to be introduced into the injected children.

Smorodintsev had a good sense of humour and told me this story with a broad smile on his face. On that occasion the Russians had been unhampered by American bureaucracy, but how tragic it would have been if the fears of the FDA had been correct. The way this great scientist told me the story, I could tell that he had been completely convinced of the efficacy of the vaccine and had no fears at all about immunizing thousands of children—some of whom, no doubt, might have suffered from poliomyelitis without this intervention.

The last in this little trio of memories of exotic travel is from 1976. By that time I had already established my own company, Advisory Services (Clinical and General). I was contacted by a firm of management consultants and asked whether I would be willing, at the invitation of the Iranian government, to fly to Tehran for a week. This was three years before the revolution that swept Ayatollah Khomeini into power and very few people in the West realized that the Pahlavi regime was gradually crumbling; I was warned not to engage in any political comment because all the hotel rooms were bugged by Savak, the notorious secret police. The Shah had apparently expressed a concern that his country had so little pharmaceutical expertise that its government was forced to buy drugs from abroad rather than manufacturing them locally under license. Could these drugs not be synthesized in Iran? My brief was to determine whether this was possible with the country's available pharmaceutical resources and expertise. I met the Iranian

Minister of Health in the biggest office I have ever seen (his name was Dr Shaikholezlamzadeh—I remember making myself memorize it, and my memory serves me still). He was later sentenced to death by the Khomeini regime and only reprieved at the last moment. I also met Dr Ali, the medical adviser of the Shah (in a few short years that ill-fated leader-in-exile would be seeking treatment for lymphatic cancer in the USA). After visiting some of their factories and hospitals I came to the conclusion that there was insufficient pharmacological training or experience for the Iranians to manufacture the requisite drugs. They would have to keep importing in bulk until they had well-trained staff. I again met the Minister of Health to whom I transmitted my findings which I would later send as a full report to Tehran. At the end of my visit I wanted to buy some silver and a Nain carpet and the Ministry of Health was kind enough to send two guides to ensure I was not cheated in the transaction. I got the distinct impression that the Shah's government had not appreciated the low marks I had given them for pharmacology, but it was a fascinating glimpse into the dying days of a declining empire. I felt danger in the air and I was relieved to come home in one piece.

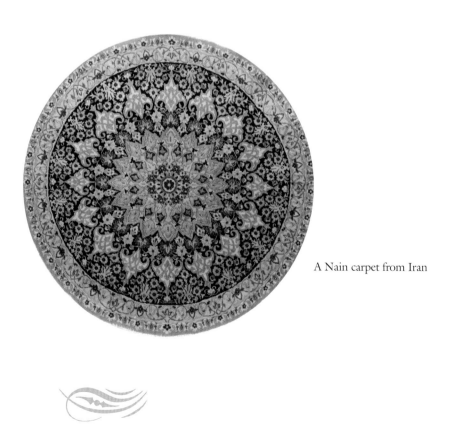

A Nain carpet from Iran

PRELUDE XIII

Moving on

I WAS HEAD OF EXPLORATORY PHARMACOLOGY at Smith Kline and French for seven years (1958–1965). The UK pharmaceutical sector was international although, apart from Glaxo, the top-selling companies (ranked by sales) were American or Swiss. Smith Kline and French was the fourth largest after Pfizer, Lederle and Glaxo. Companies could choose between the American model of mass-marketing or opt for European drugs-by-design. At Smith Kline and French we took a hybrid approach, an international outlook, searching for already proven and commercially promising drugs to take from one market to another—in this case from western Europe, eastern Europe and Asia to America—as well as doing our own research in-house.

These seven years represented an important apprenticeship in terms of what lay ahead for me in my future. I came to know the structure and function of the industry: this meant knowing all the intricacies associated with the commercial release of a drug, the various stages of experimental, pre-clinical and then clinical trials in all markets, cultures and jurisdictions—this is far more complicated than it sounds. I also came to know many of the leading researchers in Europe and Japan. This was useful because surprisingly few individuals at that time had international experience or a broad overview of the industry that transcended linguistic barriers. Many Americans and Germans understood perfectly well that they worked in an international business but felt uncomfortable outside their own respective culture zones.

Smith Kline and French operated from its UK headquarters in Welwyn Garden City in Hertfordshire (about twenty miles north of London) under the chairman-ship of Dick Pfizenmaier, a graduate of the University of Pennsylvania and of the Wharton School of Business. As the laboratories in Welwyn Garden City expanded under Pfizenmaier's control, my life with the company gradually changed. At this point I need to backtrack somewhat and talk about some of my other colleagues. In the early 1960s the development director at Smith Kline and French was a scientist with acute commercial insight named David Jack—later Sir David Jack FRS. Unfortunately for us, he was lured away from the company by Allen & Hanburys, a firm that was later bought by Glaxo. This was a great loss for us because Jack was one of the finest post-war research directors: a pharmacist and chemist with an appreciation of the commercial possibility of drugs. Perhaps the poaching of a man of Jack's distinction was regarded by head office in Philadelphia as a thrown gauntlet that required a proactive response. In 1964 it was decided that Smith Kline and French needed an internal research department of its own to cover as many opportunities as possible. The research director, Dr Alan Ratcliffe, was a clever professional, a mathematician who excelled in designing clinical trials, although not a specialist in the biological sciences. It was a terrible surprise that he committed suicide after a few years in the job, leaving the firm without a research director. The position was offered to David Jack (who would have been Ratcliffe's obvious successor) but he chose to honour his commitment to Allen & Hanburys. The job subsequently went to Dr Edward Paget, an appointment that was influenced by the after-effects of the thalidomide tragedy. Pharmaceutical companies needed to ensure that their drugs were, above all, safe; as a result Smith Kline and French felt that they needed an expert in toxicology in the job, and Paget had been head of pathology at ICI. I had been responsible for bringing new products and chemical structures into the company from other research facilities. The laboratories at Welwyn Garden City had been brought back to life by Pfizenmaier, and now Paget arrived with his new team, including Dr James Black (who had developed beta blockers).

One of the other people in the team Paget brought with him to Smith Kline and French was Shirley Cross, a botanist by training, who was an assistant in the research and development operations. Her husband had been a doctor who had been killed in a plane crash as he made his way to a scientific meeting in the US, and she had been left with two small children. She recovered from this tragedy with great personal bravery; I got to know her quite well as a colleague, but lost touch with her when I left Smith Kline and French. Some years later my wife Zahava and I spent a few days at the famous Cipriani Hotel in Venice; to my surprise I saw Shirley lying by the side of the Olympic-sized swimming-pool with a man I did not know. I was initially shy of approaching her under the circumstances, but she came up to me. He turned out to be her second husband, James Sherwood, the chairman of Orient-Express Hotels (the Cipriani was part of his empire). Shirley also played a great part in the renaissance of the Orient-Express train service. We saw a great deal of each other during the stay and we returned to London in Sherwood's private jet instead of using our tickets on Alitalia. Shirley Sherwood is now well known for her association with Kew Gardens and her considerable collection of botanical art.

I wish I could say that the kind of cordiality I enjoyed with Shirley was typical of my interaction with the new adminstration. After some months Paget wanted to extend his role and take up some of my work. He believed there was a conflict of interest between his trying to develop new drugs internally, while I was attempting to bring in new drugs from outside. If I were successful, James Black and his team would have to spend time and money on developing ideas not of their own making; Paget and Black wanted the money, time and people for their own internal projects. My search for drugs outside the company threatened Black's research strategy and Paget's managerial ambitions. I was convinced, however, that the company needed both internal research and drugs under license.

I discussed this awkward situation with Dick Pfizenmaier, who wanted me to stay with the firm and accept other responsibilities. He urged me to consider the situation carefully, and I spent some weeks in Princeton on a management training course in the autumn of 1962 thinking over my options. The one thing I could not bear was working for a firm with internal rumblings. Certain people at Welwyn Garden City thought my activity was over-supported and regarded me as something of a loose cannon. Some little time before I left, I remember I was due to negotiate a new deal concerning our drug Furadantin, a drug marketed also by the firm Abic in Israel. Before I left for that country, the managing director at Welwyn Garden City called me in and had the temerity to remind me whose side I was supposed to be on regarding the negotiation of the new agreement. It was as if he suspected that my loyalties would automatically be with my co-religionists rather than the best interests of our firm. When anti-Semitism emerges in business circles it is in ways as covert as this. I immediately offered to withdraw from going to Israel; he backed down saying that I was unduly sensitive and had misunderstood his remarks. 'I believe I have understood you correctly', I replied, and left the room.

Obviously this was an impossible situation to find myself in. I had the confidence of Pfizenmaier and of the Philadelphia head office, but I was unprepared to put up with working under these unsatisfactory conditions in the longer term. I found that I was feeling unsettled in my travels and, like the wanderer in the famous Schubert song *Der Wanderer an den Mond*, I was tempted to address my woes to the moon.

 Der Wanderer an den Mond D870 FRANZ SCHUBERT (1797–1827)   *see page 338*
CD Track 18   *for text and translation*

There was no question in my mind but that I should move on from Smith Kline and French, though not immediately of course; there was unfinished business, too many things in the pipeline, to leave in a chaotic manner. If I had had my father's volcanic temper I might have stormed out of the firm in a rage, complaining of ingratitude and so on (and regretting it later of course). Far more valuable in my paternal inheritance was my father's foresight in terms of contingency planning, and working out an adequate exit strategy. The right moment to offer my resignation came in early 1965.

I already had plans for a new life. One of the many contacts I had made during my work for Smith Kline and French in Switzerland was a German Jewish refugee by the name of Dr Werner Rosenberg. He owned Robapharm, a company name made up of the first parts of three words—Rosenberg, Basel and pharmaceutical. The firm was hardly in the same league as Smith Kline and French: it was a 'biological house' dealing with traditional—some would say antiquated—forms of medication where plant and animal extracts were used for the treatment of heart, prostate, bone and liver diseases. Rosenberg wanted to modernize and bring the company up to twentieth-century standards. The middleman in bringing the two of us together to discuss a possible collaboration was Professor Domenjoz, chairman of pharmacology at Bonn University and one of Rosenberg's advisers who had been head of pharmacology with the Swiss pharmaceutical company Geigy, now part of Novartis.

Werner Rosenberg of Robapharm (Basel) with his family

We had met in the winter of 1963 at the Carlton Hotel in St Moritz. This year had already been a turning point in my life because I had married in the spring (see the next chapter). It was now doubly important for me to investigate a position suitable to a married man with a young family. Robapharm was the kind of business, more typical in Germany and Switzerland than the UK or America, that sold both conventional pharmaceutical products and herbal remedies. Rosenberg approached me because he realized that the world of pharmacology was advancing fast, while he and Robapharm were being left behind. To my relief he did not want me to move to Basel to manage his company; on the contrary he regarded my living in London as a positive advantage for his future plans. He wanted Robapharm to have a new future in the UK with additional worldwide possibilities.

I explained to him that for his products to have credence they would have to be subject to stringent clinical evaluation. Rosenberg had not bothered to do this and it is easy to see why. Such products have always had a cult status among a minority who fervently believe in these kinds of remedies (often at the expense of conventional drugs) and they can sometimes achieve great commercial success without going through formal procedures—provided they are not actually harmful or toxic of course. Today this is truer than ever: alternative medicines and therapies, many of very doubtful efficacy, are big business with huge commercial rewards. In recent years distrust of doctors, and the medical establishment in general, has been a money-spinner; certain firms have ably exploited the feeling among some of the public that there is something almost mystical out there that is more effective than conventional pharmaceuticals.

In 1963, long before this fashionable new wave of alternative medicine, there had recently been the crisis with thalidomide that had shaken the public's confidence in inadequately tested drugs. Rosenberg wanted to draw his firm closer to the conventional world of pharmacology. Some of his remedies were based on the principle of treating organs, or parts of the body, with medication derived from the same parts of the body that were experiencing illness or discomfort. These medicines were not homoeopathic—there was no question of the dilution of substances and so on—but I felt it would be a hard task to prove the efficacy of some of them in any scientific manner. Nevertheless, Rosenberg was adamant that I was the man to help him, and that the UK was the place for these products to be rigorously tested. He wanted me to be managing director of the firm in London with worldwide responsibilities, and he offered me an excellent salary with a five-year contract. I was not free to take up his offer immediately—it would take me a year or so to make the transition—but I now realized that this was where my future lay, or rather that Robapharm would be an effective stepping-stone towards my final goal.

One of the things I have learned in life is that when things happen to me I don't usually resist; I 'go with the flow'. If things were moving in a certain direction, I moved with them. Robapharm already had a token presence in the UK with Dr Norman Levenson as medical director. In the autumn of 1965 I took over his position and moved into the company office at 44 Welbeck Street, next to the Clifton Ford Hotel (for those unfamiliar with London, Welbeck Street is one block west of Wimpole Street, and two blocks west of Harley Street, both renowned for their distinguished medical addresses). The secretary, Miss Newbold, remained to help me. I was required to fly to Basel two or three times a month, and in the next five years I travelled all over the world—including India and South America—giving presentations and lectures on Robapharm's products. I was used to travelling in Europe and further afield, and I earned my salary for the firm in that way alone. But what was most fascinating about my new job was that my brief now included meeting, and getting to know, my British clinical colleagues. That is a chapter in itself.

I had been born in Leipzig, had trained in Manchester and had worked in Europe from a base in Welwyn Garden City. Now, for the first time, and at the age of thirty-seven, I was situated in central London itself, on the very fringe of the British medical establishment. (It was also only a step away from the Wigmore Hall, London's principal recital venue—but that is to look even further into the future.) What might have been seen as a setback by an outside observer was, in reality, an outstanding opportunity.

Fugue XIII (in 2 voices) RALPH KOHN *with* GRAHAM JOHNSON

GJ As so often in your story, it strikes me how easily things might have turned out differently. What, for example, if David Jack with whom you got on very well, had remained research director at Smith Kline and French, instead of defecting to Allen & Hanburys?

RK Well Allen & Hanburys was eventually taken over by Glaxo and David Jack did great things there. There are two sides to every story. Jack and his team focused on discovering chemical substances to manipulate natural mediators such as transmitters, hormones and enzymes to cause certain effects in specific organs in patients. Early success with this approach came with Glaxo's ventolin—salbutamol—which was launched in 1969 and became a standard treatment for asthma.

GJ Well, it's clear that the loss of David Jack at Smith Kline and French must have been quite a shock. But surely there were people there who could have fought harder to keep you at Smith Kline and French? Dick Pfizenmaier for example?

David Jack

RK Dick behaved in an exemplary way and I was very fond of him. He was certainly not to blame for my needing to move on to new pastures. I admired his spirit and his courage. He had been a pilot during World War Two on carriers in the Pacific and was shot down, but rescued from the sea, badly wounded with spinal injuries. We used to travel together often—going to Moscow, Milan, Frankfurt and many other cities. Once we landed at fog-bound Geneva, the worst landing imaginable; the plane was shuddering. 'Dick,' I said, 'I never thought we'd make it.' His answer was simply: 'We used to say in the navy that any landing you walk away from alive is a good one.' One of the near-death experiences of my life was some years later, a flight between Calcutta and Madras when one of the two engines blew up on take-off and I was certain we were going to land in the sea and drown. It was absolutely terrifying, but I walked away from the incident alive. I returned to Bombay for the weekend and, when I eventually reached Madras, was taken to the races followed by a dinner with orchestrally accompanied classical dancing. What could have been a wake turned into a party!

GJ Well something of this same good fortune was evident when you walked alive from Smith Kline and French! You were about to be taken, metaphorically, to the races and then to dinner, but some of your colleagues at the firm must have believed you were picking yourself up from something of a disastrous crash and that you would have to make do with something inferior to what you had previously.

RK I daresay that is what some of my colleagues might have thought at the time. But what they could not know was that I had a plan for myself right at the back of my mind, and that five years earlier something very important had happened to my way of thinking about my own long-term future. This was the result of a meeting in the Euler Hotel, Basel, with my father's old friend, Kolomán Lauer, the intermediary who had recommended Wallenberg for his heroic work in Sweden. At the time I was in the early years of my working for Smith Kline and French. I suppose this was in 1959 or 1960 and I was very pleased with all my travelling and all the contacts I was making throughout Europe and Asia. In fact I thought I was in the ideal job.

My meeting with Dr Lauer at this time was a revelation. I have already spoken about this occasion, I know, but it was so important for me that I must emphasize that it was a watershed moment for me. At that time I had forgotten, for example, that my father's happiest days in Leipzig had been when he had been the proprietor and director of his own business. My father was independent, he was his own boss. Lauer was in exactly the same position of course, although his company was much more important than my father's. Lauer listened politely to my enthusiastic stories about my role with Smith Kline and French and then, in a few kindly but devastating sentences, made clear that the only job that was worthwhile, the only job in which I would be happy, was one where I operated as an independent. He believed that there would come a time, a turning point, when I should have the courage to 'go it alone'. 'Take my word for it,' he said, 'in life one can achieve so much more if you are independent.'

GJ Knowing something of your family history, it is very moving for me to hear this. You told me that you have inherited some of your father's *Aberglaube*, or superstition—that he would kiss the mezuzah, that he would consult the Chortkover Rebbe and take his advice almost as if it were Holy Writ. Well, it seems to me that Kolomán Lauer played something of the role of the Chortkover Rebbe in your life! These words were more than an elderly man's opinion about your future, they had the power of coming from a great Elder, and they took on the quality of something inevitable and predictive.

RK That is certainly one way of putting it. There is no doubt that Lauer played a role in my life far beyond the realms of friendly advice—and you are right, it seemed to me there was something infinitely wise about his opinion. Remember, everything he said carried a certain weight; it was not for nothing that he was a *Kohen*, a member of the priestly sect. Once this idea of independence had been planted in my mind I realized that Smith Kline and French was a temporary solution, and the same applied to Robapharm. With Robapharm I had not yet achieved my goal, but I was a step nearer to doing so. I worked with a skeleton staff, and apart from my travelling obligations, I was able to invent a rewarding schedule for myself as far as my work in London was concerned. The clinical trials that Rosenberg had required for his products did not yield much value—with one notable exception, Ossopan. But my life as an independent organizer of clinical trials began with that medication, and the experience of setting these up with the help of Professor Allan Dixon—another hero of my story—encouraged me to begin my own business.

    Talking about this new phase would have been our next task, but we now have the happy intervention of a personal blessing, my marriage in 1963. My own career must now wait in the wings as the story of my beloved wife takes centre stage.

Zahava Kohn
Photograph by Hephzibah Kohn Rudofsky

PRELUDE XIV

My wife, Zahava

I MARRIED RELATIVELY LATE, but I married extraordinarily well. Over fifty uninterrupted years of marital happiness have been the greatest blessing of the many that have been granted me in this life. I have been supremely fortunate to have enjoyed a life-partnership with a truly exceptional woman, Zahava Kanarek Kohn. Today we are closer than ever. It may be a matter of contention whether the title of 'Knight of the Realm' is befitting as far as I am concerned, but this honour applies equally to Zahava, and she is truly Lady Kohn, My Fair Lady in every possible way—although the reader might have guessed by now that I prefer operas to musicals.

Anything I write here about my wife's childhood and upbringing has been much better recounted by Zahava herself in *Fragments of a Lost Childhood* (co-authored with Ann Rosen, and published in 2010). Instead of quoting extensively from this haunting Holocaust chronicle (I will allow myself only one harrowing excerpt), I will commend it to readers in the heartfelt hope that they will read this uplifting story for themselves. Zahava and her parents suffered the horrors of Nazi concentration camps (and survived) while I, and my own immediate family, were spared that experience. Anything I write here about this phase of her life can only convey a shadow of what she went through, and I hope she will forgive me for even attempting to do so. I know she understands that everything about her story is also an indescribably dear and important part of my own narrative.

My parents had known the Kanareks (though not well) since the late 1930s in Amsterdam where both families attended the same *shtiebel*. The Kanarek family had, like my own, escaped from Germany and had mistakenly taken Holland to be a safe place of refuge. Sigmund Kanarek was born in Poland; his family moved to Düsseldorf when he was four; he spoke German without a foreign accent, and this accounts for my wife's excellent German to this day. Rosie Kanarek, Zahava's mother, was born in Czechoslovakia and moved with her parents to Zürich when she was five. Sigmund and Rosie were married in 1933 and intended to make a new life in Palestine. En route they stopped in Amsterdam while they waited for the papers for their voyage, eventually reaching Tel Aviv in 1935. Zahava was born in Palestine in August of that year and there are beautiful baby photographs of her enjoying the sunshine of the Holy Land. The reader will discover that having their first child on Palestinian soil was one of the cleverest things the Kanareks ever did.

How wise, one may say, that the family had neatly avoided all the consequences of Hitler's rise to power! But this was to reckon without the kind of hard manual work that Zahava's father was required to do, and that Palestine was far too hot for comfort; it was a climate that Rosie Kanarek found intolerable. The family returned to Amsterdam in 1937 little realizing, of course, that in three years' time their lives would change entirely. The Kanareks were not the only family who imagined that Holland would be safe from Hitler—as I have explained, the Kohns of Amsterdam were of exactly the same opinion.

I have already recounted the drama of 14 May 1940 when I, together with my entire family, left Amsterdam at the last possible moment, sailing on the SS *Bodegraven*. The Kanareks were not so fortunate; they had attempted to get visas for Honduras, but these arrived too late. In the end they were among the many Jews in Holland who hoped they could, somehow or other, weather the storms of the Nazi Occupation. As elsewhere in Europe, the descent into barbarity was incremental but inexorable. From May 1942, two years after the Kohn family left Amsterdam, the Jews remaining there were required to wear a yellow Star of David sewn onto their clothes. That summer the Nazis began the first round-up of Jews in the Netherlands, having driven many thousands from the countryside into the Jewish ghetto in Amsterdam. Many of these Jews were taken to the Hollandsche Schouwburg (the former theatre) and loaded onto trains bound for the Westerbork concentration camp.

The Kanareks lived in a comfortable home in Amsterdam but they were also transported to Westerbork. Their infant son, Jehudi, born in 1941 and now sixteen months old, had already been handed over to the care of the Dutch resistance—certainly this must have been a devastating moment for Rosie, my future mother-in-law. The Kanareks felt that the baby had a better chance of survival if he was handed over to the safekeeping of others. Jehudi had blond hair and blue eyes, and was Aryan in appearance. He was subsequently placed in a Dutch orphanage; of the forty-five children in that unfortunate institution, forty-three were later deported to Auschwitz. Jehudi was saved because of an arbitrary decision: judging by his appearance, the SS thought he could not possibly be Jewish. For almost two years he was then taken care of by Nurse Stol, a Dutch Protestant, who wrote to the Kanareks in Westerbork, using code words to tell them that my future brother-in-law was fine. She even sent a photograph of him hidden in a bag of dried beans. In the summer of 1945 Jehudi was transferred to Copenhagen by the Red Cross, and was then moved to Sweden.

In the meantime the remaining members of the family, Sigmund, Rosie and Zahava, faced the full force of Nazi brutality. The enormously strong character of my future wife is shown by the fact that on 26 May 1943 the seven-year-old Zahava faced-down the SS who had entered the Kanareks' apartment in Amsterdam: she had a bad case of chickenpox at the time, and the family was told to prepare for transportation to Westerbork. The guards wanted to separate Zahava from her mother and father and place her in a separate train for sick people. Her response, uncharacteristically, was a fit of screaming hysterics; the amazing outcome was that the SS, not wishing their work to be hampered by panic and commotion, relented. She was allowed to travel with her parents, something that almost certainly saved all their lives. I would find this incident even more extraordinary if I had not often experienced Zahava's determination and strength of will in the many years we have been together.

Life at Westerbork was no picnic, but the next destination, Auschwitz, was a place from which there was no return. A ruthless bureaucracy aided the terrible crimes of the Germans, but very occasionally this bureaucracy interrupted the death machine. Zahava had been born in British Mandated Palestine and that automatically made her a citizen of a territory that was nominally under the protection of the British Crown. The family was huddled on the platform at Westerbork, waiting to board a cattle train to Auschwitz, when they were called back at the last second. A Dutch official came on to the platform with the news: 'Mr Kanarek, I have instructions that you are to be removed, with your wife and child, from this transport.' (This official had the humanity at the time to say that he wished he had similar messages for other people.) Zahava was not exactly a British citizen, but she was 'protected'—a status good enough for someone who could potentially be exchanged for German prisoners of war. Fortunately this was sufficient reason for the Nazi authorities to detain the entire family in Westerbork for a further five months.

In January 1943 the family was 'selected' (this became the most ominous of words during the Holocaust) to go to Bergen-Belsen. This was certainly a notorious destination, but it was not, like Auschwitz, an extermination camp. In the circumstances it was an easier option, but it offered many of its inmates slow, lingering deaths rather than instantaneous execution. It had been built in 1940 as a prisoner of war camp southwest of the town in Bergen in Lower Saxony, north of Hanover. In 1941 it had been renamed Stalag 311 and held over 20,000 Russian prisoners of war. In 1943 it became a concentration camp divided into eight sections: a detention camp, two women's camps, a special camp, a neutrals' camp, a 'star' camp (mainly Dutch prisoners who wore a Star of David on their clothing, and also the destination of the Kanareks), a Hungarian camp and a tent camp. Between 1943 and 1945, 50,000 people died there, 35,000 of them of typhus in early 1945.

On arrival Rosie and Zahava were immediately separated from Sigi who was sent to the men's camp and put to hard and grinding work repairing old shoes. Rosie worked as a cleaner for the SS Kommandant—a piece of luck because she could trade cigarette ends for crusts of bread. Zahava writes of her memories as a seven-year-old: she recalls the watchtowers with searchlights and her fear of the dogs and guns. During the endless roll-calls she was forced to stand shoeless, and freezing, for hours in the snow. She was known as the 'tall girl' because she had simply grown out of her clothes; she was severely malnourished and weighed only 25 kilos. Let me allow her to recount some of the details of that living hell in her own words:

> It was a brutal place with many beatings. My father's teeth had been knocked out and I was constantly worried that something even worse would happen to him. I shared a bunk with my mother. Another woman who was also crammed into this constricted space had typhoid and kept a tin on the beam above us because she couldn't make it outside to go to the toilet. One day she knocked the bucket all over me. My mother was terrified because it was infectious and we had nothing to wash with.

As I once again read these words, as familiar as this terrible story is to me, I have tears of anger in my eyes. Man's inhumanity to man is one thing, but to think of my dignified and beloved Zahava suffering in this way is truly unbearable. I am reminded of the terrible anguish in the dialogue between the mother and starving child of Gustav Mahler's *Das irdische Leben*.

Das irdische Leben GUSTAV MAHLER (1860–1911)   *see page 338*
CD Track ⏹19   *for text and translation*

It also seems miraculous to me that throughout this time my mother-in-law somehow retained a battered old suitcase in which she kept every record, every scrap of paper, relating to these terrible times. It was the contents of this suitcase, opened only many years later, that enabled Zahava to write her book, backing up all her own memories with copious documentation.

It would have been no surprise if all three family members had succumbed to illness and died. Left much longer to rot in Bergen-Belsen, this would certainly have happened. But help arrived unexpectedly through the Red Cross: by a remarkable stroke of good luck the Kanareks were selected as part of an exchange programme by the Reichssicherheitshauptamt—the Reich's Central Security

Office—and moved out of Bergen-Belsen on 21 January 1945 at the height of the typhus epidemic. For once that word 'selected' had a positive connotation. They gathered together whatever food they could for Sigmund's uncle (Zahava's great-uncle) Saul Tugendhaft, but they could do nothing to change his fate; he died in April 1945 on a transport to Theresienstadt.

Zahava was very ill on leaving Bergen-Belsen, and her family was also near death as a result of malnutrition and other ailments. Despite the fact that the Kanareks had relations living in Switzerland and Sweden—both neutral countries—food parcels sent regularly were stolen or went astray. The family spent some months in an internment camp at Biberach near the French and Swiss borders where the conditions were considerably better, although still gruelling by any civilized standards. During this time the health of all three Kanareks was very touch and go—indeed it is a miracle they all survived.

Liberation by the French followed in April and the family eventually reached Zürich, the home of Zahava's grandparents, in the summer of 1945. Zahava was given daily treatments for the frostbite suffered at Bergen-Belsen, and was sent to various alpine retreats to recuperate (arranged by her anxious grandparents). Only on her return to Amsterdam in 1946 did she go back to full-time schooling. Just before the family left Bergen-Belsen in early 1945 a strange thing had happened: a honey cake had arrived for them from Holland. Zahava realized that this cake was a sign that her brother Jehudi was alive, and indeed he had survived. In the autumn of 1946 she travelled together with her mother to Stockholm to fetch Jehudi and bring him back to Holland. The little boy, now five, regarded Regina Hermann (the woman who had looked after him in Sweden) as his mother and he now spoke fluent Swedish. Jehudi's real mother (whom he called 'Mummy from Switzerland'), as well as his big sister, took a great deal of time and trouble to bond with their son and brother before taking him back with them to his rightful home.

On leaving school in 1951 Zahava took a secretarial course which included the study of English, little realizing how useful this would one day turn out to be. She worked as a secretary for Julius Hollander, an importer of hides and skins, and then for the financial director of the Jewish community centre in Amsterdam. Her father Sigmund was by now an independent purveyor of rainwear; in Switzerland he had seen the efficacy of waterproof capes for bicycle riders and now manufactured these garments for the Dutch—a nation of cyclists after all. But my future father-in-law's health had been severely compromised in the concentration camps and in the evenings Zahava used to help him to make the merchandise and then pack it for commercial distribution.

In 1958 she was taken to St Moritz on a skiing holiday by her mother. There she met a group of young people who lived in London. She decided, almost on the spur of the moment, that she would like a change of scene. Zahava moved to London, first as secretary to Rabbi Dr Solomon Schonfeld, founder of the Jewish Schools Movement in London (and himself a Holocaust hero), and then as nursery school teacher, first in Edgware and then Golders Green. During these years, 1958 to 1962, she was taken under the wing of the Orthodox community of Golders Green. At that time she had no idea at all that a young high-flyer called Ralph Kohn was commuting from close by in Mill Hill to Welwyn Garden City and working for an American pharmaceutical firm. Of course, devoted daughter that she was, she returned every so often to see the family in Holland and for short breaks at the sea in Scheveningen.

With the familiar name 'Scheveningen' the reader of this book will perhaps already begin to sense the turning of the wheels of fate! Scheveningen had been an important town for my father during the First World War. He was living there when he was contemplating marrying my mother, Lena Aschheim from Berlin, after having lost contact with her for some time. Fortunately for my subsequent existence he was advised by the Chortkover Rebbe to honour his earlier commitment to Lena. Scheveningen was also, in due course, a favourite holiday spot for the Kohn family, and history was about to repeat itself.

In August 1962, shortly after her twenty-seventh birthday, Zahava was due to fly to Montreux for an educational seminar. Her father then asked a favour of her: would she be willing to meet a young man who was the son of some acquaintances? I was on my way to visit the ASTA-Werke laboratories in Brackwede, near Bielefeld, regarding a potential takeover by Smith Kline and French. The owner of this firm was a Mr Kipper who was later revealed to be someone who had massively benefited from paying a risible price for a Jewish business he had acquired in Germany in the 1930s. The person whose business was thus officially stolen was Werner Rosenberg, the proprietor of Robapharm, the Swiss firm for which I was later to work in London and internationally. He told me that Mr Kipper had had the barefaced cheek to appeal to him for help in the later denazification process. On the way to see this Mr Kipper I stopped over to visit my parents who were also on holiday in Scheveningen. This seems to have been an unintentional gathering of the clans, both present and future. Fortunately for me, Zahava was so fond of her father that she indulged his request—she had no expectations of this meeting and there had been similar unsuccessful attempts to introduce her to suitable young men.

I met Zahava Kanarek, my future wife, at a kosher restaurant in Scheveningen. Three out of four parents were present—Zahava's father was ill at the time. At the end of the evening I boldly asked her if she would be prepared to postpone going to Montreux to spend a little more time with me. She refused of course, and went off on her trip. I carried on to Brackwede, but I now had a new sense of purpose. This was an independent young woman, but I was a determined young man (not quite so young at this time, admittedly, at thirty-five years old) and I telephoned her in London as soon as she had returned. What good luck that we both lived in north London! We went out with each other between September and December 1962, after which we became engaged. Our parents had definitely acted with match-making intentions, but I think even they were surprised by the speed with which their schemes had borne fruit. We were married on 12 March 1963 at the Jacob Obrecht synagogue in Amsterdam. A major part of the jigsaw of my life had fallen into place, and I have never ceased to give thanks for my extraordinary luck. With such a companion at my side I felt ready to go forward and create for myself a new destiny. I can think of no more appropriate song in connection with this epsiode in my life than an exquisite Rückert setting by Robert Kahn, a German composer of the older generation who left Germany and came to England as a refugee.

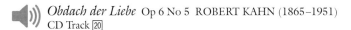

Obdach der Liebe Op 6 No 5 ROBERT KAHN (1865–1951)
CD Track [20]

*see page 339
for text and translation*

Fugue XIV *(in 3 voices)* RALPH & ZAHAVA KOHN *with* GRAHAM JOHNSON

GJ If your two families had not really been closely in touch before, may I ask you, Zahava, how was this fateful meeting in a kosher restaurant in Scheveningen arranged?

ZK The restaurant owner, Mr Berger, was a close friend of my parents. On this occasion he was the *shadchan*—the matchmaker. He knew that the Kohns were visiting from England and that they had a son, an eligible son I should say! I went along with it also to please my father.

GJ What language did you speak during your first meeting?

ZK English! I had already been living in England for four years. I suppose if we had met a lot earlier we would have spoken in Dutch. As it happened my range of languages was very similar to Ralph's, although my Dutch was perhaps better because I had lived there longer. I had German, *Hochdeutsch*, from my father and Swiss German from my maternal grandparents. The two of us share a love of languages and have always managed to get by wherever we go on our many travels—for example, it was not at all hard to understand the Afrikaans language when we visited South Africa.

RK Right from the beginning it was clear we had an enormous amount in common in terms of background. We were both from Orthodox families of course, but our shared Dutch upbringing was also important, as was the fact that we had both decided (Zahava many years later than me of course), to make our homes in Britain. As I get older it seems to me that successful relationships need this kind of common ground; the best hope for a couple is if they have similar backgrounds. I didn't exactly marry the childhood sweetheart from my village (Toscanini claimed to have done so), but right from the beginning there was between us a strong feeling of the already familiar.

With Zahava Kanarek, my future wife. Engagement photograph, Amsterdam 1962

GJ What about the music which is such an important part of Ralph's life?

ZK Before we got engaged I was invited to hear Ralph sing a recital at the Allied Circle off Oxford Street. I absolutely loved it and told him so afterwards.

RK I had asked my good friend, the late Professor William Taub of the Weizmann Institute, to accompany Zahava to the event. He was a connoisseur of lieder and French song. I asked William to report back to me if she absolutely hated what I was doing. When she was enthusiastic I knew this was the woman for me.

William Taub

ZK I had grown up with music and my mother was extremely musical; we had a piano in the home. When Ralph made records and the test-pressings were sent to the house, I was the first to sit with him and listen to the results of his hard work. As Ralph's wife I have attended countless concerts around the world—recitals, operas, symphony concerts, oratorios—and it is never a duty, always a pleasure. We enjoy these experiences together. And the music of Bach for me is always a special joy.

GJ I can vouch for that personally because I have seen how much you always enjoy being at the Royal Academy of Music for the Bach cantata series on those very special Sunday mornings. You can't wait to hear the music! You both recently invited me to a performance of Bach's 'Goldberg' Variations played by András Schiff at Wigmore Hall. On that memorable occasion I was aware of you both sitting next to me, holding hands like a couple of young lovers, listening together to the music, and absolutely absorbed in it.

ZK I would say we are remarkably suited.

GJ Have you attempted to find suitable husbands for your own three daughters?

ZK Not at all—my daughters all found their own husbands. Arranged marriages still happen of course, often most successfully, but we live in modern times and many of the old Orthodox traditions have fallen away.

RK Talking of old Orthodox traditions, did you know that at an old-fashioned Jewish wedding it is a custom that the groom should begin to make a speech that is then almost ritually drowned-out by the singing of the guests? He never gets to say anything! The reasoning behind this is that on this important day the poor fellow has other things on his mind than the making of speeches. At my own wedding dinner I had prepared nothing to say (when speaking in public I always make careful notes) but I rose as if to make a speech, expecting the traditional raucous interruption. (I am reminded here of the fake execution of Cavaradossi that is supposed to take place in Puccini's *Tosca*.) Zahava *assured* me that I would be drowned out by the guests. I rose to speak and to my absolute horror, a respectful silence fell in the room. I found myself totally at sea, improvising in various languages and making a hash of it.

GJ I take it that you didn't make a hash of everything else that evening!

ZK I will quickly come to the rescue and say that in other ways our wedding in Amsterdam was very traditional! Ralph had to sign a *Ketubah*, a kind of prenuptial agreement, that protects a woman's rights in the event of his death and so on. This is an ancient and sacred document but I find it very enlightened in many ways regarding women's rights. I also received a wedding ring that, by tradition, had to belong to the bridegroom.

GJ Talking of a woman's financial rights, Zahava, I noticed that when Ralph established his own independent firm you were a director.

ZK Well, that makes sense for all sorts of business reasons of course, but I was more than a token presence I assure you! I had very good jobs in Amsterdam before I came to Britain and I had learned quite a bit about bookkeeping and how a business is run. In the early days when Ralph became self-employed I used to put the children to bed and then sit up late at night doing the firm's books.

GJ What are the most valuable qualities you find in each other?

RK Zahava is even and balanced. She doesn't lose her sense of perspective. She is reassuring and supportive. We work things out between us and invariably see eye to eye. And if we don't there is a wonderful Talmudic saying: 'If your wife is small, bow down and whisper to her.'

Our wedding, 12 March 1963

ZK   On my side I value the fact that Ralph is positive and lively and that we do a lot
     of things together. We still do a lot of travelling and we have a shared passion for
     music. We are fortunate to have heard performances all over the world. And it is
     wonderful to go on meeting people.

GJ   And you go on meeting people almost every day, particularly in recent years because
     of your book *Fragments of a Lost Childhood*. Together with your eldest daughter,
     Hephzibah Rudofsky, you speak at many schools, charities and organizations about
     your Holocaust experiences—indeed the work you two do together on this
     project—*Surviving the Holocaust*—is a link between mother and daughter that
     mirrors the close relationship you had with your own mother. Have these terrible
     events of your childhood left you with unresolved feelings and nightmares?

RK   May I interrupt here and say that the long-term effects on Zahava's health of her
     wartime experiences have been significant. She's had a stomach bypass, a knee
     replacement, and osteoarthritis—all conditions that go back to those terrible times.
     There must be some relationship between these illnesses and the deprivations of her
     childhood.

ZK   People get ill for all sorts of reasons and I refuse to blame anyone. To answer your
     question Graham, no, I have no unresolved resentment. I've learned to let all that
     go, and that is largely due to the wisdom of my own mother who never looked
     back. That is why she chose not to open that suitcase of documents in her own
     lifetime. Instead she left it for me to discover them and use them in my own way.
     It is a real joy to go from place to place bringing this story to all sorts of people,
     including many youngsters. I am proud to have left this book for my children and
     grandchildren, and also for my brother of course.

GJ   Are you still in touch with your brother Jehudi?

ZK   Three times a week by phone! We are very close. He made his career in the Israeli
     diplomatic service. He was consul-general for Israel in Bonn, San Francisco and
     Toronto and ended his career as ambassador to Belgium and Luxembourg. He now
     lives in Jerusalem.

GJ   Are either of you disappointed that you did not have a son of your own?

ZK   Absolutely not! We have been blessed with three marvellous daughters and four
&
RK   beautiful, healthy grandchildren. Alex, the eldest of these, son of Hephzi and
     Steven, is taking a gap year and is in Israel at the moment at a Talmudical college.
     We are very proud of him.

RK   Our pride in our children, and more recently our grandchildren, has been something that has made our marriage even stronger as the years have gone by. I often think of how it could have turned out so very differently—on my side as well as Zahava's. She was saved from the Nazis by being a 'protected' citizen of British Palestine. You know that I consider myself something of an old-fashioned British patriot, but I give thanks daily that we both seem to have been 'protected' throughout our lives by a power older and more mighty than the British Crown. We both give thanks to God.

Together in Rome in 2011

Recording with the English Chamber Orchestra in 1986
Photograph by Clive Barda

PRELUDE XV

Singing

IN WRITING MY AUTOBIOGRAPHY it has been a tricky task to weave together the strands of a life that has been devoted, on one hand, to the pursuit of scientific excellence, and on the other to a musical pilgrimage. I write pilgrimage (a word with religious connotations that Bach would have understood very well) because I have always regarded myself far too dedicated a musician to consider myself merely an amateur. Of course, that is exactly what I am in terms of not having made a living in music. It is probable that I would have been unable to support my wife and family on the basis of my musical earnings, although I never actually had a go at doing so. I am, above all, a pragmatist. A life as a musician would not have permitted me, for example, to engage myself with the rewarding charitable work of the Kohn Foundation (see *Prelude XX*). Nevertheless, the word 'amateur' derives from the word meaning 'love'. It is often those who pursue a subject like music, simply for the love of it, that are able to glimpse its glories with an altruism denied to those whose main concern is building a career. In that respect I regard myself as a privileged observer. At the same time I am proud to have also been a passionate and lifelong participant—nothing less than that would have brought me any satisfaction.

The reader has already glimpsed various aspects of my vocal enthusiasms—I did not attempt, for example, to disguise my somewhat envious admiration for the great male opera singers of the New York Metropolitan Opera in the 1950s. In fact I would have been very happy to be a full-time professional musician—something also true of Sir Ernst Chain (see *Prelude X*) and another admired friend, that great statistician and former chairman of the Royal Opera House, Lord Claus Moser, both of whom were gifted pianists. As a singer I was something of an exception among the many scientists who have almost exclusively been instrumentalists. Ernst Chain delighted in accompanying me in German lieder and Italian songs; he was an amateur too of course, but a fine one, and we had a lot of fun together. The difference, however, when it comes to collaborating on a professional level is enormous—working with great accompanists (and I have known several) has been one of the greatest pleasures of my life. I have often imagined how extraordinary it must be to be able to make a living from something that is so spiritually rewarding, at the same time as being so unashamedly hedonistic!

Apart from the artistic side there was, for me, the added physical pleasure of singing. Is a singer not also a musician? The answer to that is that he should be, certainly, and the best instrumentalists are also singers in their way—their sound comes from the heart and can be as legato as any vocal line. And yet, instrumentalists, even the great ones, are denied the physical joy experienced by those who use their vocal chords and their diaphragms, their entire bodies, to produce their very own sound, not a sound that partially belongs to a Stradivarius violin or a Steinway piano, an individual sound that belongs uniquely, in all the world, to that singer alone. It is one of the physiological wonders of music that the resonators in the human body (in the facial sinuses, head cavities and chest) have the function of inbuilt amplifiers; these ensure that the singing voice, providing it is produced correctly and healthily, is carried easily into the biggest auditoriums. This is one of the great secrets of bel canto, and it is a crying shame that microphones are insidiously creeping into opera houses, via the musical theatre, as a kind of soft option for real singing. Singers are also athletes of a kind: as anyone who has ever sung in a good choir can attest, there is nothing as bracing as the joy of singing—it lifts the spirit and lightens the heart. Listening to music is wonderful, but making it is better still.

I am certain I inherited this love of vocal music from my father who adored Italian opera first and foremost—he had a collection of records with singers of the Caruso generation. There was always the thrill of liturgical music and the singing of the great cantors; in the home there was Jewish music sung in Hebrew, often with scriptural texts, but also folk songs and drinking songs. Despite all these vocal aspects of my childhood, I started off as a youngster in Amsterdam with the violin; as you may remember, my gifted cousin Gegi played the piano. I am grateful now for the musical discipline of this training; as an adolescent I was far too young to have studied singing seriously. At this earlier stage of my life, and also a few years later in Manchester, I was enraptured by orchestral concerts conducted by giants like Mengelberg and Barbirolli. A lively enthusiasm for this kind of music has never left me.

As I have already described, vocal revelation came to me when I had my first opportunity to hear a great opera singer 'live'. This was Beniamino Gigli who came to Manchester in the summer of 1949 and gave a concert for 5,000 people at the Belle Vue Stadium in Kirkmanshulme Lane. He was born in 1890 and emerged after the death of that other great Italian tenor, Enrico Caruso, in 1921. In fact he was often called 'Caruso Secondo' though he rightly preferred 'Gigli Primo'. He was famous in opera roles like Andrea Chénier (in Giordano's opera of the same name) and the Chevalier des Grieux in Puccini's *Manon Lescaut* (these are normally considered too demanding for lyric tenors, but Gigli had the stamina to handle them).

There was no opera, not even an orchestra, on that memorable occasion in Manchester. Gigli simply sang an entire recital with a pianist, and this too was a lesson for me—an induction into a world of musical intimacy where all sorts of colours and atmospheres could be created on stage just by a singer with his accompanist. I was simply enthralled by the all-round artistic experience, by the sound of the voice, like liquid gold, as well as by the beauty of the repertoire Gigli sang—largely Italian *arie antiche*, the gentle and intimate 'old songs' from earlier centuries which shy away from the drama of opera while retaining every aspect of Italianate melodiousness and style. This for me was truly heavenly music.

Five years after this life-changing experience I found myself studying in Rome (see *Prelude IX*). I have already admitted that I could have spent more time in the laboratories—my professors, Bovet and Chain, certainly thought so—but I was like a man who was engaged to a woman while postponing the wedding date and secretly retaining a beloved mistress. At this younger stage of my life I still had pipe-dreams about perhaps spending my life in music professionally; Italy was clearly the place to study singing. At the Istituo di Sanità I used to leave early in the afternoon—suffering occasional mock reproofs for doing so—and visit a famous singing teacher, Maestro Manlio Marcantoni. I was not ashamed to be supplementing my scientific studies with this kind of work—the study of bel canto is scientific in its own way. I happen to believe, by the way, that a good scientist must have artistic qualities in the same way that an artist must have discipline and approach his art in a scientific manner.

How might I define the bel canto approach to singing? The answer might be something like 'elegance, flexibility, an assured technique hand in hand with a certain gallantry and bravura, and that is nothing to do with overwhelming decibels'. This is the refined style associated with composers like Bellini and Donizetti as well as Scarlatti, Caccini and Paisiello. The whole world of *arie antiche* opened up to me.

 Delizie contente from *Giasone 'Jason'* FRANCESCO CAVALLI (1602–1676) *see page 340*
CD Track 21 *for text and translation*

My lessons with Marcantoni were formative and inspirational. It so happened he was a childhood friend of Gigli, both born near Ancona in a town called Recanati. This, incidentally, was also the birthplace of the great Italian poet Giacomo Leopardi. Marcantoni was for many years a flautist in the orchestra of La Scala,

Milan (in the Italian tradition pianists and instrumentalists are almost as often singing teachers as singers themselves).

After I had studied with Marcantoni for three years, and was due to leave for New York, he kindly arranged for me to meet my idol who had retired to a massive villa in the Via Nomentana in Rome. With a man involved in medical research like myself, Gigli was mainly concerned to discuss his illnesses (he was a diabetic and had heart problems) but he did ask me to sing for him. I had brought along Malatesta's aria 'Bella siccome un angelo' from Donizetti's *Don Pasquale*. I'm glad to say he was generally encouraging and made several helpful comments, but as Gigli died not long afterwards I often wondered whether my singing had contributed to this sad turn of events.

Beniamino Gigli

When I arrived in New York I contacted the Juilliard School of Music in search of an accompanist to study new repertoire. In Charles Wadsworth I found an invaluable friend and colleague of more or less my own age. He was one of the up-and-coming vocal accompanists and chamber music pianists on the East Coast. We met once a week and I almost entirely relied on him for my education in a field that was rather new to me—that of German lieder. It is perhaps strange that I fell in love with this branch of music after I had already fallen for Italian *arie antiche*: I was

German by birth, and German was my mother tongue, but this was also music of great sophistication and subtlety and I feel I came to it at exactly the right time in my mid-twenties. I also studied aspects of the French song repertoire in New York, although I knew that my future singing would mainly be devoted to Italian and German music.

When I returned to Britain I sought out one of the finest teachers, Helene Isepp, an émigré like myself who had arrived in London from Vienna in 1938. I met her through her son Martin Isepp who was a marvellous accompanist. We began working towards my Wigmore Hall debut in 1968. I am very self-critical but I am pleased to say that the former director of Wigmore Hall, William (Bill) Lyne, remembers the occasion rather better, and rather more kindly, than I do.

With the accompanist Martin Isepp before a recital

Following my debut I had a decently busy London diary for a singer who was not a full-time professional: concerts at St John's, Smith Square, and the Queen Elizabeth Hall singing Bach, the Fauré *Requiem* with the great Austrian soprano Gundula Janowitz, a lieder recital at the Purcell Room, and so on. In Israel I collaborated with my good friend the accompanist Jonathan Zak in various broadcasts and recitals (at the Recanati Hall in the Tel Aviv Museum of Art and at the Weizmann Institute for Science). I also collaborated with Zak in a recital disc recorded in London—the first time of very many that I worked with that amazingly talented recording producer Mark Brown. Zak was also my supportive accompanist at a seemingly disastrous audition in Tel Aviv with the Romanian-born conductor Maestro Gary Bertini—during which all the four pieces I attempted to perform were interrupted by phone calls, each of them after ten seconds of my starting to sing. To my huge surprise Bertini engaged me to sing two performances of Bach's *Magnificat* with the Jerusalem Symphony Orchestra, as well as two performances of Stravinsky's *Pulcinella*. The concerts were in the Jerusalem Theatre and at the beautiful Kibbutz Ein Hashofet, one of the finest concert halls in Israel; two of the concerts were broadcast live on Israeli radio (Kol Yisrael).

It was actually at an audition for Kol Yisrael that I encountered the most deadpan panel of jurors I had ever come across. When asked to sing oratorio, I offered 'Gibt mir meinem Jesum wieder' from Bach's *St Matthew Passion*. To lighten matters I asked if it was in order to sing this aria in Jerusalem. In a very serious way the head of the panel (the wife of an Israeli Supreme Court judge) asked me if I had forgotten that Jesus was a Jew. Nevertheless, I was invited to do the broadcast!

Although I enjoyed working with orchestras whenever I had the opportunity, my first love was lieder, and I have been unbelievably fortunate in those who have accompanied me. After Charles Wadsworth in New York, I found an equivalent song expert in Martin Isepp—who, as I pointed out, was the son of my singing teacher Helene Isepp (his father was Sebastian Isepp, a famous restorer of pictures). Martin was later a central figure at Glyndebourne, as head of the music staff, for over forty years. Another name on my pianists' list was Marcel Lorber (elderly when I met him) who had been the accompanist of those great tenors Richard Tauber and Leo Slezak. It was thanks to Marcel and his enthusiasm for collecting Japanese netsuke that I also began to be interested in this field. Then there was Paul Hamburger who, like Isepp, was a Viennese who had come to London in 1939. In the early years of the war Paul was interned in the Isle of Man (as were all German or Austrian nationals) and remarked that 'it was such fun being around so many artists from my homeland'. It was legendary that he was one of the very few people who had found a kind of Viennese *Gemütlichkeit* and solace in the conditions of internment. As an official accompanist at the BBC Hamburger worked with many prominent singers, including Janet Baker and Elisabeth Söderström. I had listened to Hamburger's analysis of Schumann's song cycle *Dichterliebe* on the BBC, and our working relationship was based on a mutual respect for the European traditions of song performance. He had the same kind of rigour in his own field as I had attempted to develop in my own professional life as a pharmacologist.

Paul had a gifted accompaniment pupil named Roger Vignoles, today one of the country's most distinguished in the field. I collaborated with Roger on a record of Beethoven lieder. For many years I also worked with Stephen Wilder, a wonderfully gifted coach and superlative sight-reader, who worked at Covent Garden and who helped me prepare for many of my recordings. Many years ago I also did a Purcell Room recital with perhaps the most celebrated of the accompanists in the direct line of succession from the legendary Gerald Moore (sadly I never had the chance to work with this most renowned of all 'Unashamed' accompanists). This was the Australian Geoffrey Parsons who for many years was considered the country's most distinguished vocal accompanist. Parsons, together with Gerald Moore, was the teacher of the next, and final, lieder collaborator who came into my life. I will not attempt to flatter him by saying I saved the best until last because this extraordinary man has become one of my closest friends and needs no such buttering up! I would now introduce readers to Graham Johnson were it not for the fact that he has clearly played a part in this book from the very first chapter.

Fugue XV *(in 2 voices)*   RALPH KOHN *with* GRAHAM JOHNSON

GJ   So far, in working with you on this book, I have often felt like a rather ignorant bystander when it came to discussing scientific matters. But now at last we are approaching a subject in which I have some first-hand experience! Almost all the people you mention in this chapter are familiar names to me, and some of them were teachers and friends.

RK   Well I am more than twenty years older than you, so you couldn't have met Gigli …

GJ   No, I was still in primary school in Rhodesia when you were in Rome. Neither have I met Charles Wadsworth who was enormously powerful at the Lincoln Center for many years—I am certain I would have done so if I had lived for any length of time in New York. It was there, actually, that I first met Martin Isepp who was working at the Juilliard at the time as head of that school's vocal programme.

RK   When I first telephoned Martin's mother, Helene, and asked her to teach me in London on her son's recommendation, her reply was: 'But Martin knows I have no experience with men!'

GJ   Well, apart from that being an amusing story, it is true that her most famous pupils were women, Janet Baker for example, and that highly gifted singer, almost forgotten today, Ilse Wolf who was a German refugee. What a great deal we owe to all those fine artists who left Germany and Austria and went on to enrich the musical life of Britain! Apart from the people you mention in this chapter—and I was a great admirer of Paul Hamburger (there is now a yearly prize in his honour at the Guildhall School)—I am, thinking of other such figures as Otto Erich Deutsch the Schubert scholar, the publisher Erwin Stein, the coach Peter Gellhorn …

RK   I worked with Gellhorn also!

GJ   … and the Amadeus String Quartet, Egon Wellesz, Hans Keller, the list is virtually
     endless … all coming to live and work in what had been termed 'Das Land ohne
     Musik'—Britain, 'the country without music'.

RK   Did you know this was said by one Oskar Schmitz as part of an anti-English
     polemic in 1904? It is one of the unfairest things ever written! Britain has always
     been a profoundly musical country in my opinion.

GJ   I think that old jibe was meant to be about our lack of home-grown composers—
     and that is also unfair. In any case, Britain had imported the best of Continental
     music since the time of Haydn. There was no place where Brahms was more
     revered than England in the late Victorian age.

RK   I think I would have enjoyed Victorian Britain far less than the country I came to
     know during, and after, the war. It was an amazing piece of luck that I began to
     study singing in London just at the point when there was a marvellous combination
     of innate British musicality and a recently acquired layer of European know-how
     and sophistication.

GJ   … thanks to the Jewish refugees …

RK   Helene Isepp typified this influx of a different and rarefied sensibility. No one could
     dispute that the Viennese temperament is very different from an Anglo-Saxon way
     of thinking!

GJ   I know she was not your only teacher.

RK   I went on to study with the Czech operatic baritone, Otakar Kraus—he was yet
     another émigré of course. He was still working at the Royal Opera House at the
     time I first met him but he retired from singing in 1973. He trained many of the
     outstanding basses and baritones of the time, John Tomlinson and Willard White
     among them. The last of my trio of male singing teachers was Derek Hammond-
     Stroud, principal baritone of the English National Opera. He was a singer
     renowned in roles from Gilbert and Sullivan to Wagner, and also admired for his
     ability as a comic. His first love, however, was German song and he had studied
     with the soprano Elena Gerhardt and the baritone Gerhard Hüsch, both legendary
     names in the lieder world of the 1930s and 1940s. I started working with Derek in
     1979 and until the time of his death, quite recently, we had a fixed time for our
     lessons—10am on a Sunday morning—that became almost a sacred tradition.

The Czech baritone Otakar Kraus

The British baritone Derek Hammond-Stroud

GJ I remember that was the case, and it was Derek who was your teacher when we made our many recordings together. I am truly privileged to have been part of such an extraordinary line-up of your musical associates. You seem always to have been searching for new leads.

RK This is all part of a drive in my own nature—the desire to surround myself with people from whom I can learn, who can give me the things which I needed in my life for my own development—whether you call it artistic or spiritual, it was a dimension of my life that would have been sadly neglected had I confined myself to working strictly within the sciences. Robert Schumann wrote: 'Es ist des Lernens kein ende' ('There is no end to what one can learn'). If there are people who can help me learn, I seek them out! For example, I heard about you, Graham, from the cellist Raphael Sommer—one of the very few people I have known to share my real first name of Raphael. His mother, Alice Herz-Sommer, a fine pianist, has recently died aged 110. She became quite a famous personality thanks to a film made about her music-making and optimistic love of life. A truly inspiring person! She was a fine pianist and also a Terezín survivor of course, as was her son Raffi who was with her in the concentration camp as a little boy. Many years ago Raffi had seen you giving masterclasses in Finland, I think it was. He phoned me up and said: 'If you want to meet someone who really knows about lieder you must meet Graham Johnson.' I simply followed up that advice.

GJ   Our meeting was also a very important one for me. In the beginning I found it hard to believe, and very touching, that someone whose family had lost so much under the Nazis was so enthusiastic about German culture. And then I had to remind myself that 'German' culture was not the same as 'Nazi' culture, it did not belong to them at all but had been hijacked for twelve terrible years, and here you were, claiming it back as your birthright! I could also hear straight away with your first vocal phrases that you were singing in your mother tongue—after listening to the bad German of many British singers, what a pleasure this was!

I also remember thinking how youthful your voice was. At the time of our first collaboration, a recording of *Winterreise* in 1995, you were in your late sixties, the time when almost all singers are worn out and forced to retire. Because you had not made singing your career, the instrument was astonishingly well preserved. It was in much better shape than it would have been if you had been a singer who had used his voice on the opera stage year in, year out. And then there is also a part of you, even today, that doesn't allow himself to even think of getting old. That is one of the many exceptional things about Ralph Kohn.

RK   Thank you for that. All I would say in reply is that I am a very tenacious individual and I applied some of the same qualities to mastering the task in hand as I had to advancing my scientific career.

GJ   Well that approach is a good thing in a way, but it also has its limitations. I have scarcely ever heard you sing a note out of tune and you have an admirable sense of rhythm. Your early training as an instrumentalist has stood you in remarkably good stead. But we all get better at what we do as we go along—just think how my spoken German has improved over the years. We can now talk conversationally with each other and that was not the case when I first met you. I hope you will take it as a compliment when I say that that your artistic expressivity has grown with each recording we have done together. Mark Brown, who produced all our records, absolutely agrees with me.

RK   I intend to write about the happy experiences of the recording studio later in this book.

GJ   The challenge in making music is accessing one's imagination, allowing oneself to 'let go', placing oneself in the position of being vulnerable. In the earlier days that side of your music-making—little to do with determination, efficiency and hard work (and nothing to do with having a beautiful voice either)—was not easy for you. It belongs to those imponderable areas of the soul where an artist has to listen to his inner voice. This inner voice has slowly revealed itself to you over a period of time with increasing clarity, and your patience has paid dividends. You may not have made a great deal of money from your musical career, but it has been a journey that has hugely enriched you.

RK I am aware of that, and very grateful, but I remember feeling almost broken-hearted when I had to relinquish my early dreams of becoming a full-time singer …

GJ I wanted to be a composer more than anything, and I relinquished my dream of doing what I really wanted to do in favour of something more realistic. A lot of us do this in life. I secretly wanted to be like Benjamin Britten, whom I knew and venerated. He was a great composer and he also played for singers. I had to give up the idea of the first career in order to concentrate on the second, infinitely less glamorous one.

RK I wanted to do more than just listen to concerts; I wanted to take part.

GJ And so you did, and for quite some time! You will laugh at me for donning the hat of an amateur psychiatrist, but it seems to me that your attachment to music is your attempt to make sense and to complete the circle of a life that has been strangely disrupted by events outside your control. It is a reaching back into the past, an attempt to make things whole. 'Unfinished business', you may say. You and Zahava, after all you have been through, have told me that neither of you have ever been in therapy. Well, they say that music is the best therapy there is!

RK Making music has given me a very different kind of fulfilment to any of my work in science and medicine. At times it has been a real life-saver …

GJ It is also one of the tragedies of the dwindling power of classical music that fewer and fewer people in the audience can claim to have 'had a go' themselves with the music that is being heard in the auditorium. If the younger generation had half as much experience of actually singing the music as you, classical music and its audience figures, the numbers of bottoms on seats, would be in much better shape.

RK Well, you have navigated a few murky pyschological waters before bringing the subject, full circle, around to statistics! As far as this book and our conversations are concerned, I think we must return to the real world where I was attempting to make a professional difference in the complex world of clinical trials. There is quite a lot of explaining to do, so I hope that our readers will reward us with their patience.

Paul Ehrlich

Vorderansicht (Nordufer)

Kgl. Institut für Infektionskrankheiten „Robert Koch", Berlin N. 39

Rückansicht Buchstraße—Föhrerstraße

The Institute of Infectious Diseases in Berlin

PRELUDE XVI

Clinical trials A POCKET HISTORY

THE CLINICAL TRIAL is nothing new. In former times, whenever a physician gave a patient a new treatment, he or she was performing a clinical experiment. If several patients were treated with a new drug or procedure, and the efficacy of the treatments was measured and the results recorded, then the physician had conducted a form of clinical trial. If the treatment worked, the physician added it to a list of things that might be prescribed and told others about it.

A great many treatments were local and traditional, and an individual physician in his career might have become convinced of the efficacy of certain treatments entirely due to his personal interaction with patients. The pioneers of the standardization of pharmacological information worked at the turn of the twentieth century at the Institute of Infectious Diseases in Berlin: Paul Ehrlich and his mentor Robert Koch. Koch had demonstrated that organisms were responsible for infectious diseases, and Ehrlich established that chemicals could affect pathological conditions in specific ways. It was Ehrlich who envisaged a 'magic bullet', killing only the organism at which it was specifically aimed. Specificity of this kind, not only in infectious diseases, has been an important aim of pharmacologists ever since.

Microscopes and electron microscopes (which contributed to the science of bacteriology) contributed enormously to examining the way a chemical worked in a particular context. In the twentieth century, physiological testing of chemical agents took place first in animal subjects with a condition which matched the ones to be treated in humans, and then moved to humans, healthy and paid volunteers. The purpose of this physiological testing was to establish dose levels for optimum activity and to determine the nature and extent of adverse effects. Only if the appropriate safety ratios could be met would the drug proceed to treatment in patients. Patients, unlike the volunteers, were unpaid—they stood to gain from the potential treatment and really were suffering from the condition the drug was designed to treat.

Austin Bradford Hill was one of the great heroes of my particular corner of medicine because he brought order into potential chaos. He was born in London in 1897, and like me had first hoped to pursue a medical career. Instead he took a correspondence course in economics. In the 1920s he worked for the Industry

Fatigue Research Board alongside the medical statistician Major Greenwood. When Greenwood became a professor at the London School of Hygiene and Tropical Medicine in 1933, Bradford Hill followed and became reader in epidemiology and vital statistics. It was in 1937 that his seminal work *Principles of Medical Statistics* was published. In it Bradford Hill suggested randomization in the selection of individuals (he wrote in 1990 about how radical an idea that had seemed at the time); in 1947 he became professor of medical statistics.

Bradford Hill worked on two studies that changed the way clinical trials were established and interpreted. In 1948 he was statistician on the Medical Research Council and was

Austin Bradford Hill

responsible for one of the first randomized trials with the new antibiotic, streptomycin, in the treatment of pulmonary tuberculosis. This eliminated bias in the selection of patients; one collateral benefit was that it provided a proper estimate of random error; both problems were addressed in one move. This was reported on 30 October 1948 in the *British Medical Journal*:

> Determination of whether a patient would be treated by streptomycin and bed-rest (S case) or bed-rest alone (C case) was decided by reference to a statistical series based on random sampling numbers drawn up for each sex at each centre by Professor Bradford Hill; the details of the series were unknown to any of the investigators or to the co-ordinator and were constrained in a set of sealed envelopes, each bearing on the outside only the name of the hospital, and a number. After acceptance of a patient by the panel, and before admission to the streptomycin centre, the appropriate numbered envelope was opened at the central office: the card inside told if the patient was to be an S or a C case, and this information was then given to the medical officer of the centre.

With this report the world's first randomized multi-centre, double-blind clinical trials set the standard for all that were to follow. There was a similarly established Dutch trial on the effects of paludrine in the treatment of malaria; this was also reported in 1948. These two trials set the appropriate clinical and statistical benchmark for clinicians and statisticians, at least until trials of this kind came to be questioned in the early years of the twenty-first century.

Sir Austin Bradford Hill then went on to run a series of studies with Sir Richard Doll on smoking and lung cancer. They began work at the Medical Research Council in 1949. Government statisticians had noticed a recent increase in lung cancer deaths. At the time even Doll himself remarked that smoking seemed a normal, harmless habit—eighty percent of men smoked. Doll and Hill both believed that the most likely cause would prove to be pollution. They designed a questionnaire, administered by social workers, for 650 patients in London hospitals. Their interviewees were patients suspected with lung, liver, or bowel cancers. To reduce the possibility of bias, the teams of interviewers were not told the suspected diagnosis. They interviewed hospital patients with other diagnoses. After the proper diagnoses had been made, it was clear that those whose lung cancer was confirmed were smokers, and those that did not have lung cancer were non-smokers.

The results were compelling and unexpected; Bradford Hill and Doll thought that the close correlation they found may be peculiar to London, given that one theory of the high incidence of lung cancer was that pollution from engines or buildings could be the cause. So they studied 750 similar patients in Bristol, Cambridge, Leeds and Newcastle. They published their results in the *British Medical Journal* in 1950, spurred on by some parallel research in America also published that year. The first of their papers on smoking, published in 1950, was a case-control study designed to compare lung cancer patients with matched controls. The report concluded:

Richard Doll

> The risk of developing the disease [lung cancer] increases in proportion to the amount smoked. It may be 50 times as great among those who smoke 25 or more cigarettes a day as among non-smokers.

The *BMJ* paper on smoking and lung cancer was largely ignored by the public. The Department of Health's cancer committee was unconvinced by the findings; it thought that telling people to stop smoking might start a mass panic. It was shortly following this controversy that Bradford Hill memorably addressed the department of preventive medicine at the Harvard Business School in May 1952. He pointed out that there had long been tensions between statisticians and clinicians: 'The medical man charged with a responsibility to the patient was contemptuous of the statistician's fundamental approach through the group; and the statistician took a jaundiced view of the conclusions light-heartedly drawn by the practitioner from a handful of cases without allowance for the play of chance.' Behind these remarks lies the idea that all in science is measurement, and that all measurement is essentially comparative. At the time we might remind ourselves that many doctors smoked in their surgeries, sometimes offering cigarettes to patients.

In February 1954 the British health minister, Iain Macleod, officially accepted the link between smoking and lung cancer, smoking while doing so. It was when the Royal College of Physicians brought out a report in 1962, linking smoking and death, that public opinion began to change.

The questions raised by Bradford Hill were many. How might clinical trials be run? How might their results be interpreted? What might those results mean for practitioners, regulators and drug producers? The concern of the pharmaceutical industry was that the results of trials—pre-clinical and clinical—in one country should be transferable to another. Without common intellectual foundations, there could be no commercial crossover between a drug that had proved successful in, for example, Japan, and its commercial future in the USA. In 1954 Bradford Hill was made a Fellow of the Royal Society. His citation, written by one of his severest critics, R A Fisher, contains these words:

> Since the war he has demonstrated in an exact and controlled field the association between cigarette smoking and the incidence of cancer in the lung, and has been the leader in the development of medicine of the precise experimental methods now used nationally and internationally in the evaluation of new therapeutic and prophylactic agents.

In the design of trials and their intellectual grounding, Sir Austin Bradford Hill and Sir Richard Doll were the pioneers of the 1940s and 1950s.

As years went by, what changed most in this scenario were the methods by which evidence was gathered, and what counted as evidence. By the time I was working with Gilman in New York there was a history of advances in chemistry, physiology, biochemistry and pharmacology which had collectively established the effects of chemicals on physiological systems. There was no doubt that whatever Bradford Hill and Doll had achieved there was now quite a different attitude towards the conducting of clinical trials; we were about to move into an entirely new age.

Fugue XVI *(in 2 voices)*   RALPH KOHN *with* GRAHAM JOHNSON

GJ On reading these words I am reminded that the history of medicine is also, in part, a history of the substances that have been used to treat people down the ages. How did the practitioners of the past manage before there was any information about these substances?

RK In the past herbalists and alchemists treated patients by guesswork and tradition. There were also any number of learned tomes, some far more hocus-pocus than others, concerning the medicinal qualities of plants and plant extracts. For example morphine, curare, quinine … these turned out to be important drugs.

GJ Your professor in Italy, Bovet, spent a lot of time looking into curare—so these substances have passed into orthodox therapy?

RK Indeed they have, and many others like salicyates, digitalis, colchicine and atropine. Alchemists of the past used preparations of sulphur, gold, silver, copper, lead mercury or iron.

GJ Well, I've heard of iron treatment for anaemia.

RK Compounds of iron have long been used exactly for that purpose. Some of the traditions of old medicines with a continuing amount of guesswork thrown in have prospered. I know something about this branch of the industry having worked with Robapharm in the second half of the sixties. They had an antiquated catalogue of medicaments, but it would be wrong to suppose there was nothing effective on their list. After all, compounds of gold have been used for rheumatoid arthritis, platinum in anti-cancer drugs, bismuth for indigestion, and selenium to cure dandruff. Mercury was a purgative …

GJ As a lover of lieder I associate mercury with the treatments for syphilis that were meted out to Franz Schubert and Robert Schumann in the earlier part of the nineteenth century. They were made to consume quantities of mercury as part of the syphilis cure (Schubert lost his hair in the process). Schumann and Wolf were killed by tertiary syphilis but Schubert never reached that stage—he died before the tertiarty stage of the disease had presented itself, but many people think he was terribly debilitated by mercury poisoning and had an impaired immune system.

RK Quite possibly. There used to be an old saying in London medical circles regarding the treatment of syphilis: 'Two minutes with Venus, then two years with Mercury.' Side-effects are risks in the taking of all medicine that has not been subject to clinical trials. Arsenic was also thought to be useful to treat syphilis, as well as leukaemia. This was a very early kind of largely ineffective chemotherapy, but there was some evidence at the time that such drugs worked, at least up to a point.

GJ What kind of evidence? What kind of laboratory testing existed in Schubert's time?

RK Well that is a very straightforward and modern question, and the answer is 'very little'. The fact is that drugs were introduced by trial and error and news of their efficacy spread both culturally and professionally. Although there was any amount of quackery in the early history of drugs, there was also a certain amount of anecdote-based evidence. My colleague Allan Dixon would have referred to these as 'narrative' or observational trials and they are not entirely without merit.

GJ As a matter of fact I know of only one song by Schubert which describes the working of a drug on the body. This is *Florio*, a setting from a play called *Lacrimas* by Wilhelm Schütz. Florio imagines a powerful poison seeping into his veins, a metaphor for an impossible love.

 *Florio* D857 No 1 FRANZ SCHUBERT (1797–1827)   *see page 341*
CD Track 22   *for text and translation*

RK After that Schubertian diversion, we should return to the subject of clinical trials. A distinct improvement was the use of concurrent controls whereby patients were treated by one or other of two treatments. This was a method adopted at times in the nineteenth century, and as late as the 1930s. But the method of allocating alternate patients to one of two treatments had a drawback. It was simply that the investigator knew which treatment the next patient would receive. That knowledge in turn had a bearing on the decision to include the patient in the trial in the first place, and could be based on an assessment of that patient's suitability. In this way bias about the relative efficacy of the two treatments could easily emerge. One could overcome this by dividing the patients before they were allocated to a particular course, and at the last minute selecting one group for a treatment …

GJ … by tossing a coin?

RK Exactly. But the trouble with this is that it did not permit the investigators to measure random error—aside from the obvious fact that it was almost impossible to match cases. Both of these problems—bias in the selection of patients, and proper estimating of random error, were solved by Austin Bradford Hill when he suggested randomization in the selection of individuals for clinical trials.

GJ We have talked a lot here about human volunteers—those who volunteer to take part in trials, and patients who might stand to benefit concerning improvements in medicine. I would be failing, however, were I not to raise the question—posed by many people when confronted with the idea of drug trials—of whether it is humane to use animals for this purpose.

RK Well, first it is absolutely necessary in the fields in which I worked. I can understand people's distress about animals being in pain. This seems unjustifiable in the case of cosmetic tests and other vanity products, and there are certain animals, like dogs, cats and monkeys, that are only used in very special and highly regulated cases. But we are, after all, talking about saving human lives. I have found that there are many people who feel very strongly about this issue and yet are quite happy to remain meat-eaters: they have never bothered to visit the abattoirs that provide their daily meat, or the tanneries where their shoes and belts and other leather possessions are made. I assure you that the atmosphere of a laboratory with animals can't even begin to match the chaos of fear and pain that is everywhere to be felt, and heard, in an abattoir on a daily basis. People can certainly live without meat, if they choose to do so, but they can often die without the right drugs. In my time (and this may change in the future) toxicity studies were indispensable in the development of new drugs.

GJ Are there any checks and balances preventing people from torturing animals just for the pleasure of it?

RK There will always be people who are sadists, but I have never come across this in a laboratory or among professional clinicians. This would be a kind of mental sickness—like that of Dr Josef Mengele, the sadist who invented medical experiments for Jewish and gypsy children. Look, when I joined Macdonald's laboratory in Manchester I had to obtain an animals' licence. I had to describe, define and justify what my research would involve. We are taught right from the beginning that an animal is not to be subjected to undue pain. A Home Office inspector has to be informed if experiments have to be done which are likely to cause pain. My own licence was for rats, mice and guinea pigs. (I was not authorized to experiment with animals larger than this; for other animals I would have required additional authorization). All the annual licences had to be signed by the presidents of the Royal College of Physicians and the Royal College of Surgeons. We are quite simply unable to develop new drugs without toxicity trials and these have to be done before we begin testing the products on humans.

GJ Are there similar animal licences required throughout the world?

RK I wonder if you know that Hitler, the vegetarian, passed laws in Germany that animals had to be anaesthetized before slaughter? No such concessions for human beings however! I am not up-to-date with present-day requirements, but when I worked in Rome in Bovet's laboratory, I asked how long it would take before I received a licence to work with animals. Bovet was astonished—'But you are working in a registered laboratory'. I said that in the UK we nevertheless needed individual licences. He looked at me with a wry smile: 'Les Anglais!', was all he could say.

GJ Well such laissez-faire on Bovet's part is unlikely to win admirers for the pharmaceutical industry in this country …

RK When a young mother is told that there is a new drug that will save the life of her child, she will not question how many animals' lives were sacrificed during the development of that life-giving medicine. Drugs are like flood-defences: extremely expensive and seemingly a waste of money, questionable on any number of grounds when the weather is fair, but suddenly essential to avert the tragedies that occur in their absence. We take a lot for granted about medicines—we need them when we need them, and not otherwise—and certainly the sacrifice of animals' lives to this end is part of the story, but decreasingly so as laboratory testing becomes ever more sophisticated. So your question about animals is already rather old-fashioned—animals are being replaced by cultured cells and computer simulations. My friend of many years, Lord Turnberg, was chair of the National Centre for the Replacement, Refinement and Reduction of Animals in Research founded in 2004—the three 'Rs' of this title go back to a ground-breaking book from 1959. Apart from these recent developments, you would be surprised how gentle, even affectionate, some scientists are with their animal helpmates when they are working on an ongoing project. They have a respect for their animals some of whom will certainly have died in a very good cause.

Norman Heatley, one of the pioneers in the development of penicillin, described sitting up until 4 in the morning in Oxford in May 1940, monitoring six mice. Four of these died, but he had given penicillin to the two who survived. One might truly say that the death of these mice, and the survival of the others, signified a turning point for humanity—or as Heatley noted exhaustedly in his diary that night: 'It really looks as though penicillin could be of practical importance.'

Over many years it is these kinds of revelations that we have owed to the animals in our laboratories. Our decision to sacrifice their lives has never been taken lightly and as far as humanity is concerned the loss of those animals' lives has led to unimaginable medical progress for mankind.

PRELUDE XVII

To thine own self be true

IN THE PREFACE to the second edition of his *The Pharmacological Basis of Therapeutics*, Alfred Gilman wrote that he intended to equip the reader with what he called 'a way of thinking about drugs', the better to withstand the flood of unsubstantiated claims often made for new drugs, and to evaluate the literature written about new therapeutic agents in comparison with well-established compounds in the same class. In Shakespeare's *Hamlet*, Act I Scene 3, Polonius lectures his son Laertes who is about to travel abroad to France. 'Keep close to old friends,' says Polonius in essence, 'while being careful about new ones.' By substituting the word 'drugs' for Shakespeare's original 'friends', and 'remedy' for 'comrade', Dr Gordon Millichap, the distinguished paediatric neurologist (and with whom I had a close research relationship at the Albert Einstein College) wittily saw the significance of this advice with regard to the dangers and challenges of working with new pharmaceuticals:

> The friends [drugs] thou hast, and their adoption tried,
> Grapple them to thy soul with hoops of steel;
> But do not dull thy palm with entertainment
> Of each new-hatched, unfledged comrade [remedy].

In this remarkable speech Polonius goes on to offer further words of father-to-son advice that have resonated through the ages: 'Give every man thine ear, but few thy voice. / Take each man's censure, but reserve thy judgement', as well as 'Neither a borrower or lender be' and 'This above all: to thine own self be true'.

Dr Millichap's paraphrase of Shakespeare with regard to pharmacology is indeed ingenious but, as a matter of fact, the ethical advice of Polonius in its original form is valuable enough to me without any need to change it. By the late 1960s, having experienced clinical trials in most of their forms, I knew that it was to be my role in life (and I do not wish to sound over dramatic, or big-headed, in saying so) to bring clinical trials into a new order where organization, efficiency, honesty and integrity—including affability and humanity—could be every bit as important as scientific know-how. I take the phrase 'To thine own self be true!' to mean also being true to one's own talents and abilities. My task was not to invent clinical trials, that had already been done, but I did believe I could put them on a new footing. Now I had to work towards that goal, and it could not be achieved overnight.

When exactly does a new friend become an old friend, someone whom I would 'grapple' to my soul with 'hoops of steel'? The fact is that after beginning to work for Robapharm I had begun, dramatically and with ever-deepening effect, to broaden my circles of professional acquaintance and personal friendship within the British medical and scientific establishments. Several new British colleagues became deeply respected and enduring associates. One of these was Professor Allan Dixon, a distinguished rheumatologist at the Kensington and Chelsea hospitals and later at the Royal National Hospital of Rheumatic Diseases in Bath. He was passionately committed to the Bradford Hill revolution in clinical trials, having taken part in the streptomycin trials of 1948. This was also a wonderful year for rheumatology which had previously been associated more with physical medicine and spa therapy. The advances in antibiotics, starting with sulphonamides, penicillin and anti-tubercular drugs, had important applications in rheumatology and Allan Dixon was at the forefront of the development of his discipline into a respected speciality in its own right. His marvellous book *Rheumatology in the United Kingdom. 50 years of progress* is a celebrated chronicle of these amazing developments. The cartoon by Watson Buchanan reproduced opposite, wittily depicts the struggle experienced by rheumatologists in being taken seriously by their more highfalutin clinical colleagues. It was what might be termed a 'Cinderella' discipline. Actually at this time some people might have placed pharmacology in the same boat, and been happy to see it similarly thrown to the sharks.

In 1970, at a turning point of my life

The plight of rheumatology
Cartoon by Watson Buchanan from Allan Dixon's book

Allan Dixon was on Professor Eric Bywaters' unit at the Hammersmith Hospital, one of the finest in the country. I first met him at St Stephen's (a hospital that has since been demolished—it is now the site of the present Chelsea and Kensington Hospital in Fulham Road) and explained to him that I wanted to do a clinical trial of a Robapharm product named Rumalon. This was a biological extract of young bone and cartilage marketed for the treatment of osteoarthritis. I presented him with the basic scientific background and he agreed to collaborate on the project. It should be emphasized that British clinicians at that time were mostly unwilling to work with this type of preparation—they claimed that this was going back to the dark days of therapeutics.

This clinical trial for patients with osteoarthritis of the hip was the first of the many times we worked fruitfully together. Dixon insisted that he and I should also both receive an injection of the materials he was about to administer to patients, simply to see what it felt like, and if there were any adverse effects. He knew that the patients talking to each other would not be able to guess who had received the active injection of Rumalon and who the placebo. Far from regarding patients in a clinical trial as guinea pigs or dupes, Dixon actually felt they were at an advantage if they took part. Patients in a clinical trial were often those who were best looked-after; they were visited at regular intervals, a set of observations was made, if something was going wrong or they were unhappy or in pain they were attended to immediately. He also emphasized the fact that clinical trials should not be solely drug trials. In his field, rheumatology, there was scope for non-drug trials (with appliances and mechanical aids) and for using other means of treating patients which could in due course be tested and assessed. All of this showed a remarkably enlightened attitude.

The rheumatology team at the Hammersmith Hospital, 1959. Allan Dixon (*second from left, standing*) is next to Barbara Ansell (*also standing*), another distinguished rheumatologist. Eric Bywaters (*standing, wearing glasses*) is the leader of the team, as well as the tallest man in the photograph

Ripason, a liver remedy, and another product of Ropapharm, was the subject of a clinical trial in 1966 conducted by Professor Roger Williams at King's College, London. Williams had established the Institute of Liver Studies at King's College and was its first director. I had a long and rewarding collaboration with this great hepatologist. A few years later, in 1968, he was part of the medical team that performed the first liver transplant in the UK, working in conjunction with Professor Sir Roy Calne FRS (Calne was the distinguished liver transplant surgeon at the Addenbrooke's Hospital in Cambridge, and a great personal friend of mine). I quickly realized at the time that the opportunity to work with people of the calibre of Dixon and Williams, both working within easy reach of my London office, was an incredible blessing. I was learning all the time and they, without realizing it, were my teachers and exemplars.

Roger Williams

While discussing Rumalon and Ripason, I should record that in 1970, when my contract with Robapharm came to an end and I had left the firm, an important commercial opportunity arose for me; this was connected with a remedy called Ossopan that was also manufactured by Robapharm. This was a natural product of young ground-up animal bones, rich in calcium and hopefully more valuable in treating calcium deficiency than simply administering pure calcium. Robapharm had a moribund UK subsidiary and the head office in Basel were willing to sell it off to me. If I succeeded in increasing sales of their products they would finally make a profit. I had a feeling—today it would be called a 'hunch'—that Ossopan would do well in the UK and that buying the UK part of the firm would be a worthwhile investment regarding this product alone. The Swiss parent company sold me this loss-making subsidiary for a negligible sum. The UK was a very small part of Robapharm's market and most of my work for the company—involving a great deal of travel—had involved the firm's worldwide interests.

A study on Ossopan was carried out at University College Hospital by Professor C E Dent FRS, an authority on metabolic bone disease. He used Ossopan in children with brittle-bone disease (*osteogenesis imperfecta*) where bones fractured frequently and where sufferers generally died at a young age. Dent's work indicated that patients treated with ground-up bone fractured less than the control group given pure calcium. A number of additional positive papers in the treatment of osteoporosis gave rise to greater interest and the product gradually became well known within the UK where, until now, it had had zero impact.

This challenge of actually owning a small subsidiary of a large Swiss company was only a temporary diversion from my overriding interest in how best to run clinical trials. Meeting Allan Dixon was fundamental to my developing thoughts on the matter. I remember having a crucial discussion with him in Bürgenstock,

Switzerland. We were together there at an Anglo-Swiss conference on rheumatology in the late 1960s and discussed the commercial significance of independently setting up controlled clinical trials of new drugs. British controlled trials had an outstanding reputation in Continental Europe and indeed worldwide, so why not, I said, set up a company to act as an intermediary between British trialists and drug manufacturers? Allan Dixon also believed that this type of high-powered independent organization could have a great future and would be much in demand. We both realized that large-scale, multi-centre trials were needed to push forward research not only in rheumatology, but in other specialities. We also understood that if such trials were to succeed, the clinicians involved must commit to the idea of an independently run clinical trial. Money that came from the pharmaceutical companies, however well directed, ran the risk of putting clinicians under pressure. It was a problem that needed to be solved and I cannot adequately express my gratitude to Allan Dixon for his guiding support at this crucial junction of my career.

If I was to establish a firm of my own, I needed to gather together a group of highly qualified, multilingual and professional men and women to provide not merely competence but an exceptional range of services to pharmaceutical companies. I knew that the UK was respected for the stringency of its regulatory authority in granting approval for new therapeutic agents—this trend towards oversight by the authorities was to become more pronounced in the 1970s. At the back of my mind I had a clear commercial objective: to provide a variety of services to allow pharmaceutical companies to evaluate and test medical and ancillary products in the UK, taking advantage of the UK's excellence in research and regulation.

Everything now began to fall into place. I understood that my new company would need to maintain a roster of contacts in the international pharmaceutical community. How glad I was that these contacts already existed and that many of these people were

Allan Dixon

already colleagues, some of them friends! It would also be essential to call on the resources and expertise of leading distinguished clinicians and scientific investigators in most areas of clinical medicine. How lucky that the years between 1965 and 1970 were rich for me in new and rewarding associations of this kind! It was indeed fortunate for me that the UK was renowned throughout the world for its medical expertise and for the quality of its experimental and clinical research. Moreover, all these factors were present in the British business and regulatory environment in which I had worked for some time.

Above all what I wanted and needed was independence, the independence that Kolomán Lauer had gently revealed to me as the sine qua non of professional fulfilment. He might just as well have given me that famous fatherly advice that Laertes received from Polonius: 'To thine own self be true.' What I had perhaps not fully realized at first was that financial independence, rewarding as that was, was less important to me than professional independence. To put it in a nutshell, for years I had surveyed the territory occupied by the drug companies on the one hand and the clinicians on the other, and found there was a real need for an independent third party. My new company would bring this much-needed independence, but also professionalism and speed of delivery to an area that had not yet realized its own deficiencies. My five-year contract with Robapharm had come to an end and I was ready for the next phase of my life.

Fugue XVII (in 2 voices) RALPH KOHN *with* GRAHAM JOHNSON

GJ In this chapter you've mentioned the names of Professors Allan Dixon, C E Dent and Roger Williams. Before I began to take an interest in your life and career, these were all names unknown to me. The layman knows about some of the really famous figures in medicine, like Sir Alexander Fleming for example, but I am always fascinated to hear you speak about some of the lesser-known heroes, important names in their own fields of science and medicine who are by no means international, or even national, celebrities. There are lots of such important, but little-known, people in my own musical world, but it takes a group of musicians talking and enthusing together adequately to celebrate their importance.

RK   Well, let's do some celebrating right now of the people who were involved in the development of clinical trials. I have been enormously privileged that my life has been deeply influenced by the work of extraordinary clinicians like Philip D'Arcy Hart in the field of tuberculosis, Francis Avery Jones in gastroenterology and Sheila Sherlock in hepatology. Of these I knew Professor Sherlock personally, Dame Sheila as she became, as well as her fellow hepatologist, Professor Roger Williams. In the commercial sector great discoverers and drug developers emerged, able to use development in trials to test their ideas reliably and quickly. Sir James Black FRS,

Philip D'Arcy Hart

and Sir John Vane FRS (both Nobel prizewinners) and Glaxo's research director Sir David Jack FRS (my former colleague at Smith Kline and French) all contributed significantly from the pharmaceutical sector. We were later very fortunate that for five years Sir John Vane was to be chairman of the medical advisory committee of my company, Advisory Services (Clinical and General)—this was after Allan Dixon had held that position for a couple of decades.

GJ   Philip D'Arcy Hart is an unusual name, and so is Francis Avery Jones. They sound like characters from another epoch, Victorian or Edwardian perhaps. Were they both equally extraordinary clinicians?

RK   Such altruistic people seem much rarer in our own times, although I hope this is not the case. D'Arcy Hart was born in 1900 into a banking family, very well-to-do, but his political sympathies were with the working class. In 1937 he ran a large-scale clinical examination of miners. Those who had quarried mine shafts developed silicosis and received compensation; on the other hand, those who worked at the coalface developed chronic lung disease and received nothing. Hart demonstrated that their disease was occupational and recommended that they receive compensation—something of a bombshell. Hart's work straddled the period of private mine-ownership, nationalization of the coal industry and the coming into being of the National Health Service. Between 1937 and 1948 he lived in Cardiff and drove a van through the south Wales valleys with a portable X-ray machine. He was regarded as a 'traitor' by some of his London colleagues who were more interested in their lucrative consultancies. He took part in the streptomycin trials of 1948—as we have discussed, these were a turning point in the history of clinical trials. He was later director of the Medical Research Council's tuberculosis research unit. He officially retired at the age of sixty-five but spent a life devoted to research until the age of 102. He died at the age of 106.

GJ   I'm impressed you have all this at your fingertips.

RK   Since beginning to write this book I have reacquainted myself with the life-stories of those who were closely associated with the Bradford Hill revolution. D'Arcy Hart was something of a legend, a real mover and shaker. Francis Avery Jones was another giant but a quieter kind of personality. He was a consultant physician and gastroenterologist at Central Middlesex and St Mark's Hospitals; he opened a gastrointestinal unit at the Central Middlesex Hospital, building the first British clinical and research base in that speciality; his interest was in peptic ulcers. I can think of few people more renowned for the teaching of clinicians. Hundreds of young doctors flocked to work with him and many went on to found their own units. They had been taught how to be calm, caring and methodical in questioning the old and evaluating the new.

GJ   Over the years I have heard you mention the name of Dame Sheila Sherlock many times. I have always gathered both that she was a redoubtable woman and clinician and that she played a very important part in your career.

RK   Sheila Sherlock! Where could one begin to pay tribute to her? She has been called, rightly in my opinion, one of the most dazzling medical personalities of the latter half of the twentieth century, and I am very proud that over the years she became a close friend of mine, and also of my family. She was world-renowned for elucidating the anatomical, physiological and biochemical pathology of liver disease. She identified the relationship between hepatitis B and liver cancer. She also made major contributions to the epidemiology, immunology and pathology of viral and other forms of jaundice, hepatitis and the effects of drugs on the liver. I am very proud to say that I collaborated closely with her in the 1970s and 1980s. Together we ran numerous clinical trials on a variety of liver conditions and it was thanks to her confidence in

Francis Avery Jones

Sheila Sherlock

me and our collaboration with Roger Williams that my firm, Advisory Services, began organizing medical symposia on a large scale with visitors from all over the world. Some of these, in turn, became contacts and close friends. I truly owe Sheila Sherlock a very great deal. She was made a Fellow of the Royal Society some months before her death in 2001. I can think of few people who were of greater help to me in my career.

GJ A number of your contemporaries are still active in the field.

RK Some of them remain in remarkably good health! Roger Williams, for example, is only a few years younger than me and still very active. One of his most famous patients was the footballer George Best, but not even a liver transplant and the best medical care were able to save the life of that brilliant and tragic figure. The Institute of Hepatology that was once part of University College London, is now a private research institute supported by the Foundation for Liver Research, and affiliated to Birkbeck College. Roger Williams is director of that institute and a few years ago he became visiting professor at King Saud University in Riyadh, Saudi Arabia, where he heads a collaborative biomarkers research programme. I am a trustee of his Hepatology Trust and we still see a great deal of each other. He is an outstanding physician and a great personal friend. Another great friend and influence on me is Professor Victor Dubowitz, world authority on muscular disorders in childhood and a man of immense *joie de vivre* and humour.

GJ You have described how you were learning from all these great figures, but also that you had become something of a businessman by acquiring Robapharm UK, a loss-making subsidiary of the Swiss firm. You had a hunch that Ossopan was a useful product as far as the UK was concerned, and this was backed up in clinical trials. Where did you go from there?

RK This was the kind of undertaking that appealed to an energetic young man with an extraordinary wife. It turned out to be an extremely profitable venture and this despite the fact I had, of course, no sales force at all. In due course we moved from 44 Welbeck Street to larger premises at No 28 Welbeck Street. Marketing was done through sales literature and by word of mouth. Moreover, the orders had then to be packaged and sent out. Here, as with the later development of my own company, Zahava played a key role. If you remember, she had helped her father develop his rainwear business, first in the area of actually manufacturing the garments and then sending off orders.

GJ So it was Zahava who was not only looking after two—subsequently three—young daughters, but was also packing and posting boxes of Ossopan, while also keeping the firm's books?

RK Exactly! She was a tower of strength, not only in this particular project but also advising me on the main work of the company. She was not medically trained but you might be surprised at how astute she is in this field …

GJ I'm not surprised at all!

RK And it was not only that she packed and posted Ossopan. As my plans for the new firm grew, so did our social obligations. Zahava hosted events in our home on countless occasions, and was always a gracious and unflappable hostess. She did not tend to travel with me on short trips, but came with me on those involving the USA or Japan, of which there were many. She always made immaculate arrangements for our children so that she could go away—sometimes for periods of up to two weeks or more.

GJ So now at last the time has come to talk about your very own firm. You had to wait quite some time for the realization of this dream, but the reader is impatient to find out what happened next.

RK And I was impatient to begin the work for which, in many ways, I felt I had long been destined. In the meantime, I am sorry to say, I had come to the conclusion that there was a great deal wrong with the status quo.

Photograph by Clive Barda

INTERLUDE 4: SARABANDE

Bad Pharma

I HAD SURVEYED THE TERRITORY occupied by the drug companies on the one hand and the clinicians on the other, and found there was a desperate need for an independent third party. Medical departments of pharmaceutical companies at that time were often of poor quality and patchily and sporadically supported. There was a received opinion that some of the doctors they employed were often those who had failed to become hospital consultants or to establish themselves in academic medicine—they were often perceived to be 'second division'. Whether or not this was true, the British class system, affecting all aspects of professional and social life, did little to lessen this feeling, and if anything reinforced it. I noticed that medical doctors in pharmaceutical employment often felt inferior when dealing with clinicians. In this rather demoralized atmosphere the protocols of their trials (in other words, the basis on which they were conducted) were often deficient, as were the record forms (the means by which results were charted and finally turned into statistical evidence). Furthermore, follow-up tended to be poor. There was often a notable lack of energy, enthusiasm and persistence in bringing trials to a speedy conclusion with a reliable result. I aimed to create an organization that provided that indispensable sense of urgency, quite apart from everything else that was necessary in this complex field.

When I was observing clinical trials during the 1960s there were often no well-defined dates for starting; there was often no clear idea of when the study could be concluded, nor of the number of patients required for a definitive answer. Such lack of rigour was harmful to the patients (who were not receiving new treatments as soon as possible), detrimental to the clinicians (who took far longer than necessary to judge whether a treatment was useful) and irksome for the pharmaceutical industry (which lost time and money in not being able to make an early decision on the safety of a new treatment). The marketing departments of these companies rarely knew how long it would take before they found out whether they had a product to market at all, and if so, when. Budgets and resources had to be allocated; shareholders and investors had to be informed of the company's prospects: all depended on the next big thing.

When it comes to the development of a new drug, few people outside the industry realize the complexity of the timetable. Without going into technical detail here, the complete process may now take up to twelve years on a major drug and up to one billion pounds may be spent. Exploratory research is followed by applied research; then comes exploratory development and, finally, full-scale development—the marketing necessary for the launch of a new product and its registration. Clinical trials are only a part of this extended process, but the pharmaceutical companies have already invested huge amounts of money and the expeditious execution of these trials is crucial.

Money is not necessarily a dirty word—pharmaceutical companies are certainly money-making concerns (and enjoy, in some quarters, the present unpopularity of bankers), but highly trained medical professionals also need, and deserve, to be rewarded for their hard work. One of the very first things I had to do was to promote a realistic attitude to the financing of trials. Clinical departments in hospitals were accustomed to government funding and were not valuing at a commercial rate the time and expertise they gave to trials; in essence, they were doing the drug company's work for nothing. I knew that research, equipment and the clinicians' time needed to be paid for; I equally understood that the direct financial involvement of a pharmaceutical company might be an uncomfortable intervention into the culture of public service medicine and research. If the pharmaceutical companies were separated from the recipients of their money, both sides would have a far more transparent relationship.

On the other hand, why should money not be involved in the exchanges that took place during a clinical trial? The taboo that had grown up around this subject seemed to me as nonsensical as were the many problems that arose due to the lack of clarity in financial arrangements. Clinicians were not paid to do clinical studies in my early years. What kind of strange Victorian altruism did that represent? A hospital doctor who did a great deal of work might be invited to present his findings at an enjoyable conference abroad, but the essential expense of the trial was actually carried by the hospital (X-rays, scans, blood tests and so on). The trials were thus being funded by the NHS, but the benefits, if the results were positive, went straight to the pharmaceutical company. I thought this was wrong and that it should be changed.

At first clinicians thought that I wanted to 'bribe' the medical profession by introducing the concept of payment, whereas in reality I simply proposed the obvious fact that all parties should derive an advantage from their collaboration, and that money should be paid for time spent in a proper, transparent way. Together with clinicians it was necessary to establish that we needed x patients in y months (or weeks) and that the following tests were necessary. I never expected a clinician to spend valuable time exclusively for a pharmaceutical company's benefit; I simply proposed to pay for these services by supporting a research fund or an appointment. This would be paid for by my company as an independent, and therefore only indirectly by the pharmaceutical company. This rational working arrangement would raise the whole relationship into a proper scientific, medical and commercial footing. All procedures, timetables and money matters were to be part of a budget discussed at the outset of the trial. The advantage of this was that clinicians never felt that positive results were expected of their trials, and were in fact freer to deliver only the facts that derived from them.

My work had always had an international perspective. While conditions in the UK favoured the possibility of a well-run trial, those in many countries of Continental Europe did not. There the situation was even more chaotic than in the UK. In certain countries I had seen manipulation of the results of clinical trials. This could have serious consequences—a number of drugs were marketed which should not have been. In other cases, such as the famous Chemie Grünenthal drug thalidomide, the company continued to promote its drug as a treatment for morning sickness and as a night-time hypnotic even after serious adverse effects had been reported; these were at first ignored by the manufacturers.

While working at Smith Kline and French I encountered an out-and-out fraud played out (unsuccessfully in the long run) in a laboratory in Naples which had many of the qualities of buffo operatic comedy. The Italians claimed that they were developing a remedy against the influenza virus (PR8)—potentially a very exciting prospect. Mice injected with the new chemical compound survived, while untreated mice died. None of the Italian results could be reproduced in laboratories in Philadelphia or London; eventually we agreed to visit Naples and view the trials there at first hand. The learned professor from Naples University and Hospital expressed his utmost confidence in his young doctors. After a few days I came to the conclusion that these men were fiddling the results by substituting live mice for dead ones when we were not closely observing their actions. This was a fraud that went to the top, although it was impossible to say so openly. The Italian consultant who had made the compound insisted that we had not done the experiments correctly in Philadelphia and London, but Smith Kline and French dropped the project.

This is an extreme case of a clumsy plot that had been designed in the hope of making a lot of money. In many cases pharmaceutical companies were guilty of something far less blatant; their attitude to their results was sometimes an affair of compromise and a genuine inability to see what was before them, rather than one of outright fraudulence. As we all know, when there is a great deal at stake you often see what you want to see, while psychologically suppressing the undesirable result. On the Continent, however, results which did not 'help the cause' were frequently simply suppressed.

Somewhat ironically I have taken the title of this segment of my book from a recent publication by Dr Ben Goldacre who is Wellcome Research Fellow in epidemiology at the London School of Hygiene and Tropical Medicine, a centre where I conducted a clinical trial in the 1980s. In *Bad Pharma* (2012)—a pun no doubt on 'bad karma'—Goldacre describes a crisis in present-day pharmacology. The book's theme is encapsulated by Sir Michael Rawlins, former president of the Royal Society of Medicine and former head of the National Institute for Health and Care Excellence (NICE), in a review he wrote for *The Lancet* (27 October 2012):

> Goldacre's anger is directed not only at bad pharma. He also criticizes bad academia, bad drug regulators, bad patient advocacy groups, bad journal editors, and bad doctors more generally.

Goldacre makes many points and accusations, among which is the fact that the industry in the USA, with its celebrity endorsements of medical products, spends twice as much on marketing as on research. Sir Michael Rawlins counters, in defence of the UK's regulations, that companies in this country can only spend up to 6% of their sales to the NHS on marketing, but 30% on research and development. Things are still very different here in the UK than they are in the US, but increasing globalization sometimes plays a destructive role. Although Rawlins finds much of Goldacre's polemic exaggerated, he agrees that many of the points raised in this large book are valid.

It is now over twenty years since I have been involved in clinical trials; I am no longer au fait with this aspect of the industry in a world ruthlessly streamlined for shareholders' interests (I never floated my own firm on the market). There have no doubt been many changes in pharmacology, some of them of debatable value, which I have not experienced at first hand; the industry, and the financial stakes at play, have become gargantuan in a way that could scarcely have been imagined. But Goldacre's arguments, when taken to their logical conclusion, would ask his readers to believe that most of the drugs licensed in the 1970s, 1980s and 1990s underwent corrupt or inadequate trials, and were thus no better than placebos. What, then, of ibuprofen, statins, or angiotensin-converting-enzyme inhibitors, to name only a few of the very many important drugs that have been introduced in the past thirty years? This part of Goldacre's argument can be refuted.

There is also the matter of publication. Goldacre accuses academics of not only failing to publish the results of their own trials, but of conniving with pharmaceutical companies in the selective reporting of the results of studies with which they have been involved. This is very old news; it is the very danger that I saw undermining the integrity of clinical trials in the late sixties. When I was in charge of Advisory Services—the organization described in the next chapter—

I introduced the condition of publication irrespective of the results obtained. Companies were compelled to agree to this before beginning the trials; in this way there could be no suppression of results, and no adverse effect could be concealed. All of the company's agreements at the outset of every study expressly stipulated that publication should not be withheld. This of course helped to maintain the professional independence of the company. My company would never make a contract with a pharmaceutical company without its agreement in advance to the full disclosure of results in their reporting and in the medical press.

I am in fact a great admirer of the pharmaceutical industry and its huge achievements, but it is not infallible. As Sir Michael Rawlins points out there are some who regard pharmaceutical companies as saints and some, like Goldacre, who find them to be sinners. I think neither epithet is tenable. I am not a whistle-blower like Dr Goldacre (and whistle-blowers have an honourable part to play in any area of fallible human endeavour) but he is certainly not the first to have been troubled by certain aspects of this industry. There are things that need to be fixed but the situation is not irremediable; 'Medicine is broken', Goldacre dramatically declares at the very beginning of the book, but I do not believe this to be the case. He is forty

Michael Rawlins

years old or so, more or less the age I was when I felt a burning desire to make my own contribution to greater honesty and transparency in clinical trials. I attempted to do so, however, from within the industry, and in a way that was quietly revolutionary. I admit, however, that we held our position for no more than twenty-five years—between 1970 and 1996, and that time marches ruthlessly on. Nevertheless, we were imitated and emulated, and although I cannot speak for the conduct of the firms that came after us, I refuse to believe that ethical standards were not exemplary in many of them.

Sir Michael Rawlins makes a very important point at the end of his review:

> The only organization with the knowledge and skills to develop new medicines is the pharmaceutical industry ... The environment needs to ensure the industry's creativity is appropriately rewarded. At the same time, the industry's unacceptable practices, that Goldacre describes in *Bad Pharma*, must be confined to history. It is this balance between the beautiful and ugly that Goldacre fails to achieve.

Achieving a balance has always been for me a golden rule. I strove to create a working environment (however temporary it turned out to be) that both encouraged the industry to develop the drugs that society desperately needed, while providing a level playing-field that ensured that the interests of patients and clinicians were not pushed aside and marginalized in favour of big business.

I also believe that a close working relationship between science and industry is essential in view of one of the major concerns of our times—the fact that many bacteria are now resistant to antibiotics after seventy-five years of use, and that a solution for this daunting problem can only be achieved by a problem-free collaboration between great scientists and those with the means to finance their research. This is a sufficiently disturbing problem to have engaged the serious attention of world leaders, including our own prime minister who recently referred to the danger of our returning to the 'dark ages of medicine'.

PRELUDE XVIII

Advisory Services (CLINICAL AND GENERAL)

MY NEW ORGANIZATION, founded in 1971, was named Advisory Services (Clinical and General) Ltd. When I look back on it, this pioneering venture represented something of risk; branching out on one's own is never easy. Fortunately I am not someone who allows my better ideas to be submerged by self-doubt. The advice of Kolomán Lauer about my becoming independent had been at the back of my mind for several years. Moreover, my devoted wife was behind me all the way, and I have already described how Allan Dixon, that great lateral thinker, also encouraged me to go ahead.

In the early days there was no company doing our type of work in Europe and we made a difference—a large claim, but an accurate one. We aimed to make a highly professional job of clinical trials with first-class investigators, getting the work done within the time we said we would, irrespective of what the results might be. We sought to apply a level of scientific and commercial rigour in the hope and expectation of bringing order to an area that had become chaotic. Independent auditors, crucial in any major industry, were entirely lacking in this kind of work before Advisory Services came into being. As a result clients came to us from all over the world. They came to us often because Advisory Services was more precise, comprehensive, reliable and swift than their own organizations. We selected the best clinical units in the country, wherever possible at teaching hospitals, in order to guarantee the highest clinical and procedural standards.

Medical doctors in pharmaceutical companies were often not well versed in the basic sciences and not looked on as 'equals' by busy clinicians. I approached the medical profession with a completely different attitude: I was not a clinician but a basic medical scientist, and I made this clear to the consultants I met; neither was I part of the drug company's research and sales function. Both groups, therefore, respected what I did.

There are four distinct phases in modern clinical trials. In the first phase manufacturers test the effects of a drug in healthy volunteers. They look at how the drug is handled in the human body, particularly with respect to the immediate short-term effects of higher doses. In the second phase, trials test dose-response curves and the benefits that might be seen in patients with a specific condition or disease, and undesirable side-effects which might arise. Phases one and two may be classified under the heading 'clinical pharmacology'.

In the third phase the drug is tested in a controlled way in a large patient population and compared with a standard treatment or placebo; this is derived from the Bradford Hill type of trial. A drug succeeds or fails with respect to its safety and efficacy at this point. This third phase became known as the 'pivotal study' by which a drug may gain a license to be prescribed for a specific disease (in this area Advisory Services had a particular expertise).

The fourth phase is the post-marketing study conducted after the drug has gained the appropriate regulatory approval and licence. These studies are important for gathering safety information from larger groups of patients in order to determine long-term adverse effects. Within each trial, separate protocols and specific designs are applied.

Advisory Services applied a strict discipline to the management of each and every aspect of the trial and in each of its phases. It first established what the pharmaceutical company needed from the trial. This entailed advising the client on how those needs could be met, not only in practical but regulatory terms, and thus meant ensuring compliance with the Medicines Control Agency (formerly the Medicines Division of the Department of Health). We would then determine the trial protocols (the numbers of patients and clinical centres, and the methods of providing the drug or testing the treatment). The company then oversaw the trial with meticulous attention and great persistence. Our studies were always blind to avoid any bias that might invalidate results, and they always involved a statistician. We had patient record forms, consistent monitoring and measurement, as well as a timely and accurate completion date. Our work entailed frequent and regular visits to monitor progress, gathering and collating data, remaining alert to adverse effects, helping the clinical centres to deliver their undertakings on time, and liaising with the client as the process moved forward.

It was our concern to make the clinical trial as watertight as possible in terms of conduct and outcome. This meant ensuring that sufficient numbers of patients were enrolled, and that in conducting the trial we used many centres (a multi-centre trial) with one of the senior consultants acting as chairman of the participating clinical units. I also introduced an element of competition between the units. When we met with consultants, assuming 200 patients had to be enrolled between five units (say, forty per unit), it would look poor if some centres had enrolled significant numbers while others had hardly contributed. So there was peer pressure to ensure quick and adequate enrolment: this system worked wonders and was shown to be of the utmost importance.

After the trial we gathered the results, collated and analysed the data from all the units involved and circulated it to all the trial centres as well as to the company which commissioned the work; we then wrote the draft reports, circulated them and requested comments. After taking account of the comments we would prepare the final reports and circulate them to all parties for approval. 'Good news or bad news' about a drug was all the same to us—though not, of course, for the client. A full disclosure of the result was assured by the contract made in the first place with the drug company. It was the only way to work and it was respected by all. Advisory Services was paid whatever the results. We had no interest per se in the outcomes of any of the hundreds of clinical trials which we ran for many clients. We neither sought nor received additional payments when favourable results were obtained.

It may seem like blowing my own trumpet, but from time to time I have received compliments from highly respected, and difficult to please, colleagues that have made all the hard work worthwhile. Professor Roger Williams in an interview wrote:

> Despite the intracies of clinical trials and negotiations around them, I cannot ever recollect these leading to a cross word. This was not only because of the considerable expertise that Ralph Kohn brought to such negotiations but also his ability in seeing a way forward.

Professor Allan Dixon in another interview paid us this compliment:

> Ralph Kohn and his company made the clinical trial into a highly efficient, reliable and meaningful science, which could be trusted and was the fastest way to achieve earliest commercialization.

The pathway to this 'earliest commercialization' (in Allan Dixon's words) was a great deal more work than most people realized, but it was also part of our remit. We offered help with regulatory matters where such consent was required prior to marketing the drug or its further development. We then had to prepare material for publication in the relevant professional journals and to set up—assuming a set of positive data—a symposium to publicize the results. These were organized at prestigious venues in the UK such as the Royal Society, the Royal College of Physicians and the Royal Society of Medicine. Organizing symposia of this kind became a special part of our firm's work, an offshoot with a name of its own— Advisory Services Medical Symposia.

The operations of Advisory Services gradually grew throughout the 1970s and 1980s. I had worked with over a hundred UK, European, American and Japanese pharmaceutical and related companies in therapeutic drugs, medical equipment and foodstuffs covering a variety of clinical practice by the time we received the Queen's Award (see *Interlude 5*, following this chapter). We also took part in licensing negotiations (thus enabling products to be distributed worldwide) and arranged for the testing of prototypes, appliances, diagnostic aids and hospital equipment. This is the reason why our full title was Advisory Services (Clinical and General).

I apologize to the reader for the following lists but it seems the least fussy way of describing the breadth of our work. In the 1980s I note that we ran trials in the following centres: Aberdeen, Bath, Birmingham, Bristol, Cambridge, Edinburgh, Glasgow, Harlow, Leeds, London, Manchester, Newcastle, Norwich, Oxford, Salford, Southampton and Sunderland. We dealt with most of London's teaching hospitals: the Brompton, Charing Cross and Westminster, Guy's, Hammersmith, King's College, the London Hospital, the London School of Hygiene and Tropical Medicine, the Marsden, the Royal Free, St Bartholomew's, St George's, St Mary's, the Whittington and many other smaller hospitals.

The company's areas of medical specialization were diverse. It is worth listing them to indicate the scope of the company's expertise, and the areas in which it provided services: biotechnology, cardiovascular disease, clinical pharmacology, computer applications, dementia, dentistry, dermatology, endocrinology, gastroenterology, general practice, general surgery, geriatrics, gynaecology, hepatology, infectious diseases, medical editing, medical statistics, metabolic diseases, nephrology, neurology, nutrition, oncology, ophthalmology, orthopaedics, paediatrics, pharmaceutics, pharmacology, psychiatry, radiology, respiratory medicine, rheumatology, sexually transmitted diseases, sports medicine, urology and veterinary medicine.

By 1990 I had set up specialist divisions of the company to cover clinical research, statistics, regulatory affairs and general administration. Under a group structure, Advisory Services Medical Symposia was established in 1976 and Advisory Services Research & Development in 1986. They were gathered under Advisory Services Holdings Ltd in 1987. Revenues increased steadily throughout the 1980s—from a modest base in 1981 to sixteen times that in 1989. Nevertheless, the number of staff remained small; as revenues increased exponentially, staff numbers increased slowly, only doubling in the same period. In essence I remained responsible for contacting hundreds of clinicians and hospital staff in dozens of centres around the UK.

Advisory Services was highly profitable. The company remained privately owned and attracted several takeover bids from the US which were resisted. I was in the fortunate position of being able to expand, as required, using internal funding. More importantly, the involvement of other outside investors would have had an impact on my freedom to take the firm in any direction I chose. Neither did I wish to float the company and see it become subject to the whims of market commentators—the people I regarded as 'City scribblers'. I look back to the advice of Kolomán Lauer and realize just how right he was about being independent. It was for precisely this reason that I always approached the office with joy, and a spring in my step. Years later, when I was elected an Honorary Fellow of the Royal Society, I made a speech entitled *The pharmacological basis of the Kohn Foundation*. When this presentation was printed, the president of the Royal Society, Lord Rees, contributed a foreword in which he wrote of my activities as having been 'in the furtherance of science and innovation'. The pairing of those two tremendous nouns faithfully describes what I attempted to achieve in the field of clinical trials.

Fugue XVIII (*in 3 voices*)

RALPH KOHN & HEPHZIBAH KOHN RUDOFSKY *with* GRAHAM JOHNSON

GJ In discussing the work of Advisory Services we welcome Hephzibah Kohn Rudofsky to our conversation.

RK Well my daughter is no stranger in this office, I assure you. Hephzi worked here between 1986 and mid 1993, I think it was …

HR Absolutely correct! Trust you, dad, to have all the facts at your fingertips. I must say that my eight years here as a senior clinical research associate were very rewarding, and I really got to know the business in all its aspects …

RK … which is exactly why I suggested that you join us to discuss Advisory Services. Hephzi, I would be delighted for you to answer some of Graham's questions for a change …

GJ Before assuming my role as 'Grand Inquisitor', I should explain, for the benefit of readers, where this conversation is taking place. After you sold Advisory Services some twenty years ago, you chose to continue your work for the Kohn Foundation (of which more anon) in this beautiful building, 14 Harley Street; at the age of eighty-six, you continue to keep office hours, more or less. We are sitting in this spaciously elegant and beautifully carpeted room, the width of the entire house, on the first floor; in Victorian times it must have been the main drawing room of a gracious home, perhaps that of a prosperous doctor with patients from high society. Zahava, your wife, supervised this decor in greys and browns and the mood is calm and supremely comfortable, a room made to receive clients and welcome friends. Your large desk, full of family photographs is in the left-hand corner of the room as one comes through the large set of double doors that separates your office from that of your secretary. On entering, the visitor is faced by three imposing high windows; the traffic below is scarcely visible on account of a narrow balcony adorned with greenery; the room is bathed in light. The wall to the right, opposite the desk, has a large antique bookcase and there are numerous photographs of friends and colleagues. In an office of this size there is plenty of room for a large round coffee table surrounded by comfortable chairs; this is where many of these conversations have taken place between us.

Now, back to the questions! Do you mind sharing with me how you managed to begin your business without a large amount of capital? Or have you simply been very discreet about a number of people who invested in your company from the very beginning?

RK I had no investors and no hidden revenues. But right from the beginning I asked for the payment of 50% fees upfront for any work undertaken by Advisory Services. The remainder of the fee was paid in various stages, the final 10% on completion. By the standards of the time, when most firms submitted gentlemanly invoices that could take months to be settled, this approach took chutzpah, but it was necessary for our survival as a self-financing operation. I refused to take out bank loans that depended on us getting paid eventually. I was perfectly direct with all my clients that this was how I did business, and it was accepted. I must say that this simple decision from the very beginning spared us a great deal of trouble and needless worry and expense.

GJ At one time did Advisory Services occupy the whole of this building?

RK At one point, yes. We purchased 14 Harley Street in 1987; the lease on our previous offices at 79 Wimpole Street was about to expire. We had landed some large contracts and we required more spacious premises because we needed more staff, thus we also acquired 8 Harley Street.

GJ Hephzi, how did you come to work for your father?

HR It was by chance really. After completing my degree in geography and economics at the London School of Economics in 1986, I had initially planned to do a masters in urban and regional planning at Columbia University in New York. I think my father thought town planning an unusual choice of career, and even I had to admit that New York was rather a dangerous city at that time. I also had reservations about the amount of money this degree course would have cost my parents, although they would have certainly supported any decision of mine to go to the USA. Dad invited me to begin working for the company while I was considering my options. There was a separate branch of Advisory Services that organized medical symposia and in the autumn of 1987 an important international conference on viral hepatitis and liver disease took place at the Barbican, with some 1,200 delegates from all over the world and Professor Ari Zuckerman in the chair.

14 Harley Street, W1

RK The fact that this symposium was based in London at all, as opposed to the usual host country of the United States, was a huge coup for British liver clinicians like Sheila Sherlock and Roger Williams. When Sheila was asked by her American colleagues who in London might be capable of organizing such an event, she gave my name and that of Advisory Services Medical Symposia Ltd without hesitation. That she put her trust in us to this extent was a great honour, but it was a huge challenge for the company …

HR … and dad delegated almost the entire planning of this massive event to me! 'Do you want to run it for me?', he said. I would say he is a 'big ideas' man and he has a knack of finding people he can trust to execute the details. Fortunately, working on my degree at LSE had honed my organizational and managerial skills, but I had no experience whatever in orchestrating anything of this magnitude. These were the days before computers and e-mails and the like—so it was a huge logistical undertaking. It had only been recently that we had acquired a fax machine— I remember how fascinated you were, dad, by this new technology.

RK Well those were the days when such important advances were not to be taken for granted. In these last years it seems to me that office technology leaps forward every day and appears to have got completely out of hand …

HR When I was organizing this symposium at the Barbican I would have been so grateful for present-day technology! At the time the task represented the steepest of learning curves for me, but I somehow survived.

GJ More than survived! By all accounts the symposium was a resounding success!

RK It was indeed, and it represented a real step forward for the worldwide reputation of the company! My faith in Hephzi had been entirely justified and I was very proud of her. I have learned over the years that when there is a task to be done I can always rely on Hephzi to carry it through.

GJ Being given such awesome responsibility, Hephzi, seems to have been enjoyable for you. You were subsequently drawn into working for the firm for a longer period?

HR Exactly! In organizing the symposium and meeting so many people in the scientific and medical fields, some of them world famous in their disciplines, I had become fascinated by the whole concept of clinical trials. I decided to begin to work my way up through the company.

GJ Your father must have been delighted, and rather relieved that he was not going to lose you to New York. So what would your typical working day have been like at Advisory Services?

HR There was nothing typical about any of the days except that they always began early, and sometimes ended late. I was living at home at the time and dad and I would go to work together. We were usually there shortly after 8 am. Conversations on the way to work covered a multitude of topics and I learned a great deal about the business and all the personalities involved. They also took my mind off dad's driving in his beloved ancient Volvo; when he was preoccupied with a thousand issues at any one time, and seemingly in command of them all, he was not the most reassuring driver—sorry dad!

RK Well, I've given up driving entirely now, and I'm sure you are all relieved …

GJ When you got to the office, presumably in one piece, who were some of the people you might have encountered there?

HR There was a relatively small number of people for such a large enterprise. I was one of several clinical research associates but gradually we took on more staff as the workload increased—although we were very conscious of trying to keep the number of employees under careful control. At the back of the building was our scientific expert, Dr Jeff Harper (he was a man of few words but had a sharp sense of humour), who was absolutely brilliant. He was a fine chemist and was primarily involved in registration matters. He provided the scientific and medical backbone of much of our work and was also excellent at the preparation of abstracts and of papers for publication. On the less intellectual level there was dad's fiercely loyal secretary, Jock Heiden, a feisty spinster despite the name, and later Margaret Treanor.

with my daughter Hephzi in Japan (the other young lady is the daughter of a Japanese colleague)

GJ Did you accompany your father on his numerous trips abroad?

HR Very rarely. I travelled with him to Japan, but I was mainly concerned with the company's activities in the UK.

RK This was because most of our clinical trials were conducted within the United Kingdom and Hephzi's job entailed identifying suitable centres for those trials to take place. She then acted as a kind of visiting inspector to monitor how they were progressing.

GJ So fewer flights and more train journeys?

HR Yes, I always went second class by train because I was hugely conscious of being the boss's daughter and I never wanted my colleagues to be able to say I got preferential treatment.

RK So they went first class as a permitted perk of the job, and Hephzi decided to go second!

HR I always flew to Belfast because I was working there at the Queen's University during the so-called 'Troubles' with the IRA, and I never wanted to stay there overnight—first flight in, last flight out. But I went on any number of long train journeys and flew up to Edinburgh and to Glasgow where I worked in various hospitals and general practices. I became quite expert at identifying potential centres suitable for conducting whatever kind of trial was required.

GJ Give me an example of that.

HR One of the trials was in post-episiotomy pain relief. Women who are torn during childbirth need medication for the pain. For the clinical trials of suitable drugs we needed mothers who were not breastfeeding …

RK There are certain drugs, those containing steroids for example, that must not be given to breastfeeding mothers.

HR I found that breastfeeding was not really in vogue in the less prosperous parts of Glasgow or Belfast at that time. As a result there were more women suitable for this particular trial in Scotland than further down south. In cases like this I had to look at the inclusions and exclusions criteria of the trials and think 'out of the box'. But making this kind of informed decision was only part of a very much larger overall picture. Much of my work was to conduct spot checks on how the trials were being conducted and to monitor proceedings. I never found any evidence of 'fiddling the books', thank goodness, but it is a field where this can happen unless a careful eye is kept on all aspects of the trial.

RK Hephzi really did learn the business from the bottom up and became very good at it. When I decided to retire and devote myself to the work of the Kohn Foundation I asked her seriously to consider whether she wanted to take over the running of Advisory Services. In that way it would have been possible for the company to remain within the family.

HR This was a moment of truth for me. I had to ask myself what I could do in comparison with my father. I was certainly organized and meticulous, I knew I was a hard worker, but I had limited scientific and medical knowledge—apart from what I had already picked up on the job—and I lacked my father's great ability with languages. What he had created was something that so entirely reflected him as a person that he was literally irreplaceable—he was synonymous with Advisory Services. The last thing I wanted to happen was for the company to lose the reputation my father had worked so hard to achieve …

RK I very much doubt if you would have allowed that to happen Hephzi …

GJ　But Ralph, I do understand Hephzi's point. In many ways you had created a company entirely around your own talents and personality, not exactly a one-man band, but something along those lines. In any case, Hephzi, by the time Ralph decided to sell his company you had already married and were living abroad.

HR　Yes, I married Steven Rudofsky in March 1993. As he is American, our wedding guest list was very international, and it also included a number of friends I had made while working for dad. The president and the research director of one of our large client companies in Japan attended our wedding, together with their wives of course: the ceremonial kimonos worn by the ladies must have taken three hours to put on. I was most honoured by their presence and that they had made such a long journey simply to be with us on this happy occasion. Steven and I lived in Switzerland for two years where I worked for a laboratory in the field of clinical trials. For the past ten years I have become involved in the running of various Holocaust-related projects—something very close to my heart. Many of the interpersonal skills needed for this work were certainly learned in those crucial years at Advisory Services.

GJ　Since then you have become the mother of a son and a daughter. And now a question for Ralph. Would it have been easier for you to pass on your business to a son?

RK　Of course not. Hephzi had been at my right hand for so many years that if she was not willing to take on the task, no one could have done it.

GJ　Actually, I think it would have been far worse dealing with a son, and there might have been a much greater source of conflict if a son had not been at all interested in the business.

RK　Perhaps so. I was certainly completely uninterested in taking up the same line of business as my own father, and my cousin Gegi never followed in Uncle Jacob's footsteps. Hephzi's fascination with the work she did here with me was genuine and spontaneous. The same was the case with my second daughter, Michelle, who worked here for a shorter time. For me the time spent together as colleagues with my daughters was delightfully unexpected—a real bonus.

HR　Looking back, working with my father was very enriching and fulfilling; it served as a kind of apprenticeship for many aspects of the rest of my life.

ELIZABETH THE SECOND,

by the Grace of God of the United Kingdom of Great Britain and Northern Ireland and of Our other

Realms and Territories Queen Defender of the Faith, to

ADVISORY SERVICES HOLDINGS LIMITED GROUP OF COMPANIES

Greeting!

We being cognisant of the outstanding achievement of the said body as manifested in the

furtherance and increase of the Export Trade of Our United Kingdom of Great Britain and

Northern Ireland, Our Channel Islands and Our Island of Man and being desirous of showing

Our Royal Favour do hereby confer upon it

THE QUEEN'S AWARD FOR
EXPORT ACHIEVEMENT

for a period of five years from the twenty-first day of April 1990 until the twentieth day of April 1995

and do hereby give permission for the authorised flag of the said Award to be flown during that

time by the said body and for the device thereof to be displayed in the manner authorised by

Our Warrant of the fifth day of April 1976.

And We do further hereby authorise the said body during the five years of the currency of this Our

Award further to use and display in like manner the flags and devices of any current former Awards

by it received as prescribed in the eighth Clause of Our said Warrant.

Given at Our Court at St. James's under Our Royal Sign Manual this twenty-first day of April in the

year of Our Lord 1990 in the thirty-ninth year of Our Reign.

By the Sovereign's Command.

The Queen's Award for Export Achievement, an award unusual
in that it is signed by both the prime minister (Mrs Thatcher at the time) and the sovereign

INTERLUDE 5: MENUET

The Queen's Award

MY WORK with Advisory Services was interdisciplinary, multilingual and multinational. The Advisory Services group was based in the UK but had extensive international connections with clients and investigators. We employed a number of eminent medical and scientific consultants in different countries; staff operated in all the major European languages. There is no doubt that we benefited from the reputation of clinical trials in the UK: our clients knew that a product accepted by the UK regulatory authorities was likely to achieve registration in most countries. The company therefore prepared clinical trial protocols for international clients in accordance with the standards laid down by the UK and EEC authorities and also those of the US Food and Drug Administration in order to encompass future exports to the UK. Between 1971 and 1990 treatments for diseases ranging from heart failure, cancer and Alzheimer's disease, to peptic ulcers, back pain and asthma had been tested by our team at Advisory Services.

The Advisory Services group of companies won the Queen's Award for Export Achievement in 1990. The *Financial Times* (on 23 April 1990) noted: 'Advisory Services (Clinical and General), run by Dr Ralph Kohn, has brought a Queen's Award to Harley Street for the first time.' I regarded it as very much a company success and we would never have received this accolade without the support we enjoyed from friends and colleagues in the medical profession.

The award ceremony took place at a lunch at the Royal Automobile Club in London on 25 October of that year. The application had been supported by the deputy chief medical officer of the Department of Health, Dr Michael Abrams, by the president of Marks and Spencer plc, Lord Sieff, and by the director of the William Harvey Institute, Sir John Vane FRS, a Nobel laureate. At the lunch, Field Marshall Lord Bramall (representing the Queen) made the award.

The Queen's Award for Export? Eyebrows may have been raised by those unaware of our work: the question may have been, 'What exactly have you been exporting?' We received this particular accolade because the services provided by my firm were specifically, although not exclusively of course, tailored to the requirements of overseas clients. Scientific data provided by foreign clients was frequently not of a standard acceptable in the UK, and we offered programmes of investigations that produced internationally recognized British-generated data.

The group's personnel were fully conversant with scientific, regulatory and marketing considerations in major overseas territories and had a wide range of linguistic abilities to facilitate contact with foreign clients. Added to this, a drug accepted by our health authorities would be registered in practically all the countries of the world. The controlled clinical trial was developed in Britain and we were recipients of this award thanks to the excellence of British drug and clinical research. As Sir John Vane pointed out in a speech given on that occasion, our work had encouraged major international pharmaceutical companies to invest large-scale research

John Vane

funding in Britain; this, in turn, had made a huge contribution to maintaining the UK as the recognized centre of excellence in this field.

The following, rather more personal, tribute came from Sir David Jack FRS, research director at Glaxo. Needless to say I am embarrassed to print praise of this kind, but I take heart in that it comes from someone who has always been disinclined to do anything other than speak his mind:

> Ralph Kohn is a very unusual and gifted man … his achievement with Advisory Services is particularly unusual in that very few small companies, built up from nothing in less than twenty years, would be honoured in this way. He has succeeded in finding the most distinguished people in the UK to undertake research of the highest quality and competence—no one else could have done it so well.

PRELUDE XIX

Collecting

I THINK THAT COLLECTING is a hobby that must have come down to me directly from my father. In May 1940 we turned our back on our home in Amsterdam and left behind books, paintings and furniture without a second thought. They were only objects after all, and our lives were at stake. And yet, as someone who has spent my life in England gathering around me things that give me and my family pleasure—paintings, musical autographs and first editions, Japanese netsuke and so on—I am aware that it must have cost my father considerable pain to leave behind those dear possessions that he had acquired with care and affection over a lifetime. (My mother was more practical and less poetic in this respect.) I think in particular of the leather-bound volumes of the Talmud, an edition from Vilnius and a huge bibliophilic rarity that had brought my father so many hours of contemplation and joy. I have often wondered what happened to these books—whether they were stolen and sold (who would dare buy them at the time?) or whether the Germans burnt them along with so many sacred Jewish texts. A famous burning of the books took place in Berlin and other German cities on 10 May 1933. Works by a vast list of authors—not only Jewish writers but writings in English, French, and Russian that were in any way considered unfriendly to Nazi ideology—were destroyed in a series of grotesque public ceremonies whereby each book was named, as it was consigned to the flames, like a public enemy about to be executed. There are present-day memorials to these events in the Bebelplatz in Berlin and Römerberg Square in Frankfurt.

The Nazi ideologues like Goebbels, some of them well read, put a great emphasis on the power of books, indeed they were terrified of the power of the printed word, but the young men tasked with consigning countless treasures to the flames were mostly thugs and philistines. This was to the advantage of Jews who were forced to emigrate and had put their money into autographs or precious books. The ignorant guards at the German border searched people for hidden money or jewels, but were oblivious to bundles of what they considered to be meaningless old papers. In this way many precious musical or literary items were brought into this country and America, helping to finance the emigration of these poor exiles; after many years these treasures eventually found their way into museums. A lot of this was to do with the sheer portability of paper items. If my father had possessed a priceless first edition or a musical autograph, a matter of a few pages, he would have been able to bring it with him aboard the SS *Bodegraven* on that fateful day. (If he had been a violinist he might have carried a priceless Stradivarius—people used to say that so many Jews were violinists, rather than pianists, because a fiddle is supremely portable in times of trouble.) We did indeed leave a piano behind in Amsterdam (and I left my violin, fortunately of no great value). But my father was able to slip into his pocket the document that was more precious to him than any other—the letter he had received years before from the Chortkover Rebbe (see page 31). Though of little commercial value at the time, these days I suspect it would fetch a considerable sum at an auction, if only because there are so many knowledgeable collectors of Judaica. It remains for me a family treasure with which I would never part.

When I first began to sing with any seriousness I bought simple working editions of the music that I needed for my studies. The most important thing for me, as for all musicians, was to lift the music from the page and bring it to life. But I had been brought up to have the utmost respect for old religious books, and for me music is something of a religion in its own right. It gives me enormous pleasure to hold a piece of musical history in my hands and to contemplate the myriad connections between past and present. In the 1980s (once Advisory Services was on a solid financial footing) I began to turn my attention to what I might call my 'Talmusical' studies—and this entailed the acquisition of items related to those great figures in the musical world whose work was of almost sacred significance to me. In this I was aided by two great men in the world of book- and music-dealing—the late Albi Rosenthal of the firm Otto Haas (Albi was undoubtedly the premier music-dealer of the twentieth century) and Dr Stephen Roe of the musical department of Sotheby's, a world expert on musical autographs and early editions who has also become a close family friend.

In 2001 Stephen Roe prepared a printed catalogue of my collection. In the foreword he wrote the following words: 'One can almost think of the catalogue as a fugue, with several themes, almost all of them related to the great Johann Sebastian, who dominates.' I make no apology for the fact that this is the case; by now the reader will have realized the extent of my devotion to this composer. At the heart of my collection is the autograph manuscript of Bach's cantata *Auf Christi Himmelfahrt allein* (*By Christ's Ascension alone*), BWV128; this belongs to the second great cycle of cantatas (1724/25) that the composer produced in Leipzig, the town of my birth. This autograph, that had first belonged to Bach's son Wilhelm Friedemann, is on 16 pages (8 folios); it is one of only two or three major autographs of Bach that are still in private hands. The work is dated 10 May 1725, 208 years to the day before the burning of the Jewish books in Berlin, a contrast

The first page of the autograph score of J S Bach's cantata *Auf Christi Himmelfahrt allein*, BWV 128

Another page from the autograph score of J S Bach's cantata *Auf Christi Himmelfahrt allein*, BWV128

between the highest and lowest levels of Germanic endeavour. On the first page we read Bach's personal epigraph: 'J[esu]. J[uva]. Festo Ascensionis. Xsti. Auff Christi Himmelfahrt allein' ('Jesu. Help. For the feast of Christ's Ascension. By Christ's Ascension alone').

The other items of Bach's handwriting in my collection—three handwritten receipts for music performed in annual memory of one Gottfried Krell—come from near the end of his life (1748 and 1749) when he was struggling with blindness. The 1749 entry is in a much larger hand (and thus more easily visible to the composer). This is also the late handwriting characteristic of the B minor Mass. I also possess a manuscript copy of four English Suites, Nos 1, 3, 5 and 6 (BWV806, 808, 810 and 811). Bach's autograph is lost, but these pages were written out by his pupil Heinrich Nicolaus Gerber and date from 1725, the same year as the cantata. Gerber made a number of copies of Bach's works as part of his studentship; this beautifully penned collection had clearly been seized from its rightful owners in the 1930s and it went to a German library in Halle. It was restored to its rightful owners and came up for sale in 1997.

I have autographs by five other composers, two of these again connected with Bach: Felix Mendelssohn's arrangement for violin and piano (made in Leipzig in 1846) of the opening movement of J S Bach's Partita in E major for unaccompanied violin, BWV1006, and Gustav Mahler's arrangement, in 1909, of an orchestral work based on the Bach Suites. (I also possess Mahler's copy of Bach's complete works published by the Bach-Gesellschaft with numerous annotations by Mahler who was clearly an avid student of Bach's works.) Although it may seem to the reader that Bach is the sole focus of my interests, it is not so— lieder have also been a passion of mine for over fifty years. (Stephen Roe wrote of the Bachian 'fugue subject' of my collection but noted that it also had 'counter-subjects' and 'counter-melodies'.) Franz Schubert's *Hagars Klage*, D5 (1811), is an extended ballad of 369 bars, modelled on the Swabian composer Zumsteeg, and based on the biblical theme of Hagar, Abraham's concubine, who was sent into the desert together with her son Ishmael. This is among the earliest, as well as the longest, of Schubert's compositions. Also in the collection is an autograph of Mendelssohn, a duet for female voices (later published as *Sonntagsmorgen*) entitled *Sonntagslied*, Op 77 No 1 (Uhland), and a particularly beautiful autograph of Brahms's immortal song *Feldeinsamkeit*, Op 86 No 2. I also have an album leaf dating from 1936 of an extract from Kurt Weill's *Die Dreigroschenoper*.

Although there is no doubt that viewing and touching a composer's autograph produces a very special frisson, the printed scores of the eighteenth and nineteenth centuries are far more beautifully produced than most modern editions, and one

The title-page and first page of music of the first edition of
J S Bach's *Clavier-Übung IV* ('Goldberg' Variations)

also feels a very strong connection with the past when reading and studying them.
My collection of printed music encompasses several main areas: Bach with various
offshoots, Gluck, Mozart, Beethoven, Mendelssohn and Schubert. I am not a
rigidly systematic collector so there are also miscellaneous items: for example, a first
edition of Haydn's *Die Jahreszeiten* (*The Seasons*, 1802), a vocal score inscribed by
Puccini of his *La Fanciulla del West* (1911) and a page of Gregorian chant from the
late fifteenth century. In addition there are items of Judaica, including ten volumes
of Abraham Zvi Idelson's *Hebräisch-Orientalischer Melodienschatz*, an anthology of
the liturgical songs of the Jewish traditions of Europe, the Middle East and North
Africa.

Among early editions of Bach's printed works I have the *Choralgesänge*, four
volumes from 1784–87, with a preface by C P E Bach and once the property of the
French pianist Alfred Cortot; also from Cortot's collection the *Motteten* (*Motets*)
from 1802 (the editions of both these works were printed in Leipzig); an edition
of the Bach *Magnificat* from 1811 printed in Bonn; the piano edition of the
St Matthew Passion prepared by Adolph Bernard Marx and published in Berlin

in 1830, and also the libretto of that great work with a preface by Carl Friedrich Zelter. This was printed for the performance of 1829, the first of that work since Bach's own time. Zelter, a composer and a builder, was the closest friend of Goethe's later years and the teacher of Felix Mendelssohn. His music influenced Schubert.

My most recent acquisition of a printed work has probably given me the most pleasure of all. This is one of the rarest of all printed editions of Bach, the 'Goldberg' Variations printed in 1741 in Nuremberg in Bach's own lifetime. There is no such title on the cover. This is the fourth book of *Clavier-Übung* that Bach published; at first glance it seems to be handwritten musical script—in fact this is the musical handwriting of the publisher, Balthasar Schmid, turned into print. As I hold this slim volume of music in my hands, recent performances of this incomparable work by my dear friend András Schiff (both at the Royal Society, and at the Wigmore Hall for his sixtieth birthday celebrations) come vividly alive for me.

Fugue XIX (in 2 voices)   RALPH KOHN *with* GRAHAM JOHNSON

GJ   There is only a small part of your collection ranged before us this afternoon but it would make any music-collector's mouth water! Of Gluck you have the first edition of *Orfeo ed Euridice* (1764) and the French first edition of *Alceste* (1783) which once belonged to Hector Berlioz. Mozart is represented by two collections of lieder as well as the first complete edition (1793) of the vocal score of *Die Zauberflöte*, K620; the first edition (1800) of the *Requiem*, K626; the first edition of the full score (1801) of *Don Giovanni*, K527; an early edition of the vocal score of *Le Nozze di Figaro*, K492, and Mozart's arrangement (published in 1803) of Handel's *Messiah* (*Der Messias*), K572. That's a lot of wonderful Mozart!

RK   Do you remember what Karl Barth said? 'When the angels sing to God, they sing Bach. When they sing amongst themselves they sing Mozart—and God eavesdrops.'

GJ   Beautifully said, but where does that leave Schubert and Beethoven? Let's see, as far as Beethoven is concerned, and apart from lieder, there is a first edition (1811) of his oratorio *Christus am Oelberge*, Op 85; the first edition of the full score (1826) of Symphony No 9, Op 125; and a handsome piano score of *Fidelio*, Op 72 which had once belonged to Joseph Tichatschek.

RK He was a tenor who gave up a life in medicine in order to be a singer—and became the first great Wagner singer—performing the role of Rienzi in 1842. Even if I had given up pharmacology I very much doubt whether I would have ended up singing Wagner.

GJ For the purposes of this conversation I asked if I could look at some of your collection of first editions of German lieder because that is my own field. Here they are, all ranged about us, but before we get to these exquisite nineteenth-century publications of music dear to us both, let's talk about the eighteenth century! On two memorable occasions I have been witness to the effect that sight of your Bach cantata manuscript has had on those who have been privileged to see it. It has to be kept in a bank safe, like many of your great treasures, but from time to time you permit it to emerge. I will always remember the enraptured face of the great tenor Peter Schreier in 1997 (he was on the Wigmore Hall Song Competition jury at the time) when he slowly leafed through its densely written pages.

RK Well, it is such a beautiful object and it tells us so much about Bach. The immense piety of the man is evident from the very first words he wrote at the top of the first page—here is someone who led a life that he daily dedicated, through music, to the service of God. The pressure under which he had to work must have been enormous. We feel dizzy with the complexity of task that he has taken on and the speed with which it had to be accomplished. We can somehow feel the sheer energy and the flood of inspiration that clearly carried him along, the economy with which he used the paper, with music flowing right to the edge of the page, the manner in which he made his revisions! It is all overwhelming and it somehow transports us back to 1725. My admired Stefan Zweig was one of the greatest collectors of manuscripts of the last century and he commented on how much he learned from studying the works of great composers and writers from their manuscripts. It is like being there at the moment of their creation. In studying the autograph of this cantata it is almost as if we are in Bach's presence and watching him at work.

GJ There is very little in any musical collection that could match this cantata, and yet that slim volume of piano music entitled simply 'Clavier-Übung' and containing the 'Goldberg' Variations, not the autograph of course but the first printed version, has a similar magic.

RK Bach himself must have held a volume exactly like this one in his hands. In seeing, even with some short-sighted difficulty, the fruit of his labours, I hope it gave him profound satisfaction.

GJ It is a most beautiful object, but I notice there is no mention of Goldberg on this title-page.

RK The story that led to this work being named the 'Goldberg' Variations was first revealed by Johann Nikolaus Forkel in his biography of Bach of 1802. According to Forkel, it was the task of one Goldberg, in the retinue of Count Kaiserling, the former Russian ambassador to the electoral court of Saxony, to play music in the middle of the night to his insomniac employer. Kaiserling commissioned the work from Bach, paying him handsomely. According to Forkel, young Goldberg became both Bach's pupil and his virtuoso interpreter. It is a very nice story but it is probably not true. I have the first edition of this biography by Forkel—*Über Johann Sebastian Bachs Leben*—as part of my collection …

GJ Is that what you mean by collecting Bach 'with various offshoots?'

RK Exactly. Everything that has touched Bach's life has a fascination for me. Because Forkel was Bach's first significant biographer I have an autograph letter of his, and also one by Johann Gottlieb Naumann from 1801 regarding plans for the new complete edition of Bach's work. Not to mention the autograph draft of a newspaper advertisement for a performance of Bach's *St Matthew Passion* that Mendelssohn himself wrote out in 1841.

GJ Perhaps Mendelssohn is important to you because he was the original, and most important, Jewish connection with Bach—the man who did so much to bring this composer back into the public eye with the first performance of the *St Matthew Passion* in modern times in 1829?

RK That is true, but I also love Mendelssohn as a composer in his own right of course. I have a copy of his quartets arranged in 1838 for piano duet, and a first edition of the full score of *Elijah*, actually the German version *Elias* published in 1847 shortly before his death …

GJ And you have the autograph of a beautiful Mendelssohn duet which brings us back to the world of the lied. You have some very fetching early editions of Mozart's lieder but it is Schubert who always first engages my attention. My eyes are drawn to this amazing Schubert autograph. *Hagars Klage* is the first song in the famous chronological complete edition of Schubert's lieder made by Eusebius Mandyczewski in 1894 …

RK And it is no longer considered to be Schubert's first song?

GJ Actually Schubert composed two rather long and rambling settings of *Lebenstraum* by Gabriele von Baumberg before *Hagars Klage*, real apprentice stuff, but that fact has emerged only in the last thirty years or so. For nearly a century *Hagars Klage*, with the Deutsch catalogue number 5, was taken to be Schubert's very first setting for voice and piano. He was only fourteen years old. I also believe that Schubert's choice of a poem about Hagar and the young Ishmael being cast into the wilderness reflects an adolescent composer's difficulties with his own tyrant of a father.

RK I had always wanted to own a Schubert manuscript and when this particular item came on the market it felt right—a substantial Schubert work on a famous Old Testament theme …

GJ Yes of course, it has a Jewish connection which is also one of the background themes of your collection as a whole. I have recently heard a fine young Israeli soprano named Hagar Sharvit accompanied by a pianist I admire very much, Ammiel Bushakevitz.

Autograph of *Hagars Klage* D5 by Franz Schubert

RK He won the accompanist's prize in the Wigmore Song Competition in 2013, didn't he?

GJ He did indeed! I wonder whether Hagar would ever sing this song that shares her name? Because of the young Schubert's inexperience in writing for singers it makes great demands on the voice. I see in looking at this autograph that there is a very lightly written-in second text above the text of the original poem by Clemens Schücking.

RK What was the point of a second text?

GJ It is a sign that this work was so well known to Schubert's friends and contemporaries at the Imperial Konvikt in Vienna (where he was a pupil) that they furnished the piece with a light-hearted alternative text, a kind of parody. You mentioned the effect the Bach manuscript has on people—for me this autograph of Schubert's *Hagars Klage* is powerful evidence of a young fourteen-year-old genius in the making, surrounded by his school friends, and engaging in the kind of pranks that young people have always got up to at their informal gatherings. The replacement text, though incomplete, is risqué by the standards of the time. That Schubert's friends made fun of this piece in this way is a sign that they knew and admired the original version. At fourteen years old, Schubert was already something of a celebrity in the eyes of his own circle.

RK Well as you know Schubert is an incredibly important composer for me. Here are the first editions of the *Gesänge des Harfners*, Op 12, and *Die Sehnsucht*, Op 39.

GJ This music is much later than the teenage composer's autograph *Hagars Klage*. Remember that Schubert was twenty-four when his music first appeared in print. These editions are both beautiful in appearance but, if I may say so, the second of these, with *Die Sehnsucht* on the title-page, is an example of how inefficient the whole world of Viennese publishing was—bogged down by laziness, ineptitude and *Schlamperei*. The real title of the song, a setting of Schiller, is simply *Sehnsucht* without the 'Die'. In other editions there are examples of the wrong names of poets being printed and so on.

RK Well what about *Winterreise*? A lot of people refer to *Die Winterreise*, but on this title-page it is simply *Winterreise*.

GJ In this case the publisher Tobias Haslinger, a favourite of Beethoven's, has got it right! The poet Wilhelm Müller had referred to *Die Winterreise* but Schubert himself excised the definite article. This is a beautifully printed edition and all the more poignant because it is said that the proofs of the second part of the cycle were read by the composer on his deathbed. It appeared in Vienna only a few days after the composer's death. *Schwanengesang* is also a Haslinger publication but there remains a controversy about whether the two poets' groups of songs contained in this work, seven by the poet Rellstab and six by Heine, plus a stray Seidl masterpiece, *Die Taubenpost*, all belong together.

RK But they work so well together in performance! When we recorded them the sequence seemed utterly right, almost inevitable.

GJ Exactly! You make the most valid point that most of the musicologists have missed. I think it possible that Schubert talked about the shape of this project with Haslinger in the last days of his life; it is very possible also that the collection is not simply a botched arrangement by an irresponsible publisher, but a cycle that could well have represented the composer's final wishes. This is rather an unfashionable view, but it is gaining ground in some academic circles.

RK As far as I can see there is nothing wrong with title-pages of *Auf dem Wasser zu singen* and the Op 92 songs beginning with *Der Musensohn*.

GJ They are both sumptuous editions, a pleasure to hold in the hand, but there is always a background story to precious objects of this kind. The two publishers were very different personalities. Diabelli, who issued *Auf dem Wasser zu singen*, was the kingpin of all the Viennese publishers but he was also a wheeler-dealer of the first water. When he was first asked to publish Schubert's songs he was haughtily contemptuous of the young man's music, agreeing only to publish the works 'on commission', at no risk to himself with Schubert's friends meeting all the expenses. When Diabelli discovered that this music was selling like hot cakes he cornered the composer (who was ill and very vulnerable at the time) and conned him into selling him the copyright of songs, including the immortal *Erlkönig* and *Gretchen am Spinnrade*, at a cheap price. These songs made Diabelli a lifelong fortune while the composer remained short of money.

RK I hope you are not going to tell me that Diabelli was some type of villainous Jewish businessman? The kind of stereotype the Nazis tried to pillory?

GJ Far from it, Diabelli was Catholic; he was extremely lucky to become immortalized by the fact that Beethoven contributed a massive piano work—the so-called 'Diabelli' Variations—based on a banal little waltz theme the publisher sent out, calling for a variation of it from every composer in Vienna. Schubert replied with the requested single variation. Beethoven, insulted to be considered just one of the herd, wiped the floor with his rivals by providing thirty-three variations! I was sitting next to you at Wigmore Hall when András Schiff played this masterpiece, together with the 'Goldberg' Variations, for his sixtieth birthday.

RK That was one of the most extraordinary concerts I have ever attended, a super-human marathon.

GJ I agree! Now, back to Schubert … the other publisher we have here, Maximillian Leidesdorf who brought out Schubert's Op 92 (*Der Musensohn*, *Auf dem See* and *Geistes Gruss*) was Jewish and was one of Schubert's good friends. Leidesdorf did not have a dishonest bone in his body, but he was inefficient and slow-moving, a bit of a schlemiel. He was a depressive and had made a hash of publishing the *Die schöne Müllerin* cycle in 1824—it was late, badly publicized, full of printer's errors and failed to make any impression on the public. Schubert was depressed about this, but he realized that Leidesdorf was a much nicer person than Diabelli. As a result he allowed Leidesdorf to publish this late opus number from 1828.

But this is enough about the long-suffering Schubert, I am anxious to look at your Beethoven collection, songs that are much rarer for collectors than those by Schubert. You have three beautiful items and once again they were all printed in Vienna.

RK This is music that is very dear to me. I have recorded with you *Adelaide* and some of the Op 52 settings and of course the *An die ferne Geliebte* cycle.

GJ I don't think there is a music-collector in the world who would not envy you this *Adelaide* edition (see illustration on page 232). It dates from 1797 and it is extremely rare—I've never seen one of these. It is this music that somehow unites your own love of Italian *arie antiche* and the German lied. The Op 52 collection, although it contains songs of comparatively minor importance, is very handsome. But what a jewel you have in this edition of *An die ferne Geliebte*! This is an example of another hidden Jewish theme in your collection because Alois Jeitteles, the poet Beethoven had chosen to provide him with a text that would enable him to write the first song cycle, was in fact Jewish.

RK This played no part in my decision to acquire the edition, I simply loved this music very much and have often performed the cycle, recording it on several occasions.

GJ It seems that Beethoven had a very clear idea of the interconnected cycle he wanted to write and commissioned a sequence of poems to provide the framework he required. There is no doubt that the appearance of this work in 1816 provoked an enormous crisis for the nineteen-year-old Schubert who had imagined himself the preeminent composer of lieder in Vienna. Beethoven had composed no lieder since 1810 and Schubert had composed literally hundreds in 1815 and 1816. And suddenly, just when Schubert was feeling secure about being the most important lieder composer in town, Beethoven emerged with this ground-breaking work that pointed song in an entirely new direction. The younger composer spent the rest of his life searching for an answer to the question of how best to match that innovation and compose his own song cycle. His eventual answers to this conundrum, seven and eleven years later, were the cycles *Die schöne Müllerin* and *Winterreise*.

RK   We have recorded both these great works of course. It astonishes me how a great genius like Schubert felt himself insufficient in comparison to Beethoven.

GJ   In the same way a great composer like Johannes Brahms felt himself unworthy in comparison to Schubert. And speaking of Brahms, what could be more beautiful than your Brahms autograph of *Feldeinsamkeit*, written out on manuscript paper with a pattern printed in beautiful blue borders? I note that this is exactly the same key in which you sing the song and that Brahms here writes out the vocal line in the bass clef.

RK   There is no doubt that sharing these things with someone who knows the music well, and loves it as I do, is a very special pleasure.

GJ   What a privilege it has been to spend this time here with you and all these mementoes of some of the world's greatest composers. The emotions aroused by this experience give rise to the kind of inspiration that is not only intellectual but somehow physical. One can actually touch the past and hold it both in one's hands and in one's heart.

RK   That is exactly how I feel. If the possession of a fragment of a great man's output does not necessarily teach one anything about how to perform the music, it heightens one's sense of belonging to the same tradition, of being privileged to exist in the same world as these great people, even if separated by hundreds of years. There is no doubt that I feel unaccountably closer to composers like Bach, Schubert and Brahms after spending time in the company of their handwriting. It is as if in acquiring a fragment of their output I have been able somehow to travel towards them. I'm sorry if that sounds pretentious …

Autograph of *Feldeinsamkeit* by Johannes Brahms,
with the composer's signature on the fourth page of the manuscript

GJ Not at all. My own collection is very small in comparison to yours, but I feel exactly
the same way. We are clearly both men who believe in the unaccountable spiritual
power of the talisman, or holy relic, translated here into secular terms. In your case,
it may go back all the way to your father's belief in the protective power of the
letter he received when he carried with him the wonderfully ornate and evocative
handwriting of the Chortkover Rebbe.

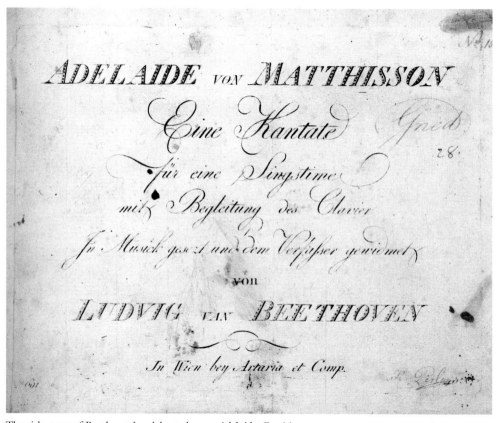

The title-page of Beethoven's celebrated song *Adelaide*, Op 46

INTERLUDE 6: DOUBLE

A question of attribution

I ALWAYS REMEMBER having pictures in the home and collecting paintings in a modest way has always been important to me. In Amsterdam we had a large watercolour of a *shadchan* who made a circle between his thumb and first finger signifying that he had pulled off a good match on behalf of his clients. I suppose it is inevitable that perhaps the most important picture in my collection should have something to do with music, and a great deal to do with Bach in particular. The painting is ascribed to Balthasar Denner (1685–1749)—thus he was born in the same year as Bach, but died a year before the composer. It almost certainly dates from the 1730s. Although there is an illustration below of this

Presumed to be Johann Sebastian Bach and three of his sons by Balthasar Denner

family portrait, the verbal description by Stephen Roe from the catalogue of my collection published in 2001 is eloquent and reveals details that merely glancing at a picture often fails to provide:

> The fine portrait depicts a family of four musicians: a middle-aged man, a small boy and two youths. The man is seated, holding what seems to be a cello, the bow in his right hand as if to play; but, in fact, the back of the instrument is facing the bow. The second figure is a young boy, wearing a blue coat, the fingers of his left hand touch a violin resting on the table. Manuscript music is placed variously, some lying under the boy's violin and elsewhere on the table and on a small music stand. The third figure, a much older boy, dressed in red, clutches a wooden transverse flute. The fourth is older still, resplendent in a dark coat trimmed with gold, with a scarlet and gold waistcoat and holds a violin in his left hand. An empty seat stands on the far right of the picture, the music stand with manuscript music lies open before it. Although the music has titles and notes on the paper, all are schematic and no definite words or music is legible. In the background, a swagged curtain is pulled back to reveal a blue sky with many white clouds and a landscape of trees.

The question is: is this a picture of J S Bach and his family? The attribution to Denner, and the claim that this was a portrait of Bach *en famille*, was first made in 1982 by the art historian, Helmut Börsch-Supan. There is another copy of this portrait in Stuttgart (also depicted in *The Kohn Collection of Music*) which is very similar (although of somewhat inferior quality according to Christoph Wolff). This is the property of the Internationale Bachakademie in Stuttgart. Nicholas Kenyon identified the other sitters here (left to right) all as Bach's sons: Gottfried Heinrich Bach (1724–1763), Johann Gottfried Bernhard Bach (1715–1739) and Carl Philipp Emanuel Bach (1714–1788) to the far right of the picture. The empty chair would have represented the eldest of the Bach sons, Wilhelm Friedemann Bach (1710–1784) who left the Leipzig home for Dresden in 1733. If the painting dates from 1733 or 1734 Johann Sebastian paterfamilias would have been forty-eight or -nine, Gottfried Heinrich nine or ten, Johann Gottfried Bernhard eighteen or nineteen, and Carl Philipp Emanuel nineteen or twenty. The fact that this copy exists in duplicate seems to me something of importance, or at least it shows its principal sitter was considered a person of some significance. Is it simply a coincidence that the most famous portrait of Bach, that of Elias Gottlob Haussmann (1695–1774), court painter at Dresden and official portraitist at Leipzig, also exists in two versions? At this point in talking about the finer details of Bach iconography, I have to emphasize how greatly enriched my life has been by my friendship with two remarkable men who are deeply associated with Bach:

Christoph Wolff, emeritus professor of music at Harvard, and until recently director of the Bach Archive is without doubt the greatest living expert on the composer. He was recently presented with the Medal of Honour of the City of Leipzig. Christoph's cousin, Christian Wolff, Vicar of St Thomas Leipzig, has also become a dear friend. Both Christoph and Christian attended our Golden Wedding celebrations in London in 2013.

Now back to the Denner portrait! In his foreword to *The Kohn Collection* Graham Johnson admits he is not at all a Bach expert while making a case for 'The Kohn Portrait' as one actually depicting J S Bach and three of his six surviving sons:

Christoph Wolff

Does this genial, but not handsome, broad-faced man in early middle-age not resemble the face we have come to recognize as Bach's in the famous portrait? It is surely of little importance that he is not sitting in front of a keyboard, for this is an off-duty portrait which reflects the pride of the father who had boasted in 1730 that he could form out of his own family a vocal and instrumental concert ensemble; also, how might a painter have efficiently organized three full-faced children's portraits around a keyboard with the composer in profile? Balthasar Denner (and it seems likely, although not certain that he was the painter) was not the technician to do it. There is something about the portrait, a decent piece of work but not masterful, that suggests a sitting at short notice: four people gathered round a table was surely an easier and quicker task for the painter, and an effective means of showing Bach as head of a dynasty and teacher to his prodigious brood. One of the nicest things about this picture is that it seems that we have opened a door by mistake and interrupted a music lesson; the mood is relaxed but also serious—just as one would expect when the Master imparted his wisdom to his children.

The domestic background (rather than a portrait posed in the Thomaskirche) surely reflects the composer's pride in the newly refurbished apartment that his family had occupied since April 1731 (even if this was not as grand as is suggested by the background here). It is plausible that Denner, who also made a portrait of Handel, should wish to paint Bach; it is also possible that the painter passed through Leipzig on a visit to Dresden—it was difficult to do otherwise when travelling on the post-chaise routes of the time. It also makes much sense that the composer himself, at an especially proud period of his life as a family man, should have chosen to be painted in a way that suggests both fecundity and prosperity.

And there is one other point. Just how many fathers could muster such a line-up of talented and musical children? If there are other contesting contemporaries for this line-up, who are they? Would we not know about them somehow? There were other musical dynasties of course—Graun and Naumann, for example—but no one has yet suggested that this portrait concerns one of those families. Christian Ferdinand Abel (1683–1737) is the most recent contender, but there has been no proof that this portrait represents this very much less celebrated musician and his children. On the basis of a chain of circumstantial evidence, and in the absence of a positive identification of who these musicians are, if not the Bachs, I cast my vote for Johann Sebastian as a proud paterfamilias who is confident enough in his growing fame to pose as a member of an ensemble rather than as a soloist. And who knows, it may have hung for a time on the wall of that very apartment—the sort of snapshot which would grace the home of any up-and-coming eighteenth-century householder. It is a fact that there was a portrait in the Bach family's possession until 1820. If this is not the picture, how many other contenders are there? When pondering such questions as this I come to the limit of my knowledge of Bach iconography and retire as gracefully as possible from the scholastic fray.

In the twelve years since Graham Johnson wrote that passage nothing has changed in terms of the picture's attribution. After I bought the picture at Sotheby's I contacted the previous owner whose family had possessed the portrait for many years. He told me that the picture had always been referred to as 'J S B and three of his sons'. Few people argue now that this group portrait was painted by anyone other than Balthasar Denner, but whether or not it is a portrait of Johann Sebastian Bach is still unproven. There has been a recent biography of Bach that has used this portrait (or the Stuttgart copy) for a cover, but this has no real meaning in terms of the disciplined field of the composer's iconography. If this were ever proved to be a picture of the great composer, the value of the portrait would be enormous (so

Christoph Wolff informs me), and as such an extremely good investment. But as with so much else in my life, clever investment was the last thing that motivated me. I bought the picture because it gave me pleasure, and the mere possibility that it might depict my favourite composer is enough to justify its being an honoured part of my collection.

I am also delighted to own a pastel of Bach's distinguished son, Carl Philipp Emanuel Bach. The painter is A F Oeser, although there were copies made by other artists such as Johann Friedrich Reifenstein.

A F Oeser's portrait of Carl Philipp Emanuel Bach

By the way, Zahava and I are delighted to be friendly with the only surviving blood member of the Bach clan—Hans-Jürgen Smekal, a descendant of one of the great composer's sons, Johann Christoph Friedrich Bach, also known as the 'Bückeburger Bach'. We met Herr Smekal first at the Bach festival in Leipzig in 2009 and he always sends us *Lebkuchen* at Christmas time.

Enjoying a moment of relaxation with Herr Hans-Jürgen Smekal

PRELUDE XX

Beyond business THE KOHN FOUNDATION

IN MANY WAYS the Queen's Award, and the recognition it bestowed, was the high point and culmination of my time at Advisory Services. It was some three or four years after this that I decided that I no longer wished to continue to be actively involved in clinical trials. In 1995 I decided to sell the company to the management; there were some of my colleagues at 14 Harley Street who wished to continue there with the work in progress and I happily passed on to them, for next to nothing, the name and good will of the company. They managed to keep it going for another couple of years but, as my daughter Hephzi noted in *Fugue XVIII*, the success of Advisory Services was perhaps overly dependent on my rather singular way of doing things. By then I was sixty-seven, retirement age for most people. I had no intention of retiring, as such, but once again in my life I needed to change direction. The time had come to begin giving back something to the communities of science and music that had given me so much joy throughout my life. It was fortunate that the good management of my finances (much helped by my astute solicitor and dear friend Morty Rabin as well as my ever-vigilant and brilliant accountant and close friend Tony Forwood) enabled me to begin a new kind of professional activity, the same kind of turning point as my decision, twenty-five years earlier, to establish my own company in the field of clinical trials.

This is how the Kohn Foundation, and my work as philanthropist, came into being. I find this is rather too pompous a word to use, but I can truly say that the happiest years of my life have been these more recent ones when I have worked almost daily in trying to make a difference to organizations that are associated with both the sciences and music, as well as Jewish causes and certain deserving individual cases and humanitarian aid.

The motto of the Kohn Foundation is taken from something Winston Churchill said: 'We make a living by what we get, but we make a life by what we give.' People who have been successful and made enough money to provide for themselves and their families have an obligation, it seems to me, to help the community in which they have experienced that success. For me charitable work is a necessity, and it saves one from death in both a spiritual and physical sense—and this is according to the Talmud!

I have had various near-death experiences in my life, but the following incident was the most hair-raising. On Christmas Eve sometime in the early 1990s, my wife Zahava and I were in Johannesburg in South Africa. We had signed up from our hotel to take a bus tour of the famous black township of Soweto. By that time bus tours were apparently regarded as a safe way of visiting the locale. We missed the bus (it had departed early, without us) and the tour agency offered to arrange a private driver so that we could visit Soweto. The driver concerned had a large, new Combi vehicle and took us to various interesting (as well as distressing) places within the large township. At the end he offered to

with Tony Forwood

drive us to Diepkloof, off the beaten track of the tourist vehicles, so we could see the poverty of the 'real' Soweto. We agreed, perhaps rather foolishly. Zahava and I got out of the car and entered into a hut, the poverty and dirt of which were indescribable. It was incomprehensible to me that human beings should live like this; I had never seen poverty of this kind, even after many years of travelling in India. There was a sick old man lying in this hell-hole. Without thinking about it I bent down and gave him a certain amount of money and said that he should buy himself something for Christmas. I don't know whether he fully understood my words but I remember he thanked me in a weak voice.

As we turned round and left the hut we found ourselves face-to-face with three youths in their late teens pointing guns. We were ordered to give them everything we had. I quickly emptied my pockets and handed over my wallet and my watch; Zahava gave them her handbag and took off her rings and jewellery. There was no physical violence but there was an alarming amount of anger and aggravation in the air. The young men climbed into the Combi and at first had difficulty starting it. Fortunately, they got the car going, and roared into the distance in a cloud of dust leaving Zahava and me (and the tour guide) deeply shaken.

There was a police station just up the road that we were able to reach on foot. This small fortress in the midst of what was a very violent and dangerous area was manned by an Afrikaans police officer, and we told him our story. 'Folks,' he said, 'I'm finding it difficult to believe that you are standing here with this story. This is the first time in Diepkloof that anyone has come out alive from this kind of incident.' (Two New Zealand tourists who had been in the same area recently had been murdered after giving up their valuables.) This of course brought home to us that it would have been the easiest thing in the world for those young men to have gunned us down without giving it a second thought. We have pondered why they did not do so: was it because the sound of gunshot would have alerted the police up the road? They certainly wanted to get away with the new Combi without the inconvenience of being chased.

Soweto is one of the most complicated places on earth for outsiders to visit; I still have no idea whether the driver who delivered us to that place was 'in on the plot', and I have no idea whether our assailants knew or cared about the old man to whom I had given money. It is possible that made a difference to the way we were treated, and perhaps we were seen as somehow not typical of the white people of that country, not immediately recognizable as 'the enemy'. What I do know is that seconds before that potentially fatal confrontation, something age-old and dignified had taken place between that old man and myself: the giving and receiving of alms. I had felt compassion at his plight and I had given him a token, however inadequate, of my wanting to make a small difference in his life. And this is where I repeat that old Talmudic saying 'Zedaka tazil mimavet': 'Charity saves one from death'.

Where, and how, did the work of the Kohn Foundation begin? The large liver disease symposium held in 1987, which was magnificently organized by my daughter Hephzi (as recounted in a previous chapter), had been preceded, five years earlier, by a very important symposium on osteoporosis chaired by my great friend Allan Dixon; this had been held at the Royal Society in 1982, and was organized by Advisory Services. Allan Dixon believed that a patient group might bring pressure to bear on public authorities to allocate more resources to the treatment and prevention of this insidious disease. In 1986 he had founded the National Osteoporosis Society with Commander Dickie Rowe in Bath. The society was launched with backing from the Department of Health and from the government's chief medical officer. It worked to raise public awareness of the condition. In 1999 I decided to establish the Kohn Award for achievement and excellence in the field of osteoporosis. One of the earlier recipients of the award was the remarkable Linda Edwards who was the director of the National Osteoporosis Society until she died in 2002; in this case the award was posthumous. The eighth recipient of the award, in 2007, was HRH The Duchess of Cornwall who has been a supporter of the society for over ten years, as well as a patron and president. Over this period she had undertaken a variety of activities on behalf of the society, including opening

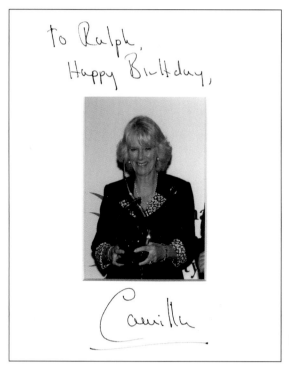

To Ralph,
Happy Birthday,

Camilla

HRH The Duchess of Cornwall

scanners, visiting hospitals, invigorating support groups and hosting dinners. The Duchess continues to be of enormous importance to the National Osteoporosis Society as a truly 'hands-on' president.

It was the establishment of this prize that signalled a change in my outlook (there is a list of the recipients on page 349). There is no doubt that giving away money to good causes is easier in America, where the tax issues involving charitable giving are much more generous, but I feel this is used as an excuse by a number of British people who imagine they might suddenly become extremely giving by nature if American taxation conditions miraculously pertained here. My response to that is that giving to good causes is a good deal more rewarding for its own sake than merely being tax efficient. As early as 1991 I had established the Ralph and Zahava Kohn Charitable Trust—this now became the Kohn Foundation. I had been a regular contributor to charitable causes for most of my life—I can truly say that I was raised that way—but now it became possible to give on a larger scale.

I had long known about the work of the Royal Society through organizing symposia, but this great and historic organization now became an important part of my life. The next chapter in this book is devoted to my work with the Royal Society. Other recipients were the Foundation for Science and Technology, the Academy of Medical Sciences, the Royal College of Physicians and the Institute of Hepatology. My decades of work with clinicians made me an enthusiastic donor who was often something of an old friend and insider. On other occasions I first came into contact with some of these august institutions as a result of being introduced to them by an intersection of old friendships and long-standing professional associations. I continued to support the National Osteoporosis Society which came into being thanks to the visionary Allan Dixon (and thus has a great claim on my loyalty and affections). We also supported the Vega Science Trust set up by my distinguished friend and Nobel laureate Sir Harold Kroto FRS (whose parents came to the UK from Berlin in the 1930s). After seventeen years' activity this organization closed in 2012, but it has left an amazing legacy of science films that can be viewed online.

The Kohn Foundation is also very active in Israel. We have an ongoing association with the Weizmann Institute through my Alma Mater, Manchester University, and the eminent Dame Nancy Rothwell FRS, professor of physiology and also president and vice-chancellor of the university. The Kohn Foundation has

with Ephraim Katzir, the fourth president of Israel (1973–1978), who had also been head of the department of biophysics at the Weizmann Institute of Science

To Dr. Ralph Kohn, with best wishes —

Jerusalem   Ephraim Katzir   September 1976

twice supported three-year programmes whereby students from Manchester University are enabled to complete their doctoral studies at the Weizmann Institute. We have also supported the Haifa Technion, the Hebrew University in Jerusalem, and the Hadassah Hospital.

The late Adam Klug, son of Sir Aaron and Lady Klug, was a lecturer at Ben Gurion University of the Negev, Beersheba, Israel. He was an economic historian stricken with pancreatic cancer and he died in his forties. My admiration for Aaron and Liebe in facing this great tragedy in their lives knows no bounds. In speaking to Lady Klug I had learned of her late son's passion for the history of Palestine under British rule. In memory of Adam Klug the Kohn Foundation donated to the Ben Gurion University library a century's worth of volumes of Hansard, the official record of British parliamentary proceedings—Adam had always wanted this reference work to be available to his students. This reminds me that the world-famous Weizmann Institute in Rehovot, south of Tel Aviv, began with a building in memory of Daniel Sieff, the son of Israel Sieff (the Sieff family were co-founders of Marks and Spencer), who had died at the age of eighteen. Thanks to Chaim Weizmann the Daniel Sieff Institute, built in 1933, stands at the core of the huge and impressive centre of learning as it is today, the jewel in the crown of Israeli science.

The Weizmann
Institute, Rehovot

Fugue XX *(in 2 voices)* RALPH KOHN *with* GRAHAM JOHNSON

GJ Apart from donations to deserving institutions, it seems to be very much a part of your desire to remember and honour certain significant men in science and music.

RK This is true. In 2003 the Foundation endowed the Ernst Chain prize at Imperial College. The idea of instituting this award came from Sir Richard Sykes FRS, the rector of Imperial College, who realized there was no overt recognition of Chain on the Imperial College campus. How often had I visited Chain in his apartment within Imperial College and sung lieder to this enthusiastic accompaniment! I felt this was a fitting way of repaying my personal debt to someone who had been at the centre of my studies in Italy, and later a very close friend. Moreover, Chain had been instrumental in bringing certain aspects of the esoteric academic world of science kicking and screaming into the second half of the twentieth century where the pharmacological application of scientific discoveries changed the lives of millions for the better. The Ernst Chain prize was designed to be awarded to a career scientist who has made an original and substantive contribution to the field of science which had furthered, or was likely to further, understanding or management of human diseases. The recipients of the Chain Prize are listed in an appendix to this book (see page 348).

   The other scientific prize with which the Kohn Foundation is associated is connected with the Royal Institution (a venerable organization founded in 1799 with the aim of introducing new technologies and teaching science to the general public). This is the Sir Henry Dale prize in memory of the English pharmacologist and physiologist who received the Nobel prize in 1936 for his study of acetylcholine as an agent in the chemical transmission of nerve impulses. A list of the Henry Dale prizewinners is similarly given in an appendix (see page 346). By strange coincidence Henry Dale was the brother of a distinguished composer named Benjamin Dale who was warden of the Royal Academy of Music, an institution that has also had a great deal to do with the Kohn Foundation.

GJ Some of your charitable donations are one-off gifts, but you seem interested in fostering longer-term relationships with institutions. Three of these, the Royal Society, the Wigmore Hall and the Royal Academy of Music you write about in following chapters.

RK The Royal Society is a very special place for me. I began by organizing clinical trials and symposia there in the 1970s and have grown closer and closer to this venerable institution over the years. The friendships I have made with the other Fellows of the Royal Society are among the most precious to me.

Steven Pinker, linguist and psychologist, recipient of the Henry Dale prize in 2004

GJ For the moment let us concentrate on the Kohn Foundation's work in the musical sphere. I know that from time to time you help deserving individuals, because I was closely involved in one such case.

RK You are talking about Laurie Rubin, the American mezzo-soprano?

GJ Yes, as you well remember, Laurie is blind. She was born without retinae and yet she became a considerable singer. Some years ago now, I heard her at a masterclass in California and was immediately struck by her musical ability and her amazing spirit. She is an exceptional woman. I came back to London, told you all about her, and you were fascinated with the story.

RK I was indeed. She came to London under our auspices to make a CD with Mark Brown that was supported by the Kohn Foundation. She, and her pianist David Wilkinson, gave a charity recital at our home that made an unforgettable impression. The audience were beside themselves with the grace and passion with which Laurie presented her programme. I have seldom seen a person handicapped in this way who is as vivacious, amusing and completely without self-pity. A lot of the credit for this goes to her remarkable mother, Lilly Rubin, who seems to have brought up her daughter to believe that there is no reason why she should not achieve anything she wishes.

GJ Laurie claims to dream in colours. Indeed she has recently written a moving autobiography entitled *Do You Dream in Color? Insights from a Girl without Sight*. She had originally written a poem entitled *Do You Dream in Color?* which was set to music by the composer Bruce Adolphe and given its first performance by Laurie herself. There is still a great deal of prejudice about blind people, and the viability of a singing career is often judged in regard to its operatic potential. Of course working on stage in a dramatic production with other members of the cast is an enormous challenge, but Laurie has managed even this on occasion; she needs a helpful and imaginative producer however, and most of them would not even begin to try to be helpful. Everywhere Laurie goes she seems always able to transcend her own limitations and the prejudices of others. She now lives in Hawaii with her partner Jenny and takes a very lively part in the state's musical life.

RK Getting to know Laurie and her family was inspirational for me. Helping her to make a recording here in London was a stepping stone that the Kohn Foundation was able to provide.

with *left to right* Lilly Rubin (the singer's mother), the accompanist David Wilkinson, the mezzo-soprano Laurie Rubin, and Brian Rubin, the singer's brother

GJ   With your work at the Royal Academy of Music you make it possible for a great
     many young people to get to know and perform music they otherwise would not—
     the music of Bach above all. But you also take part in special projects for
     established, even world-famous musicians.

RK   I presume you are referring to Sir John Eliot Gardiner and his Bach Cantata
     Pilgrimage. Once we had clarified that this project was primarily musical (and not
     a theological celebration), I was delighted to become committee chairman of that
     project, as well as an honorary trustee of the Monteverdi Choir and Orchestra.
     I felt that John Eliot's idea was truly inspired—he took on the gargantuan task
     of performing all the church cantatas of Bach—this was in 2000, the 250th
     anniversary of the composer's death—in fifty cities across thirteen European
     countries. There was a total of 198 cantatas in 59 concerts. No fewer than 282
     musicians were involved. As if this was not sufficiently impressive, all these cantatas
     were all to be performed at the appropriate time in the liturgical year for which they
     had been originally composed! Whenever possible the pilgrimage followed Bach's
     own footsteps in Thuringia and Saxony, including many of the beautiful churches
     where Bach himself had performed. The whole thing was a vast logistical enterprise
     executed with dazzling precision. The pilgrimage started off in Weimar on
     Christmas Day 1999 and ended a year later with three concerts in New York.
     Getting to know John Eliot and his charming wife Isabella was a great pleasure.
     We have Bach in common—I am able to recognize a fellow Bach-fanatic when I see
     one! I simply felt that an idea as inventive and adventurous as this required backing.
     We had a committee that raised funds from various sources but the Kohn
     Foundation was solidly behind the enterprise. John Eliot has recently written a
     fascinating book about Bach and I have learned a great deal about the composer in
     reading it. Between Christoph Wolff and John Eliot I feel I would always be well
     informed about even the smallest detail of this composer's life and work.

GJ   Apart from as to whether he and his sons really posed for a portrait by Balthasar
     Denner! The magic name, as always with you, was Bach. But as I well know,
     because I have accompanied you in German lieder so often, you have a strong
     sympathy for the vocal music of the nineteenth century, as well as instrumental
     music and chamber music.

Presenting John Eliot Gardiner with the Bach prize at the Royal Academy of Music

RK For this reason we began the Kohn concert series at Jesus College, Oxford, where my dear friend John Krebs is the highly musical principal (besides being a world-renowned zoologist). He is the son of the famous German-born biochemist and Nobel prizewinner, Hans Adolf Krebs, who was a friend and colleague of Ernst Chain. There is another Kohn series of concerts at Trinity, Cambridge, and one at Peterhouse (the former master of the college was John Meurig Thomas about whom I will write in a later chapter).

GJ I have taken part in recitals in two of these series, at Jesus as well as at Peterhouse, and I must say they are attended by a wide range of students and staff. And I realize that the concerts at Trinity and at Peterhouse are not just vocal recitals—they occupy a broad spectrum of classical music-making.

RK I had always hoped that some of the students would be hearing this kind of music-making for the first time, that the chance to hear music on the doorsteps of their own colleges might make a difference to how they think about music for the rest of their lives. I would like to share with you a letter I received from just such a university student—the letter is undated, but I received it a couple of years ago:

Dear Sir R Kohn,

I am writing to you to express my gratitude.

My name is Sam Channon and I am currently studying for a master's degree in mathematics at Trinity College, Cambridge. Until fairly recently I had almost forgotten about classical music entirely. It is with regards to this that I write to you.

From a young age my mother exposed me to lots of music, not only classical, but a very varied collection. However, as a musician and student of the Guildhall School of Music and Drama, she was able to kindle an appreciation for orchestral and choral music that is rarely seen in young children today, especially where I was born in Devon.

As a result of this influence I learned to play the trumpet as a child. Unfortunately this skill ended up escaping me as the lures of rugby and other teenage distractions took most of my time. By the time I arrived to study maths at Cambridge, my connection with traditional classical music was gone.

However, at Trinity, I was lucky enough to be given the opportunity to experience a vast range of classical music performed by fantastic musicians, often for free. In my second year I responded to an e-mail about the chance for free tickets to a Kohn concert in Trinity College Master's Lodge. Someone called György Pauk was bringing along a group of young violinists and pianists to play to a small audience, and I was fortunate enough to get the tickets.

Wow. The only word needed to describe my reaction. I was truly shocked at the ability of these performers, all younger than me, and all unbelievably talented.

At the time of writing this, I have just been to another Kohn concert in the same location. Last night I heard Alessandro Taverna play an exquisite rendition of Beethoven's 'Moonlight' Sonata, and other fantastic pieces. This experience was one I shall not forget.

On the bottom of the programme was a remark which read: 'We are extremely grateful to Sir Ralph Kohn and the Kohn Foundation for making this series of concerts possible.'

So after the performance I used the fantastic tool that is Google to look up the man behind this Foundation.

I am writing to tell you my story, because I believe it is important for you to know the impact you are having, not just on the musically well versed, but also the uninitiated among us who are lucky enough to get a second chance at discovering the marvellous human collaboration in the musical arts. All I have left to say is thank you, and I hope you have not been too bored by the scribbles of a mathematician with too much spare time.

Many thanks, Sam Channon – Trinity College, Cambridge.

When a testimonial of this kind comes out of the blue it means a great deal to me—and of course also to my good friend György Pauk who is a world-class violinist. I have never met Mr Channon but I believe his own case, as he eloquently describes it, is typical of a lot of people of the younger generation. It is extremely easy to lose one's connection with classical music if it has been fostered at a young age, and it is even easier never to have had a connection at all. The times are against it and these days we read more reviews of pop concerts and such events in the national press than of plays or classical concerts. If the relatively small contribution of the Kohn Foundation can bring someone like Mr Channon back into the fold of classical music, I am very proud and very optimistic that we can continue to do more work of this kind to the advantage of musicians of the future, and their sadly dwindling audiences. One step at a time, I say, and this was one important step.

Some of my recordings, representing a great many hours of work over the years

INTERLUDE 7: BOURRÉE

Recordings (1995 to 2007)

A FTER MY Wigmore Hall debut in 1968 I gave a certain number of concerts and recitals as a working baritone. As anyone who has been a performing musician knows, live music-making represents a considerable strain. One has to be note-perfect on the night, all the songs should be by memory in a recital (the younger generation increasingly ignores this discipline) and there is only one opportunity, a fleeting moment in time, to get everything right. The nerves and tension (the Germans call this stage-fright *Lampenfieber*, literally 'spotlight fever') generated by these experiences are very challenging. I think live performing may become more routinely manageable if one were working very regularly under these conditions; in my case I had the proverbial 'day job'. Performing in concerts was never for me something that was an everyday experience and the effort it cost was not always rewarded. Sometimes audiences were small: every classical musician has had the experience of literally months of work leading to an excruciatingly tense twenty minutes on stage, and at the end of it one wonders why one has bothered to put oneself through the mill for so little reward, and for so few people. In fact the great baritone Fischer-Dieskau refused to give recitals at such places as Wigmore Hall because he felt the effort of giving a recital for only 500 people at a time (a factor that also affects box-office takings) was not worth his while. He was the only singer, as far as I know, to have given lieder recitals in the vast expanses of the Royal Albert Hall, although lieder have very occasionally been performed there as part of the Proms.

I had recorded broadcasts from time to time for various radio organizations. These could also be very tense engagements because quite a lot of music had to be fitted in to a tight time-slot—normally something like three hours. The red light (a sign that recording was in progress) in those circumstances was very intimidating and it was some time before I came to regard the red light as a friend. Indeed, it was only eventually that I realized that the ideal conditions for the making of music, as far as I was concerned, were those attached to commercial recordings—by that I do not mean recording for radio stations on a tight budget, but the making of self-financed compact discs where I could be in control of every aspect of the schedule. Certainly this was a more expensive way of making music, but it was also something permanent; all one's efforts were not doomed to disappear into the ether and never be heard of again.

I have already described working with the pianists Roger Vignoles and Jonathan Zak on recording projects. I put my toe into the water as far as recording was concerned quite early on, and on certain occasions I have made recordings with orchestra, but it was not until the 1990s that I decided to embark on a series of recordings with piano (the same kind of intimate teamwork I had admired when I first heard Gigli). These experiences both challenged me as a musician and offered me the most propitious conditions in which to 'up my game'. I suppose the difference here is between the stage and the cinema. If I were an actor I would have come to the conclusion that I was happier making movies (with all the possibilities of re-takes and editing) rather than baring my soul nightly on the stage. There are, incidentally, quite a number of great movie actors who are not interested in working in the theatre, but rather few who despise the cinema when the chance arises.

Everyone knows the huge EMI recording studios in Abbey Road (made famous by The Beatles) and the Decca studios that used to be in Broadhurst gardens NW6 (now rehearsal studios for English National Opera). In the 1970s, as soon as smaller record companies began to emerge, like Hyperion and Chandos, suitable buildings all over London began to be used as recording studios. On the top of the list were churches with their generally roomy, reverberant acoustics. This new wave of recording took the wind out of the sales of the major labels because it soon became obvious that teams of producers and engineers, working freelance for smaller companies, were able to deliver products that were equal, in technical terms, to anything recorded in the vast and impressive studios at Abbey Road. Add to this two further things: a huge pool of talent—wonderful artists of every kind living within easy reach of London and unaccountably ignored by the major labels—and sophisticated, compact recording equipment, the result of an ever-advancing digital age. These factors accelerated the process whereby the giants that had controlled the industry (EMI, Decca, DGG, Philips, RCA) now had to share the classical music recording market with ambitious newcomers, streamlined firms with far lower expenses than the increasingly challenged dinosaurs from the 1950s and '60s.

These developments in a sense freed all of us from the need of waiting in vain to be invited by some condescending bigwig to make a recording. It was now something that could be organized with considerably less fuss than the vast medical symposia undertaken regularly by Advisory Services. This is not to say that the task was a simple one. In order to make a recording to the highest commercial standards there is a list of preparatory tasks. First, singer and pianist have to be fixed, and repertoire decided. Dates have then to be found when all the participants are available; a venue, often a church, has to be hired, and heated if necessary (like countless other artists I have made discs in Rosslyn Hill Unitarian Chapel in

Hampstead, St Paul's Church in Southgate, and All Saints' Church, Durham Road, in East Finchley in the depths of winter …). It goes without saying that these churches, although happy to derive extra revenue from recordings, are also places of worship and we have to work around church services and other events that are taking place. The piano has to be selected and delivered from Steinway, together with the services of a tuner on a daily basis. In charge of all this coordination is a highly skilled and experienced producer. He must be a fine musician, and it helps if he is good at handling people. He sits in the control room (usually a short walk from where the music is actually being made) and follows every detail of the musical score with great attention, judging when, and if, re-takes are necessary (they usually are!). This producer (in German he is called a *Tonmeister*, a 'sound master') must lead the recording process every step of the way. A sound engineer has to be present throughout. He will have set up the array of microphones and is responsible for the balance between voice and piano, the general sound of the product as a whole (apart from the actual singing and playing of course!) as well as the working of the recording machinery, the tabulation of takes and so on.

At a recording session in 2010

For a song recital record a period of three days is set aside with open-ended schedules and one can make music more or less at one's leisure (and in any order, all the takes are edited at the end to make an end-product). It is difficult adequately to describe the pleasure of these sessions which were always exploratory without any of that stress that comes from someone dictatorial in the control room. This is relaxed music-making with a friendly team that is supportive and helpful (as opposed to threatening and judgmental, as is the case with many producers of ill-paid radio recordings). There was usually a nearby kitchen where copious amounts of tea and coffee were dispensed and where we gathered to chat and tell anecdotes before the morning's work began. On occasions such as these I found myself drawn into the conversations of people who spent their whole lives in music; on the other hand, I found that they in turn were fascinated to hear anecdotes about the world of science and medicine. If things were going well we continued the session, and if not, we curtailed it. Everything was informal but also, of course, very serious and focused when it came to the music-making. A happy presence at many of our recordings has been that great photographer Clive Barda who has the extraordinary knack of taking wonderful shots while melting into the background. Over the years he and I have become really good friends. I think this is because he is a genuine music-lover and regards a day in the recording studio as something far more pleasurable than a grinding day of work. Clive is of course renowned for his photographs of musicians and is honoured with a permanent exhibition of his work at the Wigmore Hall.

On one hand there is the advice and encouragement of the producer, and on the other there is the accompanist—a key person in the process. I always felt buoyed up, truly supported, from both sides. As a recording producer Mark Brown has a touch of genius—there is no question of that. He was once a singer himself (we joke about his being a 'light counter-tenor', anxious to be invited to record all the repertory, and never being invited to do so) and he understands singers and the singing voice from the inside. Above all he seems to understand what singers like or dislike about their own voices, and he edits accordingly. Mark is something of a miracle worker; unlike many producers who indulge in unnecessary 'takes' he records just as much as he needs for the track, and no more. This makes an enormous difference to the singer in terms of tiring the voice which should remain fresh for as long as possible.

All artists need encouragement, and all artists need to be comforted when things are not going well. Many people in this field delight in destroying confidence, as if they somehow wish to shock the artist into doing his best. (I am told the legendary Walter Legge was this kind of producer.) But I have often said to Mark Brown: 'When you are done with the recording business you must come to Harley Street and set up as a psychologist or psychotherapist. You will be a huge success and put the other characters in the business out of work.'

With the recording producer Mark Brown in 2010

In working with all this exquisite German poetry, it makes a difference to me that Mark studied German at university. Graham Johnson is also a fine German-speaker and he reads a great deal in the language. As one of the world's most celebrated accompanists he is a fount of wisdom and experience in this repertoire, the navigator and steersman of the music-making. Most of the pianists I have worked with over the years get the notes right—most of the time—and much more, of course. But when it comes to the creation of 'magic'—the musical poetry and atmosphere with a 'halo' over it, I don't believe Graham has an equal in the world. He has been a huge inspiration to me.

He and I got together before each recording and selected some of the loveliest art songs by a variety of composers. The choice posed enormous difficulties—we had an 'embarrassment of riches' as far as the songs were concerned. At the forefront were the great lieder composers Schubert, Schumann and Brahms. Our performance of Schubert's *Winterreise* was released on the Capriole label in 1995, and, in the same year, further Schubert and Beethoven songs. Beethoven is also a song composer very important to me. It is said that he was not gifted at writing for the human voice but this reputation, as far as the lieder are concerned, is undeserved—I think he is a marvellous song composer. In 1999 we made a recording of Mahler songs (a very important composer to me, perhaps the greatest of the Jewish musical masters) together with Brahms and Robert Kahn, a composer more or less forgotten now. He was a German who was invited to study with Brahms in Vienna but was too shy to take up the offer. Kahn emigrated to England in 1937 at the age of seventy-two, too late to begin a career in a new country. Graham and I also included the French composer Ravel in our recording schedule for 2000, together with a selection of my beloved *arie antiche*. Between 2001 and 2003 there were further collections of Schubert, Schumann, Mahler and Beethoven. In 2004 there was a disc entitled *An die Musik—A Musical Journey* that charted my own voyage through music, from the early Italian arias through to the great lieder repertoire. We also made a recording of English music, Vaughan Williams songs and so on, with which I was not satisfied; it was never released. From the musical point of view it was fine, but it was a question of diction. Everyone assures me that when I speak English no one can detect the slightest trace of a German accent. But when I sing in English I sound as if I am someone with an accent that combines German and Italian. I suppose Graham might attempt to find some psychological reason for this! There is no detectable German accent in my speaking voice, but when I sing I revert to an accent that is a combination of my mother tongue and the Italian vowels I heard as a child on my father's Italian opera records. I might add that Charles Wadsworth made the same comment many years ago when we worked together in New York.

Excerpts of all these recordings assembled on a single CD are interpolated at appropriate places throughout this book. Of course the reader of my life-story need not listen to any of the music—this part of *Recital of a Lifetime* is purely optional. I will say, however, that those with the patience to listen to some of the songs that have been very dear to me over many years will perhaps understand far more about me than what I am simply able to express in verbal terms. I speak quite a few languages—and this was a factor in my success as a pharmacologist and businessman—but there is no language more vital to my happiness than the language of music.

PRELUDE XXI

The Royal Society

THERE IS SO MUCH MUSIC all around us, piped into shopping malls and restaurants, that we can take it for granted. We find a means to turn it off in our heads and take no notice. We live in a world where science is also taken for granted, but where almost every day new scientific discoveries are being made that change the lives of ordinary people. There are many who are excited by these kinds of changes in their lives; but there are also those who resist, and even fear, the newest developments in science and technology. Throughout history there has been this kind of Luddite resistance—a fear that science is a kind of Frankenstein that is out of control and will destroy the jobs and livelihoods of ordinary people who would prefer to keep what they have, and stay where they are. Some of this is human nature—as we age most of us tend to become more reactionary and resistant to change. The period of the Cold War and the nuclear threat (the Cuban crisis in 1962, for example) did little to convince people that the inventions of science were uniformly to mankind's advantage. The result was a growing split between the work and achievements of great scientists, and the public's perception of those achievements. It was possible for a scientist to be lauded by his colleagues for some fantastic new discovery while generating distrust and a distinct lack of enthusiasm from the public at large.

It was Sir Aaron Klug (awarded the 1982 Nobel prize in chemistry for his development of crystallographic electron microscopy) who realized that it was an essential role of the Royal Society (of which he was president from 1995 to 2000) to bridge this gap between science and the general public. Indeed, he spoke of a 'social contract' whereby there should be greater public involvement in the uses of science, and more public accountability and transparency from science. He saw the task of the Royal Society—the independent scientific academy of the UK—as not only strengthening science, promoting research, advising governments and fostering excellence in UK science, but also encouraging a dialogue with the public in ways that had not been tried before.

Ever since Francis Bacon's essays on scientific method, there had been wide intellectual engagement in the uses of science. Bacon, Hooke, Locke, Newton and the other founders of modern science in Britain had mapped out the territory for scientific discoveries in the succeeding three hundred years. Their legacy had enabled the economic and social progress of the nineteenth and twentieth centuries.

Francis Bacon

The heritage and the traditions it engendered remained strong. And yet there was, in the 1990s, a growing scepticism about the uses of science. The media and the government had begun to question what scientists did with their time and the public's money.

There was now clearly a growing need to communicate with a public that had become out of touch with, and sometimes fearful of, what was happening in the sciences. There needed to be a carefully planned bringing together of two somewhat alienated worlds, similar perhaps to the turning point, sixty years earlier, when Ernst Chain, in the face of tremendous professional hostility, had espoused, for the public good, the healthy commercialization of important scientific discoveries through the collaboration of industry and academia. I am pleased to say that the Royal Society and the Kohn Foundation began to work together. One of the society's lecture rooms was dilapidated and in need of refurbishment, but I felt this was a sticking plaster to a problem that required a more radical solution. I agreed that the society should have a state-of-the-art communications centre, a modern venue for lectures and events of all kinds. This was the beginning of the Kohn Centre. At the beginning of the new millennium, we then happily embarked on a five-year project entitled *Science in Society*—the title attracted me because I had made my entire career in the very area where science intersects with society. I had never been interested in shutting myself off from ordinary people, researching in the groves of academe, and I felt I had developed some expertise as someone in the middle (in my case standing as a go-between for the worlds of science and medicine on the one hand and the pharmaceutical companies on the other). I felt that it would be a privilege to assist the Royal Society to explain and clarify its important work to the public.

This was certainly the time for the scientific community to engage in a more constructive dialogue with the rest of society based on a mutual understanding of common concerns hopes, beliefs and values. The *Science in Society* project covered, among other things, genetically modified animals and foods, the fear of BSE ('mad cow disease'), genetic testing for humans, nanotechnology (the manipulation of matter on an atomic, molecular and supramolecular scale), pharmacogenetics and communications in science. As Stephen Cox, executive director of the Royal Society at the time, noted: 'Here at the Royal Society we began to realize that there was a danger of the public turning against science, and if the public turned against science, since so much of it is publicly funded, then the funds would dry up … there was a huge threat to science at that time.'

The society had never attempted anything as ambitious as this in terms of outreach. Sir Aaron Klug and Sir Robert May (who succeeded Sir Aaron as president of the Royal Society, and who is now Lord May of Oxford) were at the centre of this new initiative. I told them I wanted to be involved in this important project and the Kohn Foundation contributed a significant sum, funded over a period of five years, to *Science in Society*. Public debate was necessary because decisions about genetically modified technology, stem cell research, environmental or energy policy were not solely scientific—they clearly had political, ethical and economic dimensions. One of the pressing questions for society and its relationship with its scientists was the direction of scientific research: which avenues were open and which closed? It was clear that dialogue was of crucial importance, but on the other hand, and as Lord May remarked in the 2004 report for *Science in Society*, it was 'lunatic' to suggest that the public ought to be involved in setting the agenda for research. He continued:

Isaac Newton

We must attempt to understand the effects of unintended consequences … People are living longer: the life expectancy of a child born in the developing world is hugely better than it was in the developed world 150 years ago. Really remarkable! But that means population growth. We now feed people better, and we've doubled food production in thirty-five years. But the impact of that and of the high-tech things we've done to achieve it has increased the destruction of habitat. We subsidize our activities with energy of all forms—differently in different countries, and the epiphenomenon of that is climate change … Wouldn't it be better if we had a more effective way of thinking about the unintended consequences of our increasing knowledge that's reaching down the molecular machinery of life? That is what *Science in Society* is all about.

What wise words these are from Robert May—he is one of our greatest thinkers in the field of theoretical ecology and biodiversity. On the *Science in Society* project I also worked with Sir Paul Nurse (Nobel laureate, 2001) who became president of the Royal Society in 2010. He has been one of the most eloquent spokesmen against what he terms 'pseudo-science' or 'anti-science'. He believes that it is the scientist's duty to 'expose the bunkum', 'taking on politicians and exposing nonsense during elections'. In an article in *New Scientist* (17 September 2011) he criticized Republican Party candidates in US presidential nomination for opposing the teaching of natural selection, research on stem cells from human embryos, and anthropogenic climate change. He blamed scientists for not speaking up on these issues and was alarmed that this could happen at all in the US, a world leader in science, the 'home of Benjamin Franklin, Richard Feynman [the great physicist] and Jim Watson [James Watson, the molecular biologist, geneticist and zoologist]'. Nurse pointed out that scientific discussion cannot be treated as political debate, 'using rhetorical tricks rather than logic'. 'We need to emphasize why the scientific process is such a reliable generator of knowledge with its respect for evidence, for scepticism, for consistency of approach, for the constant testing of ideas.'

Sir Paul Nurse expresses his views very directly. My natural approach has always been conciliatory and I have never engaged in politics, but his last sentence as printed above could serve as the credo on which I based my entire career in clinical trials: the belief in science as a generator of knowledge, together with a respect for evidence, an enlightened scepticism, consistency of approach and the constant testing of ideas. I might add that the motto of the Royal Society is very applicable to this approach: 'Nullius in verba' (which means 'Take nobody's word for it'). In connection with this I must mention the prize, supported by the Kohn foundation and the journal *Nature*, and administered by Sense about Science, an organization that promotes the idea of research 'free from intimidation, hysteria and political pressure'. This prize is named after the late Sir John Maddox FRS and goes to a scientist who has 'stuck up for science' in the face of adversity or pubic opprobrium. Sir John's widow, the writer Brenda Maddox, remains a close friend.

The practical changes brought about by *Science in Society* were many: focus groups were established; there were improvements in the way reports were prepared; an MP–scientist pairing scheme was established (six pairs in 2001, fourteen in 2002, twenty-two in 2003 and twenty-five in 2004) whereby both members of parliament and scientists benefited from raised awareness and new friendships; there was an engagement with schoolchildren aged between fourteen and sixteen in a programme entitled *Genetic Futures*, with eight regional events and 800 participants; there was a collaborative project with the Royal Academy of Engineering—an important report on nanoscience and nanotechnology. The Royal Society had been able to inform the strategy of government (through the Office of Science and Innovation), advise on public engagement, work with the research councils (particularly those of the biotechnology and biological sciences, the natural environment, and engineering and physical sciences) and advise on and help form education policy through the Higher Education Funding Council. The Royal Society also helped develop social science in risk management by the Food Standards Agency.

In 2004, at the end of the five years of this important project, I told Lord May (now president of the Royal Society) that I would like to carry on supporting other initiatives. We came up with the idea of the Royal Society Kohn Award for excellence in engaging the public with science. The recipients of this award are listed in an appendix to this book (see page 346). Between 2005 and 2010 I was a member of the committee, convened by Lord Rees and chaired by Lord Sainsbury, tasked with raising funds to commemorate the 350th anniversary of the founding of the Royal Society. Among my distinguished fellow committee members were Sir David Attenborough FRS and the world-famous American writer Bill Bryson. I arranged a concert at St James Palace in the presence of HRH The Prince of Wales where students from the Royal Academy of Music performed a Bach cantata programme. The work of this committee raised £106m on behalf of the Royal Society during the five-year period. I was made an Honorary Fellow of the Royal Society (FRS) in 2006 and this was certainly one of the proudest moments of my life.

In this chapter I have already discussed my working association with the present president of the Royal Society (since 2010) Paul Nurse; I also count as friends of long-standing three former presidents: Aaron Klug, Bob May and Martin Rees from whom I received my Honorary Fellowship. Rees, apart from being a renowned cosmologist and astrophysicist, is in fact the second Astronomer Royal I have known (the first is my good friend Sir Arnold Wolfendale FRS who lives in Durham). Sir Isaac Newton was president of the Royal Society from 1703 until his death in 1727, but he is said to have become rather too all-powerful in his dealings with scientific matters, and such long periods at the helm are no longer permitted.

Four presidents of the Royal Society
clockwise from top left Sir Aaron Klug OM (1995–2000), Lord May OM (2000–2005),
Lord Rees OM (2005–2010), Sir Paul Nurse (2010–2015)

My admission lecture to the Royal Society was entitled *The pharmacological basis of the Kohn Foundation*; the president, Lord Rees, did me the very great, and most unusual, honour of introducing this inaugural address. This speech gave me the opportunity to thank a number of people who had been crucial mentors in the story of my life. The reader has already encountered them all in considerable detail: Professor A D Macdonald in Manchester; Professor Daniel Bovet, foreign member of the Royal Society, and Sir Ernst Chain FRS in Rome; Professor Alfred Gilman in New York; Sir David Jack FRS, Professor Allan Dixon and Sir John Vane FRS in the UK. These are all great men in their different ways, and in my admission lecture I did not apologize for using the words of Isaac Newton, said to have been addressed to Robert Hooke: 'If I have seen further, it is by standing on the shoulders of giants!' Unlike Newton I cannot even claim to have seen further, but I have certainly stood on the shoulders of giants during the course of my life—and probably worn them down in the process! This presentation was subsequently published in the proceedings of the Royal Society. I must also not fail to mention my gratitude to the executive director of the Royal Society since 2011, Dr Julie Maxton, who has become a staunch friend and colleague. She is the first woman to have been appointed to this position in the 350-year history of the Royal Society.

Fugue XXI (in 2 voices) RALPH KOHN *with* GRAHAM JOHNSON

GJ Your writing of 'standing on giants' shoulders' reminds me of a work written towards the end of Isaac Newton's life, *Gulliver's Travels* by Jonathan Swift.

RK Well I remember that Gulliver is taken to be a giant when he is washed ashore in Lilliput, and pinned down by the Lilliputians who are only six inches tall.

GJ I am thinking now of Gulliver's later journey to the island of Laputa. This was a flying island, a rock with an adamantine base. All the inhabitants of that island are given to a blind pursuit of science without any practical results. This is, in fact, Swift lampooning the members of the Royal Society in the first quarter of the eighteenth century, men who were so lost in thought, so abstracted by mathematical and musical calculation, that they had no idea that their wives were having adulterous affairs with the men of the neighbouring island of Balnibarbi!

RK Well at least Swift made the men of Laputa equally interested in science and music! At that time it was accepted that science and music went together—as indeed they do, in my experience at least. I don't know about sex.

GJ You mention your admiration for Bacon, a figure much earlier than Newton. Although a lofty discussion such as this needs a few jokes to lighten the seriousness, I hereby refrain from making any jokes with a distinguished Jewish man of science about Bacon!

RK Well you are right about Bacon being no laughing matter—although the claim that he was the one who wrote Shakespeare's plays has met with some derision. Francis Bacon was the kind of man who understood what the future might look like. He was also, of course, one of

Jonathan Swift's vision of the island of Laputa

the spiritual founding fathers of the Royal Society—although he died some thirty-five years before the society was actually founded in 1660. Have you read his book *New Atlantis*? He had a version of the Royal Society in mind as early as 1626. Bacon was a man who clearly lived at the crossroads of medieval and modern culture. He was certain that life could be transformed by science and by the correct method of dealing with the world. His heroes were people like Copernicus, Galileo, Gilbert and Harvey, and the inventions he regarded as life-changing were gunpowder, the seaman's compass, printing, microscopes, and so on.

GJ Mentioning all those great names from earlier centuries makes one realize that many of the people you have mentioned in this chapter are the direct descendants of the scientific traditions founded by Sir Francis Bacon in this country, and some of them very famous men.

RK Well I was acutely aware of that, I can assure you, when I was offered an Honorary Fellowship of the Royal Society. In my admission lecture I told the story of Sir Henry Dale who was offered an Honorary Fellowship of the Physiological Society on his seventieth birthday (he was already a Nobel prizewinner, a president of the Royal Society and a member of the Order of Merit) and he replied: 'But I am still far too young for this honour!' This echoed the sentiments expressed by the great nineteenth-century Japanese woodblock artist Hokusai, who at the height of his fame aged eighty, exclaimed: 'Should I be granted ten more years I promise to become a real artist.'

GJ What were your earliest memories of the Royal Society?

RK My company, Advisory Services, organized a number of symposia at Carlton House Terrace, and of course I knew a number of the Fellows individually over the years. I was drawn into a closer relationship with this august organization through Sir David Jack FRS with whom I had worked at Smith Kline and French in the late fifties. I also got to know the great molecular biologist Dr Max Perutz OM—one of the few people at this level of achievement to have refused a knighthood, but certainly distinguished enough to have earned that honour many times over. In fact, he was recently honoured posthumously by having a British stamp created in his memory—this depicts him looking into a microscope, underneath which are the words: 'Max Perutz, 1914–2002, molecular biologist and Nobel laureate'. Like Chain, Perutz was an émigré, having left Vienna in 1936 to work with Sir Frederick Gowland Hopkins at the Cavendish Laboratory in Cambridge. He had won the Nobel prize for chemistry in 1962.

Max Perutz with a model of haemoglobin

One evening Max, that great and humble man, kindly took me along to a meeting of the Foundation for Science and Technology—a pleasant evening of informal discussions with fellow scientists followed by a dinner—and it was there that I was introduced to Aaron Klug who had himself come to the UK from Durban in South Africa, although he was originally of Lithuanian extraction. He was the first Jew to be president of the Royal Society. This was perhaps the most crucial meeting in relation to my subsequent involvement with this world-renowned body. David Jack knew that I was supporting various scientific efforts; he suggested that I should be invited to lunch at Carlton House Terrace where I could meet the president and treasurer.

GJ   But the president was Sir Aaron Klug and you had already met him!

RK   Our lunch at Carlton House Terrace was in an official capacity—our chat at the Foundation for Science and Technology had been very informal. The treasurer, I should add, was Sir Eric Ash FRS, also an émigré from Berlin. It was also on this occasion that I was introduced to Stephen Cox, the executive director at the time. I have already written about how this meeting led to the creation of the Kohn Centre. But the important thing was that I felt increasingly at home at the Royal Society and I became friends with a great many other scientists. Many of these were well known to me in terms of their reputations, but this was a chance to get to know them on a personal level. I suppose one might say that I fell in love with the society and everything it represented in terms of its history, its aims, and its roster of truly immortal Fellows, past and present. I owe some of the closest and dearest friendships of my later life to the Royal Society.

GJ   Tell me about some of these fellow-Fellows, if I can put it in that way …

RK   I have already mentioned a dear friend, Sir Arnold Wolfendale FRS, a recent Astronomer Royal and a world authority on cosmic rays. He was a star pupil of Patrick Blackett (Lord Blackett OM), the great experimental physicist with whom I had also studied in a very humble capacity at Manchester University. Two further Nobel laureates must be mentioned: my good friend the great chemist Sir Harold Kroto FRS (whose parents were émigrés from Berlin, and whose brilliantly inventive Vega Foundation the Kohn Foundation supported) and the nuclear physicist and disarmament spokesman, Sir Joseph Rotblat FRS, originally from Warsaw, who was involved with Bertrand Russell and the famous Pugwash Conferences on science and world affairs. And then of course there is the brilliant chemist Sir John Meurig Thomas FRS, former master of Peterhouse, Cambridge.

His historical hero is Michael Faraday, of course, another early member of the Royal Society. When Sir John was director of the Royal Institution in Albemarle Street he occupied, with his wife and family, the same living quarters in the building as had been occupied by Michael Faraday and his wife. He has become a very dear friend, as has his charming wife, Jehane.

Arnold Wolfendale

GJ   I have had the pleasure to meet Sir John Meurig Thomas through you on a number of occasions. He is a great favourite of mine—a man of incredible energy and charm. He has a very special, and very disarming, Welsh charisma!

RK   At John's seventy-fifth birthday party in Cambridge I found myself seated next to the German chancellor, Angela Merkel; she attended the event to honour her old friend, and she flew back to Berlin after the banquet. John Meurig Thomas is the kind of man who inspires that kind of loyalty and devotion in his colleagues. Chancellor Merkel had been, of course, a physicist by training, receiving her degree from the University of Leipzig, a city in which she lived for ten years.

GJ   I suppose you were able to speak in German to her throughout the evening, and Sir John would have delighted in providing her with such a fellow guest?

RK   The German Chancellor and I got on so well that after an evening of warm conversation I thought we could address each other less formally. After all 'Frau Bundeskanzler' ('Madam Chancellor of the Federal Republic') is a bit of a mouthful. When I proposed a relaxing of formality, she readily agreed, responding in a way that perhaps only those of us with German as a mother tongue can savour to the full: 'Yes, we should be more relaxed!' she said: 'Please call me "Frau Doktor Merkel"'!

John Meurig Thomas looking on benignly as I chat with the German Chancellor, Angela Merkel, at his 75th birthday party in Cambridge

GJ   I know that some members of the Royal Society wanted to confer an Honorary Fellowship on Margaret Thatcher but that this was a controversial issue as that prime minister had both staunch admirers and equally staunch opponents within the Royal Society. I suppose Frau Merkel might be a recipient of an Honorary Fellowship one day, assuming non-English people are permitted.

RK   Indeed they are! Professor Bovet was a ForMemRS, and the custom of according foreign membership goes right back to eighteenth century, and probably earlier. Chancellor Merkel was awarded the Charles II Medal by the Royal Society in 2010, an honour received by the emperor of Japan in 1998 and the president of India in 2007. Since Charles II, by the way, every English monarch has been a patron of the Royal Society. There was someone else in the distant past—and other than 'Frau Doktor Merkel'—who had a link to both Leipzig University and the Royal Society. Thanks to the great Bach scholar and Harvard professor of music, Christoph Wolff, I discovered that a German professor of physics at Leipzig University, Johann Heinrich Winckler, was elected a Fellow of the Royal Society in 1747. Let me read you his citation written in eighteenth-century English:

This Gentleman was the first who favoured the Royal Society by communicating to them those most surprising and wonderfull Experiments in Electricity, whereby he produced actual fire from the Electrical flash, kindling thereby rectified Spirit of Wine and many other inflammable Substances as mentioned in his German Book published on this Subject, and in his Letter to the Society published in the Phil Trans No 475 he was for the year 1745 rector of the University of Lipsick the post of the highest Honour in that Society, and now being desirous of the favour of becoming a member of the Royal Society, we whose names are under written do on account of his Great Learning and merit recommend him as a Candidate and a person who will be a very usefull member of the Same.

GJ   Discovering that must have pleased you—an ancient FRS all the way from Leipzig!

RK   Yes, but there is something else that is important about Herr Winckler. He was not only professor of physics at Leipzig University, he taught Greek and Latin at the famous St Thomas School where Johann Sebastian Bach instructed his pupils in music.

GJ   It always comes back to Bach! 'Back to Bach' was certainly the motto of many musicians of the twentieth century in their neo-classical phase.

RK   With me a great deal always comes back to Bach. Winckler was the librettist of Bach's lost cantata *Froher Tag, verlangte Stunden* (*Blessed day, yearning hours*), BWV Anh. 18, performed on the occasion of the dedication of the renovated St Thomas School in 1732, where Winckler and Bach worked side by side. Here we have a supreme example of the union of science and music—and the Royal Society.

GJ   Although it might be said that the FRS was the greatest of your honours (certainly preceding your knighthood), you have received many other awards and accolades both formal and informal. You were, for example, selected to appear on two very important BBC radio programmes: Michael Berkeley's *Private Passions* as well as the celebrated *Desert Island Discs*.

RK   And I am proud to say that I have become really good friends with Sue Lawley, the newsreader and presenter of the programme at the time—a most charming lady.

GJ   Permit me to continue with the list of honours: in 2003 an Honorary Fellowship of the Academy of Medial Sciences; in 2008 an Honorary Fellowship of the British Pharmacological Society …

RK   That award was made in my adopted city of Manchester I am proud to say …

GJ You were made an honorary member of the European Academy in 2008 as well as receiving the degree of doctor of music, honoris causa, from the University of Manchester …

RK If you don't mind, as grateful as I am for each of these honours, and several others, I want to end our conversation today by bringing the focus back to the Royal Society and my enormous affection for a noble and venerable institution that has immeasurably enriched my life, both in terms of what I have learned as a scientist and through the remarkable friendships I have made there over the last twenty years or so.

GJ Having spoken so much about science in the last hour or two are you prepared to embark on a discussion of musical matters?

RK Certainly! Well, you have just mentioned the musical honour from Manchester, and that fragment about Bach a little earlier in our conversation has put me in the mood to return to his music as a theme for a newly written Prelude followed by a conversational Fugue.

PRELUDE XXII

Wigmore Hall
& Royal Academy of Music

THE READER of these memoirs will by now be very aware of how closely science and music have been entwined throughout my life, like fugal subject and counter-subject. As I write these words I realize how fortuitous it has been that for the last fifty years or so music has been for me literally 'just round the corner'. Wigmore Hall is situated exactly halfway between my first premises in Welbeck Street and the present offices of the Kohn Foundation in 14 Harley Street—in fact the hall is just a stone's throw from either address. For a while I had an office in Wimpole Street which is even nearer Wigmore Hall than Harley Street—indeed Welbeck Street and Wimpole Street are linked by Welbeck Mews along which countless famous artists have made their way to the artists' entrance behind the hall.

Wigmore Hall was a German import. The piano maker, Friedrich Wilhelm Carl Bechstein, built the Saal Bechstein in Berlin in 1891. This became a successful recital hall (as did similar halls in St Petersburg and Paris). Because half the firm's pianos were sold in England, Bechstein decided to build a hall adjoining his London showrooms in Wigmore Street. Work on London's new Bechstein Hall began in 1899 and was completed by 1901. The architect was Thomas Edward Colcutt who also built the Savoy Hotel on the Strand (since modified) and the Palace Theatre on Cambridge Circus. The hall, in Renaissance style, is rectangular in shape with marble and alabaster walls, and a small raised stage. This is an ideal size for recitals and chamber music concerts, but on occasion, such as the premiere of Britten's *Serenade for tenor, horn and strings* in 1943, a string orchestra has been squeezed onto the stage. The cupola above the stage is decorated with a mural by the painter Gerald Moira; this figure, Apollo-like, is said to represent the Soul of Music. Graham Johnson told me the story of how Gerald Moore, appearing on the Wigmore stage after his eightieth birthday concert, pointed up to this Gerald Moira figure and said to the audience: 'It is some years since I modelled for that!' This was followed by general uproar in the house.

Front of house, an imposing staircase in the hall's lobby leads up to the balcony, usually closed for concerts with less than full attendance. There are 545 seats in the hall as it stands today, and the acoustic is widely acknowledged as being one of the best in the world for classical music—perhaps on account of that unusual cupola executed by the sculptor Frank Lynn Jenkins.

Bechstein Hall opened on 31 May 1901 with the Italian pianist Ferruccio Busoni, the Belgian violinist Eugène Ysaye and the Estonian-born lieder singer Raimund von zur Mühlen (all three world-famous). On the following evening, 1 June, the hall fielded a cast of another famous pianist, this time the Russian-German Vladimir de Pachmann, and the British singers Ben Davies and Harry Plunket Greene. The accompanists were Hamilton Harty and Landon Ronald, both later celebrated as composers and conductors. From the very beginning the hall was a place where the London public was able to hear the greatest pianists, chamber music musicians and singers, both international and local.

During the Second World War, German-speaking refugees who found themselves in England were treated with courtesy; there were frequent German lieder recitals given at The National Gallery as part of the concert series master-minded by Myra Hess. But things were very different during the First World War when, it is said, even Dachshunds were kicked in the street for being German. After the Trading with the Enemy Amendment Act was passed in 1916, Bechstein's hall and showroom were seized as alien property and closed. The MP James Boynton, acting as an agent for the firm of Debenhams, bought the hall (as well as the showrooms, offices, studios, 23,000 square feet of warehouse space, underlettings, tuning contracts, furniture, fixtures and fittings and 137 Bechstein pianos) for £56,500. This must have been the bargain of the century as the hall alone had cost £100,000 to build. Reopened in 1917 as Wigmore Hall, the premises now had to be leased from the new owner. The Arts Council of Great Britain secured a twenty-year lease in 1946, but by the middle sixties the future of the hall was in doubt. Its situation on Wigmore Street, parallel to Oxford Street, the busiest shopping area in central London, made it a most desirable piece of real estate for property developers. Thanks to the generous contributions of those members of its audience who value this hall above all others, as well as the inspired leadership of William Lyne, and the present director of the hall, John Gilhooly, in 2008 the Wigmore Hall Trust purchased a 300-year lease for £3.1m which has secured the hall's future.

It was over half a century after Wigmore Hall was built that I gave my own debut recital there in 1968, accompanied by Martin Isepp. Since then I have spent countless hours of pleasure in this beloved auditorium as a devoted member of the audience. My closer association with the administration of the hall began in the

Wigmore Hall is a valiant island of music, holding its own in the face of London's ever-changing architectural and aesthetic values. How easily it might have been swallowed up by commercial forces were it not for the work of its two last directors and countless music-loving supporters. They may be rebuilding next door, but this far and no further!

middle 1990s with the demise of the Walther Grüner Lieder competition; for a number of years it had been held in various of the City guilds under the auspices of the City of London. Grüner had been a distinguished teacher of lieder at the Guildhall School of Music and had left money for a competition in his name, funding that had now run out (the Grüner had been specifically targeted at German song—Grüner, like myself, had been a lieder-singing German refugee).

There was a very strong feeling that it would be a pity if London should have no international song competition. Graham Johnson brought an idea to me (discussed at great length with William Lyne, manager of Wigmore Hall, and Virginia Harding who had run the Grüner) whereby the hall might be the host of a new competition for art songs in different languages—a reflection of London's position as an international crossroads of culture between Europe and the Americas.

I am proud to say that the Wigmore Hall/Kohn Foundation International Song Competition has been held eight times since 1997. I got on very well indeed with the charming William Lyne who was the first director I encountered there (he was present at my debut in 1968) and also with the present director, the delightful and very able John Gilhooly. Between these two there was an awkward interregnum when the gentleman initially chosen to succeed Bill Lyne (not a long-lasting appointment as it turned out) decided that he did not approve of competitions—preferring, as he put it, to pick winners for himself. As a result the Kohn Foundation was unceremoniously turfed out of Wigmore Hall, and there was no competition in 2005. I am pleased to say that 'normal service' resumed in 2007 when the jury was chaired by the new director, as it has been on three subsequent occasions, most recently in 2013.

The other musical institution that is dear to my heart is the Royal Academy of Music. I suppose one may say that I have that much in common with one of their greatest recent benefactors, Sir Elton John, even though I was not a pupil there—I believe he actually studied as a Junior exhibitioner in his teenage years. As it happens the academy's position on Marylebone Road, just south of Regent's Park, forms a kind of geographical triangle with my office in Harley Street and Wigmore Hall. It is very much a part of a north London axis—and by 'north' I mean north of Oxford Street. My connection with the academy is very specific in that, once

Royal Academy of Music   *Photograph by Hephzibah Kohn Rudofsky*

again, it is related to Bach—and this is quite apart from the fact that I have been generously appointed an Honorary Fellow of that august institution (FRAM), an honour I believe I share with my friend and colleague Graham Johnson. From 2006 the Kohn Foundation funded the Royal Academy of Music Bach prize (the inaugural prize was given to the great scholar Christoph Wolff, already mentioned frequently in these pages). This award, dear to my heart, was initiated with the support of Sir Curtis Price who was principal of the RAM at that time (he went on to become warden of New College, Oxford). The 2007 Bach prize went to the brilliant pianist András Schiff (who has recently been knighted in the 2014 Birthday Honours list), and the 2008 prize to Sir John Eliot Gardiner. Curtis Price's successor as principal at the Royal Academy of Music in 2008 was Professor Jonathan Freeman-Attwood, a remarkable musician—he is a virtuoso trumpeter, a wonderful record producer, a Bach scholar and a man with both the imagination and gravitas to lead a major British musical institution. He has also become a close and much admired friend.

In January 2009 a cherished dream of mine came into realization, discussed first with Curtis Price in general terms, and then planned in detail over three delicious lunches with Jonathan Freeman-Attwood at Fishworks in Marylebone High Street—turbot, halibut and sea bass. I am sorry to say that once I saw the possibility that my dream might be realized, I pursued poor Jonathan until we had nailed down all the plans firmly—'Nägel mit Köpfe', as my favourite saying goes. This was a series of concerts, nine per year, in the academy's Duke's Hall and devoted to the Bach cantatas. These take place (the series is ongoing, and all 215 cantatas will eventually be performed) on Sunday mornings at 12 noon and they have achieved a remarkable and instantaneous critical success. There are two or three cantatas performed in each concert, depending on the length of the works. The vast majority of these concerts are in the wonderfully capable hands of Iain Ledingham who is a 'Kapellmeister' of the very highest order; he coaches all the singers superbly, and conducts with great authority and understanding. The orchestral players and singers are drawn from the ranks of the very best young artists from the academy; the orchestra itself is led by an alternating trio of great baroque violinists: Rachel Podger, Margaret Faultless (presently head of historical performance at the RAM), and the Australian Madeleine Easton. The series also boasts distinguished guests. In January 2010 the great Bach tenor Peter Schreier, who is also a fine conductor (he received the Bach prize that year), directed a cantata concert—he happily returned to conduct the so-called 'Easter Oratorio' in April 2011.

The 2011 series began with a concert conducted by that outstanding international Bach figure, from the University of Glasgow, John Butt—he had been awarded the Bach prize for 2010. In March 2012 the Thomanerchor came from Leipzig (where they sing daily in the celebrated Thomaskirche, as described in the *Prologue* of this book) to take part in the RAM series, although their Bach programme was not devoted to

Peter Schreier, a wonderful conductor as well as a great tenor

the cantatas). This great choir received the Bach prize collectively—a unique and thoroughly deserved award. Their concert was directed by Georg Christoph Biller, only the sixteenth 'Thomaskantor' since Johann Sebastian Bach himself (an indication that each of these men held this life-enhancing post for very many years). In March 2012 the cantata concert was conducted by Sir John Eliot Gardiner, no less, with great éclat. Another guest of honour was the Japanese scholar, harpsichordist and conductor Masaaki Suzuki. He came to direct a concert of cantatas in March 2013 and was able to collect the Bach prize awarded him in 2012. The 2013 prize went to the great pianist Murray Perahia KBE, and the 2014 prize to the harpsichordist, organist and conductor Ton Koopman.

The press for these concerts has been magnificent. The important newspapers, including *The Times*, have been unanimous in their praise, but one review from *The Tablet*, the Roman Catholic newspaper, made a remarkable observation: it claimed that these cantata concerts were 'a central feature of London's cultural and religious life'. There is certainly something remarkable about these noonday concerts that gives them a certain interdenominational uplift. The music does the soul good, and one feels somehow, without the slightest touch of false piety, that one has taken part in a significant, soul-enriching, if not exactly religious event. For me to listen to this beloved music in such beautiful surroundings, formal in terms of architecture and musical history, but relaxed and comfortable in every other respect, is certainly a spiritual experience. As that superb violinist Margaret Faultless put it: 'These concerts are a great gift to our cultural well-being.'

Fugue XXII *(in 2 voices)* RALPH KOHN *with* GRAHAM JOHNSON

GJ   With this chapter I feel on home ground—there has been so much discussion of the sciences that it is a relief to return to the Royal Academy of Music, my Alma Mater, where I came from Rhodesia to study in 1967. I was six years a student there and played many a concert on the stage of the Duke's Hall, even performing Beethoven's Piano Concerto No 2 there in 1969. I was made a Fellow in 1984.

RK   It is a surprise to me that you are not a professor at the academy. Instead you are senior professor of accompaniment at the Guildhall School of Music in the Barbican.

GJ   Many years ago Sir Curtis Price kindly invited me to return to teach at the academy, but I remain loyal to a distinguished school with a very different style, and where I have taught for nearly thirty years. As someone who is a member of staff at another institution, I see the RAM as having blossomed in a most extraordinary way in the last fifteen years or so. When I arrived in London in 1967, access to the academy library was via a hole in the wall in the basement, and there was still a certain post-war bleakness about the place—at that time the Royal College of Music seemed so much more upbeat.

RK   Yet looking at the academy now, everything has been wonderfully refurbished, the library is splendid and there is a great deal of expansion with new teaching and practice rooms in the Nash building on York Gate—to the west of the original building—as well as the David Josefowitz Recital Hall built between the two main buildings, and current plans to build a new theatre.

GJ   Yes, the academy has changed from the poor relation of the London conservatoires to the whizz-kid on the block. By the way, I thank my lucky stars I studied there: it was at the academy as a student that I met my lifelong musical recital partner the soprano Felicity Lott, also a student, and I had some truly wonderful teachers.

Graham Johnson outside the Royal Academy of Music as a student in 1967

RK Have you heard the magnificent new organ in the Duke's Hall? Sir Elton John donated a large amount of money to ensure it was one of the best in the country.

GJ When I heard the organ was a Kuhn I thought for an unguarded moment that you had paid for it, and they had named it in your honour—only getting a single letter slightly wrong!

RK Well, it is a strange coincidence that my name is very near to that of one of the foremost organ builders in the world! There were two Bach recitals at the end of last year given in conjunction with the cantata series that demonstrated the fine qualities of the new instrument. It looks most impressive in the beautiful Duke's Hall, a name that derives, I understand, from the Earl of Westmorland, also known as Lord Burghersh, the founder of the Royal Academy of Music. Am I right in thinking the academy is a much older institution than the Royal College of Music?

GJ Indeed you are—it is exactly sixty years older—founded in 1822, and Britain's oldest degree-granting music school, and the second-oldest in the world, after Paris. I was astonished to discover the other day that the sister of Charles Dickens was a student there in the 1820s when the academy premises were still in Hanover Square, the place famously visited by Mendelssohn, Berlioz, Liszt and Tchaikovsky. The present building on Marylebone Road dates from 1911 and was built on the site of an orphanage at a cost of £51,000. By the way, historically it has always been a place where Jewish students have felt at home. This is partly to do with its north London location—it was always a far less 'establishment' or 'high-society' conservatoire than the Royal College (it had more foreign teachers than the college) and partly to do with a liberal, left-of-centre attitude that was still evident in the sympathies of Sir Thomas Armstrong, the principal I knew when still a teenager. I think it doubtful that my composition teacher when I was at the RAM, Alan Bush, a staunch communist, would have been employed in those Cold War years at any other such institution—but those were the days when a great many Jewish intellectuals outside Russia were communists, or at least very left wing.

RK I remember you mentioned to me that the roll-call from the 1920s and '30s of Jewish alumni is particularly wonderful: the pianists Myra Hess, Harriet Cohen, Irene Scharrer, Clifford Curzon, the violinist Sidney Griller, as well as your own first teacher, Harry Isaacs, and many others. None of those were communists! I must say it is a luxury to have such a noble institution almost on our doorstep—it is an easy drive from where we live in Hampstead, and it is only a twelve-minute walk from my office in Harley Street. I have always felt very welcomed there. Prior to the cantata concerts, when our invited guests all meet for coffee in the principal's

My investiture as an honorary doctor of music (London University) in July 2014
Jonathan Freeman-Attwood (principal of the RAM) is in the middle of the picture
with the distinguished broadcaster and Beethoven scholar John Suchet on the right

beautiful office (a room complete with Mozart's table and Wagner's music stand) there is always a wonderful mood of delighted expectation.

GJ Yes, it seems very obvious that Jonathan Freeman-Attwood runs a very happy ship and the whole of the cantata project seems singularly blessed.

RK I do agree with you. We are very lucky to have Jonathan at the head! And not so far from the academy, at the other end of Marylebone High Street, is another musical institution very dear to us both. When did you first play in Wigmore Hall?

GJ It was a recital in 1974—about six years after your appearance there, although you and I didn't know each other at the time. Funnily enough, Wigmore Hall was another place that was rather run-down when I first encountered it. Difficult as it is to believe now, the chic place for young people to give recitals, circa 1970, was the Purcell Room on the South Bank. When I began my student career, Wigmore Hall was definitely in the doldrums. I think that the lack of effective concert lighting and comfortable seating had a lot to do with its eclipse in those days, and most people simply took it for granted, a forgotten jewel. It always had the advantage, of course, of marvellous acoustics, and those people who understood the importance of such things remained loyal. Its present position as one of the great concert halls of the world, the nerve-centre of the song recital in Europe, was unimaginable forty years ago.

RK   There is no doubt that it was William Lyne who fought to re-establish the hall in its rightful place in the audience's affections, and John Gilhooly has continued this work and has a certain genius in finding effective sponsorship. In the first instance Bill Lyne did a magnificent job of luring big names back to the hall in the 1970s— Arthur Rubinstein and Elisabeth Schwarzkopf for example—and then encouraging younger artists to move from the South Bank back to Wigmore Street.

GJ   Well, I had personal experience of this. The Songmakers' Almanac, the team of solo lieder singers with whom I began my career, had its first three seasons at the Purcell Room and then switched without any regret to Wigmore Hall.

RK   I would like to think that the hall's present great reputation worldwide has been reinforced by the song competition. I have heard that young singers from around the world are eager to appear there, and a chance to sing at the hall even under competition conditions is taken as a serious opportunity.

GJ   I think this is the case, and I also think we have been able to attract marvellous jury members.

William Lyne   John Gilhooly   *Photograph by Ben Ealovega*

RK I have a list of them here! If I pick out the sopranos, beginning in 1997 and ending in 2013, we have Margaret Price (twice), Elisabeth Söderström, Edith Mathis, Elly Ameling, Grace Bumbry, Felicity Lott, Christine Brewer, Anne Evans—and alongside these, the mezzos Felicity Palmer, Ann Murray (twice), Bernarda Fink and Sarah Walker.

GJ I remember we have had many fewer tenors—Peter Schreier, Robert White, Christoph Prégardien and Robert Gambill, and then an array of baritones—the first of whom was Matthias Goerne in the third competition in 2001.

RK I will never forget that Tuesday afternoon, after lunch on the second day of the competition, when Goerne received a call on his mobile phone during one of the rounds (this fact was strange enough) and became very agitated. The news he distressingly brought to us seemed too impossible and mad to be true—that a plane had flown into the World Trade Center in New York killing thousands of people. As the terrible scenario unfolded, and the second plane flew into the second building, we were all transfixed and horrified in the hall's upstairs balcony, uncertain of what to do. There was some feeling that we should halt proceedings and wind up for the day—but of course with the scheduling already tight, this would have more or less finished the competition. It was the doughty Elly Ameling who declared that under no circumstances should terrorism triumph over music. You were chairman of the jury that year, and made a speech to that effect. We carried on with the competition, although on that day, 9 September 2001, the world had changed for ever.

GJ As you say, Matthias Goerne was the first of our baritone jury members; others were François Le Roux, Robert Holl, Wolfgang Holzmair and Thomas Quasthoff. We should not forget the pianists apart from myself—my colleagues Rudolf Jansen from the Netherlands, Bengt Forsberg from Sweden, Dalton Baldwin who lives between France and America, the Austrian Helmut Deutsch, and the British accompanists Roger Vignoles, Iain Burnside and Malcolm Martineau.

RK I have worked with many fine accompanists as a singer and I have already written on these pages that I know from first-hand experience what a huge difference they can make to a performance. I am reminded that the baritone Raimund von zur Mühlen, whose recital opened Wigmore Hall in 1901, is reputed to have said to his Dutch accompanist, Coenraad Valentijn Bos, 'You must have played remarkably well. I didn't notice you'.

Masaaki Suzuki conducting a Bach cantata in the Duke's Hall at the Royal Academy of Music

GJ That kind of back-handed compliment is a thing of the past, thank heavens! It is now acknowledged that the art song—whether German, French, English, Spanish, American or Russian—is a musical form that evolved from a strong pianistic foundation. The composers themselves, in performing their own music very often acted as regular pianists for great singers from the past.

RK One has only to think of Schubert and Vogl, Poulenc and Bernac, Britten and Pears …

GJ Exactly—and many others! There is no doubt that song pianists who take part in the Wigmore competition will find themselves listened to on their own account, taken seriously and valued as they are at few other such events. Apart from the prizes awarded to singers, there is a substantial pianist's prize, a duo prize for a singer–pianist team that has worked very well together, and a prize for the best performance of a Schubert song.

RK We decided to put an accent on the music of Franz Schubert right from the beginning—something I don't think you were averse to, dear Graham, as a great authority on this composer.

GJ Well, I believe that if one were running a competition for actors, a fine performance of a Shakespeare monologue may be a very telling indication of talent—not the whole picture, of course, but an indication that aspects of the craft had been mastered. Schubert is the Shakespeare of song in many ways, and in our competition there are certain songs by him, carefully chosen for each vocal category, that every applicant must sing (and every piano applicant play) in the audition process. My experience is that in the performing of a Schubert song there is no hiding place for the singers—whether technically, musically or emotionally. This is also because Wigmore Hall with its wonderfully truthful acoustic has had such a special connection with this supremely truthful composer.

RK As far as I know there is no other composer whose birthday is yearly celebrated there with a concert.

GJ Yes, 31 January is always Schubert Day at Wigmore Hall.

RK On our jury there have been a number of critics, hall administrators, scholars, directors of festivals and so on. With so many famous names it is perhaps inevitable that there has sometimes been disagreement between the jurors. I have usually been a non-voting member of the panel and have been fascinated to see how very differently people evaluate what makes a great recital singer. It is a perpetual battle to balance or off-set the advantages of a God-given instrument with the necessary intelligence, musicality, warmth of personality, choice of repertoire and so on and so on. Since William Lyne retired we have been marvellously guided by his successor, John Gilhooly, as chairman of the panel. He has a background in singing and has taken the hall from strength to strength both artistically, and in terms of its finances.

GJ John is a great blessing for the hall! But even under the most judicious and fair circumstances the judges can never get it right as far as many members of the audience are concerned. If only such people realized how difficult it is to organize an event like this, and how many people are involved! From the house manager, David King, to the enthusiastic royal patrons, HRH The Duke and Duchess of Kent, not to mention John Gilhooly at the head of the team, Wigmore Hall is filled with enthusiasts who are devoted to music. I take my hat off to Helen Granger at Wigmore Hall who is in charge of all the competition's logistics and does a magnificent job. The only person who could probably do it equally well is your daughter Hephzi!

RK I think one would have to be a trained musician to take on this job: we have candidates coming from all over the world and Helen Granger finds herself dealing all the time with such issues as repertoire choices and transpositions of songs, intricate changes of programme in many languages and so on—after all, music has a technical, almost scientific, language of its own that is often not understood by the most ardent music-lover.

GJ Well your own understanding of the language of music has always made you a very hands-on patron. You have been with us every step of the way in the decisions taken to make this competition special.

RK Giving prizes at a competition like this reminds me of something that Sir Clifford Curzon once said about competitions: 'It is such a pleasure to push up-and-coming young talent a little closer to the stars.' On the other hand, I know that singing is a supremely personal thing. Looking at the list of winners (published as an appendix to this book, see page 344) some of the second and third prizewinners of the more distant past may seem to be doing better than some of those who won first prize. I know from my own experience that one can improve a great deal at every stage of one's career, and at any age, and that careers in this field can be remarkably fluid. I have reminded some of the singers not winning the first prize that Johann Sebastian Bach, no less, was third choice for the job of Thomaskantor, after Telemann and Graupner.

The jury of the Wigmore Hall/Kohn Foundation International Song Competition, September 2001
left to right William Lyne, Matthias Goerne, Graham Johnson, Felicity Palmer, Ralph Kohn, Elly Ameling, Mark Brown, Dalton Baldwin

For me the Wigmore Hall competition is about all the contestants and all the music. It is like attending a massive symposium devoted to the subject of recitals with many different presentations and approaches. On each occasion it takes place it is a fascinating international snapshot of the state of the art, and all the youngsters coming to take part, some of them the great artists of the future, give me enormous pleasure and confidence that the art of song will survive, come what may.

The birthday celebrant, Sir Ralph Kohn,
FRS, FMedSci FRCP (Hon), DSc, MAE, FRAM, DMus

INTERLUDE 8: GIGUE

GRAHAM JOHNSON TURNS THE PAGES OF

The Birthday Book, 2007

WHEN RALPH KOHN turned eighty in December 2007, the most precious of gifts was undoubtedly a large and sumptuously arranged Birthday Book that his daughter Hephzi had lovingly, and painstakingly, assembled over many months in order to give him a huge surprise on the day—a kind of *This is Your Life* without the accompanying television interview. This large volume is a combination of photographs and messages written especially for that occasion—the result of Hephzi corresponding with many of Ralph's friends and colleagues from all over the world.

When I suggested to Ralph that he should write about this book and its contents he refused, saying that quoting such words of praise was inappropriate. I replied that he had written about his collection of music, but that his collection of friends was his most precious possession; in my opinion it was the quality and depth of those friendships that best explained both his worldly success and his enviable well-being. Hephzi offered to show me the book and, with some difficulty, I persuaded Ralph that I might choose extracts to form the last of the eight *Interludes* in this book. The selection that follows can only feature a few of the contributors; I am able only to skim the surface of the book's contents and the depth of feeling expressed therein. Unlike the book itself, these tributes are here arranged alphabetically.

from Dayan (rabbinical judge) Ivan Binstock,
Talmudical scholar and Ralph's teacher:

> There are three levels of friendship. The first level of friendship, *chavar ledavar*, is friendship at a pragmatic level. The second level, *chavar leda'agah*, is friendship at the empathetic level. The third level, *chavar ledei'al*, is friendship at the idealistic level. Visiting your home for our *chavruta* [in Talmudic study, the analyzing, discussing and debating of a shared text] I have been able to see at first hand the wonderful model of friendship that you and Zahava are able to enjoy at all three levels.

Dayan Ivan Binstock

from Professor Allan Dixon (the great rheumatologist whose support and advice was crucial to the founding of Advisory Services, and whose name features so often in these pages):

> Businessman, philanthropist, musician, scientist, who came to this country as a boy refugee, seeking sanctuary, and has repaid this country a thousand times …

Professor Victor Dubowitz (the famous neurologist and pediatrician) and his wife Lilly provided an acrostic:

> **R**alph the Renaissance man, Scientist, Scholar, Musician, from
> **A**lpha to Gamara he knows it all.
> **L**yrical with Lieder, passionate for Bach, *meshuga* for Science,
> **P**harmacologist, philanthropist, Patriarich,
> **H**earty, hospitable, *haymish*,
>
> **K**ayn *ein hora* you have so many friends and admirers, an
> **O**scar for your achievement, a *l'chaim* for your future
> **H**ere's wishing you continued jollity and joy with much
> **N**achas and *simchas* and choral resonance, and eternal youth
>   of your creative spirit and soul in the golden years ahead.

Ralph Kohn sharing a joke with Victor Dubovitz

from John Gilhooly OBE, manager of Wigmore Hall:

You (and all of your family) are very much part of the Wigmore Hall family and I hope you feel that.

Lady Jakobovits, widow of the former Chief Rabbi, Immanuel Jakobovits, wrote of

the strength of your deep committment to *Yiddishkeit*, coupled with your exquisite love of the best that the secular world can offer.

from Jehudi Kanarek (brother of Zahava Kohn, living in Israel):

Sadly enough for my self-esteem I was not even asked to approve of my sister's choice of husband. Knowing her however, and being aware of how picky and choosy she could be, I am (now) sure my counsel was not needed!

from Sir Aaron Klug FRS, the Nobel laureate frequently mentioned in the pages of this book:

I feel it is acknowledgement of our continued commitment to our ancestral cultures, and our pleasure in talking about them, that has helped forge an enduring bond between us.

from Sue Lawley (journalist and former presenter of 'Desert Island Discs'):

A castaway who became a friend and man whose great achievements have not prevented him from enjoying and encouraging the achievements of others.

from Claus Moser (Lord Moser, world-famous statistician, former master of Wadham College, Oxford, and former chairman of the Royal Opera House):

You, Ralph, are a remarkable man, and above all such a lovely person. You are the greatest credit to the sort of background we share. I am proud to be your friend, and not only proud, happy!

from John Julius Norwich (son of Duff, Viscount Norwich, and Gladys Cooper)—writer, wit and old friend:

How best to describe you when push comes to shove?
Your life is pharmacology, but music is your love …

A test-tube in your left hand and in your right a score
We wish you Happy Birthday—and so many, many more.

from Lord Jonathan Sacks, Chief Rabbi, writing of when he first met Ralph:

> You were—I thought—a true *Mensch*. Little did I know how true that was …
> You have brought pride to the Jewish people, happiness and blessings to many,
> and inspiration to all who have had the privilege of knowing you.

from Sir John Meurig Thomas FRS:

> Unlike you, Ralph, I can't sing, but
> like you I cannot do without music.
> I have discovered some people
> whose company and passion for
> communication and discourse I
> also cannot live without. You are
> one of them—your whole life
> seems imbued with the noble desire
> to spread good and happiness.

John Meurig Thomas

*from Leslie Turnberg (Lord Turnberg, former president of the Royal College of Physicians,
and fellow Salford man):*

> I first set eyes on him in 1952 in Manchester University's crowded and
> infamous Joint Common Room. I was a 'Fresher' and there was this suave man
> of the world playing poker or bridge in the romantic gloom of JCR—the
> height of sophistication to my fresh-from-school eyes, where male and female
> students were allowed to mix … But few clues there were of his hidden talents.
> Perhaps bridge gave him a facility with sums, and poker his acute acumen, but
> from where came his generosity of spirit and humanity?

The rhetorical question posed by Lord Turnberg remains unanswered, although a
reader of this book from cover to cover may be nearer to uncovering some answers.
My small selection here has permitted me only to pick out a handful of the tributes,
almost at random. There are many more, so permit me a few more examples. Those
great musical entrepreneurs, Victor and Lillian Hochhauser, speak of Ralph's 'great

charm and gaiety'; the great photographer Clive Barda praises Ralph's 'wisdom and lack of cynicism'; David Josefowitz (after whom the Royal Academy of Music's recital hall is named) sees him as 'Bigger than Life' (Josefowitz also contributes to the book an enchanting painted design); the Kohns' friends Stanley and Barbara Green refer to the fact that he worthily wears the 'Crown of Good Name'—counted in the Talmud (by Rabbi Simeon in the *Ethics of the Fathers*) to be more important that the 'Crown of Priesthood' or the 'Crown of Royalty'. Other good friends Kurt and Margaret Stern refer to him as 'the perfect friend Bach could and would have been proud of'. András Schiff, the great pianist, after paying affectionate tribute to Ralph, playfully refers to the fact that 'Kohn' is the stock character in Hungarian Jewish jokes, and proceeds to tell a hilarious story of a Kohn attempting to leave the Soviet Union for Israel. Equally playful is the record producer Mark Brown who draws a parallel between Ralph's singing voice and the purring engine of his favourite Volvo (a beloved car, by no means the latest model, in which he always drove himself to recording sessions). Sir John Eliot Gardiner and his wife Isabella contributed a beautifully printed card of greetings from a Bach cantata with the wording appropriately changed for the occasion. And so on, and so on.

The amazing thing about me going through this Birthday Book for Ralph's eightieth birthday (2007) is that it makes me realize how many new friends have come into his life since then. To tell the truth, any list of the interesting people with

A portrait of Leslie Turnberg

SIR JOHN ELIOT GARDINER

Jauchzet, frohlocket! auf, preiset die Tage,

Rühmet, was heute der Höchste getan!

Lasset das Zagen, verbannet die Klage,

Stimmet voll Jauchzen und Fröhlichkeit an!

Dienet dem Höchsten mit herrlichen Chören,

Laßt uns den Namen Ralph Kohn verehren!

... With a little help from papa Bach, and fon-
dest memories of Christmas Day 1999 in Weimar,
when yp and Zahava joined us for the start
of the Bach Cantata Pilgrimage – which would
not have happened without yp!
With love and warmest wishes for ypr birthday!

A tribute from John Eliot Gardiner and his wife Isabella

whom Ralph Kohn comes into contact would need to be updated almost every week of his life. It is not as easy to meet new people as one might think; most of us are contented to stay within a familiar rut. Ralph, however, manages to break new ground as an everyday fact of life whereas, for many older people, new faces and new friendships represent a burden, an effort of memory (among other things) they are unwilling to make. Ralph's achievement is that so very many of these new acquaintances, once they have experienced his warmth and humanity, are proud and happy, regardless of their age, to begin to count themselves as his friends.

When Ralph Kohn was knighted at Buckingham Palace in 2010, for services to science, music and charity, his family tells me he received a huge number of letters of congratulation—but those letters I have not been permitted to see!

Sir Ralph and Lady Kohn outside Buckingham Palace on the the day of the investiture, 2010
Photograph by Hephzibah Kohn Rudofsky

At my wedding in 1963—my three dear siblings, Celia, Maurice and Toni

PRELUDE XXIII

Family

I WAS THE YOUNGEST of my family, and my brother and two sisters, Maurice, Celia and Toni, married before I did. I am delighted to say they all came to my wedding in Amsterdam in 1963. Sadly, all three have died, as well as their spouses, but I have eight nephews and nieces on this side of my family. The three children of my brother Maurice and his wife Annie all live in Israel: Eli is a Rabbi—Zahava and I went to Australia for his wedding—and my two nieces are Janette Segal (an excellent writer and teacher, married to Johnny who works in the insurance business) and Sharon Gur, who is a hospital nurse and has a heart of gold. Celia and her husband Rudy Stern had three children: Allan, a successful businessman in Los Angeles, Martin who lives in Jerusalem (he is an accountant by training and active in communal affairs) and Rhona, a devoted wife and teacher of infants. My sister Toni and her husband Joe Reid had two children: Rosalind, who trained as a potter and lives in London, and Walter, a successful businessman who also lives in London but spends a lot of time in Los Angeles.

I owe much of the happiness in my life to my own three daughters, and my grandchildren, but before writing about them I will allow myself a few moments of *mea culpa* when I compare myself to the fathers of the present day who, it seems to me, are much more 'hands-on' when it comes to bringing up their children. These days there seems to be a kind of intimate participation right from the beginning, with fathers-to-be attending antenatal classes with their wives. I do not scoff at this involvement, but decades ago this kind of attitude would not have entered anyone's head, and I am not sure that the wives of the time would have welcomed it with any enthusiasm. For people of my generation and background there was no question of a father being a helpmate in the delivery room and participating in the birth of his children. This now seems almost to be a statutory requirement, and I understand that some proud fathers take a video of the birth. (Is this technology fulfilling a long-standing need, or does the need arise simply because such technology exists?) We regularly went on holidays *en famille* (all over Europe, Disneyland in California, Florida, Hawaii, and also to Israel) but fifty years ago it would not have occurred to me to take leave from my work because of an event in the school calendar, an appearance in a concert or school play. Of course, if any of the girls were seriously ill, everything else was immediately dropped, but if I was going to be away on business, a child's birthday party would not have been grounds to cancel or rearrange my commitments (although I would be certain to have brought back appropriate presents). With some certainty I can say that the same held true for those of my contemporaries and colleagues who were also fathers. I suspect that many a young father of today, with the financial means to do so, would hire a helicopter to get back to that all-important birthday party, and would be most proud to have done so. It is, as they say, another world.

History is full of cruel and tyrannical parents, but I can assure you I was neither Mr Barrett of Wimpole Street, nor Dickens's Mr Dombey who hard-heartedly ignored his beautiful daughter Florence (not, by the way, that Dickens was an ideal parent himself). Unlike the protagonist of Bach's 'Coffee Cantata', BWV211, I cannot complain of a thousand troubles with my children, and I am not the kind of father (depicted in Mozart's song *Warnung*) who would heed the advice to lock up his daughters.

Hat man nicht mit seinen Kindern from Cantata No 211 JOHANN SEBASTIAN BACH
CD Track 23   *see page 341 for text and translation*

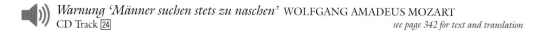

Warnung 'Männer suchen stets zu naschen' WOLFGANG AMADEUS MOZART
CD Track 24   *see page 342 for text and translation*

I suppose what could be said was that I was, by today's standards, rather unaware of the importance of both parents spending daily 'quality time' with children. It goes without saying that I never took paternity leave from my firm—an idea unheard of in those days! The whole perception of who children are, and what they need, has changed and developed enormously in the last half-century. I am not sure that I agree with all the modern conclusions, and I think things may have gone too far in the direction of over-indulgence and over-protectiveness, but there is no denying that our generation overestimated the resilience of some children, treating them as small adults, able to bounce back after sorrows and setbacks of which their parents were sometimes scarcely aware. The phrase 'children should be seen and not heard' was accepted by my generation as quite a sensible dictum rather than a recipe for later trauma, low self-esteem and so on.

My dear girls were always the apples of my eye, and yet, owing to the nature of my work when I was constantly travelling, I left much of the day-to-day responsibility of their upbringing to Zahava; I knew she would be there to look after them in every waking hour when they were not actually at school. Hephzi and Michelle were born in 1963 and 1965 respectively—this was the period of my final, rather unsettled, years at Smith Kline and French (see *Prelude & Fugue XIII*) and I was travelling a great deal. When they were toddlers my energies were taken up with the change of direction in my career as Robapharm's London representative—

this also entailed much international travel. Maxine was born seven years after Michelle, in 1972. At that time I had other pressures—the establishment of my ground-breaking new company, Advisory Services. There is no doubt that I was a proud family man, but if I were to be judged by today's standards, it might be said that I could have attempted to be more involved in the daily routines of the children and in some of the tasks that most mothers of today would not tolerate doing on their own. Once again, I pay tribute to my beloved Zahava who put the children to bed, calmly supervising that daily ritual, and then often worked until midnight packing up parcels of the bone-supplement Ossopan to keep our small, but profitable, business venture going at the time (see *Prelude XVII*). During this time I was often 'out on the road' as the hard-working breadwinner, but this generally involved meeting interesting people, staying in comfortable hotels, and rising refreshed in the morning without having been involved in the small domestic crises that on various occasions Zahava had to cope with on her own. I was no different from all the other fathers of the time whom I knew as colleagues, but I will admit I was different from what is now regarded as the ideal 'available' dad. The idea of a little girl telephoning her father, or texting him, using her own mobile phone, would never have occurred to anyone at that time, even to a writer of the most outlandish science fiction. Once again technology—e-mails, Skype, and so on—has played a major part in forming the duties of modern parents, and the expectations their children have of them.

That having been said, I can say that our three daughters have always been close to me and Zahava. Over the years this closeness has increased and now I enjoy a more loving relationship with each of them than at any other time of my life. I am also on the warmest terms with my sons-in-law and, all in all, I would describe the Kohns as an extremely happy, tightly knit family. Hephzibah (the reader has already met my eldest daughter, Hephzi, in *Fugue XVIII*) and Michelle (my second daughter) both live not far from the parental home in Hampstead. The youngest, Maxine, lives in west London, convenient for all the jet-setting in connection with her work—like me in the old days! She spent eighteen months in Hong Kong, and now has a very senior position with Google here in London, flying to the USA regularly to report to the company's world-famous proprietors in San Francisco. Maxine's son, our youngest grandchild, Sam (born in 2009) will be five this year; her husband, Matt Judge, is in corporate finance and works for Manchester United without being employed as a footballer—although he seems fit and youthful enough to be so! Michelle also has an adorable son, Theo (born in 2007); her husband Michael Da Costa works in the food and supermarket industry. Hephzi has two children with her American-born husband Steven Rudofsky (the children are

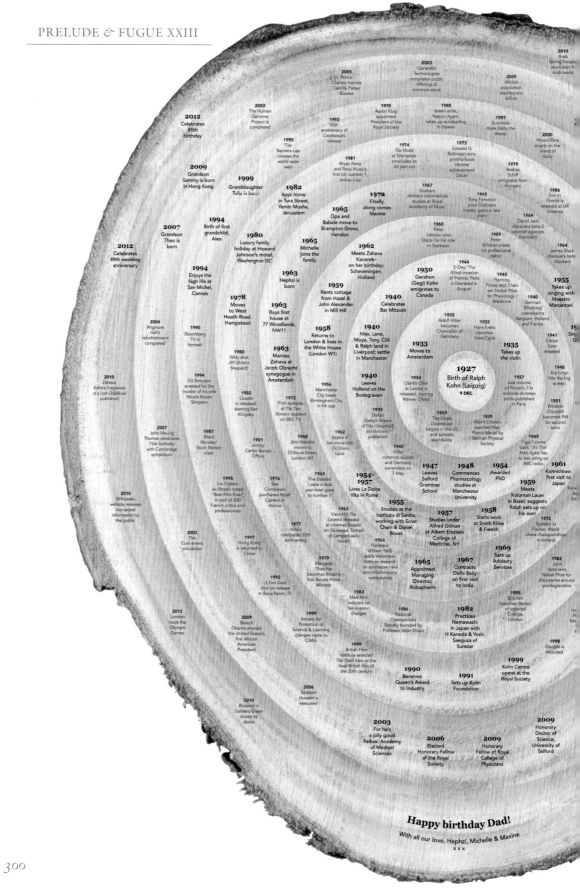

2012 Celebrates 85th birthday

2005 Prince Charles marries Camilla Parker Bowles

2003 The Human Genome Project is completed

2003 Genelabs Technologies completes public offering of common stock

2010 Arab Spring heralds revolution in Arab world

1995 Aaron Klug appointed President of the Royal Society

1988 Israeli artist, Yaacov Agam, takes up windsurfing in Hawaii

2009 Africa's population reaches one billion

2012 Celebrates 85th birthday

1992 50th anniversary of *Casablanca's* release

1997 Scientists clone Dolly the sheep

1990 Tim Berners-Lee creates the world wide web

1974 *The World at War* series concludes its 26 part run

1973 Edward G Robinson wins posthumous lifetime achievement Oscar

2000 Mount Etna erupts on the island of Sicily

2009 Grandson Sammy is born in Hong Kong

1999 Granddaughter Tallulu is born

1981 Bryan Ferry and Roxy Music's first UK number 1, *Jealous Guy*

1979 Andras Schiff emigrates from Hungary

1982 Buys home in Tura Street, Yemin Moshe, Jerusalem

1970 Finally, along comes Maxine

1967 Graham JOHNSON LONFINMEAG studies at Royal Academy of Music

19AR Tony Forwood joins Chalmers Impey; gains a new client

1986 *fem de Flavette* is released at UK cinemas

2007 Grandson Theo is born

1994 Birth of first grandchild, Alex

1965 Opa and Babele move to Brampton Grove, Hendon

1960 Peter Ustinov wins Oscar for his role in *Spartacus*

1969 David Jack discovers beta-2 selector agonists (Ventolin)

2012 Celebrates 49th wedding anniversary

1980 Luxury family holiday at Howard Johnson's motel, Washington DC

1965 Michelle joins the family

1962 Meets Zahava Kanarek— on her birthday; Scheveningen, Holland

1959 Peter Schreier made his professional debut

1964 James Black discovers beta blockers

1994 Enjoys the high life at San Michel, Cannes

1963 Hephzi is born

1959 Rents cottage from Hazel & John Alexander in Mill Hill

1950 Gershon (Gegg) Kohn emigrates to Canada

1944 D-Day: The Allied invasion of France; Paris is liberated in August

1945 Fleming, Florey and Chain win Nobel Prize for Physiology / Medicine

1955 Takes up singing with Maestro Marcantoni

1978 Moves to West Heath Road, Hampstead

1963 Buys first house at 77 Woodlands, NW11

1940 Celebrates Bar Mitzvah

1940 German 'Blitzkrieg' overwhelms Belgium, Holland and France

2004 Wigmore Hall's refurbishment completed

1990 Bloomberg TV is formed

1980 Who shot JR? (Kristin Shepard)

1963 Marries Zahava at Jacob Obrecht synagogue in Amsterdam

1958 Returns to London & lives in the White House (London W1)

1940 Max, Lena, Moya, Tony, Cilli & Ralph land in Liverpool; settle in Manchester

1933 Adolf Hitler becomes Chancellor of Germany

1932 Hans Krebs identifies Urea Cycle

1935 Takes up the violin

1941 *Citizen Kane* released

2010 Zahava Kohn's *Fragments of a Lost Childhood* published

1994 OJ Simpson arrested for the murder of his wife Nicole Brown Simpson

1982 *Gandhi* is released, starring Ben Kingsley

1956 Manchester City beats Birmingham City in FA cup

1933 Moves to Amsterdam

1934 *Charlie Chan in London* is released, starring Warner Oland

1927 Last volume of Proust's *A la recherche du temps perdu* published in Paris

1948 *Key Largo* hits the big screen

1927 Birth of Ralph Kohn (Leipzig) 9 DEC

1929 The Great Depression begins in the US and spreads worldwide

1929 Albert Einstein awarded Max Planck Medal by German Physical Society

1951 Winston Churchill becomes PM for second term

2007 John Meurig Thomas celebrates 75th birthday with Cambridge symposium

1987 'Black Monday' Stock Market crash

1981 Jimmy Carter leaves Office

1968 Jimi Hendrix moves to 23 Brook Street, London W1

1962 *Stephie & Son* move into Old Drum Lane

1939 Stefan Zweig's *Beware of Pity (Ungeduld des Herzens)* published

1949 'I go; I come back.' *It's That Man Again* has its last airing on BBC radio

1961 Konnichiwa: first visit to Japan

1995 *Les Enfants du Paradis* voted "Best Film Ever" in poll of 600 French critics and professionals

1976 Sea Containers purchases Hotel Cipriani in Venice

1963 The Beatles' *I want to hold your hand* goes to number 1

1954-1957 Lives La Dolce Vita in Rome

1947 Leaves Salford Grammar School

1948 Commences Pharmacology studies at Manchester University

1954 Awarded PhD

1959 Meets Koloman Lauer in Basel; suggests Ralph sets up on his own

1972 Spassky vs Fischer, World chess championships in Iceland

2002 The Euro enters circulation

1997 Hong Kong is returned to China

1977 Volvo celebrates 50th anniversary

1963 Visconti's *The Leopard* released at cinemas (based on Giuseppe Tomasi di Lampedusa's novel)

1955 Studies at the Instituta di Sanita, working with Ernst Chain & Daniel Bovet

1957 Studies under Alfred Gilman at Albert Einstein College of Medicine, NY

1958 Starts work at Smith Kline & French

1982 John Vane wins Nobel Prize for discoveries around prostaglandins

2012 London hosts the Olympic Games

2009 Barack Obama elected the United States's first African American President

1979 Margaret Thatcher becomes Britain's first female Prime Minister

1966 Professor William Taub leads Weizmann Institute research to synthesise new anti-inflammatory compounds

1965 Appointed Managing Director, Robapharm

1967 Contracts Delhi Belly on first visit to India

1969 Sets up Advisory Services

1985 Eric Ash becomes Rector of Imperial College, London

1992 *A Few Good Men* on release in Boca Raton, FL

1999 Society for Protection of Science & Learning changes name to CARA

1983 Marc Rich indicted on tax evasion charges

1986 National Osteoporosis Society founded by Professor Allan Dixon

1982 Practices Nemawashi in Japan with H Kaneda & Yoshi Saegusa of Sunstar

1998 Google is founded

2010 Bloom's in Golders Green closes its doors

2006 Saddam Hussein is executed

1999 British Film Institute selected *The Third Man* as the best British film of the 20th century

1990 Receives Queen's Award to Industry

1991 Sets up Kohn Foundation

1999 Kohn Centre opens at the Royal Society

2003 For he's a jolly good Fellow: Academy of Medical Sciences

2006 Elected Honorary Fellow of the Royal Society

2009 Honorary Fellow of Royal College of Physicians

2009 Honorary Doctor of Science, University of Salford

Happy birthday Dad!

With all our love, Hephzi, Michelle & Maxine
xxx

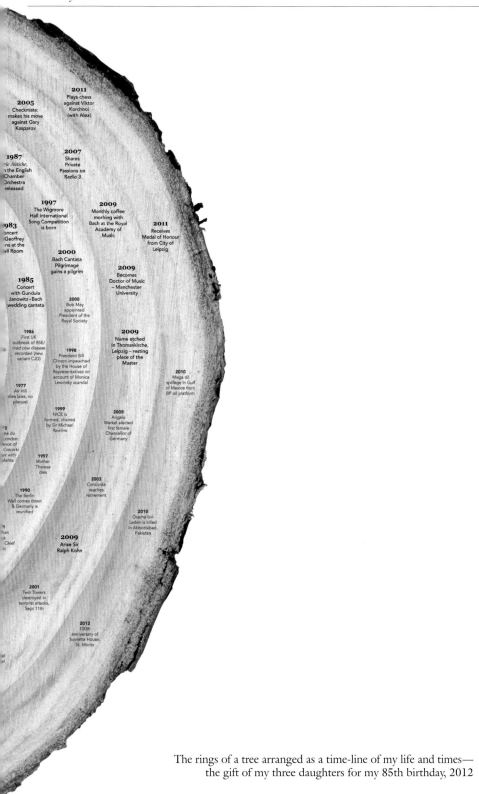

2005
Checkmate:
makes his move
against Gary
Kasparov

2011
Plays chess
against Viktor
Korchnoi
(with Alex)

1987
...ie Antiche,
...n the English
Chamber
Orchestra
released

2007
Shares
Private
Passions on
Radio 3

1997
The Wigmore
Hall International
Song Competition
is born

2009
Monthly coffee
morning with
Bach at the Royal
Academy of
Music

2011
Receives
Medal of Honour
from City of
Leipzig

...983
...oncert
...Geoffrey
...ns at the
...ll Room

2000
Bach Cantata
Pilgrimage
gains a pilgrim

2009
Becomes
Doctor of Music
– Manchester
University

1985
Concert
with Gundula
Janowitz–Bach
wedding cantata

2000
Bob May
appointed
President of the
Royal Society

1986
First UK
outbreak of BSE/
mad cow disease
recorded (new
variant CJD)

1998
President Bill
Clinton impeached
by the House of
Representatives on
account of Monica
Lewinsky scandal

2009
Name etched
in Thomaskirche,
Leipzig – resting
place of the
Master

2010
Mega oil
spillage in Gulf
of Mexico from
BP oil platform

1977
AV Hill
dies (alas, no
plaque)

1999
NICE is
formed, chaired
by Sir Michael
Rawlins

2005
Angela
Merkel elected
first female
Chancellor of
Germany

...3
...ne du
...London
...ance of
...Concerto
...r with
...Aehta

1997
Mother
Theresa
dies

2003
Concorde
reaches
retirement

1990
The Berlin
Wall comes down
& Germany is
reunified

2010
Osama bin
Laden is killed
in Abbottabad,
Pakistan

...1
...han
...a
...Chief
...i

2009
Arise Sir
Ralph Kohn

2001
Twin Towers
destroyed in
terrorist attacks,
Sept 11th

2012
100th
anniversary of
Suvretta House,
St. Moritz

...al
...l

The rings of a tree arranged as a time-line of my life and times—
the gift of my three daughters for my 85th birthday, 2012

both dual citizens of Britain and the USA): Steven is an American lawyer and works as an investment banker in the natural resources sector in emerging markets. My only granddaughter, Talia, was born in 1999, and my eldest grandchild, Alex, in 1994.

In studying medicine at university Michelle achieved what I had hoped, and failed, to do when I left school—she became an MD after studying at University College London, graduating with honours in clinical pharmacology and specializing in oncological research. Like Hephzi, she worked for me as a clinical research assistant at Advisory Services, but for a much shorter period. I would have said Michelle is, by nature, more interested in research than in one-to-one relationships with patients (she would have no interest in being a GP for example). Nevertheless, she has recently made a spectacular success of running *Living Well* at the London Oncology Centre in Harley Street. This involves giving lectures and working closely with patients while taking a holistic approach to their illness—what is termed 'whole-body therapy'. She is utterly dedicated to this work and rarely goes to bed before midnight. She is amazingly quick on the uptake and does everything with energy and zeal.

As a girl, Maxine was perhaps the quietest and most intellectually focused of my daughters, while retaining a steely determination always to do things in her own way. She went to the University of Bristol to study law but found she was not enjoying it; she changed to an honours degree in English at the same university and went on to do her MA (Hons) at King's College in London. I was not surprised by this affinity with English as she was always a great reader. For a while she worked for the communications agency Fishburn Hedges, and was then headhunted by Google. Maxine has an extraordinary brain that is wonderfully attuned to the unfolding marvels of the modern world—a world of which her present employers are global representatives, setting the pace for technological innovation in the twenty-first century.

The reader has already met Hephzi Rudofsky in an earlier chapter. Our eldest daughter, tremendously organized and highly intelligent, supervises and manages many of our business interests and, besides attending to her own family, keeps an eye on us and looks after us devotedly. Creator of the *Surviving the Holocaust* programme associated with Zahava's book, Hephzi has travelled the country, together with her mother—the two of them have connected amazingly with hundreds of young people who are shattered and moved to hear these reminiscences. The Friday evening family gatherings for *Shabbat* usually take place in the beautiful Rudofsky home in a wonderfully quiet corner of north London. My only granddaughter, Talia, is growing up to be a most beautiful and vivacious young lady, keen on the visual arts. There is no sign as yet of a talent for classical music in any of my grandchildren, but the world's perception of music has changed so much that I suppose it is possible that the Kohn musical gene will declare itself by one of the grandchildren excelling in a different kind of music from the one familiar to me. In the meantime I am grateful for the companionship of Talia's brother Alex, Hehpzi and Steven's son. Alex, my eldest grandson, is presently making the entire family proud by spending a gap year in Jerusalem pursuing a course in Talmudical studies. While he is away I miss him as an opponent in chess. It was a most moving experience for me to help prepare Alex for his bar mitzvah in 2007; the work we did together paid off handsomely as I have seldom seen a boy at this important ceremony as confident and fluent as he was on that occasion.

In this book I have talked a great deal about my musical enthusiasms, far less about my passion for chess. The Kohn Foundation has contributed to the remarkable initiative of Pete Davies (of Lansdowne Partners) whose *Chess in Schools and Communities* scheme has provided schools with chessmen and chessboards. This enlightened sponsorship is the best way to initiate a passion for chess in the young. In recent years, purely for fun, I have played Garry Kasparov and Viktor Korchnoi—both in London at simultaneous displays where the grand master takes on a number of opponents, all at once. The occasion with the great Korchnoi (a Russian Jew who lives in Switzerland) was in 2011 at a simultaneous display in Olympia. The great man walked unperturbed from one board to another, making his moves seemingly effortlessly, as if all his opponents were so many flies casually to be brushed off the sleeve of his jacket. For me the important (and very proud) thing about this match was that I had gone into battle against Korchnoi together with my grandson Alex, then seventeen years old. Together we came up with a move that we hoped would floor Korchnoi. This was to hope in vain of course; nevertheless we did give him pause for thought. He stopped at our board and said: 'Das ist aber interessant!' ('Now that is interesting!'). This was a thrilling moment for both of us, even if it did nothing to avert our eventual and inevitable defeat at Korchnoi's ruthless hands. How well I remember playing chess with my older cousin Gegi—I even beat him on occasion despite the age-gap between us—and Alex has come perilously near to beating me.

There is nothing more blessed than family life. How lucky I am, and this is largely thanks to Zahava, that I have been able to pursue my twin passions of science and music while always being able to count on the continuity of loving support at home. The love and admiration of my three girls, my four girls including Zahava, has buoyed me up in times of doubt and uncertainty—this kind of devotion is unconditional and everlasting and is not to be expected from business associates or even close friends. I would be less than human to disguise the fact that at times I have felt, as a mere male, overwhelmed by the line-up of females in my family, each of them a remarkably strong human being in her own right, and each subtly different from the other. I have often proven pathetically unequal to the task of pressing home the male viewpoint in the teeth of such opposition, but I am far from subjugated or hen-pecked. Instead I would claim to be as spoiled, and shamelessly indulged, as an Oriental Pasha: I have been surrounded, for as long as I can remember, by a group of loving women such as any man might envy, and these four unbelievably special women have immeasurably enriched and ennobled my life as a husband and father.

Maxine, Hephzibah and Michelle Kohn in 2013 on the occasion of their parents' Golden Wedding Anniversary

Fugue XXIII *(in 4 voices)*

The three daughters of Sir Ralph Kohn (Hephzibah Kohn, Dr Michelle Kohn and Maxine Kohn—respectively, Mrs Rudofsky, Mrs Da Costa and Mrs Judge) with Graham Johnson. Hephzi was born in 1963, Michelle in 1965 and Maxine in 1972.

GJ Hephzi, Michelle and Maxine, we are having this conversation in your parents' home in Hampstead, within walking distance of Hampstead Heath. For the reader I should explain this is a family residence par excellence—on two floors, comfortable and roomy, beautifully furnished, with a lovely garden behind the house. Nevertheless, coming into this dwelling one immediately feels an atmosphere that is *haymish* (Yiddish for cosy) rather than conspicuously luxurious. Although this is certainly a home for entertaining—I have attended any number of convivial gatherings here, and there have been several informal recitals in the downstairs drawing room with its fine grand piano—there is no ostentation.

HEPHZI I remember moving here from our first family home in the Woodlands in Golders Green—it was smaller than this, but it was closer to my grandparents who lived a twenty-minute walk away in Hendon. I have fond memories of our first home as we used to play outside with our many neighbourhood friends. Dad used to call us 'street children'. I love this home; it has a lot of character and charm and I think it exudes the warmth and interests shared by my parents. The house is filled with books, photographs and artefacts which they have collected over the years. My sisters and I visit our parents regularly—and now with our children too.

GJ You and Michelle went to North London Collegiate, a very fine school indeed—and later on, also Maxine.

HEPHZI My parents always attached great importance to an excellent education, and I'm sure they made sacrifices at the time in order to send us to this school. I hope they feel it was worthwhile!

MAXINE At NLC there were plenty of girls with rich parents who lived a very different lifestyle … at school we never really fitted into an obvious category. Many girls, both Christian and Jewish, came from very materialistic families …

MICHELLE … we were never given big gifts—they were always very thoughtful gifts—but nothing too lavish …

MAXINE … at school holidays, many of the kids at North London Collegiate went off on glamorous beach, or skiing, holidays with their parents, while we were taken to Italy to see the frescoes of Piero della Francesca in Tuscany.

GJ It might not have seemed very 'cool' at the time, but I would consider that kind of artistic pilgrimage very glamorous in its own way!

MAXINE Yes it was—and I realized that to a far greater extent when I got a bit older.

MICHELLE We were incredibly lucky in that way. Dad was not one to talk a lot about his innermost feelings, but he always shared his passions with us. I am mad about opera and it definitely goes back to all those childhood memories—hearing Mozart in Salzburg, for example, and eating Sachertorte in Vienna. I was even allowed to experience Wagner in Bayreuth at the same time as being made aware of all the more negative issues surrounding that composer. Wonder and mystery, travel and music, this was all part of growing up.

MAXINE And yet there were no cosy bed-time stories, no doing puzzles on the floor with the kids. Dad was always very busy at his work. I am quite a bit younger than my sisters, but it seemed to me he was always travelling while our amazing mother managed on her own. We certainly didn't have the typical soft, liberal parents of today; we fitted around them.

GJ Your father admits to that now, and acknowledges how differently children are brought up in the present-day world!

MAXINE I think there was even a difference by the time I was born—I expect that Hephzi and Michelle were more strictly brought up than me. Even ten years makes a huge difference.

MICHELLE On the other hand, when the parents were at home, we were always allowed to mix with the adults. From the age of six I can remember family meals with medics, artists, musicians. It was not all science but a wonderful mixture of science and music, as well as history and languages. I wanted to be a doctor from early on because, in our home, medicine seemed to be something far bigger and more interesting than simply scientific facts. Medical men and women came to the house and spoke about the arts with such knowledge and such love … I thought that's what a life in medicine automatically entailed …

GJ And a life in medicine is what you have had, Michelle. And what about each of you in terms of artistic education? Music, languages and so on?

HEPHZI It's a pity that Dad never spoke anything but English to us. I think it was part of a loyalty to the adopted country that refugees wanted to bring their children up to be thoroughly British. Languages are something he shares with our mother, and many of his friends, like yourself, but not with us. Of course we all picked up quite a lot of Yiddish over the years—ironically this was the language he spoke to my mother when he didn't want us to understand what they were saying! We all studied the piano—I also had flute lessons and Michelle played the oboe. Dad was a hard taskmaster when it came to piano practice. Practice times were sacrosanct as far as he was concerned and there were consequences if we didn't practise. I wish I had adopted his discipline vis-à-vis my children.

GJ So your father was quite a disciplinarian?

MICHELLE In his way … he had incredibly high expectations of us. We had it ingrained in us that 'genius was 10% inspiration and 90% perspiration'! When things were getting out-of-hand in terms of dicipline, he used phrases from his own school years in Salford, like 'If there's any more of it, there will be less of it', or 'Chance come to the mind made ready'. He could be quite stern and I think we were all worried about letting him down by not doing our best.

HEPHZI I can't begin to count the gifts of growing up in our home. Our musical education has left us with a huge respect and love of music. And we all have a deep appreciation of the arts, which may have stemmed from our weekly Sunday morning outings to Kenwood House—or other art galleries. This took precedence over any other activities.

MAXINE That's certainly true of me! I have thoroughly enjoyed the Bach cantata performances I have attended, but you are right—being younger I suppose I was the musical rebel of the family. I had piano lessons, but my tastes went off into rather more modern directions. I adore pop culture and modern comedy, for example.

MICHELLE Well my little boy, Theo, also adores pop music—perhaps he is a Mick Jagger in the making, and my niece Talia, Hephzi's daughter, is a great drummer. I am completely in love with opera now, so who knows what the children will be like when they get older. We are all changing all the time.

GJ One does, however, have the impression that the trajectory of pop music is unstoppable. And your work for Google, Maxine, couldn't be more modern in terms of technology—the sending of texts and e-mails, and so on, is hardly Ralph's strongest point.

MICHELLE He is quite resistant to technology …

HEPHZI True—to this day Dad doesn't own a mobile telephone and nor is he computer literate. And yet, I think we can all agree that Dad's way of conducting business and his way of corresponding with people has an old-world charm that I would be sad to see disappear.

MAXINE If someone writes to him he will send a 'thank you' letter—dictated to his secretary, and then, if there is a 'thank you' for the 'thank you' the correspondence thread can go on for ever!

MICHELLE One thing that is very important to say is that he never, ever made any of us think that being girls made us intellectually inferior or less able to do things that were ostensibly reserved for men. As far as he was concerned, the sky was the limit as far as our careers were concerned. When you consider the entirely domestic life of his own mother and many others of his female relations, dad was a really forward thinker. He believed in equal opportunities for women.

GJ Does that go against any Jewish Orthodox precepts of women's role in society?

MICHELLE I think everyone has a slightly different idea about what being a Jew entails, a different set of priorities. For dad it is a question of being proud of being a part of a great cultural background, studying the Talmud and so on, reading Hebrew, and examining the philosophical and historical sides of the religion. There are many people who have very Jewish lifestyles, and sometimes very narrow Orthodox beliefs, but have no real knowledge of the religion. I can't imagine my father allowing himself to be lectured or reproved by any of those types on account of the fact that all three of his daughters went to university and married relatively late!

HEPHZI Of course he was rather an old-fashioned paterfamilias in that he was very protective of us girls, concerned for our safety and happiness, worrying whether I should go to study in New York, or whether Michelle should visit the Solomon Islands on her own, but that was something physical. Mentally we were free to follow our dreams.

MICHELLE And there were many of our school friends, with that fantastic education behind them, who were simply expected by their parents to grow up, marry well, have a family … end of story.

GJ What about your dad's faults?

MAXINE I think we all agree that he has very little patience. When he gets an idea in his head to do something he wants it done yesterday. And he goes on and on until he gets his way. He doesn't always win, but he wins quite a lot of the time! It is my mother who handles him better than anyone else.

HEPHZI Dad can be quite stubborn too. I have a particular recollection of our being on holiday in Hawaii many years ago when he bought a shiny black-and-white blazer. After asking our opinion (which was unanimously negative) he proceeded to buy the jacket, and continued to wear it with complete determination and sheer delight. We were quite embarrassed. We used to tell him that he looked like a clown—but I think he continued to wear it just to spite us! I think he still has this jacket in his wardrobe …

GJ Perhaps it was just his way of asserting a bit of independence! I can only imagine what it must be like for him to have four ladies ganging up on him!

MAXINE We have all had our ups and downs with our parents—of what family is that not true? But the fact is that my relationship with mum and dad is closer and more comfortable than it has ever been. Dad is a kind person and not ashamed to show his vulnerabilities. For me that is incredibly endearing.

MICHELLE This is so true of me also. For the last ten years of my life my dad has been a kind of hero, an elder statesman to whom one can always go for guidance. And however busy he was in years gone by, these days he always has time and infinite concern for each one of us.

HEPHZI I have a deep love and respect for my father—as we all do. I continue to value and marvel at his amazing mental acuity, his drive, and passion for whatever he pursues and the fact that at all times he is thinking about us, and our own families, with our best interests at heart. He has a wonderful sense of humour too and can be very playful. I find this side of Dad very endearing. I have learned so much from my father and I'm sure Michelle and Maxine feel the same. My father's achievements make me incredibly proud of him.

MICHELLE & MAXINE Yes! … Absolutely!

Photograph by Hephzibah Kohn Rudofsky

PRELUDE XXIV

With Johann Sebastian Bach in London

I THINK I MUST OPEN THE LAST of these autobiographical Preludes by expressing gratitude, not to a person, but to an entire country. I have had an exceptionally happy life, but none of it would have been possible without the humanity and decency with which the United Kingdom welcomed me, and my family, in May 1940. We arrived penniless and downtrodden; from the moment we arrived, the older among us were treated with compassion and dignity, and the younger were given the chance to remake their lives in any direction they chose. I was fed and clothed and educated by Britain when I had nothing, and in return I have contributed whatever I can to a country of which I remain immensely proud and grateful to be a citizen. I have always regarded my residency here as a privilege.

Of course I have always been keenly aware that I am only one of the very many who owe a similar debt to Britain. In 2009 I was immensely honoured to give a lecture at the Royal Society to mark the seventy-fifth anniversary of the organization now known as CARA (the Council for Assisting Refugee Academics) which had begun in 1933 as the AAC—the Academic Assistance Council. Doing the research for this project truly brought home to me the miracles wrought by certain people in this country, as soon as Nazism began to assert itself, in order to secure new positions in England for the very many distinguished scientists who had been unceremoniously ejected from their jobs in Germany. The title of my lecture was *Nazi Persecution—Britain's Gift*; it is clear that in throwing out some of the greatest minds in science (and the arts, of course) Hitler had stupidly, and quite unintentionally, bequeathed a priceless gift to his enemies. I was far too young to belong to this amazing group of refugees who had brought their wonderful skills, and in some cases their genius, to this country, but the reader of this book will already know the names of many of the famous scientists—Ernst Chain, Max Perutz and Hans Krebs among many others—whose careers were saved by the efforts of the AAC. Their subsequent contributions to this country have been justly praised and honoured in many quarters. When I was approached by CARA, I realized that it was high time to pay adequate tribute to the distinguished group of British scientists and politicians who had brought about this rescue in the first place. It seemed to me that they had not received their full due. The very joy of a German refugee being able to work in Britain was best expressed by Hans Krebs (later Sir Hans Krebs) who found himself working in Sir Frederick Gowland Hopkins's

Hans Krebs and his son John Krebs

laboratory in Cambridge—and these words are, in themselves, a tribute to the British character: 'The laboratory included people of many different dispositions, connections and abilities. I saw them argue without quarrelling, quarrel without suspecting, suspect without abusing, criticize without vilifying, and praise without flattering.' Hans Krebs's son John is the distinguished zoologist Lord Krebs.

These words express supremely well the feeling of an outsider's delight in being permitted to become British among the British; I have heard similar sentiments expressed countless times by others. The problem in 1933 was how to place all these out-of-work Germans in appropriate British positions. As Oscar Wilde observed: 'It is personalities, not principles, which move the age.' My CARA speech paid tribute to such names as William Beveridge (Lord Beveridge) who had happened to be in Austria with Sir Lionel Robbins in 1933 at the time the mass-sackings of Jewish academics were taking place. Beveridge had been among the first to assess the scale of the catastrophe, and the sheer waste of human talent that would ensue unless something was done immediately to help.

His AAC colleagues included such luminaries as Ernest Rutherford (Lord Rutherford) and Archibald Hill (A V Hill)—these two were Nobel laureates in 1908 and 1922 respectively—and Patrick Blackett (P M S Blackett) who later attempted to teach me physics at Manchester University. My undistinguished studentship in that subject coincided, as it happened, with Blackett winning the Nobel prize in 1948. The roll-call of honour as far as the AAC is concerned is a long and distinguished one, mostly non-Jewish, and it includes people across the political spectrum—for example, Blackett was very left wing and Frederick Lindemann (Lord Cherwell), a friend of Churchill, was a man of the wealthy right.

Their tactics differed but both were essential to the scheme. Tribute should also be paid to the nuclear physicist Leó Szilárd, a Hungarian Jew, who had worked together with Beveridge in the early stages of bringing the AAC into being.

The truly unsung heroine of the enterprise, the heart and soul of this extraordinary employment exchange for exiled German academics, was the executive assistant to the general secretary, Esther Simpson, affectionately known as Tess. She was a fluent German speaker and she was Jewish by birth—although she chose not to make an issue of this; there was some fear at the time, as astonishing as it now may seem, that the appearance of English Jews doing their best to save German Jews would stir up feelings of anti-Semitism. She was also a musician—a fine violinist and chamber music player. I never knew Tess Simpson personally, but I find her a particularly endearing character because I feel she inhabited, like me, the fascinating border-country between science and music. The original remit of the AAC had been to help scientists, but Tess's musical skills brought her into contact with such great personalities as Ernst Gombrich (whom I knew quite well), the great Schubert scholar Otto Erich Deutsch (one of Graham Johnson's heroes), the violinist Max Rostal, the members of the Amadeus String Quartet, the architectural historian Sir Nikolaus Pevsner and the philosopher Karl Popper. According to her own memoirs, Tess Simpson was better able to achieve the aims of the organization for which she worked because she shared a love of music with those who came to her for help.

For someone who has lost everything, a couple of hours of music-making is magically capable of rebuilding a sense of safety and security, of reawakening a belief in civilized values, of reaffirming trust in man's humanity to man. It is this aspect of great music that has become dangerously underestimated by those who are

Esther (Tess) Simpson

William Beveridge

Leó Szilárd

responsible for educating the young. The kind of world-threatening disaster experienced by my generation made for a time when great music was not merely an entertainment, it was a moral force and an inarguable blessing I have a feeling it may be called upon, at some time in the unknown future, to perform a similar function right at the heart of society.

Music has certainly been a major blessing in my own life. Science and music, music and science—I have spent my life moving between these two disciplines while trying to decide which I love more, and which has played a more important part in my story. Certainly, without my career in science it would never have been possible for the Kohn Foundation to play a meaningful part in the activities of the Wigmore Hall and the Royal Academy of Music. But, looking back, something seems clearer to me than ever before: without music, my career in science would have been less successful and far less enjoyable.

I have already spoken about the recitals I used to do, accompanied by Ernst Chain, and I have lost count of the number of times I have been called on to sing something—perhaps not an entire recital, but a few songs—in connection with a scientific conference or symposium. My passion for music—my desire to listen to it, enthuse about it and share it, as well as sing it myself—turned out to be a kind of totally unplanned 'Open Sesame' into some of the greatest scientific companies in Europe. These organizations were headed by rounded individuals, bored with discussing scientific and business matters twenty-four hours a day; many of these highly educated people rejoiced in the chance to go to concerts or the opera, either in their own countries where I was their guest (often together with Zahava) or when they were in Britain where I was their host at exciting musical events. It meant something to them that I was able to discuss music knowledgeably—that I had real opinions and enthusiasms. When it later came to our business discussions, a barrier had been miraculously broken down: music prepared the way for a civilized conversation between us, rather than purely commercial negotiations.

I have lived long enough to see some sponsorship of classical music as a means to a rather hollow end: these days, companies' guests are taken to Glyndebourne or Covent Garden as an elite outing where the actual opera being sung is the least interesting part of the evening for almost everyone concerned. I can only come to the sad conclusion that these people were never given the chance at a younger age to listen to classical music and appreciate what it has to offer. The modern businessman often bypasses music altogether: he plays golf with clients or takes them to the races—whether Ascot, Epsom or Formula One. But my clients were not ordinary businessmen, and neither was I. It did not seem to matter to them that I could not play golf (chess was another matter!) and I am not a drinker; my version of a round of golf ended at a different kind of clubhouse, one equipped with a concert stage or orchestra pit. I have always admired the reputation of the great Edwardian baritone, the first singer to present Schubert's *Winterreise* in England, Harry Plunket Greene, and I can tell you I would much rather be known for my Plunket Greene skills than be associated with the Putting Green!

I must have been incredibly lucky to have worked for companies where, time after time, music was really appreciated by the people in charge. A shared love of music has laid the foundation of countless friendships in my life—this surely goes back to my early days in Amsterdam when my much older cousin Gegi was my mentor. He already had amazing medical knowledge and was, in many ways, a dashing man of the world—he had the sophistication and cynicism that are so often found in the young who think they know it all, but these completely melted away when it came to Gegi's open-hearted reverence for the great conductor Mengelberg, and the chance of attending a concert at the Concertgebouw. There was no question but that this was spiritual food, something almost mystical capable of uniting an audience as if in a sacred rite of passage. We all came out of those concerts changed people, somehow transfigured by what we had heard, this was even the case with me at eleven years old. And it was important that we had all been together in that great concert hall to hear and share the same thing. This above all is the importance of live music-making.

I have written about how much I enjoy recording and how it enables me to concentrate on certain aspects of singing and interpretation. I have listened to many hundreds of recordings in my time, and learned a great deal from them. But I have no doubt that my greatest musical experiences have been in a concert hall, or opera house, sitting together with other people—all the better if they are loved ones or friends—and hearing (as well as seeing) that magical moment when the imagination of the great performer, on whatever instrument, becomes a sonic reality created entirely for us, and when the score, imprisoned in its black-and-white pages, springs into life, blazing with musical colours. There is absolutely nothing like it!

This is certainly one of the reasons why the Bach cantata mornings at the Royal Academy of Music are so dear to me. These performances are not only for me and my family but for the hundreds of people I have never met—and yet I somehow feel I know them all, thanks to Bach and our shared enthusiasm for this great composer. I sit next to Zahava at these concerts and hear the great unfolding of Bach's extraordinary music, an unending fount of inspiration and genius, and feel particularly fortunate that we are able to enjoy this music together in the company of close friends, acquaintances and countless strangers.

The extent of these concerts' renown is demonstrated by the following story concerning our recent return from a visit to Amsterdam, landing at City Airport. We proceeded to immigration where an official examined my passport. Normally this takes thirty seconds, but on seeing my picture he looked very carefully again, then enlarged it to cover his screen and then, on returning my passport, said: 'You are the Kohn of the Kohn Foundation.' I thought I was about to be delivered to MI5, the Inland Revenue, or flown to Guantanamo Bay for further investigation! I said in a subdued voice: 'Yes, I am.' 'Well, I wish to congratulate you on those marvellous Bach cantatas performed at the Royal Academy of Music. Every month I normally attend them and I cannot tell you how much pleasure and happiness it gives me.' I was quite bowled over and lost for words. I had not realized that the British immigration authorities expected a knowledge of Bach as part of their required qualifications. The good thing is that if only Bach-lovers were to be allowed back into the country, I know I would always qualify for residence! We have certainly come a long way from being labelled by Oskar Schmitz in Edwardian days 'Das Land ohne Musik'!

We all come out of the Duke's Hall at lunchtime on those special Sundays with radiantly happy faces, united in the veneration of Bach's greatness. I also experience this feeling in the Thomaskirche in Leipzig—as I explained in the first Prelude of this book. This series is a gift Zahava and I made to ourselves in the knowledge that it would give Londoners of all ages the chance of hearing these great works performed live. I suppose in a way we have created, nine times a year, a little corner of Leipzig for ourselves in Marylebone Road. At the same time it gives singers and players at the academy a chance to study this divine music (an epithet I have chosen carefully) in a way that might otherwise never have come their way. It is thanks to them, and Jonathan Freeman-Attwood, that our dreams of hearing Bach in this way have come true. The Kohn Foundation has done many worthwhile things, I am proud and happy to say, but few have brought me such personal joy.

We are almost two-thirds of our way through the cycle now—the current projection is that the cycle will take eight or nine years in total. If, by some miracle, we were suddenly able to have available to us the fifty-to-a-hundred cantatas we know Bach composed but which are now lost to us, the series would last another two to four years. I would be certain to be there, come what may, for each and every concert. In fact, if there were a chance to hear the music of Bach once every

Awarding the Bach prize at the Royal Academy of Music in 2007. *left to right* Curtis Price, Peter Schreier (the recipient of the award on this occasion), András Schiff, Christoph Wolff

week at the academy, I would have to make up my mind to live for ever! In closing this final chapter, however, my thoughts turn to Franz Schubert's *Die Taubenpost*. The singer tells us about a faithful carrier-pigeon whose name is 'Sehnsucht'—a metaphor for longing. Nothing will deter this valiant bird from continuing to fly in hope and devotion. There is a kind of selfless bravery and persistence described in this wonderfully beautiful music which touches me enormously—also because it is the very last song that Franz Schubert ever wrote.

 Die Taubenpost No 14 *of* Schwanengesang, D965a　FRANZ SCHUBERT (1797–1827)　*see page 343*
CD Track 25　　　　　　　　　　　　　　　　　　　　　　　　　　　　　*for text and translation*

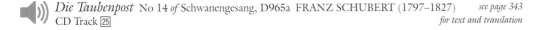

Fugue XXIV (*in 2 voices*) RALPH KOHN *with* GRAHAM JOHNSON

GJ Reading your closing words of this final Prelude leaves one in no doubt that you are a man of great determination! Positive thought seems to have played a crucial role in your life. Anyone who knows you well has heard your favourite German expression—'Nägel mit Köpfe'—an old saying that brings to mind a carpenter hammering in the heads of nails in order to finish a job, the idea of bringing something energetically to a successful conclusion, come what may.

RK One of my favourite sayings comes from the American president, Calvin Coolidge. I have a note of it here somewhere and can read it to you:

> Nothing in the world can take the place of Persistence.
> Talent will not; nothing is more common than unsuccessful men with talent.
> Genius will not; unrewarded genius is almost a proverb.
> Education will not; the world is full of educated derelicts.
> Persistence and determination alone are omnipotent.

The slogan 'press on' has solved and always will solve the problems of the human race.

GJ Well you have been true to those ideals and pressed on with your writing task until you have reached this final Prelude and Fugue of your autobiography. As you note in your introduction, it is something that many people never get round to doing. Have you enjoyed the experience?

RK It has been hard work! Fortunately I have been blessed with a reasonably good memory, a complete set of diaries that goes back almost fifty years, and a tendency to make copious notes about things—sometimes in the middle of the night. I must also say that since the Kohn Foundation began I have given a number of lectures. Preparing the scripts for these many public appearances has been the best possible practice for undertaking a larger task like this book.

GJ These lectures are mostly published in booklets—and there are a number of them here: I have already read *The pharmacological basis of the Kohn Foundation*—it makes excellent background reading to your life-story.

RK There you are!—that lecture which I gave as my introduction to the Royal Society in 2006 was really the origin of this book.

GJ In 2009 you gave the Bynum Tudor lecture at Kellogg College, Oxford, entitled *Challenges and opportunities in a changing world*. Also autobiographical was the

presidential address given at the Birmingham & Midland Institute in 2011—
In Pursuit of Passion.

RK   Yes, both of those are about my own life and times, but I am really a lot happier when I am talking about the achievements of others. I gave a lecture on Sir Ernst Chain when the Ernst Chain prize was initiated at Imperial College, and one on Sir Henry Dale when the prize named after him was initiated at the Royal Institution. And of course, there was my lecture at Manchester University on A V Hill. In 2009 my distinguished friend Dame Nancy Rothwell invited me to open the A V Hill building (together with A V Hill's grandson) and I gave a lecture on this great occasion entitled *A V Hill: Physiologist, Humanitarian, Parliamentarian*. During the writing of the CARA lecture in 2009 I had realized how important this wonderful man had been in the setting up of the Academic Assistance Counsel, and then I did a lot more research about him. It is a wonderful thing to discover new heroes late in life and A V Hill certainly comes into that category for all sorts of reasons—he was as great a human being as he was a scientist, as passionate a family man as he was a researcher and politician. He seems to me to have been altogether admirable.

GJ   Discovering new heroes, like discovering new pieces of music, is certainly exhilarating. It is a new kind of journey. With all the work you do daily at the office in Harley Street and your various writing projects, do you have time to travel, and do you enjoy it as much as ever?

RK   I travel far less than I used to when I was a businessman, but it still brings me enormous pleasure. We have our favourite spots to which we regularly return: we have an apartment in Cannes, quite near the sea; we love going to the spa town of Bad Ragaz—Zahava is always very happy in Switzerland, the country where her maternal grandparents lived—and of course we visit Israel often. If we go further afield than this, to America or Australia for example, the journey is usually associated with family celebrations of one kind or another—like the *Bris* of my youngest grandson in Hong Kong a few years ago.

A V Hill

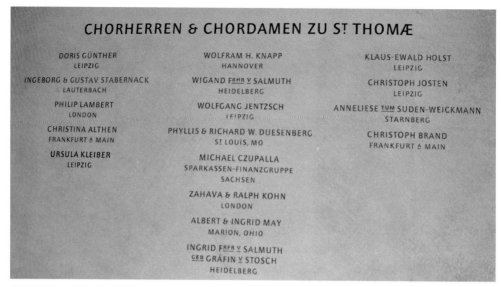

Our names engraved on a wall of the Thomaskirche, very near to the grave of J S Bach

GJ   And of course you visit Leipzig regularly. In some ways it seems as if you had never been exiled from Leipzig in the first place.

    At the very least you have taken great care to somehow repair the damage represented by the disruptions to your life in your earliest years. Is that a fair way of putting it? It is as if the cantatas you have made possible at the academy are a way of reconciling, and of bringing together, your twin heritages from Germany and Britain.

RK   This has not been a conscious decision, but things have worked out that way. There comes a time, as you will see when you get a bit older, when the ideas of early days and later days join up to become one large picture, the totality of one's life. When he was an old man, Goethe wrote a poem about this with the title of _Um Mitternacht_ in which he describes how, at midnight, thoughts of the past and the future embrace each other and come full circle.

GJ   As a matter of fact there is a wonderful musical setting of that poem by Goethe's friend Zelter …

RK   Trust you to know that! In answer to your question, there is a great deal that has remained the same, and some things that have changed for the better. And the reason some things have remained as they are is precisely because I have changed. I am reminded of a wonderful quote from a favourite film of mine, Visconti's _Il Gattopardo_ (_The Leopard_), based on a story by Lampedusa: 'If we wish things to remain as they are, we have to change.' As a result of such changes in these last years I feel closer to my wife and three daughters than ever before—an enormous blessing. We are truly a united and happy family, and what more could a man want of life than that? My love for music and my admiration for the achievements of science are unshakeable. I believe we must all nurture the best within us and make the most of our talents. I remain convinced I can still learn more about singing and how to make the best of my voice—I vocalize daily after breakfast and Zahava says she would be lost without the sound of me singing around the house. I study the Talmud every week, without fail, with Dayan Binstock; this gives me an ever-deepening understanding of my cultural heritage as a Jew, and of the faith of my fathers.

It has sometimes been quite hard for me in the pages of this book to untangle the strands of my life so that I could write about them more or less chronologically; in truth, nothing happens in this well-ordered way. Our lives are lived in a continual state of change and growth. In truth, everything happens at the same time and every facet of our lives is constantly changing.

GJ Well, an acceptance of this seems to keep you in very good form, both physical and mental.

RK During my childhood, after the loss of my brother Simon, my parents were always worried about my health. You remember I spent six months in a sanatorium in Holland as a boy, but since then I have had remarkable stamina that has stood me in good stead for decades. I have been fortunate to survive two bouts of serious illness in the last fifteen years or so, the second of these relatively recently, but as I sit here talking to you I feel as fit as the proverbial fiddle—or, at the very least, as fit as a viola, that rather more portly instrument! There is no point in too much nostalgia and looking back with regret: if one castigates oneself continually in thinking 'I could have done better' in this or that way, or if one dwells in a glorious past, rather than the present—both these attitudes are unhelpful. The same applies at looking back at the horrors of the past, and my dear wife remains an amazing example of the power of positive thought in this respect. I look forward to waking up and discovering what each new day has in store for me: new experiences, new discoveries, new thoughts and new friends, as well as the reaffirmation of everything that is glorious about tried-and-trusted discoveries and dear old friends. For me, learning is my deepest pleasure. As life is all about learning, it follows that life is a pleasure beyond compare. Today perhaps I will have the chance to hear a piece of Bach that has so far eluded me, or I will rediscover a Yiddish saying that I had forgotten from my youth. Perhaps I will meet someone who has an insight on something that opens new doors for me, and those doors will, in turn, lead to the recovery of a memory or feeling from the past that had slipped out of my grasp. In this way the old and the new blend for me into a single, joyous whole. I feel I am in continual pursuit of an understanding of life that comes into sharper and more meaningful focus with each day.

GJ   I have long thought that your pharmacological researches have provided you with a kind of elixir of youth that preserves your energies and determination. Thank you for your geniality and openness over these months of extended conversations. Now that the questions have come to an end, and in presenting you with a transcribed typescript of all our work together, I can only echo the words of the famous television personality, Eamonn Andrews: 'Ralph Kohn, This is Your Life.'

RK   Thank you from the bottom of my heart, dear Graham, for your collaboration, as much on the printed page as in many years of music-making. I don't want to alarm you, but I hope you realize this volume is only my opening gambit, the first part of a continuing story ... ?

GJ   Perhaps next time I can persuade you into what might be termed 'best-selling' tactics: a story brimming with bitterness and indiscreet criticisms of colleagues, the paying-back, with interest, of criticism and insults. We will also require a few tearful confessions of your own peccadillos, even if we had to make the details up. We would need a good libel lawyer of course, but armed with spectacular details such as these we may manage to get the next book serialized in a national newspaper! If you emerged as a kind of Napoleon of clinical trials, opposing the big corporations who wished to guzzle from the trough, we would have to think of an arresting new title for the sequel: how about *Animal Pharma*?

RK   Well Graham, it's a good joke, but I am certainly no George Orwell, and no Napoleon. I'm rather too tall for a start. As you might expect, I refuse to be cast as an Orwellian pig. There are many things in life that are better left unsaid. Decency and also a kind of reticence were part of my upbringing, and if we really need an animal analogy, old dogs and new tricks come to mind. One should hold on to the best and simply leave the rest behind. A sequel to this book would also have to be about family, faith, and passion for music, the continuing blessings of my life. If we could find a pharmacological way of distilling all these blessings into many tiny perfume phials, give them away with the book and then allow readers to inhale ...

GJ   Yes, you are right Ralph, the books would fly off the shelves ...

RK   ... and pigs can't fly, not even in Orwell's *Animal Farm*!

The next generation—my four grandchildren
left to right: Sam Judge, Alex Rudofsky, Talia Rudofsky, Theo Da Costa
Photograph by Martin Shaw

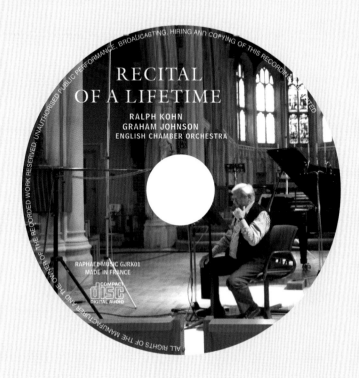

Recording Producer: Mark Brown
Recording Engineers: Antony Howell [1] [4] [9] [10] [13] [20] [23] & Julian Millard
English translations © by Richard Stokes
℗ Raphael Music, London
This compilation ℗ Raphael Editions, London, 2014
© Raphael Editions, London, 2014

*Schubert
& Müller*

FRANZ SCHUBERT (1797–1827)   PRELUDE & FUGUE I *page 1*

 Der Lindenbaum No 5 *of* Winterreise, D911 (1827)

with GRAHAM JOHNSON piano

The linden tree is the traditional centre of village life in old Germany.

Am Brunnen vor dem Tore,	*By the well, before the gate,*
Da steht ein Lindenbaum;	*Stands a linden tree:*
Ich träumt' in seinem Schatten	*I used to dream in its shade*
So manchen süßen Traum.	*So many a sweet dream.*
Ich schnitt in seine Rinde	*I used to carve in its bark*
So manches liebe Wort;	*So many a word of love;*
Es zog in Freud' und Leide	*In joy and in sorrow*
Zu ihm mich immer fort.	*I felt ever drawn to it.*
Ich mußt' auch heute wandern	*I had to pass it again today*
Vorbei in tiefer Nacht,	*At the dead of night,*
Da hab' ich noch im Dunkel	*And even in the dark,*
Die Augen zugemacht.	*I closed my eyes.*
Und seine Zweige rauschten,	*And its branches rustled,*
Als riefen sie mir zu:	*As though calling to me:*
Komm her zu mir, Geselle,	*Come to me, my friend,*
Hier findst du deine Ruh'!	*Here you shall find rest!*
Die kalten Winde bliesen	*The cold winds blew*
Mir grad' in's Angesicht,	*Full into my face,*
Der Hut flog mir vom Kopfe,	*My hat flew from my head,*
Ich wendete mich nicht.	*I did not turn back.*
Nun bin ich manche Stunde	*Now I have journeyed*
Entfernt von jenem Ort,	*Many hours from that place,*
Und immer hör' ich's rauschen:	*Yet still I hear the rustling:*
Du fändest Ruhe dort!	*There shall you find rest!*

WILHELM MÜLLER (1794–1827)

Beethoven
& Goethe

LUDWIG VAN BEETHOVEN (1770–1827) PRELUDE & FUGUE I *page 5*

2 Aus Goethe's Faust 'Flohlied' Op 75 No 3 (1809)

with GRAHAM JOHNSON piano

Auerbach's cellar in Leipzig, still a hostelry in that city, is where Mephistopheles (from Goethe's 'Faust') is said to have sung his celebrated Flea Song.

Es war einmal ein König,	*There was once a king*
Der hatt' einen grossen Floh,	*Who had a large flea,*
Den liebt' er gar nicht wenig,	*Whom he loved not a little,*
Als wie seinen eig'nen Sohn.	*Just like his own son.*
Da rief er seinen Schneider,	*He summoned his tailor,*
Der Schneider kam heran:	*The tailor appeared:*
„Da, miss dem Junker Kleider	*'Here—make robes for this knight*
Und miss ihm Hosen an!"	*And make him breeches too!'*
In Sammet und in Seide	*In silk and satin*
War er nun angetan,	*The flea was now clothed,*
Hatte Bänder auf dem Kleide,	*With ribbons on his coat,*
Hatt' auch ein Kreuz daran,	*And a medal too,*
Und war sogleich Minister,	*And became a minister straightaway*
Und hatt' einen grossen Stern.	*And wore an enormous star.*
Da wurden seine Geschwister	*His brother and his sisters*
Bei Hof auch grosse Herrn.	*Became grand at court as well.*
Und Herrn und Frau'n am Hofe,	*And courtly lords and ladies*
Die waren sehr geplagt,	*Were most grievously plagued,*
Die Königin und die Zofe	*Queen and maid-in-waiting*
Gestochen und genagt,	*Were bitten and were gnawed,*
Und durften sie nicht knicken,	*Yet they were not allowed*
Und weg sie jucken nicht.	*To squash or scratch them away.*
Wir knicken und ersticken	*We squash them and we smother them,*
Doch gleich, wenn einer sticht.	*As soon as any bite.*

JOHANN WOLFGANG VON GOETHE (1749–1832)

*Mahler
& Rückert*

GUSTAV MAHLER (1860–1911)   PRELUDE & FUGUE II *page 16*

3 Wenn dein Mütterlein No 3 *of* Kindertotenlieder (1901)

with GRAHAM JOHNSON piano

The song mirrors the family sorrow after the death of six-year-old Simon Kohn in February 1927.

Wenn dein Mütterlein	*When your dear mother*
Tritt zur Tür herein,	*Comes in through the door*
Und den Kopf ich drehe,	*And I turn my head*
Ihr entgegen sehe,	*To look at her,*
Fällt auf ihr Gesicht	*My eyes light first,*
Erst der Blick mir nicht,	*Not on her face,*
Sondern auf die Stelle,	*But on that place*
Näher nach der Schwelle,	*Nearer the threshold*
Dort, wo würde dein	*Where your*
Lieb Gesichtchen sein,	*Dear little face would be,*
Wenn du freudenhelle	*If you, bright-eyed,*
Trätest mit herein,	*Were entering with her,*
Wie sonst, mein Töchterlein.	*As you used, my daughter.*
Wenn dein Mütterlein	*When your dear mother*
Tritt zur Tür herein,	*Comes in through the door*
Mit der Kerze Schimmer,	*With the flickering candle,*
Ist es mir, als immer	*I always think*
Kämst du mit herein,	*You are coming too,*
Huschtest hinterdrein,	*Stealing in behind her,*
Als wie sonst ins Zimmer!	*As you used.*
O du, des Vaters Zelle,	*O you, the joyful light,*
Ach, zu schnell, zu schnell,	*Ah, too soon extinguished,*
Erloschner Freudenschein!	*Of your father's flesh and blood!*

FRIEDRICH RÜCKERT (1788–1866)

Ravel

MAURICE RAVEL (1875–1937)   PRELUDE & FUGUE III *page 31*

4 **Chanson hébraïque** No 4 *of* Chants populaires (1910)

with GRAHAM JOHNSON piano

A song in Yiddish recalls the father-and-son relationship in the Kohn family.

Mejerke, main Suhn,	*Meyerke, my son,*
Oi Mejerke, main Suhn,	*O Meyerke, my son,*
Zi weiss tu, var wemen du steihst?	*Before whom do you stand there?*
"Lifnei Melech Malchei hamlochim",	*'Before Him, the King of Kings',*
Tatunju.	* my father.*
Mejerke, main Suhn,	*Meyerke, my son,*
Oi Mejerke, main Suhn,	*O Meyerke, my son,*
Wos ze westu bai Ihm bet'n?	*And what do you ask of Him there?*
"Bonej, chajei, M'sunei",	*'Children, a long life and bread',*
Tatunju.	* my father.*
Mejerke, main Suhn,	*Meyerke, my son,*
Oi Mejerke, main Suhn,	*O Meyerke, my son,*
Oif wos darfs tu Bonei?	*But why children, tell me?*
"Bonim eiskim batoiroh",	*'To children we teach the Torah',*
Tatunju.	* my father.*
Mejerke, main Suhn,	*Meyerke, my son,*
Oi Mejerke, main Suhn,	*O Meyerke, my son,*
Oif wos darfs tu chajei?	*But why a long life, tell me?*
"Kol chai joiducho",	*'All that lives sings glory to the Lord',*
Tatunju.	* my father.*
Mejerke, main Suhn,	*Meyerke, my son,*
Oi Mejerke, main Suhn,	*O Meyerke, my son,*
Oif wo darfs tu M'sunei?	*But still you wish for bread?*
"W'ochalto w'sowoto uweirachto",	*'Take this bread, sustain yourself, bless it',*
Tatunju.	* my father.*

TRADITIONAL

*Beethoven
& Gellert*

LUDWIG VAN BEETHOVEN (1770–1827)   PRELUDE & FUGUE III *page 33*

5 **Die Ehre Gottes aus der Natur**
No 3 *of* Sechs Lieder von Gellert, Op 48 (1802)

with GRAHAM JOHNSON piano

A song of noble simplicity in memory of Lena Kohn.

Die Himmel rühmen des Ewigen Ehre;	*The heavens extol the glory of God,*
Ihr Schall pflanzt seinen Namen fort.	*Their sound propagates His name.*
Ihn rühmt der Erdkreis, ihn preisen die Meere;	*The earth extols, the seas praise Him,*
Vernimm, o Mensch, ihr göttlich Wort!	*Hearken, O man, to their godly word!*
Wer trägt der Himmel unzählbare Sterne?	*Who supports the heaven's countless stars?*
Wer führt die Sonn' aus ihrem Zelt?	*Who leads the sun from its tabernacle?*
Sie kömmt und leuchtet und lacht uns	*It comes and gleams and smiles on us*
von ferne	*from afar,*
Und läuft den Weg gleich als ein Held.	*And like a hero runs its course.*

CHRISTIAN FÜRCHTEGOTT GELLERT (1715–1769)

329

*Schumann
& Heine*

ROBERT SCHUMANN (1810–1856)　　　　　PRELUDE & FUGUE IV *page 47*

6 Ein Jüngling liebt ein Mädchen
No 11 *of* Dichterliebe, Op 48 (1840)

with GRAHAM JOHNSON piano

A memory of tactfully avoiding the match-making suggestions of the highly esteemed Kolomán Lauer.

Ein Jüngling liebt ein Mädchen,	*A boy loves a girl*
Die hat einen andern erwählt;	*Who chooses another;*
Der andre liebt eine andre,	*He in turn loves another*
Und hat sich mit dieser vermählt.	*And marries her.*
Das Mädchen nimmt aus Ärger	*The girl, out of pique,*
Den ersten besten Mann,	*Takes the very first man*
Der ihr in den Weg gelaufen;	*To come her way;*
Der Jüngling ist übel dran.	*The boy is badly hurt.*
Es ist eine alte Geschichte,	*It is an old story,*
Doch bleibt sie immer neu;	*Yet remains ever new;*
Und wem sie just passieret,	*And he to whom it happens,*
Dem bricht das Herz entzwei.	*It breaks his heart in two.*

HEINRICH HEINE (1797–1856)

ROBERT SCHUMANN (1810–1856)　　　　　PRELUDE & FUGUE V *page 51*

7 Belsatzar Op 57 (1840)

with GRAHAM JOHNSON piano

The tyranny and death of the Babylonian king Belshazzar, one of the biblical enemies of the Jewish people, finds its parallel in the rise and fall of Nazism.

Die Mitternacht zog näher schon;	*The midnight hour was drawing on;*
In stummer Ruh' lag Babylon.	*In hushed repose lay Babylon.*
Nur oben in des Königs Schloß,	*But high in the castle of the king*
Da flackert's, da lärmt des Königs Troß.	*Torches flare, the king's men clamour.*
Dort oben in dem Königssaal	*Up there in the royal hall,*
Belsatzar hielt sein Königsmahl.	*Belshazzar was holding his royal feast.*

Die Knechte saßen in schimmernden Reihn,	*The vassals sat in shimmering rows,*
Und leerten die Becher mit funkelndem Wein.	*And emptied the beakers of glistening wine.*
Es klirrten die Becher, es jauchzten die Knecht';	*The vassals made merry, the goblets rang;*
So klang es dem störrigen Könige recht.	*Noise pleasing to that obdurate king.*
Des Königs Wangen leuchten Glut;	*The king's cheeks glow like coals;*
Im Wein erwuchs ihm kecker Mut.	*His impudence grew as he quaffed the wine.*
Und blindlings reißt der Mut ihn fort;	*And arrogance carries him blindly away;*
Und er lästert die Gottheit mit sündigem Wort.	*And he blasphemes God with sinful words.*
Und er brüstet sich frech, und lästert wild;	*And he brags insolently, blasphemes wildly;*
Die Knechtenschar ihm Beifall brüllt.	*The crowd of vassals roar him on.*
Der König rief mit stolzem Blick;	*The king called out with pride in his eyes;*
Der Diener eilt und kehrt zurück.	*The servant hurries out and then returns.*
Er trug viel gülden Gerät auf dem Haupt;	*He bore many vessels of gold on his head;*
Das war aus dem Tempel Jehovas geraubt.	*Plundered from Jehovah's temple.*
Und der König ergriff mit frevler Hand	*With impious hand the king*
Einen heiligen Becher, gefüllt bis am Rand.	*Grabs a sacred beaker filled to the brim.*
Und er leert' ihn hastig bis auf den Grund	*And he drains it hastily down to the dregs,*
Und rufet laut mit schäumendem Mund:	*And shouts aloud through foaming lips:*
Jehova! Dir künd' ich auf ewig Hohn,—	*Jehovah! I offer you eternal scorn—*
Ich bin der König von Babylon!	*I am the king of Babylon!*
Doch kaum das grause Wort verklang,	*Those terrible words had hardly faded,*
Dem König ward's heimlich im Busen bang.	*Than the king was filled with secret fear.*
Das gellende Lachen verstummte zumal;	*The shrill laughter was suddenly silent;*
Es wurde leichenstill im Saal.	*It became deathly still in the hall.*
Und sieh! und sieh! an weißer Wand	*And see! And see! On the white wall*
Da kam's hervor wie Menschenhand;	*A shape appeared like a human hand;*
Und schrieb und schrieb an weißer Wand	*And wrote and wrote on the white wall*
Buchstaben von Feuer, und schrieb	*Letters of fire, and wrote*
und schwand.	*and went.*
Der König stieren Blicks da saß,	*The king sat there with staring eyes,*
Mit schlotternden Knien und totenblaß.	*With trembling knees and pale as death.*
Die Knechtenschar saß kalt durchgraut,	*The host of vassals sat stricken with horror,*
Und saß gar still, gab keinen Laut.	*And sat quite still, and made no sound.*
Die Magier kamen, doch keiner verstand	*The soothsayers came, not one of them all*
Zu deuten die Flammenschrift an der Wand.	*Could interpret the letters of fire on the wall.*
Belsatzar ward aber in selbiger Nacht	*Belshazzar however in that same night*
Von seinen Knechten umgebracht.	*Was done to death by his own vassals.*

HEINRICH HEINE (1797–1856)

Brahms

JOHANNES BRAHMS (1833–1897)   PRELUDE & FUGUE VI *page 60*

8 Ich wandte mich No 2 *of* Vier ernste Gesänge, Op 121 (1896)

with GRAHAM JOHNSON piano

A song recalling the darkness of the war years, and the sense of utter hopelessness experienced by the wounded and persecuted.

Ich wandte mich, und sahe an alle,	*So I returned, and considered all the*
die Unrecht leiden unter der Sonne;	*oppressions that are done under the sun;*
und siehe, da waren Tränen derer,	*and behold the tears of such*
die Unrecht litten	*as were oppressed,*
und hatten keinen Tröster;	*and they had no comforter;*
und die ihnen Unrecht täten,	*and on the side of their oppressors*
waren zu mächtig,	*there was power;*
daß sie keinen Tröster haben konnten.	*but they had no comforter.*
Da lobte ich die Toten,	*Wherefore I praised the dead*
die schon gestorben waren,	*which are already dead*
mehr als die Lebendigen,	*more than the living*
die noch das Leben hatten;	*which are yet alive.*
Und der noch nicht ist,	*Yea, better is he than both they,*
ist besser als alle beide,	*which hath not yet been,*
und des Bösen nicht inne wird,	*who hath not seen the evil work*
das unter der Sonne geschieht.	*that is done under the sun.*

ECCLESIASTES (DER PREDIGER SALOMO) 4: 1–3

Bach

JOHANN SEBASTIAN BACH (1685–1750)   INTERLUDE I *page 71*

⑨ Schlummert ein, ihr matten Augen
from Cantata 82 'Ich habe genug', BWV82 (1727)

with ENGLISH CHAMBER ORCHESTRA *conducted by* IAN WATSON

*After a terrifying and exhausting journey at sea, an aria of thanks for safe arrival
in Liverpool in May 1940.*

Schlummert ein, ihr matten Augen,	*Close in sleep, you weary eyes,*
Fallet sanft und selig zu.	*Fall soft and blissfully to!*
Welt, ich bleibe nicht mehr hier,	*World, I shall dwell no longer here,*
Hab' ich doch kein Teil an dir,	*Since I have no share in you,*
Das der Seele könnte taugen.	*That might avail my soul.*
Hier muß ich das Elend bauen,	*Here it is misery that I must tend,*
Aber dort, dort werd' ich schauen	*But there, there I shall behold*
Süßen Frieden, stille Ruh.	*Sweet peace, silent repose.*

ANONYMOUS

JOHANNES BRAHMS (1833–1897)   PRELUDE & FUGUE VII *page 83*

⑩ Wenn ich mit Menschen No 4 *of* Vier ernste Gesänge, Op 121 (1896)

with GRAHAM JOHNSON piano

*Reflecting on the differences between the past and present in terms of religious customs, a song
confirming the paramount spiritual importance of Love.*

Wenn ich mit Menschen- und mit	*Though I speak with the tongues of men*
Engelzungen redete und hätte der Liebe nicht,	*and of angels, and have not Love,*
so wär ich ein tönend Erz,	*I am become as sounding brass,*
oder eine klingende Schelle.	*or a tinkling cymbal.*
Und wenn ich weissagen könnte und wüßte	*And though I have the gift of prophecy,*
alle Geheimnisse und alle Erkenntnis,	*and understand all mysteries, and all knowledge;*
und hätte allen Glauben,	*and though I have all Faith,*
also, daß ich Berge versetzte,	*so that I could remove mountains,*
und hätte der Liebe nicht, so wäre ich nichts.	*and have not Love, I am nothing.*

Und wenn ich alle meine Habe	And though I bestow all my goods
den Armen gäbe, und ließe meinen	to feed the poor, and though I give
Leib brennen, und hätte der Liebe nicht,	my body to be burned, and have not Love,
so wäre mirs nichts nütze.	it profiteth me nothing.
Wir sehen jetzt durch einen Spiegel	For now we see through a glass,
in einem dunkeln Worte,	darkly;
dann aber von Angesicht zu Angesichte.	but then face to face:
Jetzt erkenne ichs stuckweise,	now I know in part,
dann aber werd ichs erkennen,	but then shall I know
gleich wie ich erkennet bin.	even as also I am known.
Nun aber bleibet	And now abideth
Glaube, Hoffnung, Liebe, diese drei;	Faith, Hope, Love, these three;
aber die Liebe	but Love
ist die größeste unter ihnen.	is the greatest of these.

1 CORINTHIANS 13: 1–3, 12–13

GUSTAV MAHLER (1860–1911)   PRELUDE & FUGUE VIII *page 89*

11 **Scheiden und Meiden**

with GRAHAM JOHNSON piano

A song of departure for pastures new—the joy of new experiences and the sorrow of leaving behind what is familiar.

Es ritten drei Reiter zum Thore hinaus, Ade!	Three horsemen rode out of the door. Farewell!
Fein's Liebchen, das schaute zum Fenster hinaus. Ade!	A sweetheart looked out of the window. Farewell!
Und wenn es denn soll geschieden sein,	And if a parting it must be,
So reich' mir dein goldenes Ringelein! Ade!	then give me your little golden ring! Farewell!
Ja, Scheiden und Meiden thut weh, thut weh. Ade!	Yes, parting and absence are sad, are sad. Farewell!
Es scheiden das Kind schon in der Wieg'. Ade!	The child is already left in the cradle. Farewell!
Wann werd' ich mein Schätzel wohl kriegen? Ade!	When will I win my darling? Farewell!
Und ist es nicht morgen, ach wär' es doch heut'!	And if it is not tomorrow, O were it today:
Es machte uns Beiden wohl grosse Freud'! Ade!	It would give us both great joy. Farewell!
Ja, Scheiden und Meiden thut weh, thut weh. Ade!	Yes, parting and absence are sad, are sad. Farewell!

ANONYMOUS from *Des Knaben Wunderhorn*

JOHANNES BRAHMS (1833–1897)   PRELUDE & FUGUE IX *page 99*

12 Vergebliches Ständchen Op 84 No 4 (*c*1878)

with GRAHAM JOHNSON piano

A song reflecting early years in Salford as a shy and unsuccessful suitor.

Er Guten Abend, mein Schatz,	He *Good evening, my sweetheart,*
Guten Abend, mein Kind.	*Good evening, my child.*
Ich komm aus Lieb zu dir,	*I come because I love you,*
Ach, mach mir auf die Tür!	*Ah! open up your door to me,*
Mach mir auf die Tür!	*Open up your door!*
Sie Mein Tür ist verschlossen,	She *My door's locked,*
Ich lass dich nicht ein;	*I won't let you in;*
Mutter, die rät mir klug,	*Mother gave me good advice,*
Wärst du herein mit Fug,	*If you were allowed in,*
Wär's, mit mir vorbei.	*All would be over with me.*
Er So kalt ist die Nacht,	He *The night's so cold,*
So eisig der Wind,	*The wind's so icy,*
Dass mir das Herz erfriert,	*My heart is freezing,*
Mein Lieb erlöschen wird,	*My love will go out;*
Öffne mir, mein Kind!	*Open up, my child!*
Sie Löschet dein Lieb,	She *If your love goes out,*
Lass sie löschen nur.	*Then let it go out.*
Löschet sie immerzu,	*If it keeps going out,*
Geh' heim zu Bett, zur Ruh,	*Then go home to bed and go to sleep,*
Gute Nacht, mein Knab!	*Good night, my lad!*

text arranged by ANTON VON ZUCCALMAGLIO
after a folksong from the lower Rhine

RAFFAELLO RONTANI (*c*1570–1622)   PRELUDE & FUGUE IX *page 103*

13 Se bel rio *arranged by* CHRISTOPHER PALMER (1946–1995)

with ENGLISH CHAMBER ORCHESTRA *conducted by* ANTHONY HALSTEAD

The beauties of Italy as expressed in one of the most beautiful of the old 'arie antiche'.

Se bel rio, se bell' auretta, tra l'erbetta,	*If a beautiful brook and a beautiful breeze*
Sul mattin mormorando erra;	*Wander amidst the grass, murmuring in the morning;*
Se di fiori un praticello si fa bello,	*If a meadow makes itself beautiful with flowers,*
Noi diciam: ride la terra.	*We say: the earth is laughing.*
Quando avvien che un Zeffiretto per diletto	*When a little Zephyr for pleasure*
Bagni il piè nell'onde chiare,	*Bathes its feet in the clear waves*
Si che l'acqua su l'arena scherzi a pena,	*So that water plays gently on the sand,*
Noi diciam: che ride il mare.	*We say: the sea is laughing.*
Se giammai tra fior vermigli,	*If among the red flowers and the lilies*
Se tra gigli veste l'alba un aureo velo	*The dawn puts on a golden veil*
E su rote di zaffiro move in giro,	*And moves around on sapphire wheels,*
Noi diciam: che ride il cielo.	*We say: the sky is laughing.*

Ben è ver: quando è giocondo	Well it is true: when the world is happy, it laughs,
Ride il mondo, ride il ciel quando è gioioso;	And the sky laughs when it is joyful.
Ben è ver: ma non san poi, come voi,	All this is true: but then,
Fare un riso grazioso.	They cannot, like you, smile so charmingly.

ANONYMOUS

Scarlatti

ALESSANDRO SCARLATTI (1660–1725)

PRELUDE & FUGUE X *page 114*

14 **Le violette** *realized by* GRAHAM JOHNSON (b1950)

with GRAHAM JOHNSON piano

One of the most renowned of 'arie antiche' by the most famous composer of the Neapolitan school, and one of the songs performed with Sir Ernst Chain as accompanist.

Rugiadose,	Dewy,
Odorose violette graziose,	Fragrant charming violets,
Voi vi state vergognose,	You who are so shy,
Mezzo ascose,	Half-hidden
Fra le foglie e sgridate	Among the leaves, you chide
Le mie voglie	My desires
Che son troppo ambiziose.	That are too ambitious.

ADRIANO MORSELLI (*fl*1674–1691)

RAFFAELLO RONTANI (*c*1570–1622)

PRELUDE & FUGUE XI *page 120*

15 **Caldi sospiri** *arranged by* MARK BROWN (b1941)

with ENGLISH CHAMBER ORCHESTRA *conducted by* STEPHANIE GONLEY

Falling in love at a distance during a maiden voyage to New York.

Caldi sospiri, che uscite dal core,	Ardent sighs that come from the heart,
Gite volando nel seno al mio amore:	Please fly to the heart of my love:
Dite alla cruda ch'io l'amo e l'adoro	Tell the cruel one that I love and adore her
Che miri—ch'io moro	So that she might see that I am dying
Fra tanti martiri,	Amid so much suffering,
O caldi sospiri.	O ardent sighs.

Caldi sospiri, correte da Clori,   *Ardent sighs, run to Chloris,*
Pungete il bel petto, temprate i miei ardori   *Pierce her lovely breast, temper my ardour,*
E poi felici cangiatemi incanto.   *Thus changing my enchantment to happiness.*
È gioia il mio pianto   *My weeping would be joy,*
Se cangia desiri,   *If her desires change,*
O caldi sospiri.   *O ardent sighs.*

ANONYMOUS

ROBERT SCHUMANN (1810–1856)   PRELUDE & FUGUE XI *page 124*

16 Das ist ein Flöten und Geigen No 9 *of* Dichterliebe, Op 48 (1840)

with GRAHAM JOHNSON piano

A musical portrait of the trumpet-playing of Professor Alfred Gilman at Jewish weddings in New York in the 1950s.

Das ist ein Flöten und Geigen,   *What a fluting, what a scraping,*
Trompeten schmettern darein;   *With trumpets blaring in;*
Da tanzt wohl den Hochzeitreigen   *That must be my dearest love*
Die Herzallerliebste mein.   *Dancing at her wedding feast.*

Das ist ein Klingen und Dröhnen,   *What a clashing, what a clanging,*
Ein Pauken und ein Schalmei'n;   *What a drumming, what a piping;*
Dazwischen schluchzen und stöhnen   *And the lovely little angels*
Die lieblichen Engelein.   *Sobbing and groaning in between.*

HEINRICH HEINE (1797–1856)

LUDWIG VAN BEETHOVEN (1770–1827)   PRELUDE & FUGUE XII *page 131*

17 Marmotte Op 52 No 7 (*c*1790–92)

with GRAHAM JOHNSON piano

A humorous evocation of travels for Smith Kline and French in the late 1950s and early 1960s.

Ich komme schon durch manches Land   I've travelled already through many lands
Avecque la marmotte,   *Avecque la marmotte,*
Und immer ich was zu essen fand   And always found something to eat
Avecque la marmotte,   *Avecque la marmotte,*
Avecque si, avecque la,   *Avecque si, avecque la,*
Avecque la marmotte.   *Avecque la marmotte.*

JOHANN WOLFGANG VON GOETHE (1749–1832)

FRANZ SCHUBERT (1797–1827)PRELUDE & FUGUE XIII *page 143*

18 Der Wanderer an den Mond D870 (1826)

with GRAHAM JOHNSON piano

Another song of wandering, this time rather less contented.

Ich auf der Erd', am Himmel du,	*I on earth, you in the heavens,*
Wir wandern beide rüstig zu:	*Both of us journey briskly on:*
Ich ernst und trüb, du mild und rein,	*I sad and cheerless, you pure and gentle,*
Was mag der Unterschied wohl sein?	*I wonder what the difference can be?*
Ich wandre fremd von Land zu Land,	*I journey, a stranger, from land to land,*
So heimatlos, so unbekannt;	*So homeless, so unknown;*
Bergauf, bergab, Wald ein, Wald aus,	*Up and down mountains, into forests and out,*
Doch bin ich nirgend, ach! zu Haus.	*But nowhere, alas! am I at home.*
Du aber wanderst auf und ab	*But you journey up and down*
Aus Ostens Wieg' in Westens Grab,	*From eastern cradle to western grave,*
Wallst Länder ein und Länder aus,	*Wander, a pilgrim, from land to land,*
Und bist doch, wo du bist, zu Haus.	*Yet are, wherever you be, at home.*
Der Himmel, endlos ausgespannt,	*The infinite expanse of sky*
Ist dein geliebtes Heimatland:	*Is your beloved native land:*
O glücklich, wer, wohin er geht,	*O happy is he who, wherever he goes,*
Doch auf der Heimat Boden steht!	*Still stands upon his native soil!*

JOHANN GABRIEL SEIDL (1804–1875)

GUSTAV MAHLER (1860–1911)PRELUDE & FUGUE XIV *page 154*

19 Das irdische Leben (1892/3)

with GRAHAM JOHNSON piano

A searing musical prophecy of hunger and deprivation in a concentration camp.

Mutter, ach Mutter! es hungert mich,	*Mother, ah mother! I am starving,*
Gib mir Brot, sonst sterbe ich.	*Give me bread or I shall die.*
Warte nur mein liebes Kind!	*Wait, only wait, my beloved child!*
Morgen wollen wir ernten geschwind.	*Tomorrow the reaping will be swiftly done.*
Und als das Korn geerntet war,	*And when at last the corn was reaped,*
Rief das Kind noch immerdar:	*Still the child kept on crying:*
Mutter, ach Mutter! es hungert mich,	*Mother, ah mother! I am starving,*
Gib mir Brot, sonst sterbe ich.	*Give me bread or I shall die.*
Warte nur mein liebes Kind!	*Wait, only wait, my beloved child!*
Morgen wollen wir dreschen geschwind.	*Tomorrow the threshing will be swiftly done.*

Und als das Korn gedroschen war,	And when at last the corn was threshed,
Rief das Kind noch immerdar:	Still the child kept on crying:
Mutter, ach Mutter! es hungert mich,	Mother, ah mother! I am starving,
Gib mir Brot, sonst sterbe ich.	Give me bread or I shall die.
Warte nur mein liebes Kind!	Wait, only wait, my beloved child!
Morgen wollen wir backen geschwind.	Tomorrow the baking will be swiftly done.
Und als das Brot gebacken war,	And when at last the bread was baked,
Lag das Kind auf der Totenbahr.	The child lay dead upon the bier.

ANONYMOUS *Verspätung* from *Des Knaben Wunderhorn*

Kahn

ROBERT KAHN (1865–1951)   PRELUDE & FUGUE XIV *page 157*

20 **Obdach der Liebe** Op 6 No 5 (1889)

with GRAHAM JOHNSON piano

The German-Jewish composer Robert Kahn came to England in 1937 when he was already in his early seventies—an expression of new-found love for Zahava Kanarek in a song by a fellow refugee.

Ein Obdach gegen Sturm und Regen	A shelter against the storms and rain
Der Winterzeit	Of winter
Sucht' ich, und fand den Himmelssegen	Was what I sought, and I found the heavenly gift
Der Ewigkeit.	Of eternity.
O Wort, wie du bewährt dich hast:	O how right the saying proved:
Wer wenig sucht, der findet viel.	He who seeks little, finds much.
Ich suchte eine Wanderrast,	I sought rest from journeying,
Und fand mein Reiseziel.	And found my journey's goal.
Ein gastlich Thor nur wünscht' ich offen,	I only wished for an open door
Mich zu empfahn,	To receive me,
Ein liebend Herz war wider Hoffen	Against my hope a loving heart
Mir aufgethan.	Opened up to me.
O Wort, wie du bewährt dich hast:	O how right the saying proved:
Wer wenig sucht, der findet viel.	He who seeks little, finds much.
Ich wollte sein ihr Wintergast,	I intended to be her winter guest,
Und ward ihr Herzgespiel.	And gained her heart.

FRIEDRICH RÜCKERT (1788–1866)

Cavalli

FRANCESCO CAVALLI (1602–1676) PRELUDE & FUGUE XV *page 167*

21 **Delizie contente** *from* Giasone (1649) *arranged by* MARK BROWN (b1941)

with ENGLISH CHAMBER ORCHESTRA *conducted by* STEPHANIE GONLEY

As a singing student in Rome, further exploring the beauties of Italian 'arie antiche' first revealed at a concert given by Beniamino Gigli in Manchester.

Delizie contente, che l'alma beate,	*Happy delights that bless my soul,*
Fermate, fermate.	*Stop, stop.*
Su questo mio core—deh più non stillate	*On this heart of mine pour no longer*
Le gioie d'amore.	*The joys of love.*
Delizie mie care—fermatevi qui:	*My dear delight, stop here:*
Non so più bramare—mi basta così.	*I can desire no more; this is enough.*
In grembo agli amori, fra dolci catene	*In the arms of love between sweet chains,*
Morir mi conviene.	*It is better I should die.*
Dolcezza omicida—a morte mi guida	*Murderous sweetness guides me to death*
In braccio al mio bene.	*In the arms of my beloved.*

GIACINTO ANDREA CICOGNINI (1606–1651)

FRANZ SCHUBERT (1797–1827)   PRELUDE & FUGUE XVI *page 182*

22 Florio D857 No 1 (1825)

with GRAHAM JOHNSON piano

This song with an oriental background refers to hopeless love as a poison (disguised by sweet sherbet) and how it slowly takes its effect by circulating through the veins. It is the only lied that attempts to depict, in musical terms, the gradual working of a drug on the body.

Nun, da Schatten niedergleiten,	*Now that the shadows glide down,*
Und die Lüfte zärtlich wehen,	*And the breezes blow gently,*
Dringet Seufzen aus der Seele,	*Call forth sighs from the soul*
Und umgirrt die treuen Saiten.	*And caress the faithful strings.*
Klaget, dass ihr mit mir sterbet	*Lament that you die with me*
Bittern Tod, wenn die nicht heilet,	*A bitter death, unless she*
Die den Becher mir gereichet,	*Who handed me the cup,*
Voller Gift, dass ich und ihr verderbet.	*Filled with seductive poison, cures me.*
Erst mit Tönen, sanft wie Flöten,	*First with sounds as soft as flutes*
Goss sie Schmerz in meine Adern;	*She poured pain into my veins;*
Sehen wollte sie der Kranke,	*The invalid desired to see her,*
Und nun wird ihr Reiz ihn töten.	*But now her charms will kill him.*
Nacht, komm her, mich zu umwinden	*Come, O night, and envelop me*
Mit dem farbenlosen Dunkel!	*In your colourless darkness!*
Ruhe will ich bei dir suchen,	*With you I shall seek the rest*
Die mir Not tut bald zu finden.	*Which I need to find quickly.*

CHRISTIAN WILHELM VON SCHÜTZ (1776–1847)

JOHANN SEBASTIAN BACH (1685–1750)   PRELUDE & FUGUE XXIII *page 298*

23 Hat man nicht mit seinen Kindern
from 'Coffee' Cantata 'Schweiget stille, plaudert nicht', BWV211 (c1734)

with ENGLISH CHAMBER ORCHESTRA *conducted by* IAN WATSON

The narrator of this cantata talks of the difficulty of communicating with his children: what he says to his daughter Lieschen goes in one ear and out the other!

Hat man nicht mit seinen Kindern	*The troubles one has*
Hunderttausend Hudelei!	*With one's own children!*
Was ich immer alle Tage	*Whatever I say each day*
Meiner Tochter Liesgen sage,	*To my daughter Lieschen*
Gehet ohne Frucht vorbei.	*Goes in one ear and out the other.*

CHRISTIAN FRIEDRICH HENRICI ('PICANDER') (1700–1764)

Mozart

WOLFGANG AMADEUS MOZART (1756–1791)   PRELUDE & FUGUE XXIII *page 298*

24 Warnung 'Männer suchen stets zu naschen'

with GRAHAM JOHNSON piano

A buffo aria by Mozart giving fathers eighteenth-century advice to 'lock up their daughters'.

Männer suchen stets zu naschen,	*Men always try to nibble,*
Läßt man sie allein;	*If they are left alone,*
Leicht sind Mädchen zu erhaschen,	*Girls can easily be caught,*
Weiß man sie zu überraschen,	*If you take them by surprise.*
Soll das zu verwundern sein?	*Is that to be wondered at?*
Mädchen haben frisches Blut,	*Girls have fresh young blood,*
Und das Naschen schmeckt so gut.	*And nibbling is so pleasant.*
Doch das Naschen vor dem Essen	*But nibbling before meals*
Nimmt den Appetit,	*Takes away the appetite.*
Manche kam, die das vergessen,	*Many a girl who's forgotten that*
Um den Schatz, den sie besessen	*Has lost the treasure she possessed,*
Und um ihren Liebsten mit.	*And with it her beloved.*
Väter, laßt's euch Warnung sein,	*Fathers, let this be a warning,*
Sperrt die Zuckerplätzchen ein,	*Lock your sugar-drops away,*
Sperrt die jungen Mädchen ein.	*Lock young girls away!*

ANONYMOUS

Seidl

FRANZ SCHUBERT (1797–1827)   PRELUDE & FUGUE XXIV *page 317*

25 **Die Taubenpost** No 14 *of* Schwanengesang, D965a (1828)

with GRAHAM JOHNSON piano

The recital closes with the last song that Schubert wrote before he died.

Ich hab' eine Brieftaub in meinem Sold,
Die ist gar ergeben und treu,
Sie nimmt mir nie das Ziel zu kurz,
Und fliegt auch nie vorbei.

Ich sende sie vieltausendmal
Auf Kundschaft täglich hinaus,
Vorbei an manchem lieben Ort,
Bis zu der Liebsten Haus.

Dort schaut sie zum Fenster heimlich hinein,
Belauscht ihren Blick und Schritt,
Gibt meine Grüsse scherzend ab
Und nimmt die ihren mit.

Kein Briefchen brauch' ich zu schreiben mehr,
Die Träne selbst geb' ich ihr:
O sie verträgt sie sicher nicht,
Gar eifrig dient sie mir.

Bei Tag, bei Nacht, im Wachen, im Traum,
Ihr gilt das alles gleich:
Wenn sie nur wandern, wandern kann,
Dann ist sie überreich!

Sie wird nicht müd', sie wird nicht matt,
Der Weg ist stets ihr neu;
Sie braucht nicht Lockung, braucht nicht Lohn,
Die Taub' ist so mir treu!

Drum heg' ich sie auch so treu an der Brust,
Versichert des schönsten Gewinns;
Sie heisst—die Sehnsucht! Kennt ihr sie?
Die Botin treuen Sinns.

JOHANN GABRIEL SEIDL (1804–1875)

I've a carrier-pigeon in my pay,
She's so devoted and true,
She never stops short of her goal,
And never flies too far.

I send her many thousands of times
Each day to spy out the land,
Past many a beloved spot,
Till she reaches my sweetheart's house.

There she peeps in at the window,
Observing every look and step,
Delivers my greeting cheerfully
And brings hers back to me.

I no longer need to write a letter,
I can entrust to her my very tears;
She'll certainly not mistake the address,
For she serves me so fervently.

Day or night, awake or dreaming,
It's all the same to her:
As long as she can range and roam,
She's richly satisfied!

She does not tire, she does not flag,
To her the route seems always new;
She needs no enticement, no reward,
That pigeon is so loyal!

That's why I cherish her in my heart,
Certain of the fairest prize;
Her name is—Longing! Do you know her?
The messenger of faithfulness.

WIGMORE HALL / KOHN FOUNDATION
INTERNATIONAL SONG COMPETITION

FIRST PRIZE FOR SINGERS

Marcus DeLoach *USA* (1997)
Stephan Loges *Germany* (1999)
Mattijs van de Woerd *The Netherlands* (2003)
Martha Guth *Canada* (2007)
Marcus Farnsworth *Great Britain* (2009)
Dominik Köninger *Germany* (2011)
Timothy Fallon *USA* (2013)

SECOND PRIZE FOR SINGERS

Sebastian Noack *Germany* (1997)
Håkan Vramsmo *Sweden* (1999)
Measha Brueggergosman *Canada* (2001)
Colin Balzer *Canada* (2003)
Robin Tritschler *Ireland* (2007)
Benedict Nelson *Great Britain* (2009)
Stuart Jackson *Great Britain* (2011)
Gavan Ring *Ireland* (2013)

THIRD PRIZE FOR SINGERS

Herman Wallén *Finland* (1997)
Andrea Meláth *Hungary* (1999)
Tyler Duncan *Canada* (2001)
Sophie Karthäuser *Belgium* (2003)
Ben Johnson *Great Britain* (2007)
Erin Morley *USA* (2009)
Dorottya Lang *Hungary* (2011)
Helen Sherman *Australia* (2013)

FOURTH PRIZE FOR SINGERS

James Rutherford *Great Britain* (1999)
Erik Nelson Werner *USA* (2001)
Martha Guth *Canada* (2003)
Sidney Outlaw *USA* (2009)

FINALIST'S PRIZE

Daniel Norman *Great Britain* (2001)

FIRST PRIZE FOR PIANISTS

Roger Braun *The Netherlands* (1997)
Clinton Cormany *USA* (1999)
Christopher Gould *Great Britain* (2001)
Erika Switzer *Canada* (2003)
Joseph Middleton *Great Britain* (2007)
James Baillieu *South Africa* (2009)
Timothy End *Great Britain* and Jonathan Ware *USA* (joint winners 2011)
Ammiel Bushakevitz *Israel/South Africa* (2013)

SECOND PRIZE FOR PIANISTS
Cameron Stowe *USA* (1999)
Catherine Milledge *Great Britain* (2001)
Joseph Breinl *Germany* (2003)

JEAN MEIKLE PRIZE FOR A DUO
Daniel Johannsen *Austria* and Elena Larina *Russia* (2007)
Gerard Collett *Great Britain* and James Baillieu *South Africa* (2009)
Jonathan McGovern *Great Britain* and Timothy End *Great Britain* (2011)
Johnny Herford *Great Britain* and William Vann *Great Britain* (2013)

RICHARD TAUBER PRIZE
FOR THE BEST INTERPRETATION OF SCHUBERT LIEDER
Timothy Fallon *USA* and Ammiel Bushakevitz *Israel/South Africa* (2013)

JURORS

2013
John Gilhooly *Chairman*, Pieter Alferink, Maxine Robertson, Robert Gambill, Graham Johnson
Sir Ralph Kohn *non-voting*, Ann Murray DBE, Christoph Prégardien, Asadour Santourian

2011
John Gilhooly *Chairman*, Bernarda Fink, Jeremy Geffen, Graham Johnson, Sir Ralph Kohn *non-voting*
William Lyne, Malcolm Martineau, Thomas Quasthoff, Richard Stokes, Sarah Walker

2009
John Gilhooly *Chairman*, Sir Thomas Allen, Ann Murray, Iain Burnside, Anne Evans
Wolfgang Holzmair, Anneke Hogenstijn, Graham Johnson, Margaret Price

2007
John Gilhooly *Chairman*, Christine Brewer, Hilary Finch, Robert Holl, Graham Johnson
Ralph Kohn, Brian McMaster, Ann Murray, Richard Stokes

2003
William Lyne *Chairman*, Grace Bumbry, Helmut Deutsch, Ralph Kohn
François Le Roux, Felicity Lott, Roger Vignoles, Annette Wolde

2001
Graham Johnson *Chairman*, Elly Ameling, Dalton Baldwin, Mark Brown
Matthias Goerne, Ralph Kohn, William Lyne, Felicity Palmer

1999
Graham Johnson *Chairman*, Bengt Forsberg, William Lyne, Edith Mathis
Christoph Prégardien, James Waters, Robert White, Ralph Kohn

1997
Graham Johnson *Chairman*, Rudolf Jansen, William Lyne, Frederick Noonan
Margaret Price, Peter Schreier, Elisabeth Söderström, Ralph Kohn

ROYAL SOCIETY KOHN AWARD

2013
Peter Vukusic
for his excellence in engaging with society in matters of science and its societal dimension

2012
Suzannah Lishman
for her excellence in engaging with society in matters of science and its societal dimension

2011
Christopher Lintott
for his excellence in engaging with society in matters of science and its societal dimension

2009
Lucie Green
for her leadership in building up a first-class programme of engagement, communication and outreach projects at the Mullard Space Science Laboratory (MSSL) at UCL over ten years. Her achievements include mentoring scientists with her department in public engagement and changing the overall culture of her department and university to encourage public engagement with science work

2008
Chris Smith
for his work engaging a diverse audience with science through his pioneering radio show, podcasts and website, the 'Naked Scientists'

2007
Carolyn Stephens
for creating and championing a programme of work experience and summer schools

2006
Kathy Sykes
for leading a programme to encourage the University of Bristol to become 'the engaged university'— encouraging and enabling scientists to participate in engagement activities

2005
Colin Pulham
for his work in communicating and promoting dialogue about science, through presentations, demonstrations and hands-on activities with local communities including in remote areas over the last 10 years

HENRY DALE PRIZE AT THE ROYAL INSTITUTION

2004
Professor Stephen Pinker

2003
Professor Christopher Lowe and Professor Martin Nowak

2002
Professor Tom Kirkwood

ROYAL ACADEMY OF MUSIC / KOHN FOUNDATION
BACH PRIZE

2014
Ton Koopman

2013
Murray Perahia

2012
Masaaki Suzuki

2011
Thomanerchor

2010
John Butt

2009
Peter Schreier

2008
Sir John Eliot Gardiner

2007
Sir András Schiff

2006
Christoph Wolff

IMPERIAL COLLEGE LONDON
KOHN AWARD LECTURE

2013
Sir Gregory Winter
From Antibodies to Bicycles

2012
Professor Sir Konstantin Novoselov
Graphene: materials in the flatland

2011
Lord Martin Rees
From 'big bang' to biosphere

2010
Sir Paul Nurse
Cell cycle control

ERNST CHAIN PRIZE
AT IMPERIAL COLLEGE LONDON

2008
Professor Sir Mark Pepys
Towards curing amyloidosis

2007
Professor Robin Weiss
Blocking the docking of HIV

2006
Professor Andrew McMichael
The T cell-virus interface

2005
Sir Roy Anderson
Pathogen Evolution and Bio-Terrorism—Which is the Greater Threat?

2004
Sir John Skehel
The Mechanism of Influenza Virus Infection

2003
Sir David Hopwood
Streptomyces Genes in Antibiotic Discovery & Development

NATIONAL OSTEOPOROSIS SOCIETY
KOHN AWARD

2010
Dr Frank de Vries

2009
Dr Alireza Moayyeri

2007
Her Royal Highness The Duchess of Cornwall

2006
Professor Juliet Compston

2004
Professor Richard Eastell

2003
Linda Edwards

2002
Professor John Studd

2001
Dr Jonathan Reeve

2000
Professor Graham Russell

1999
Professor Allan Dixon

Index of people mentioned in Recital of a Lifetime

Index of people pictured in Recital of a Lifetime